New Testament History and Literature

THE OPEN YALE COURSES SERIES is designed to bring the depth and breadth of a Yale education to a wide variety of readers. Based on Yale's Open Yale Courses program (http://oyc.yale.edu), these books bring outstanding lectures by Yale faculty to the curious reader, whether student or adult. Covering a wide variety of topics across disciplines in the social sciences, physical sciences, and humanities, Open Yale Courses books offer accessible introductions at affordable prices.

The production of Open Yale Courses for the Internet was made possible by a grant from the William and Flora Hewlett Foundation.

RECENT TITLES

Paul H. Fry, *Theory of Literature*
Shelly Kagan, *Death*
Dale B. Martin, *New Testament History and Literature*

FORTHCOMING TITLES

Christine Hayes, *Introduction to the Old Testament*
Ian Shapiro, *The Moral Foundations of Politics*
Steven B. Smith, *Introduction to Political Philosophy*

New Testament History & Literature

DALE B. MARTIN

Yale
UNIVERSITY PRESS
New Haven and London

Yale University Press books may be purchased in quantity for educational, business, or promotional use. For information, please e-mail sales .press@yale.edu (U.S. office) or sales@yaleup.co.uk (U.K. office).

Set in Minion type by Westchester Book Group
Printed in the United States of America

Library of Congress Cataloging-in-Publication Data

Martin, Dale B., 1954–
New Testament history and literature / Dale B. Martin.
p. cm. — (The open Yale courses series)
Includes bibliographical references and indexes.
ISBN 978-0-300-18085-5 (pbk. : alk. paper) 1. Bible. N.T.—Criticism, interpretation, etc. 2. Christian literature, Early—History and criticism. I. Title.
BS2361.3.M37 2012
225.6'1—dc23
2011045262

A catalogue record for this book is available from the British Library.

This paper meets the requirements of ANSI/NISO Z39.48-1992 (Permanence of Paper).

10 9 8 7 6 5 4 3 2 1

To all the students I've been privileged to teach over the past twenty-five years at Rhodes College, Duke University, and Yale University

Contents

Preface and Acknowledgments

When editors at Yale University Press invited me to turn the lectures of my course "Introduction to the New Testament" into a book, I think they must have assumed, as I know I did, that doing so would be a matter of editing the existing transcripts. Once I began the task, however, I quickly discovered that the lectures as I gave them needed much more than mere editing. Perhaps some instructors lecture in printable prose, but I do not. When I lecture, which I do from notes and outlines, not from fully written texts, I digress a lot, fail to finish sentences, start on one point only to discover that I must return to another, and so forth. I've found that I chatter a lot when I lecture. The way I speak resists proper prose style. I therefore used the spoken lectures as guides, but ended up having to write these chapters as if from the bottom up. The chapters follow the basic content of the lectures, but not the actual language. That writing process has allowed me sufficient freedom to bring the lectures up-to-date (they were recorded in 2009), to correct mistakes, and to fill in material sometimes unfortunately left out in the original presentation.

I owe many people thanks—people who have over the years offered comments and suggestions and who will have to remain nameless simply because there are too many of them. The person who deserves the most thanks is Sonja Anderson, a Yale doctoral student in New Testament studies. Sonja read every word and offered countless suggestions. She corrected mistakes, proposed alternative wording, and brought up needed additions. Her superb editing rid the manuscript of many infelicities. And she provided most of the references and notes. She did this, moreover, in a feverish pace over one quick summer. This is one case where the phrase "I couldn't have done this without her" is perfectly accurate and more than merited.

Matthew Croasmun, another doctoral student in the same program, did an excellent job producing all the illustrations, with the exception of the map, which was drawn by Bill Nelson, whom I also thank. I thank Matt, moreover, for his reading of the manuscript and suggestions for improvements. Others who read the manuscript and came back to me with suggestions are Chungsen Cheng and my sister, Ferryn Martin. They deserve hearty and explicit thanks.

I have been teaching college students some kind of "Introduction to the New Testament" for my entire career. The precise content of the course has naturally changed many times, and I'm still altering and trying to improve it every time I teach it. It is a nice coincidence that this book is coming out twenty-five years after I first began teaching full-time, in 1987 at Rhodes College. I deeply appreciate all the bright and eager students I have had the privilege to teach, first there, then at Duke University, and now at Yale. I dedicate this book to all those students with gratitude and fond memories.

Map

Fig. 1 The Ancient Mediterranean World in the East. Map by Bill Nelson.

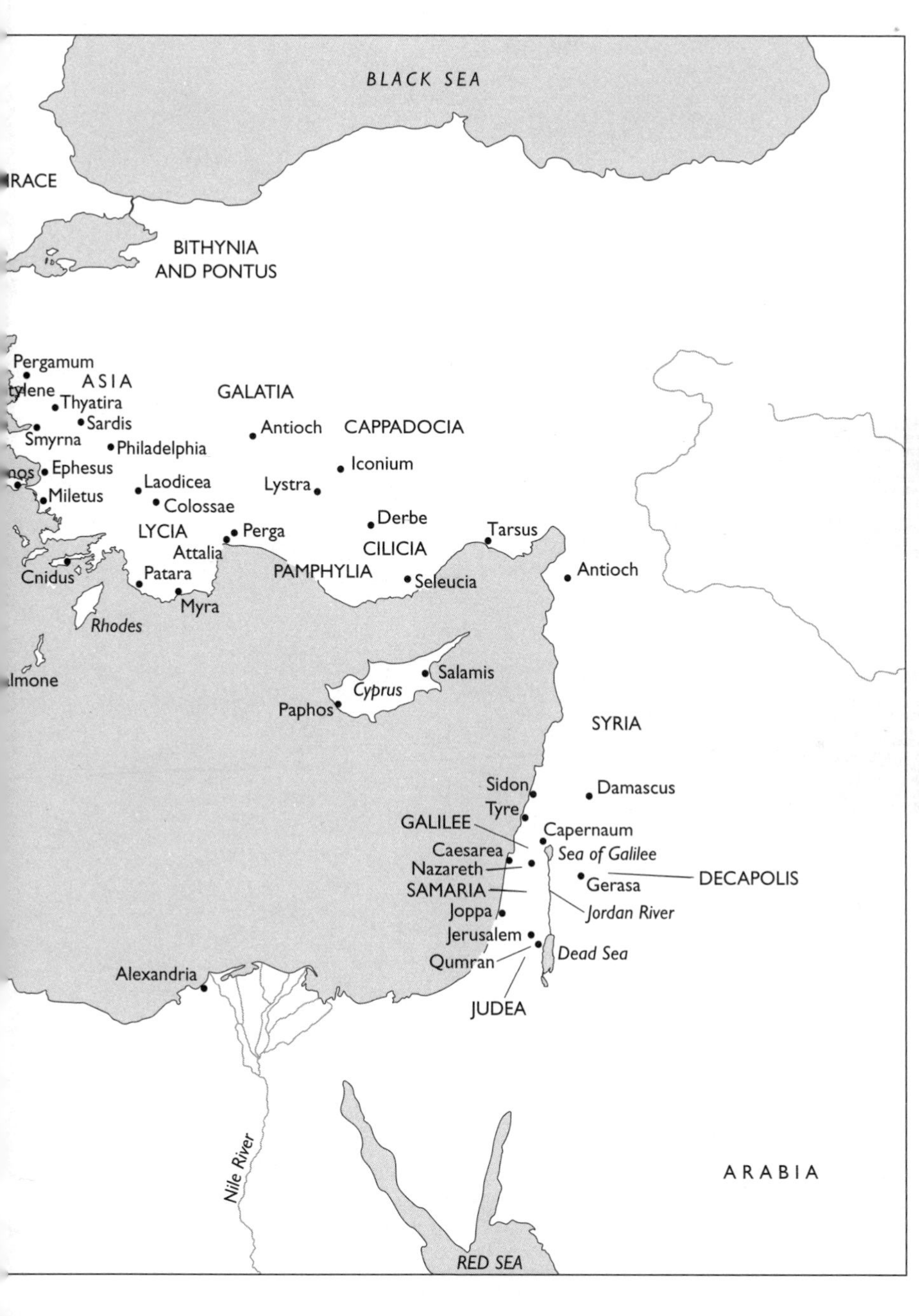

BLACK SEA
RACE
BITHYNIA AND PONTUS
Pergamum
ASIA
tylene
Thyatira
GALATIA
Sardis
Antioch
CAPPADOCIA
Smyrna
Philadelphia
Ephesus
Iconium
Laodicea
Lystra
Miletus
Colossae
Derbe
LYCIA
Perga
Tarsus
Attalia
CILICIA
Cnidus
Patara
PAMPHYLIA
Seleucia
Antioch
Myra
Rhodes
lmone
Salamis
Cyprus
Paphos
SYRIA
Sidon
Damascus
Tyre
GALILEE
Capernaum
Sea of Galilee
Caesarea
Nazareth
Gerasa
DECAPOLIS
SAMARIA
Joppa
Jordan River
Jerusalem
Qumran
Dead Sea
Alexandria
JUDEA
Nile River
ARABIA
RED SEA

CHAPTER 1

Introduction: Why Study the New Testament

Overview: This book approaches the New Testament not as scripture, or a piece of authoritative holy writing, but as a collection of historical documents. Therefore, readers are urged to leave behind their preconceived notions of the New Testament and read it as if they had never heard of it before. This involves understanding the historical context of the New Testament and imagining how it might appear to an ancient person.

Why Study the New Testament?

The first question people should ask themselves when they are taking up the study of the New Testament is why they want to study it. What is the New Testament, and why should one study it? The first answer many people give—and for many, the most obvious—is, "Because I'm a Christian." Or perhaps, "I believe the New Testament is scripture."

The problem with that answer, at least as it relates to this book on the New Testament, is that the New Testament isn't "scripture" for everyone. When we say that the New Testament is "scripture," we have to identify for whom it is scripture. What does it mean to call a document "scripture"? In Christianity, when people call the Bible scripture, that often means they intend to listen to the text for the "Word of God," whether read in church or alone at home. Christians often expect the Holy Spirit or God to communicate to them and to their church, or to some broader community, through this document.

But the text of the Bible is not scripture in itself. It is scripture only to a community of people who take it as scripture. The text itself, any text, is not holy writing. Originally, the word in Latin (*scriptura*) meant simply "something written," but we now take the word to mean holy writing, sacred writing. The writing, however, is not holy in itself. It is holy only to people who take it as holy.

I will not be assuming in this book that the New Testament is holy or sacred writing. In fact, the purpose of much modern scholarship on the Bible has been to avoid, at least momentarily and for the purposes of secular scholarship, taking the Bible to be sacred writing. Thus in my courses in Yale College, I explain that for the purpose of the course we will treat the different documents of the New Testament just as we would any other document from the ancient Mediterranean. Yale College, in spite of some of its traditions and accoutrements that might suggest otherwise, is not a religious community. We must presume that students who take our courses in religious studies are not necessarily religious. Those wanting to learn about Buddhism may not be Buddhist. In fact, for many courses, including many of those on Islam and religions of Asia, most of those taking the courses will not be adherents of the religions they are studying. Therefore, we teach these courses, including courses on Judaism and Christianity, the Hebrew Bible, or the New Testament, from a self-consciously secular, nonconfessional point of view. That means approaching the New Testament not as "scripture" but simply as ancient documents produced by the movement that eventually became Christianity.

Other people want to study the New Testament because they believe it is a "foundational document" for Western civilization. But again, what does that mean? Does that mean that people can't really get along in Western civilization unless they know something about the Bible? We might argue, though, that there are many other things more important for "getting along" than knowing the New Testament. I'd think it more important, for instance, to know how to fix one's car, or how to use computers, or how to speak other languages, or maybe even something about sexual technique. With a bit more reflection, we might decide that the New Testament would rank further down on the list of "things one must know to get along."

And what about the New Testament has been historically or culturally important? Often, the most culturally significant things about the New Testament have been not things that are actually in the New Testament studied historically, but things people think are in the New Testament. This is easily demonstrated by a little quiz. Here is a list of sayings or ideas that either are or are not in the New Testament. I provide the list first and the answers later, in case you want to play along. Just mark whether something is or is not in the New Testament:

1. The immaculate conception.
2. "Love bears all things, believes all things, hopes all things, endures all things."
3. At Jesus' birth, three wise men or kings visited the baby Jesus.
4. "From each according to his ability, to each according to his need."
5. The doctrine of the Trinity.
6. "You are Peter, and upon this rock I will build my church."
7. Peter founded the church in Rome.
8. After his death, Jesus appeared to his eleven disciples in Jerusalem but not in Galilee.
9. After his death, Jesus appeared to his eleven disciples in Galilee but not in Jerusalem.
10. Peter was martyred by being crucified upside down.
11. Jesus taught that if people wanted to be his disciples, they had to hate their parents and even their wives.
12. Satan and his demons were fallen angels who rebelled against God.
13. Jesus taught people that God forbade divorce for any reason.

Now let's check our answers.

1. The immaculate conception is actually not in the Bible. Many people think it is because they (especially Protestants) may think it refers to the virgin birth of Jesus, which is narrated in the Gospels of Matthew and Luke. But the immaculate conception refers to the conception of Mary, the mother of Jesus, and teaches that Mary was born without original sin. "Immaculate" means "without stain." This is a doctrine important in Roman Catholicism, but it is not in the Bible and is not accepted by Protestants.[1] The "miraculous conception" of Jesus is in the New Testament (Matt 1:18–25; Luke 1:27–35), but not the immaculate conception of Mary.

2. Yes, this is a quotation from 1 Corinthians 13:7.
3. No, the Bible does not say that three wise men or kings visited Jesus after his birth. Only tradition teaches that there were three of them, no doubt just because in Matthew they are said to have brought three gifts: gold, frankincense, and myrrh (Matt 2:1–12). Readers saw the three gifts and made up the "fact" that there were three men.
4. This quotation is often taken by people to be from the Bible. Ironically, it is from Karl Marx, although many of us would argue that it expresses a sentiment that should reflect Christianity in its better moments.[2]
5. The doctrine of the Trinity is not in the Bible if it is read in its historical context. Of course, one can find references to the Father, the Son, and the Holy Spirit in the New Testament, even together as a triad in Matthew 28:19. But the actual doctrine, which teaches that the three are different "persons" who each share the same "substance" of full divinity, took centuries to be developed, elaborated, defended, and established as Christian dogma. Christian theologians may be right if they say that the doctrine is at least "hinted at" in the New Testament, and that the later church was correct in "taking" the Bible to teach the doctrine, but that is a theological position, not a strictly historical one.
6. This quotation is from Matthew 16:18.
7. That Peter founded the church in Rome is part of Christian legend, and for Roman Catholics perhaps an important tradition, but it is not narrated in the New Testament.
8. This and the next are a bit tricky. Jesus did appear to his disciples in and around Jerusalem according to the author of Luke and Acts (Luke 24:33–36; Acts 1:4). Moreover, according to that author, Jesus appeared to them only in and around Jerusalem and not in Galilee.
9. But according to Matthew, Jesus appeared to his eleven male disciples not in Jerusalem but only later in Galilee (Matt 28:16–18). I explore this conundrum in a later chapter.
10. That Peter was martyred by being crucified upside down has been important in tradition and Christian art, but Peter's death is not described in the Bible, and historians actually have no reliable evidence about it at all.[3]

11. Yes, contrary to much-trumpeted, supposed "family values" of Christianity, Jesus did teach, according to Luke 14:26, that his disciples had to "hate" their family members, including their parents and wives.
12. The idea that Satan was a fallen, rebellious angel who was joined by other fallen angels, who are the same beings as those called "demons" or "evil spirits" in the New Testament, is not actually in the New Testament. It is an invention of Christians that began in the second century C.E. and became important for Christian mythology and lore.[4]
13. Yes, contrary to the teachings and practices of almost all Christian churches today, Jesus, according to Mark 10:2–12, forbade divorce for any reason.[5]

So much for the quiz. My point with this little exercise is that on the one hand, there are many things people may think are in the Bible that are not, and on the other hand, many people are utterly surprised when they learn about other sayings or actions that definitely are in the Bible (Jesus told his disciples to hate their parents?). Many of these ideas, such as the immaculate conception or the imagery of wise men surrounding a manger, are important for Western civilization, for the history of art, and for the furniture of people's imaginations. So it may be important to know, for example, that legend says that Peter was crucified upside down, but it is not part of the New Testament. And the fact that much ancient Christian tradition is not actually in the Bible raises something of a problem for the study of the New Testament: if we study the New Testament by asking about its meaning in its ancient historical context, which will be the method mostly pursued in this book, are we thereby neglecting the most important historical "meanings" of the Bible—what that text has been taken to mean in the history of culture and interpretation?

The "historical-critical" approach to the Bible, which is the method demonstrated in this book and which will be explained and illustrated throughout, anchors "the meaning" of the text in its ancient context: what the original authors "intended" or the original readers likely "understood." But one could argue, as I do and have argued in other books, that it is just as important to learn about the impact and interpretation of the New Testament through history—that is, what the New Testament has been taken to mean later in history and culture, regardless of its "original meaning."[6]

We can see this also by comparing what the New Testament actually says about some issues with what most people assume that it must say even on matters of significant beliefs. What do most people believe happens to someone after death? Some would say, "You're dead like Rover and dead all over." Some, "You go to heaven." What may we imagine that most people assume religious Christians to believe? Where is Aunt Martha during her funeral? A popular assumption, whether people actually believe it or not, would be, "She's safe in heaven. She's in the arms of Jesus. Her body may be in the casket, but her soul is up there." Many people assume that Christianity teaches the immortality of the soul.

But that, again, is not really something taught by the Bible, and it is not even the best interpretation of "official Christian orthodoxy," as would be contained, say, in the Apostles' Creed or the Nicene Creed, according to which afterlife existence is supposed to be experienced in the resurrection of the body or the flesh. Contrary to common opinion, even popular Christian opinion, the New Testament more often teaches a form of the resurrection than the soul's immortality (see, for example, 1 Cor 15).

So where do we get the very common idea of the immortality of the soul? Perhaps much more from Platonism than from the New Testament.[7] So if one is interested in learning about the origins of central aspects of Western civilization, it may make more sense to study Plato than the New Testament.

The Bible as a Historical Text

My point has been to emphasize that this book will not be approaching the New Testament as scripture, nor will I analyze how important it was for medieval and early modern literature. I will be looking mainly at what it meant in the first and early second centuries. In fact, I will be attempting to approach the New Testament "from the outside," which is not always easy for people in our culture to do because most of us have grown up with some kind of cultural knowledge of "what Christianity is" and "what the Bible is." This is true even for those who are not religious, as well as for those who are Christians.

Most of us live in a post-Christian culture, and both aspects of that term are important. It is post-Christian in the sense that it is hard to live in America without having some exposure to Christianity and seeing its influence on society, politics, culture, and art. It is also post-Christian because we can no longer assume, especially if we live in a multiethnic, pluralistic environment, that everyone we meet will be Christian. In a sense, we live in a society that has something of a "hangover" from Christianity, but one in which people do not necessarily know a lot about Christianity in a critical and educated manner.

So let's make an attempt to scrape our brains clean of what we think we know about the New Testament and try to approach it from the outside, as something new and strange. At the very beginning, we find the Gospel of Matthew, which begins like this: "The book of the origin" (*genesis* is the Greek word for "origin" here) "of Jesus Christ, son of David, son of Abraham. Abraham had a son named Isaac. Isaac had a son named Jacob. Jacob had Judah and his brothers. Judah had Perez and Zerah from Tamar" (Matt 1:1–3). These are "the begats" that figure prominently in certain parts of the Hebrew Bible and begin Matthew. The text goes on like this for many sentences. As a modern person, one might ask, "What is this? Why begin this way?" Then we arrive at the birth narratives in Matthew, the stories of the baby Jesus. If we lived in the time of the writing, this would seem fairly familiar, because people knew other stories about stars appearing as signs of the birth of a great man. In fact, this is part of the propaganda culture of the ancient world. Matthew begins as one would begin the story of the birth of a famous man, and if you lived in that time, you would recognize the genre.

But we continue in our reading and find a story of a man who travels around, giving speeches, talking to people, and teaching. He also exorcizes demons, heals people, and performs a few miracles. For a modern person with no exposure to religious narratives like this, the story would sound odd. In the ancient world, though, it would have sounded familiar because people knew of other stories of teachers who healed and performed miracles. It was not an uncommon way of talking about someone supposed to be great. Of course, in the end the man dies a gruesome death by crucifixion, a form of Roman torture and execution usually reserved for slaves, rebels, and lower-class troublemakers. But even some "philosophers" and moral teachers were known to have been martyred in a "noble death."

We arrive next at the Gospel of Mark. It appears to be something like the same story. It is shorter than Matthew, with fewer teachings. But why do we have a "second chapter" (Mark) of this same book (the New Testament) that looks basically like an abbreviated version of the first chapter? With the Gospel of Luke, we see something of the same thing. With the Gospel of John, though, we see something different. Compared with the first three Gospels we've read, it sounds different and has a different style. But it is still generally a similar story of the same man. That should look odd to us.

The next "chapter" is the Acts of the Apostles. Now we are back on more familiar ground. It starts off like the Gospel of Luke because it is written by the same person. It even begins with a paragraph that recapitulates the ending of Luke, much as different episodes of a television series begin by rehearsing the gist of the preceding episode. Then Acts begins sounding something like a Greek novel. Greek novels were usually about a man and a woman, young, rich, and beautiful, who see one another, fall madly in love, and passionately desire one another.[8] Usually they do not immediately marry, nor do they "consummate their love." Instead, one of them may get kidnapped by pirates or have to go off to war; the heroine may be captured and sold into slavery. In one way or another, though, they are separated and go all around the Mediterranean searching for one another chapter after chapter. The novel may be full of shipwrecks, battles, miracles, and meddling gods.

That is something of what the Acts of the Apostles looks like: an ancient Greek novel. But it lacks the one thing every good Greek novel had: sex and passion. An ancient reader may have been disappointed about that. But Acts has things that the novels don't, such as the "Holy Spirit" (meaning what?) serving as the main actor for most of the book. The book of Acts should look odd to us if we are not familiar with biblical texts or ancient novels. And it would look both familiar and a bit odd to an ancient reader.

We may realize, about this point, that the Acts of the Apostles is mistitled. It doesn't depict the actions of all the apostles, but for the most part those of Paul. And Paul is not really considered an apostle by whoever wrote Acts. The author is working with the assumption that an "apostle" is someone who accompanied Jesus during his lifetime (see Acts 1:21–26), and Paul didn't meet that criterion. But the issue of the title brings up another point about the New Testament: the titles these different books now bear in our Bibles were not put there by their authors, but by later Christian scribes. This will prove to be important for most of the New Testament.

Next in our initial tour of the New Testament we come to the letters of Paul. Is it strange that most of the New Testament documents are letters? They are not like modern letters, of course, but they are quite like ancient letters, at least letters passed around in philosophical schools. They are often addressed to groups of people, and they deal with philosophical-sounding issues and ethics. They give advice on group problems.

Next we get to the Epistle to the Hebrews or, in what would be a less formal translation, the "Letter to the Jews." What is odd, though, is that it isn't actually a letter. In fact, it doesn't claim to be a letter, but a "word of exhortation," that is, a sermon (13:22). It also, on closer examination, appears not to be addressed to Jews, but to gentile Christians to convince them that Jesus provides for them a liturgy that is superior to that of the Jews. It is not a letter, and it may not be addressed to Jews. But it may lead us to another insight in our tour: these letters seem to be meant to be read out loud to groups of people. So what would it mean to read this letter out loud in a community, not alone at home or in a library?

Let's come to 1 Peter. It is not written to one place. Rather, it is a circular letter, meant to be sent around to different churches. Eventually, we get to 2 and 3 John, one of which is addressed to "the elected lady and her children" (2 John 1:1). What does that mean?

Finally, we get to the Revelation of John, the Apocalypse. The word "revelation" is just the latinized and then anglicized version of the Greek word *apokalypsis*, which means "unveiling," "uncovering." This document seems really bizarre, certainly to many of us moderns—as it probably was to many ancient readers as well. It is not really like any other document we've seen in the New Testament. It starts off with a narrative about a vision (Rev 1:1–20). A man named John says something like, "I was on the island of Patmos. I was in the spirit on the Lord's day. I started having this vision and an angel appeared to me and all this happened." Then we encounter seven different letters, very short, addressed to seven different churches (Rev 2:1–3:22). Then the book turns into something like a wild action movie, a narrative of a heavenly journey of John. He goes up into the heavens. He sees the throne room of God. He sees weird kinds of beasts, animals that have strange bodies, like a lamb with horns and covered in blood. There are terrible catastrophes. The drama ends with a cosmic battle between forces of good and forces of evil. It is like several installments of *Star Wars*. Finally, it ends with the establishment of a new world and a new city of God.

That is the end of the New Testament—and a long way from the little baby Jesus and the kings in Matthew. The New Testament includes diverse literature: twenty-seven different books, probably written anywhere from the year 50 to the year 150 or so, a hundred-year period. They have different points of view, different situations, different theologies, and different genres. They use confusing in-house language, as we will encounter regularly throughout the course of this book.

Imagining an Ancient Person's Perspective

In another experiment, we can try not just to look at the documents from the outside but to imagine how an ancient person who encountered an early Christian church from the outside would think about it. Imagine that you are a seamstress who works in a cloth shop in the city of Corinth, in Greece, in the year 56. Eutychus, a guy who lives next door to you and works in a leather workshop nearby, has just joined a new club, and he tells you about it. First, they don't meet in the daytime, but either early, before light, or after dark. There are only enough of them to fill a decent-sized dining room, but they call themselves the "town meeting." You're not quite sure what they do at these meetings. They don't appear to worship any god or goddess that you can see. They use the term "god" sometimes, but this god doesn't have a name, and to you that would be bizarre. Remember, you are pretending that you're a Greek living in the year 56 in Corinth. To you, these people look as if they don't believe in gods at all; they look like atheists.

The people in this new club have a very high respect for a criminal Jew who led some kind of guerrilla war and was executed long ago, somewhere in Syria. Eutychus says, though, that this Jew is still alive somewhere. In fact, Eutychus says that the Jew "bought" him, although you didn't know that Eutychus was ever a slave. In fact, you're pretty sure he wasn't a slave. So what does it mean that this guy bought him? At these town meetings they eat meals—which is not unusual since most clubs in your society eat meals—but they call the meals the "boss's dinner," or sometimes "the thank-you." Some people say they eat human flesh at these dinners, but you doubt that because for some reason they seem to be vegetarians. You doubt whether vegetarians would eat human flesh. Eutychus says that to initiate new members into their club, they "dip them," naked, and then they "get healthy." Once you're in the club, they call you "comrade," and you have sex with anyone and everyone, because it doesn't matter anymore whether you're a man or a woman; in fact, they kind of figure you're neither—or both.

I constructed this fanciful portrait out of actual data from the New Testament and other early Christian, Greek, and Roman sources. This was, in fact, the way at least a good many ancient people saw early Christian groups. For example, a later Roman governor informs the emperor that Christian groups he knew about met early in the morning or after dark.[9] As we will see repeatedly, all the early Christian groups were "house churches" and must have been relatively small. The Greek term we translate as "church" (*ekklēsia*) in an ancient Greek context also, more commonly, referred to the public meeting of the citizens of a city. We must remember, in spite of our tendencies otherwise, that "god" is not the name of God and in the ancient context would have been used as the generic category for any god. Each god would have his or her own proper name.[10] The Christian "god" did not. And we know from many sources that Christians were considered by others to be atheists.[11]

Most people in Greece likely had no knowledge of Galilee; they would likely have taken it to be simply part of Syria, which was much better known. When Eutychus said that Jesus "bought" him, he would have been using the Greek word *agorazein*, whose older, more "religious" translation was "redeem." The meal they ate regularly would have been the Communion, the "Lord's Supper," which in the earliest days of the Christian movement was observed along with a full dinner, something like a potluck supper (see the way Paul talks about it in 1 Cor 11:17–34, where it obviously was a meal, as we will see in a later chapter). Even the common English term for the Communion, the "Lord's Supper," is actually a more "formal" way of translating the Greek, which less formally could be translated as "the boss's dinner." *Kyrios* could mean "the Lord" or simply someone's master or employer. And if outsiders heard these meals referred to with another ancient designation, the "Eucharist," they may likely have taken that Greek word, *eucharistia*, as having its normal, everyday meaning of "thanks."

We know from Christian defenses against the accusation that Christians were thought to consume human flesh.[12] After all, they do say they are eating the body and blood of this man named Jesus (John 6:53–56; 1 Cor 10:16). We also know that Christians developed a reputation at some times and in some places of avoiding meat, perhaps because they wanted to avoid eating meat that might have been part of a sacrifice to a god, which most Christians carefully avoided.[13] I said that they initiated one another by "dipping" into water: the word "baptize" in Greek meant simply "dip." We know from later Christian sources that this was often done in private, and the person baptized was naked.[14] To note that the Christians called this "getting healthy," I just translated the Greek word we usually translate as "salvation" into its more mundane, everyday sense of "health" (*sōtēria*).

Christians did call one another "brother" and "sister," and without knowing how those terms would later become theologically laden in Christianity, a Greek would likely have heard them as a rather odd, in-house, jargony use of language, much as Americans heard "comrade" during the cold war. As for that part about sex and not being male or female, Paul says that in Christ there is no male and female (Gal 3:28). And hearing Christians talk so much about loving one another, brother and sister, although there was no longer a difference between male and female—well, we may imagine how outsiders could have allowed their imaginations to run wild with salacious rumors, as does seem sometimes to have been the case.[15]

Just as early Christian house churches, with their in-house, jargony language and their often odd-seeming practices and sometimes private meetings at night, would have appeared strange to the average inhabitant of Corinth, so the Bible presents us with a strange world if we approach it without our normal preconceptions, if we approach it fresh and from the outside. This is an ancient collection of documents from different times and places, put together much later to form the New Testament.

In the next chapter, I address the process by which these twenty-seven diverse documents came to be included in the New Testament. That is the history of the canon. In much else as well, the history of early Christianity is about how a diverse group of different people—all considering themselves loyal to the man they called Jesus but differing from one another in practices, beliefs, ethnicity, class, and geography—finally became at least somewhat unified into one historical movement and institution, with at least a modicum of uniformity of belief and practice.

This book actually runs counter to that historical tendency that attempts to manufacture unity from diversity. This book takes the New Testament and even the different books of the New Testament apart. A major theme of the book, in fact, will be the diversity of early Christianity—in fact, the diversity of early Christianities. I will look at the many different ways Jesus was thought to be either divine or human or some combination of both. I'll highlight different ways early followers of the Jesus movement dealt with the fact that the movement itself came out of Judaism but before long was dominated by gentiles. I'll show how these different Christian communities treated women and their roles in churches; how they treated slaves and other servants in their households; how they related to whatever politics surrounded them; and how they reacted to the powerful Roman Empire. The book takes up not only the documents of the New Testament, but also a few other early Christian texts. Beginning with the New Testament as a now-unified text, the book pulls apart that unity to analyze the diversity of the early Christian movement and its texts.

Ancient and Academic Contexts for the Study of the New Testament

CHAPTER 2

The Development of the Canon

Overview: The Christian faith is based on a canon of texts considered to be holy scripture. How did this canon come to be? Different factors, such as competing schools of doctrine, growing consensus, and the invention of the codex, helped shape the canon of the New Testament. Reasons for inclusion in or exclusion from the canon included apostolic authority, general acceptance, and theological appropriateness for "proto-orthodox" Christianity.

Canon versus Scripture

What is scripture, and what is canon? These are not necessarily the same thing. The two words are often used interchangeably, but it is helpful to distinguish them. "Scripture" may refer to any writing taken by someone as holy and authoritative—any written text that is sacred in itself or that communicates something sacred. Some religions don't have what we would normally think of as scripture in Islam, Judaism, or Christianity. Some religions have lots of "holy writings," but they do not have one particular, bounded body of writings called "the scripture" that they cordon off from all other writings. We may see such religions, therefore, as having lots of scriptures, but no "Bible." In any case, what makes something scripture is that it is taken to be authoritative and holy by some particular community.

"Canon" refers to a more limited, defined entity. The Greek word *kanōn* originally referred to any kind of measure, such as a ruler. Thus it could also refer to a list: a list, a ruler, say, of books. Either a book was on the list or it was not. This is what "canon" means for Christian history and theology: the list of sacred writings that includes some Christian documents but excludes other Christian documents. Islam, Judaism, and Christianity have canons. For Islam, it is the Qur'an. For Judaism, it is the Hebrew Bible. For Christians, it is the Jewish scripture (the Hebrew Bible, called the Old Testament by Christians) plus the New Testament.

When we call something a "canon," we signal that we are talking about a group of writings that has boundaries. A canonical list therefore excludes as well as includes. It says, "Even if there are other writings we take to be special or holy in some sense, those on this list are special in a special sense." The canon is "closed." We may indeed talk about something like the canon of Shakespeare or the canon of great Western literature, but when we do so we are actually using the term in an expanded or metaphorical sense: we don't really consider Western literature to have an actual closed canon of authoritative texts.

Even before Christian churches came up with canonical lists, they had "scripture." In fact, the first scripture for Christians was Jewish scripture, which Christians accepted as their own. When the apostle Paul, for instance, says, "Scripture says," he is not speaking about the New Testament. He is referring to Jewish scripture, which he knew in its Greek translation. The people who wrote the documents that eventually made up the New Testament didn't realize they were writing the New Testament. They were writing a sermon, a letter, or an account of the life of Jesus. So when they talk about "scripture," they are, at least in the earliest times of Christianity, referring to Jewish scripture, accepted as their own. This chapter discusses how the particular twenty-seven books that came to be in the New Testament canon got there. How were they chosen? By whom? When did people make the decision? And what were the criteria they used? Why did they allow some books into their canon and not others?

Traditions and Texts

The oldest surviving written materials of Christianity are the letters of Paul. This comes as a surprise to some people because the Gospels come first in the New Testament. The Gospels are about Jesus, so most people assume they contain "the oldest stuff." But the Gospels were all written twenty, thirty, or forty years after the letters of Paul. Most scholars believe that the oldest of Paul's letters is 1 Thessalonians, which is dated to around the year 50 C.E. Fairly soon, though, and perhaps even during Paul's lifetime, different churches, probably those founded by Paul himself, began sending around copies of Paul's letters. We have to remind ourselves that there were no printing presses. Whenever one church received a copy of one of Paul's letters, they would have scribes, sometimes slaves, since slaves often were trained as scribes, make a copy of the letter. That church might keep the original copy it received and send the copy it made to someone else. Letters and books were copied and sent around among different communities and persons.[1]

I will eventually argue that Colossians was not actually written by Paul, but by one of his disciples after Paul's death. At any rate, the author of Colossians says, "And when this letter has been read among you, have it read also in the church of the Laodiceans; and see that you read also the letter from Laodicea" (Col 4:16). Note that the author is writing in the name of Paul, and he claims that there is another letter sent by Paul to the Laodicean church. He encourages the two churches to copy their respective letters and send those copies to one another. Even in the letters bearing Paul's name, we see this practice of letter exchange and collection.

I will later argue that the letter to the Ephesians was also not written by Paul, but it will still serve to illustrate early Christian practices of letter circulation. Ephesians, when it is examined closely and by looking at ancient Greek manuscripts, seems not to have been sent to just one church. Some scholars have suggested that it was a circular letter meant to be sent around to different churches, each one making its own copy along the way. Some ancient manuscripts lack the address "To the Ephesians," and it seems that in others the letter may have been addressed to a different city.[2] Perhaps the original writer left a blank in some copies so that a copier could fill in the addressee: "Well, we're in Laodicea, so let's fill that in, and we can act like Paul sent it just to us!"

Paul's letters are the earliest that survive (although they may not have been, and in fact probably were not, the earliest Christian letters written), but soon others were imitating Paul's practice of writing letters to churches. I have said that I don't think Paul wrote Colossians or Ephesians. What is even more interesting is that the writer of Ephesians obviously used Colossians as the model for his own letter (see Chapter 17 in this book). He takes many of the themes and images and much of the vocabulary from Colossians, which he may well have thought was an authentic letter of Paul. Notice, therefore, that one disciple of Paul is forging a letter in Paul's name, and he is using another letter, also forged in Paul's name, as his model: an imitator imitating another imitator imitating Paul.

So Paul's letters were circulating, new ones were being written in his name and added to the circulation, and all were being copied, recopied, and circulated. Eventually, Paul's letters became so famous and respected, at least in some circles of Christianity, that they themselves were called "scripture." Indeed, the only time, apparently, the word "scripture" is used in the New Testament to refer to a specifically Christian text rather than to Jewish scripture is in reference to Paul's letters. The person who wrote 2 Peter—again, not really Peter but someone writing in his name—speaks of Paul's letters: "There are some things in them hard to understand, which the ignorant and unstable twist to their own destruction, as they do *the other scriptures*" (2 Peter 3:16; my emphasis). By the time of the writing of 2 Peter, which I take to be many, many years after the death of Paul, Paul's letters had come to be regarded by at least some Christians as scripture, perhaps on a par with the long-accepted Jewish scriptures. Paul's letters attained that kind of status at least in part because they had been copied and circulated so much.

Even before the circulation of letters and other written materials, we can see that oral traditions—sayings of Jesus, stories, ethical teachings, and lists of witnesses to the resurrection appearances—were also circulating among early churches. People would tell stories about Jesus in their churches. In Romans 12:14, for example, Paul says, "Bless those who persecute you; bless and do not curse them." Paul does not say that this is a quotation of Jesus, but it sounds much like similar sayings found in the Gospels, such as Matthew 5:44.[3] In 1 Corinthians 11:23–26, Paul relates an account of Jesus' instructions establishing the Christian practice of the Communion, and he explicitly says that he is passing along an oral tradition: "For I received from the Lord what I also handed on to you, that the Lord Jesus on the night when he was betrayed took a loaf of bread, and when he had given thanks, he broke it and said, 'This is my body that is for you. Do this in remembrance of me.' In the same way, he took the cup also, after supper, saying, 'This cup is the new covenant in my blood. Do this, as often as you drink it, in remembrance of me.' For as often as you eat this bread and drink the cup, you proclaim the Lord's death until he comes."

We must remember that Paul can't be getting these sayings from the Gospels, because as far as we know, no gospels were yet written at this time. And Paul did not learn this from Jesus during Jesus' earthly ministry, because Paul was not a follower of Jesus until some years after the death of

Jesus. Paul never "saw" Jesus except in visions (Gal 1:16; for the way Acts imagines these events, see Acts 9:3–9, 22:6–21, 26:12–18). Paul says he "received" the saying "from the Lord," which is doubtless a reference to Jesus. Either Paul is claiming to have received this directly from Jesus in something like a vision, or he is just using a manner of speaking to acknowledge that Jesus was the ultimate source, even though Paul may have been taught these things by people who were followers of Jesus before Paul was. The latter is the more probable explanation.

This, in any case, is traditional Greek language about passing on tradition. So Paul knows that he is passing along very early, spoken Christian traditions. Another such example is found in 1 Corinthians 9:14, where Paul says, "In the same way, the Lord commanded that those who proclaim the gospel should get their living by the gospel." We don't actually have a verse in the Gospels where Jesus says that, although it does sound something like, perhaps, Luke 10:7.[4] But this is a saying Paul attributes to Jesus that is not found in our Gospels. It is also noteworthy that Paul is here saying that Jesus himself taught that churches should support preachers and missionaries, that it is a command from Jesus. But Paul, right there in 1 Corinthians 9, insists that he is not going to obey it. In the very next verse, Paul makes the point that he will not be taking money from his churches.[5]

The earliest surviving Gospel that pulled together sayings of Jesus, combining them in a narrative about his ministry and death, was the Gospel of Mark, written around the year 70. In following chapters, I will demonstrate how we attempt to determine when Mark was written. After Mark, the Gospels of Matthew and Luke appeared, both using Mark as one of their sources. We can see another hint at early Christian use of "sources"—including written sources—in the introduction of the Gospel of Luke:

> Since many have undertaken to set down an orderly account of the events that have been fulfilled among us, just as they were handed on to us by those who from the beginning were eyewitnesses and servants of the word, I too decided after investigating everything carefully from the very first, to write an orderly account for you, most excellent Theophilus, so that you may know the truth concerning the things about what you have been instructed. (Luke 1:1–4)

There was a "Luke" who was a companion of Paul (see Philem 24; Col 4:14; 2 Tim 4:11), but most modern scholars don't believe he was actually the author of Luke and Acts. We believe that all four Gospels were originally published anonymously, and the names they now bear were given to the four books later in order to link the books to disciples of Jesus or close disciples of disciples of Jesus, as I will explain when we get to the Gospels themselves. But the author of Luke, whoever he was, admits that he did some research. He collected sayings of Jesus; he read other written accounts; and from those different resources, oral and written, he compiled his own Gospel.

The Gospel accounts of Jesus began, that is, with oral traditions passed around, different sayings and stories about Jesus. About forty years after the death of Jesus, that is, around the year 70, the Gospel of Mark was written. Therefore, there was a forty-year period between the death of Jesus and the appearance of the first Gospel we possess, although there seem to have been other written materials circulating during that time, and there were certainly many oral traditions being passed around.

As modern people, we tend to think that a written text provides a better account than "word of mouth." Writing, we often assume, is more reliable than rumor, or hearsay, or oral tradition. Some ancient people, apparently, didn't think so. The way Plato, at least in explicit claims, ranked unwritten, that is, oral, information above written information is famous.[6] At least some ancient Christians expressed similar sentiments. Papias was a Christian leader who wrote about this issue around 130 or 140. He makes some claims about his own method of research into Christian origins:

> I also will not hesitate to draw up for you, along with these expositions, an orderly account of all the things I carefully learned and have carefully recalled from the elders; for I have certified their truth. For unlike most people, I took no pleasure in hearing those who had a lot to say, but only those who taught the truth, and not those who recalled commandments from strangers, but only those who recalled the commandments which have been given faithfully by the Lord and which proceed from the truth itself. But whenever someone arrived who had been a companion of one of the elders, I would carefully inquire after their words, what Andrew or Peter had said, or what Philip or what Thomas had said, or James or John or Matthew or any of the other disciples of the Lord, and what things Aristion and the elder John, disciples of the Lord, were saying. For I did not suppose that what came out of books would benefit me as much as that which came from a living and abiding voice.[7]

Unable to interview any actual apostles, who had long since died, Papias searched out old men who might have known the early disciples. This quotation is interesting because it gives at least an idealistic account of continuing tradition from Jesus to the second century (how historically accurate or true that continuing tradition was is another question). And it shows that at least some Christians trusted the "living voice" of tradition over written documents.

Justin Martyr lived in the middle of the second century and is so named because he was martyred for the faith around the year 150. He does not explicitly mention the four Gospels. Rather, he talks about "the memoirs of the apostles."[8] Although Justin doesn't name any gospels explicitly, we know that by this time several written gospels were in existence. Besides the four that eventually formed part of the New Testament—Matthew, Mark, Luke, and John—many other gospels were known, one of the most famous being the *Gospel of Thomas*, but there were gospels in the names of Mary, Peter, and, as a recent discovery has made famous, even Judas.[9] With all these different gospels, how did we end up with the canonical four?

The Forming of Canon Lists

The first church leader who came up with a list informing his followers that "this gospel" and "these letters" were to be given central and special attention—that is, the closest thing yet to a "canon" list of approved Christian texts—was Marcion, a man from Asia Minor (modern Turkey) who came to Rome in the first half of the second century.[10] Marcion seems to have been a successful businessman, perhaps a shipbuilder. He gave the Roman church a large sum of money and initially was welcomed and honored. He died around 160.[11]

Marcion, however, began teaching doctrines about God and the Jewish scriptures that were at odds with the opinions of much of the rest of the church.[12] The God depicted as the creator and the God of Israel in the Old Testament was not the Father God referred to by Jesus (remember that there was not yet a "New Testament," so Christians did not yet call the Jewish scriptures the "Old Testament," although I will for convenience). The God of the Old Testament, the creator god, does exist, but he is a bungling, legalistic god and even has a physical body. The God Jesus speaks of is the God of grace, love, justice, and mercy.[13]

Marcion did use the writings that later came to make up the Old Testament, but only as proof that the god there depicted cannot be the same being represented by Jesus Christ. So Marcion rejected the use of Old Testament documents to reveal the Father of Jesus Christ or to teach truths of the gospel. He taught that other Christians who interpreted Jewish scripture "symbolically" or "allegorically" so that they could discern there the Father of Jesus Christ were practicing illegitimate biblical interpretation practices. Those texts were to be read "literally," and if Christians did so, they would find an angry, vengeful god there, not the Father of Jesus Christ.

In place of the rejected "scripture" of the Jews, Marcion selected one Gospel, the Gospel of Luke.[14] Why Luke? It seems clear that Paul was Marcion's favorite apostle. In fact, he seems to have taught that the other apostles adulterated the pristine gospel taught by Jesus by introducing "judaizing tendencies." Paul had retained the true, "law-free" gospel (that is, free of Jewish regulations and writings). As we will see, Paul taught not just that gentiles need not attempt to keep Jewish law; he taught them that they must not attempt to follow Jewish law (see Gal 5:2–4).[15] Marcion believed that Paul was the only apostle to get it right. We have seen that Luke was known to be a companion of Paul, and by this time Luke's name had become attached to the third Gospel. Marcion likely chose the Gospel of Luke out of the many different possibilities because of its supposed connection to Paul.

To that Gospel, Marcion added ten letters of Paul.[16] In our Bibles, Paul is credited with writing thirteen letters.[17] Marcion did not include what we call the "Pastoral Epistles": 1 and 2 Timothy and Titus. We can't be certain why, but I think it was likely just because Marcion didn't know those letters. As we will see when we study them, they were not written by Paul himself, and they may not have been in circulation until well into the second century. In fact, Marcion's apparent ignorance of them provides some evidence that they may not have been written until sometime toward the middle of the second century. At any rate, they were not included in Marcion's "canon" list.

You may have noticed that even in the Gospel of Luke and Paul's letters there are quotations of Old Testament texts as "scripture," and the God of Israel, as depicted in the Jewish scriptures, plays a role both in the Gospel of Luke and Paul's letters. It seems that Marcion attributed such passages to the evil meddling of "judaizing" apostles. They adulterated even the "good" texts accepted by Marcion. Marcion's later critics maintained that Marcion got rid of those passages in Luke and Paul that offended his own doctrines by simply editing them out. Marcion redacted Luke and the ten letters of Paul he accepted, and that edited version was what he identified as proper Christian scripture, the list of authoritative writings for Marcion.[18]

This is the first time in Christianity we have someone attempting to say, "This is an authoritative list of accepted books. These books are what should constitute Christian scripture."[19] Marcion came to be considered a heretic by those Christians who would later be identified as "orthodox." The church in Rome kicked him out and returned his donation.[20] Of course, we must keep in mind, as this book will stress repeatedly, that there were many different kinds of Christianity. In the second century, there were no agreed-on lines between "orthodoxy" and "heresy." Therefore, it is anachronistic, in a sense, even to speak of Marcion as "heretical" and those who rejected his teachings (and accepted both Jewish scripture and four Gospels) as "orthodox." Sometimes in this book, therefore, I adopt the term "proto-orthodox," which is just a somewhat clumsy way of identifying those kinds of Christianity that happen to have agreed, more or less, with what later, in the fourth and fifth centuries, would "win out" as Christian orthodox doctrines.[21] But it is interesting that the first Christian to come up with an authoritative list of Christian scripture was one later rejected as a heretic—mainly because of his rejection of the God of Israel and Jewish scripture.

For much of the twentieth century, scholars believed that Marcion's "canon" list was a major impetus for other Christians to come up with their own canons of Christian scripture.[22] If one did not accept Marcion's list, what alternative should be suggested? Should the church choose one among the different known Gospels as its favorite? What should be read in church? Some Christian writers in the second century started arguing that the church should accept the four Gospels they believed were truly connected to real apostles: Matthew, Mark, Luke, and John. Was this a reaction to Marcion's selection only of Luke?

In the past few decades, some scholars have questioned just how influential Marcion and his list really were on the formation of the Christian canon.[23] Yet there can be little dispute that Marcion's activities and his list are the earliest attempt we know about to identify particular works—and to reject others—as constituting "Christian scripture" set apart from Jewish scripture. His "solution" does demonstrate that having four different Gospels, and these four in particular rather than others, demanded debate and defense in the second century.

There were other ways of dealing with the problem. Tatian was a disciple of Justin Martyr. He took the four Gospels and wove them together to form an edition that combined all four into one book. The product was a book one could hold up as containing everything necessary from each of the four Gospels, now in one handy Gospel. It went by the name *Diatessaron*, which is a Greek word meaning "through four."[24] Other people seemed to prefer one or another Gospel. Papias believed that Mark had followed Peter to Rome and had written down Peter's version of the gospel.[25] So Mark's Gospel gets us closest to Peter, the apostle closest to Jesus. Others seem to have preferred Matthew, who was, after all, one of the twelve, and who is named as a tax collector in the First Gospel (Matt 9:9; the tax collector is named Levi in Mark 2:14 and Luke 5:27). The author of the Gospel of John was also believed to have been a disciple of Jesus,[26] and John seems to have been the favorite of other Christians in the second century.

The problem with all of this, from our modern perspective, is that Papias and these other early Christians didn't really know what they were talking about. Papias, for example, also thought that the Gospel of Matthew had originally been written in Hebrew and only later had been translated into Greek.[27] That is wrong. It is clear to modern scholars that Matthew was written in Greek. It shows no signs of being a translation from Hebrew, and in some instances it makes a point by using Greek words that cannot have been translations from Hebrew.[28] If Papias was so wrong about those "facts" about which we can check him, we probably shouldn't trust him on those "facts" about which we have no other evidence either. So modern scholars doubt all these ancient traditions: that Mark was the disciple of Peter who wrote Peter's version of the gospel; that Matthew was written by the actual disciple Matthew; that Luke was written by the disciple of Paul; and that John was written by John, son of Zebedee. We accept none of these ancient traditions about authorship.

The four Gospels were published anonymously. Note that they are not "pseudonymous," which is the term for a document published under a false name. Rather, they seem to have been written with no authors' names attached. We don't know how or when these names were attached to these Gospels; that is lost to history. They are four of the earliest gospels that survive, all four probably dating from the first century, while most of the "noncanonical" gospels we possess were probably written in the second century or later. They are the culmination of the circulation of first-century oral and written traditions about Jesus.

Later Canonical Lists

One important canon list is known as the Muratorian Canon (see Fig. 2). This list, along with some comments on the different books, was discovered by Ludovico Antonio Muratori (thus the name given by scholars to the document) and published in 1740. It is actually a fragment of the canonical list, missing its beginning and ending abruptly. It survives in a bad Latin translation of a Greek original. For many years, scholars believed

Muratorian Fragment	Cheltenham Canon	Codex Sinaiticus	Claromontanus Canon List
<Gospel>*	Matthew	Matthew	Matthew
<Gospel>*	Mark	Mark	John
Luke	John	Luke	Mark
John	Luke	John	Luke
Acts	13 Pauline Epistles	Romans	Romans
1 Corinthians	Acts	1 Corinthians	1 Corinthians
Galatians	Revelation	2 Corinthians	2 Corinthians
Romans	1 John	Galatians	Galatians
Ephesians	[2 John]**	Ephesians	Ephesians
Philippians	[3 John]	Philippians	1 Timothy
Colossians	1 Peter	Colossians	2 Timothy
1 Thessalonians	[2 Peter]	1 Thessalonians	Titus
2 Corinthians		2 Thessalonians	Colossians
2 Thessalonians		Hebrews	Philemon
Philemon		1 Timothy	1 Peter
Titus		2 Timothy	2 Peter
1 Timothy		Titus	James
2 Timothy		Philemon	1 John
Jude		Acts	2 John
1 John		James	3 John
2 John		1 Peter	Jude
Wisdom		2 Peter	Revelation
Revelation		1 John	Acts
Apoc. of Peter		2 John	Shepherd of Hermas
		3 John	Acts of Paul
		Jude	Apoc. of Peter
		Revelation	
		Epistle of Barnabas	
		Shepherd of Hermas	

Fig. 2 Four Ancient Canon Lists

*The beginning of the Muratorian fragment is missing; it begins by describing Luke as "the third" Gospel.

**The Cheltenham Canon seems to be of two minds regarding the Johannine and Petrine epistles. The original list has the full complement of books, but a later editor has protested "just one" each.

that it might be the earliest canonical list, dating from around 200 or earlier. More recent scholarship has argued that it is from the fourth century, perhaps as late as around 400.[29] For my purposes here, the date of the document is less important than what it includes and excludes.

The author of the Muratorian Canon includes names of books he believes Christians should use as scripture, as well as those they should not consider scripture. At times, we can see that he excludes some documents from his canon not because he believes they are bad books, but just because they shouldn't be considered canonical. Note that he includes books not in a modern Bible. We do have an *Apocalypse of Peter*, but it is not included in our Bibles. And we have the Wisdom of Solomon, but it is one of the books called the Apocrypha, included in Roman Catholic and Anglican (Episcopalian) but not Protestant Bibles.

The author excludes several books by name, two of which are in our New Testament: Hebrews and one letter of John. He knows of, but rejects from his canonical list, the *Shepherd of Hermas*, a second-century document we include in a group of early Christian texts we call "the Apostolic Fathers."[30] He also excludes other books he calls "Gnostic" books. (The issue of early Christian Gnosticism and some writings attributed to "Gnostics" will be addressed in Chapter 8.) If the Muratorian Canon derives from the late second century, it is remarkable for being a very early canonical list that agrees with our own to a degree surprising for that time. It probably did begin with Matthew and Mark, and so it does have, we should note, the four canonical Gospels and no others. If it is from the fourth century, or as late as 400, it is remarkable for the way it differs from what later became the commonly accepted New Testament canon.

The first document that contains a canonical list of the New Testament that matches ours, that has the twenty-seven books of our Bible, dates from the year 367. It is an Easter letter by the bishop of Alexandria, Athanasius. Bishops of the day, especially those of major cities, would sometimes send around a "paschal letter," an Easter letter, in which they would provide instructions on doctrine or practice to the churches in their diocese. In just such a letter from 367, Athanasius says this:

> Again it is not tedious to speak of the [books] of the New Testament. These are, the four Gospels, according to Matthew, Mark, Luke, and John. Afterwards, the Acts of the Apostles and Epistles (called Catholic), seven, viz. of James, one; of Peter, two; of John, three; after these, one of Jude. In addition, there are fourteen

> Epistles of Paul, written in this order. The first, to the Romans; then two to the Corinthians; after these, to the Galatians; next, to the Ephesians; then to the Philippians; then to the Colossians; after these, two to the Thessalonians, and that to the Hebrews; and again, two to Timothy; one to Titus; and lastly, that to Philemon. And besides, the Revelation of John.[31]

Although this is the first surviving canon list that includes only those in our Bible, it is nonetheless interesting that Athanasius places the letters of Paul after those letters we call "the catholic Epistles" (so called because they are addressed not to a specific church but to a wide, general, or "catholic" audience) rather than before them, as in modern Bibles.

Athanasius's letter is sometimes described as the "culmination" of the canonical process, as if, with the publication of his letter, the church had arrived, already in 367, at some kind of agreement about the New Testament canon. Nothing could be further from the truth. We have to remember, for one thing, that Athanasius's letter was authoritative only for his own diocese of Alexandria. No one else had to take any notice of it at all. And portraying his letter as the "end point" of the historical process of the development of the canon ignores the fact that we simply don't find any real churchwide consensus on the question for many years after his letter. As we will see, real consistency on the makeup of the canon did not develop until well into the third, fourth, and even fifth and sixth centuries.[32]

The Invention of the Codex

One of the historical factors that may have contributed to the need for a developing consensus on the canon was the development of the codex.[33] Early books, at least in Greece, in Rome, and generally around the Mediterranean in the Greco-Roman period, were in the form of scrolls. It would take a fairly thick scroll to contain the entire Gospel of Matthew. If someone wanted to look up a particular passage in Matthew, say, one from the middle of the book, a good bit of unrolling, searching, and rolling back up was necessary. If readers wanted to move back and forth between two or among several different citations of different books, that would require unrolling and rerolling many different, unwieldy scrolls. Libraries, therefore, would have boxes or shelves containing scrolls. Synagogues had baskets, boxes, or cabinets that contained the scrolls of the Torah, the prophets, and the other writings of Jewish scripture. Some biblical books would be contained in more than one scroll, so sometimes even moving from an earlier place in a book to a later one (say, in Isaiah, which is a long document) would require a reader to put down one scroll and unroll another.

Around the time of the beginning of Christianity, although people seem to have known about the technology earlier for shorter or more "workaday" texts, people began cutting up scrolls to make pages and sewing the pages together so that they had a "codex," a technical name for what we modern people all think of when we think of a "book": pages sewn or glued together by their edges, or folded and sewn together at the fold, so that one could flip back and forth throughout the entire book.

The technology of the codex was known before Christianity, but by far the most common format for books even in the second and third centuries was the scroll. During the time Christianity was experiencing growth, from the second to the fourth centuries, the codex became increasingly popular as the format for books. Some of us have imagined—it can be only imagination since we don't have direct evidence—that Christians may have been a driving force in the growing popularity of the codex, and we can imagine why. Christians seem to have been an argumentative lot, debating among themselves and with Jews about the proper interpretation of Christian and Jewish texts. Although it is mere speculation (and some scholars have disputed the idea), it is at least easy to see that the codex would provide a more flexible technology for moving around in many texts at the same time than would a box of scrolls.[34]

At any rate, the invention and popularizing of the codex (plural: codices or codexes) may not have been as revolutionary as the invention of, say, the computer, but it did make a difference in the technology of book production and scholarship. As early as the fourth century, copies of the entire Bible, including the Old and New Testaments, were being put between two covers of a book. These are large, thick, heavy books. We have a few, such as the Codex Vaticanus, which resides in the Vatican Library, and the Codex Sinaiticus, which is now in the British Library and is so named because it was found in St. Catherine's Monastery on Mount Sinai. Although these codices are large and heavy, they still would be much more transportable than a whole box or closet full of scrolls. Thus the shift from scroll to codex, which, of course, took place over many centuries, was an important technical innovation.

It also necessitated firmer decisions about what was "in" and what was "out." With a box or closet of scrolls, one can just take a scroll out if the local church or bishop decides it should no longer be read in church as scripture. Once a document is sewn into a book, that decision is not nearly as easy or practicable. Once the canon begins being published between the two covers of a book, deciding what to include or exclude becomes a more permanent decision. The increasing move in Christianity from using scrolls to publishing the Bible, or parts of the Bible, in the form of the codex may have done something to encourage the church to arrive at some stability regarding the extent of the canon.[35] So it is that in the third, fourth, and fifth centuries, we get different codices containing the Bible, and along with them the lists of their contents: their canons, their Bibles.

One called the Cheltenham Canon or List dates probably from around 350.[36] It includes the four Gospels, but in this order: Matthew, Mark, John, Luke. It excludes the Epistle to the Hebrews and the letters of James and Jude. Interestingly, it argues that the number of New Testament books must be exactly twenty-four, because according to Revelation 4:10, twenty-four elders surround God in the heavenly throne room. The Codex Sinaiticus is also dated around 350 and thus is also one of our earliest. It includes the *Letter of Barnabas* and the *Shepherd of Hermas*, both of which we include not in our Bible but in the Apostolic Fathers collection previously mentioned.

The Codex Claromontanus dates from the sixth century. The codex itself contains only the Pauline letters, but inserted between Hebrews and Philemon is a fourth-century canon list in Latin that includes, in this order, Matthew, John, Mark, and Luke. It also includes the *Letter of Barnabas*, the *Shepherd of Hermas*, the *Acts of Paul* (in addition to the Acts of the Apostles), and the *Revelation* (that is, "Apocalypse") *of Peter*. The list, however, excludes Paul's letter to the Philippians, 1 and 2 Thessalonians, and Hebrews.

A Slowly Developing (and Incomplete) Consensus

Far from dating the establishment of the Christian canon to 367 with the publication of Athanasius's Easter letter, we must remember that the development of the Christian canon took centuries.[37] We find differences among canon lists for a very long time. With that in mind, though, we may note that a consensus did gradually develop. Different bishops in major cities and a few church councils attempted decisions and decrees. What is even more remarkable is that they never completely succeeded in arriving at unanimity among all Christians everywhere about the exact extent of the canon. Although this is surprising to most people, what counts as "the Bible" is still not agreed on by Christians around the world.[38]

Generally, the canon of the New Testament, our twenty-seven books, is accepted by all Christian churches, with the exception that the Revelation of John is excluded from the liturgy of Eastern Orthodox churches.[39] The canon of all of scripture, however, is much more up for grabs. The western Roman Catholic canon and the Greek Slavonic Bibles have, for example, Tobit, Judith, the Wisdom of Solomon, Ecclesiasticus, Baruch, the Letter of Jeremiah, and 1 and 2 Maccabees. They also have a longer version of Daniel and a longer version of Esther. The Greek and Slavonic Bibles also accept 1 Esdras, the Prayer of Manasseh, Psalm 151—one more than the 150 psalms of other Bibles—and 3 Maccabees, another Maccabean book. The Slavonic Bible and the Latin Vulgate also include Psalm 151 and 3 Maccabees. And the Greek canon also accepts 4 Maccabees.

Why, with all this variation, is the Protestant canon as it is? At the time of the Reformation, in the 1500s, Roman Catholics had not only the twenty-seven books of the New Testament canon we now have, as well as the books Protestants accept as the Old Testament, but also several other books that we now call the Apocrypha, such as Judith, Tobit, and 1 and 2 Maccabees. These, and several others, were books that had originally been written in Hebrew but had been translated, in ancient times, into Greek. They were taken by many Greek-speaking Jews to be part of Jewish scripture also (although we must remember that there was no firm and settled Jewish canon at that time either). Ancient Christians had tended to accept, as part of their Old Testament, these Jewish texts that survived in their Greek Bibles. Early Christians did not use the Hebrew Bible, but Greek translations of it. Eventually, these books, not part of the scripture that survived in Hebrew, but part of the Greek Old Testament accepted by ancient Christians, were called "deuterocanonical" by Roman Catholics, which means "secondarily canonical," that is, canonical but of a secondary status when compared with the other books of the Old Testament.

During the period of the Reformation, the central Reformers—Martin Luther, John Calvin, and Philipp Melanchthon—had been influenced by the Renaissance, with the scholarly concern at that time to get back to the original texts in original languages. There had been a growing practice of going back to the Greek of classical Greek texts rather than reading them in Latin translation. "Back to the fount," that is, the "origins," was a scholarly goal. So these Reformers wanted to go back to the original Hebrew of the Old Testament scriptures. They noted that some of the books in the Greek Old Testament did not survive in Hebrew. Therefore, they decided not to include those books in the Old Testament proper. They included in their

Protestant Bibles only those Old Testament books that could be translated directly from the Hebrew.

The word "apocrypha" means "hidden things," and this was the term that became associated with those books no longer considered by Protestants to be part either of the proper Old Testament or the New Testament: Jewish writings from the ancient world that might have been written in Hebrew but that survived not in the Hebrew Bible used by Jews, but in Greek Christian Bibles. The Roman Catholic Church retained the Bible it had traditionally used, which still contains those books. Thus the Roman Catholic Bible is larger than the Protestant Bible, because the Roman Catholic canon is based on the ancient Greek Christian canon, and the Protestant canon is based on the Hebrew Bible alone, the Masoretic text of traditional Judaism.[40]

Many people wrongly assume that rabbinic Judaism preceded the beginnings of Christianity because some men are called "rabbis" in the New Testament, including Jesus. But the term "rabbi" could mean simply "teacher," and its occurrence does not mean that what later became rabbinic Judaism, with its concentration on the Mishnah and the Talmuds (the Palestinian and Babylonian Talmuds), was present during the time of Jesus. Rather, what we recognize today as rabbinic Judaism grew up beginning, perhaps, in the second century, but during late antiquity. The rabbis eventually also accepted only those books that survived in Hebrew (or partly in Aramaic in a few cases) as part of their Bible.[41] Jews today often call their scripture Tanak (or Tanakh), which is an acronym for the Hebrew words *torah* (referring to the five books of Moses, the first five books of the Bible, called sometimes the Law), *nevi'im* (prophets), and *ketuvim* (writings; that is, Psalms, Proverbs, and other books not included in the prophets or the Torah).

Jews, therefore, have one Bible based on the ancient Hebrew texts. Protestants have followed the rabbis, in a sense, and accepted the Hebrew Bible as being the Old Testament. Roman Catholics followed the ancient Christian practice of accepting other Jewish texts extant in Greek though originally written in Hebrew as part of the Old Testament. Protestants have one set of texts, Roman Catholics have another, and Jews have another.[42]

But who made the original decisions about the Catholic canon, and why did they do it? As I have already noted, the process was long and complicated and probably owed more to something like a developing consensus than to a vote or firm decision that took place once and for all. A few church councils did make pronouncements on the canon,[43] but some scholars would say that those councils were simply affirming practices that had already become common in general church usage.[44]

Reasons for Canonical Inclusion and Exclusion

Why were some texts included in the New Testament and other texts not? One reason that springs to mind for many Christians is certainly not correct. Many people will answer that something is in the Bible "because it is divinely inspired." That is not the reason ancient Christians would have given. They believed that many texts were inspired (which just means "God-breathed"), and that there were different gradations or levels of inspiration.[45] Just because a text was inspired, or written under instruction from God, was not enough for ancient Christians to include it in the canon.

What they did think was important was apostolic authorship. Even if they believed that an apostle did not personally write the Gospel, for instance, it was important for them to link the author very directly to an apostle, as Papias did for Mark and Peter, or Luke and Paul. Even though we modern scholars do not accept apostolic authorship for most documents in the New Testament, that seems to have been a very important factor to ancient Christians. So if there was a book they did not want included in scripture for whatever reason—say, they did not agree with its theology—they might try to demonstrate that it was not actually written by an apostle.

Flexibly, the criteria the ancient writers seem to have been most concerned about for inclusion in the New Testament are the following:[46]

1. Antiquity and proximity to Jesus. Those texts came to be canonical that were believed to be the most ancient and to have had the closest proximity to Jesus. Even if the documents were not written by apostles, ancient Christians would argue that they were close to the apostles in antiquity and proximity.
2. Popularity in general use and geography. Apparently, the texts that were the most popular over a larger geographic area tended to be those that were accepted eventually as canonical. If many Christians in many places revered a document and used it in their churches, it would be difficult to deny their use of it as scripture in the liturgy. There were different gospels that seem to have been popular in different geographical regions. Literature about Thomas, such as the *Gospel of Thomas* and the *Acts of Thomas*, seems to have been especially popular in Syria and other regions of the East. But as time went on, it seems that Christian leaders attempted to honor as canonical those Gospels and documents that were more generally accepted.

3. Doctrine and theology. Perhaps the most important criterion was theological acceptability. The development of the canon was part of the development of Christian doctrine and theology, including what was being accepted as "orthodox" and what was being rejected as "heretical." We therefore find Christians rejecting documents by pointing out what they consider its theological errors. They reject books that are the favorites of their theological opponents, whom they label "heretics." It may well be, for example, that 2 Peter was eventually included in the New Testament precisely because it argued for "orthodox" interpretations of Paul and in opposition to "heterodox" interpretations of Paul and because it defended doctrines about the coming of Jesus, even though the letter is a later document than most others in the New Testament and was certainly not written by the apostle Peter. One reason some people argued against including Hebrews in the canon was that they thought that it was too lax in its ethics. Hebrews taught that one who repented of grave sins committed even after baptism could still be forgiven—a teaching rejected by morally stricter Christians. The inclusion of 2 Peter and the attempts to exclude Hebrews both demonstrate the centrality of doctrine and theology for the development of the canon.

It may appear cynical to suggest that Christians included those documents they considered theologically appropriate. Once we make that point, we have to ask, "Appropriate to whom?" And that, of course, raises the historical hypothesis that the establishing of the Christian canon was a matter of "who won the theological-political battle for the title 'orthodoxy.' " In the second century, there was no clear line between established orthodoxy and rejected heresy. The diversity of early Christianity predates any later consensus about orthodoxy and thus predates any stability of "canon."[47]

Those Christians in the second and third centuries whose beliefs resembled what later would become orthodox Christianity—the Christian doctrines and theology expressed in the great councils that created the major creeds such as those of Nicea and Chalcedon—were the ones who had the greatest impact on what became a book of the Bible and what did not. In the end, the canon is a list of the winners in the historical debate to define orthodox Christianity.

CHAPTER 3
The Greco-Roman World

Overview: Knowledge of historical context is crucial to understanding the New Testament. Alexander the Great, in his conquests, spread Greek culture throughout the Mediterranean world. This would shape the structure of city-states, which would share characteristically Greek institutions, such as the *gymnasium* and the *boulē*. This would also give rise to religious syncretism, that is, the mixing of different religions. The rise of the Romans would continue this trend of universalization of Greek ideals and religious tolerance, as well as implement the social structure of the Roman household. The Pax Romana and the infrastructures of the Roman Empire would facilitate the rapid spread of Christianity.

Alexander the Great and Hellenization

Religion cannot be divorced from social, political, and historical contexts and issues. In our world, we find the New Testament in the same book as the Old Testament or, as Jews call it, the Hebrew Bible or the Tanak. Clearly, therefore, early Christianity must be studied in the context of ancient Judaism, and that topic will be addressed in the next chapter. But to understand Judaism of the time of Jesus, Paul, and the development of earliest Christianity, we also need to see Judaism in the context of the larger ancient Mediterranean, which was dominated, at least in the urban areas, by both Greek and Roman cultural institutions.

Some classicists may object to the term "Greco-Roman." Because they study ancient Greece and Rome as distinct entities, with their own respective languages, social institutions, and cultures, classicists sometimes cringe when other scholars use the term "Greco-Roman" (and we in religious studies are especially guilty). They may feel that we are papering over or minimizing significant differences between Greek and Roman. But the term is so useful for us who study Christianity and Judaism in the ancient Mediterranean that we are not likely to give it up any time soon.

By the time of the first and second centuries, Rome ruled the eastern Mediterranean. We see Roman governmental institutions in all the major cities of the East. When we travel today in Turkey (the western part of which was Asia Minor in the Roman Empire), we see significant temples to the Roman emperor, as well as to Roma, the goddess and personification of Rome and its people. We see statues honoring the imperial family and other important Romans. But we also note that eastern cities are often structured around certain older institutions that made up Greek cities. The dominant language of the upper class and educated persons, and even of many others, such as merchants and businesspeople, was Greek. Although we do find a Latin inscription here and there, or a bilingual inscription in Latin and Greek, by far most of the inscriptions are in Greek. The Romans who governed the Roman provinces in the East were usually expected to speak Greek. It would be misleading to call urban culture in the eastern Mediterranean in the first two centuries C.E. (the basic limit of this book) either "Roman" or "Greek" without substantial modification. Urban culture was a mixture of older Greek elements and more recently arrived Roman elements. Judaism was neither a "Roman religion" nor a "Greek religion," but it is entirely sensible to call it a "Greco-Roman religion."

By calling the Judaism of the early centuries of Christianity "Greco-Roman," we signal that it was one among many recognized ethnicities—Egyptian, Lydian, German, Scythian, and on and on. Modern persons often have the mistaken idea that there were perhaps three cultural entities in the world that saw the advent of Christianity: Greek, Roman, and Jewish (or, in an even more misleading taxonomy, Christian, Jewish, and pagan). But that is not the case, and it elevates Judaism to an exceptionalism as an *ethnos* (the Greek word for a "people" with its own culture and language) on a par with Rome and Greece. The dominant "ethnicities" or cultures were obviously the Romans and the Greeks, but everyone recognized that there were many others, and it was assumed that each ethnic group had its own ways of dealing with its own gods and other superhuman beings, such as demons or angels or heroes or ghosts; that is, each ethnic group was expected to have its own religion, to invoke the word we (but not they) would use to group together technologies for dealing with the gods.[1]

In that case, Judaism was treated as its own ethnicity with its own cultural traditions, including ways of sacrificing to, praying to, and otherwise dealing with the gods. Those ways, though, had been influenced first by Greek culture and later, somewhat, by Roman. Thus the Judaism of our period may be designated, like Egyptian practices and culture, a "Greco-Roman religion." Therefore, in order correctly to understand the particular kind of Judaism of this period as an ethnicity, culture, and even "religion," to use the rather anachronistic umbrella term, we must place it in its Greco-Roman context. Thus the need for this chapter.

We need not go all the way back to classical Greece, however—that is, to Athens of the sixth and fifth centuries—but only to the process of "hellenization" of the East that began, we may say for convenience, with Alexander the Great. The word "Hellene" means simply "Greek" (our English "Greek" is from the Latin designation for the Greeks, whereas the Greeks called themselves, of course, "Hellenes" when they were speaking Greek). "Hellenization" refers to the "making Greek," the "Grecization," of the eastern part of the Mediterranean that accelerated with the eastern conquests of Alexander.[2]

Alexander the Great's father was Philip II, king of Macedonia, or Macedon. Philip conquered the different Greek city-states, eventually defeating Athens and its allies at Chaeronea in 338 B.C.E. Alexander was born in 356 B.C.E.[3] He was educated by Aristotle beginning in 342 and became king after the assassination of his father in 336. Alexander continued the expansion policies of his father Philip. At the time, Persia was the large empire in the region, controlling vast areas of the eastern Mediterranean, including Greece's neighbors to the east in Asia Minor.

Persia was always threatening to overrun Greece itself. Alexander defeated the Persian army in Asia Minor in the battle of Granicus, in 334, which put Alexander and his Macedonian army in control of all of Macedonia, Greece, and Asia Minor. When Darius II, the "Great King" of the Persians, died, Alexander took that title for himself. Eventually, after more battles with Persia, Alexander pushed his army all the way to the Indus River, the western boundary of India, we might say. He wanted to go all the way to the Ganges River, but his army forced him to turn back. Alexander was not yet thirty-three years old when he died of a fever in Babylon (modern-day Iraq) in 323.

After Alexander's death, his empire was divided among his generals, who fought many wars over who would get control of which parts of the formerly united empire. After much fighting, maneuvering, and negotiation, different smaller kingdoms or empires rose out of Alexander's, ruled by Alexander's former generals and their dynasties. We call these rulers the Diadochi (from the Greek *diadochoi*, which means "successors"). There were several of these kingdoms, and their boundaries, structures, and rulers changed regularly. For our purposes, however, only two of these "Hellenistic kingdoms" are important because of their importance in the history of Palestine and Judea in the centuries before Christ.

Making its primary base in Syria was a kingdom ruled by Seleucus and later his descendants. In Egypt, Alexander's general Ptolemy established his own kingdom, which was ruled for centuries by different Ptolemies. We need to keep in mind that these were actually "Greek" kingdoms, since they established Hellenistic social and cultural structures, their rulers and elite inhabitants spoke Greek, and they educated their children in Greek ways. Thus the "Syrian-Greek" kingdom of the Seleucids (as the dynasty is called) lay just to the north of Palestine, and just to its south was the "Egyptian-Greek" kingdom of the Ptolemies. It is very important for the history of Judea at this time that Judea was caught between these constantly warring and conniving dynasties, sharing a northern border with Syria and the Seleucids and a southern border with Egypt and the Ptolemies.

The different peoples Alexander had conquered obviously spoke many different languages and had different customs. Alexander himself had founded many cities around the eastern Mediterranean, often giving land to his veterans and settling them and their families in different conquered locations. These cities, though, were all founded on the model of the previous Greek cities. Gradually, this practice of Alexander, later followed also by his successors, led to the fact that the eastern Mediterranean was dotted with towns and cities that had at least a strong veneer of hellenization. The elites were expected to be able to speak Greek, and they educated their sons, and sometimes their daughters, with Greek education and in Greek ways.

The lower classes continued to live mainly in the countryside and in villages, speaking their own ethnic languages and maintaining their local customs. But those who intended to occupy the upper class and live in the cities had to accommodate themselves to the hellenizing program of Alexander and his successors. Thus those cities founded by Alexander and his successors certainly ended up being "Greek" cities no matter where they were located, and gradually, even the older cities came to be "Greek" as well, at least for the elite inhabitants. Whether this was Alexander's conscious decision and an intended program or was just an accident of history, something like a unified cultural world developed in the Hellenistic period, based on the classical institutions of the Greek *polis*, the city.

This may have been the first time in history, or at least in the Mediterranean and its environs, where an attempt was made to create a large empire in which everyone—or again, at least everyone of the upper class, everyone who "mattered"—shared one language, one culture, and a common educational system: one world. Previous conquerors—say, the Assyrians, the Egyptians, the Babylonians, and the Persians—seem to have contented themselves with defeating other peoples and deriving from them tribute—taxes, food, and money. They seem not to have cared about turning those they conquered into Assyrians or Egyptians or Persians themselves. The hellenized, urban world created by Alexander and his successors meant that the regions he had conquered shared much common language and culture.

As I mentioned, the people in these new cities or older cities that were being "hellenized" spoke Greek, but it was a form somewhat different from those dialects spoken in classical Athens or Ionia. A "common" form of the Greek language developed, a modified and popularized version of Greek that scholars call "Koine" Greek (*koinē* is the Greek word for "common" or "shared"). The form of Greek, therefore, Paul spoke, which he learned from the beginnings of his life growing up in a Greek city, probably in Cilicia (along the southern and eastern coast of modern-day Turkey and Syria), was Koine Greek. Thus the New Testament was written in Koine Greek, the "common language," the lingua franca, of the urban eastern Mediterranean in the first and second centuries C.E.

The Greek City-State

The Greek polis (plural *poleis*) had several institutions that later become important for Judaism and early Christianity.[4] We cannot think of these poleis in terms of the huge cities we have today, or Rome at that time. A Greek polis might number only one thousand citizens, or five thousand. It is often estimated that the city of Rome had one million inhabitants in the first century. No classical Greek city was ever nearly that large. Although the Greek cities were of different sizes, they tended to be similar to one another in what they contained, in their structures and institutions. The center of the town (the polis would more often look like a town to us) would have certain buildings necessary for the governing of the town and day-to-day life in it. But the town would also be the center of a much larger geographic area, the "region" (*chōra*; pronounced "kohra"), including farmland, villages, and the majority of the inhabitants of the area. Thus Athens was the polis for the entire region of Attica. There was a mutual dependency between the polis and its surrounding area: the city dwellers needed the production powers of the countryside, and the rural dwellers needed the aspects of market, culture, and government provided by the polis.

Greek methods of educating children (mostly just males) were, of course, not uniform throughout time and location, but by the time of the hellenization of much of the eastern Mediterranean, education in the different Greek cities was remarkably similar.[5] The Greek word for "education" is *paideia*, which means more than simply rote learning or memorization or learning to read. Paideia referred to the complete education, the "forming," of the boy who would become the proper citizen of a Greek polis, including reading and writing, of course, but also music, mathematics, athletics, and fighting. Girls could sometimes be given some education, but that was usually done within their own families. The state did not concern itself with the education of females. So paideia referred to the training of young men mentally, militarily, and culturally.

Education took place mostly in the gymnasium.[6] The word does not refer to a building in itself, nor simply to the place where athletic activities alone took place. The word comes from the Greek *gymnos*, which means "naked," and the reason these locations were called "the naked place" was that Greek youths stripped naked for exercise, sports, and physical training. The gymnasium, however, also was the place for all sorts of learning. Adolescent boys, for instance, were regularly taught rhetoric, the reading, writing, memorizing, practicing, and giving of speeches, and this took place in the halls of the gymnasium. The gymnasium was also a social place for the men in the city. They would gather there, watch the boys and younger men go through their exercises or compete in sports, meet their friends, make dinner plans for later, or just while away the day. Men also played games in the gymnasium, such as board games using knucklebones and such. When we travel in Greece and other countries today, we can see in archeological sites board games, with their squares, circles, or boxes, carved in the flagstones of different temples or buildings.

At first, in what we might think of as "elementary" schooling, boys were taught reading and writing and some arithmetic, mostly using Homer. Later, after the onset of puberty, boys would be taught rhetoric. Around the ages of sixteen to eighteen, the boys would be called "ephebes" and would be enrolled in the local town's "ephebate," the social organization for young men that provided their final preparation for citizenry and military service. The ephebes marched together in parades, trained together in sports and military maneuvers, and often developed strong ties of friendship and camaraderie with one another. The ephebate (or *ephēbeia*) was the institution every young man went through in order to become a citizen of the city. (In Greek cities, women and "aliens," that is, people whose ancestors had come from elsewhere, were not citizens.)

Greek cities also had particular political institutions. The most fundamental was the *dēmos*, which means, in its simplest sense, "the people," but more technically referred to all the male citizens. The dēmos became most important, of course, with the invention of democracy (rule by the dēmos) in Athens at the end of the sixth century B.C.E. (we may even date it to the reforms of Cleisthenes in 508–507).[7] Although most foreigners (including those of foreign ancestry), slaves, and women were excluded, all adult male citizens, as members of the official dēmos, had a vote. The classical democracies of Athens and other Greek cities collapsed or were destroyed later. Neither Philip nor Alexander promoted democracies, but the idea that the dēmos was a political body that had its own prerogatives was retained. Thus in Greek cities of the Hellenistic period also, although the different citizen bodies did not completely rule themselves, they did come together, usually in the theater, for debates and local decisions.

Out of the dēmos was chosen a smaller council called a *boulē*. Its size varied much among different cities. It might have, though, fifty men, or more or fewer. The council was usually charged with deliberating about new business or particular issues, perhaps voting itself, and then bringing the matter to the fuller body of citizens for final decision. This gathered body of all the citizens, the official dēmos, was called the *ekklēsia*. The word is very fecund, with many different meanings throughout antiquity. Literally, it means something like "the calling out." For the polis, it referred to the gathered assembly of the citizens that would have vigorous debates and come to a vote on measures perhaps forwarded by the council. The word occurs many times in our New Testament, where it is most often translated "church."

The typical structures of the Greek city would have included a theater.[8] Theaters were, of course, places for performances. By the first century, as Christianity was developing, theaters were no longer the site for highbrow productions of the great classical tragedies, such as those by Sophocles or Euripides. People more often would see farces or fairly crass comedies in their local theater. The Romans liked to fill the central part of a theater, the *cavea*, with water, and they staged naval battles or elaborate mock military productions. So people might enjoy all kinds of public amusements in theaters. Theaters were also the place where the ekklēsia would have its meetings, with the men all talking at once, shouting each other down, or booing some local bigwig when his speech lasted too long. The theater was a central space in the Greek city, housing both entertainments and the meetings of the political decision-making body, the ekklēsia.

Greeks are and were famous for their games.[9] Of course, the gymnasium was one place for gaming of both the running and jumping kinds, as well as the gambling kind. But for larger events, cities had a hippodrome, from the Greek words for "horse" and "running." This was a large track, often with huge stadium rows for spectators, much like our football stadiums, though narrower. Later, Romans would adopt the hippodrome, rename it the Latin "circus," and use it for the elaborate and hugely popular chariot races so loved by Romans and even by many Christians (over the objections of their priests and bishops).

The later Romans were the most energetic advocates of public baths, but these were known in Greek cities as well and were central and valued social amenities. At times, some baths were "co-ed," shared even at the same time by both men and women, but mostly they were used only by men, or by women at designated days and times. Like the gymnasium, the baths were an important venue for social networking. Baths included public toilets as well. One can scarcely wander the ruins of a Greek or Roman city today without seeing latrines. By the first and second centuries, baths would have different rooms for different purposes: rooms for dressing and undressing; a room with a cold pool; a room with a tepid or lukewarm pool; and a hot room supplied with hot water. Men especially attended the baths to relax, make a business deal, meet friends, chat, meet new people, or perhaps try to have sex. All kinds of things went on in the baths.[10]

These basic structures constituted daily life for many people in ancient Greek cities. Alexander and his successors took those basic institutions from the Greeks and transplanted them all over the eastern Mediterranean, in Egypt, Syria, Asia Minor, and yes, Palestine. That is why modern travelers to Syria, Israel, Jordan, Egypt, Turkey, and many other modern countries can see excavations of towns that look remarkably alike because they were inspired by the originally Greek model of the polis, with theaters, smaller council lecture halls, baths, public buildings, and temples. All major cities of the Mediterranean came to have a certain commonality, a *koinē*, a Greek "overlay," along with surviving original, indigenous languages and cultures.

Religious Syncretism

The English word "syncretism" derives from the Greek word for a "mixture," or a "mixing together" (*sygkrēsis* or *sygkrasis*). When Alexander arrived in Egypt, to cite just one among many possible examples, he would have encountered there the goddess Isis. She was an important deity of Egypt, well represented in literature and art. Alexander would have felt no compunction about worshiping her as Isis, an important Egyptian goddess. In the ancient world, people tended to think that one should worship local gods when in their territory. It couldn't hurt, they thought, and it might help, or at least keep the local gods from harming you because you neglected to show them proper respect. Ancient devotions to gods were seldom mutually exclusive. People cheerfully, or sometimes out of fright, worshiped many different deities of many different places and of many different levels of power.

But ancient people, often led by intellectuals such as philosophers or writers of mythologies, regularly combined the different cultural deities by equating one from one area with one more familiar to them from their own region. Thus Alexander may have worshiped Isis as Isis, but he also could believe that when he was paying homage to Isis in Egypt, he was at the same time worshiping the same goddess known by another name in Greece and elsewhere, such as Artemis, goddess of the hunt. As all high-school students well versed in Greek and Roman mythologies now know, the ancients often believed that Aphrodite was simply the Greek name for the same god called Venus in Latin. Just as people in the increasingly "international" world of the ancient world might have more than one name, one from their indigenous language and another in the more dominant language of the Greeks or Romans, so people interpreted the many different names of deities to be, at least some of the time, just different cultural names for the same gods. Moreover, they mixed together different stories about the gods from different cultures, and different images and attributes of the gods from different locations. Scholars call this mixture of religious elements and deities from different origins "religious syncretism."[11] Alexander seems to have promoted it, perhaps even self-consciously, as a propaganda technique and a unifying ideology.[12]

Alexander even claimed divine status for himself. He allowed rumors to be circulated that his mother had been impregnated by the god Apollo, who was supposed to have come to her bed in the form of a snake. Alexander's interest in attaining divine status was not new among rulers in certain parts of the ancient world; kings in some cultures had been considered gods by their people for many years.[13] Although we have no way of knowing what was in Alexander's head, we also have no reason to doubt that Alexander really believed he was divine. Contrary to modern popular assumptions, the combination of humanity and divinity in one person was not at all considered impossible in the ancient world; it wasn't even particularly rare. Alexander, the stories went, had a divine father and a human mother; he was a highly successful governor and warrior; he had conquered practically the whole world; of course he was a god.

Another means for "mixing" the gods and practices of different peoples was simply to add new ones to the old ones. People had little reserve about adding gods: the more the merrier, or safer. So sometimes Greeks, and others, would discover the goddess Isis from Egypt and simply add her to their own pantheon. Although the Romans would develop a reputation for wariness about new cults or new gods in Rome, their actual history shows them often moving from initial caution or opposition to eventually importing new gods to Rome. One of the most popular of such gods was Asclepius, the god of healing, who traveled to Rome in a boat and crawled off onto the island in the middle of the Tiber in the form of a snake. But there were many others as well.

Ancient pieties were not exclusive. The fact that one was especially attracted to one god didn't mean one shouldn't worship and sacrifice to others. This was common throughout almost all the ancient world. The spread of hellenization after Alexander also seems to have furthered practices of religious syncretism.[14] As we will see in the next chapter, this would become a problem for Jews, some of whom seemed to welcome the previously "alien" gods, but others of whom resisted. Even if Jews were willing to adopt the Greek language, some social institutions, citizenship, and other practices, many of them ended up resisting the tendency toward religious syncretism.[15]

The Roman Household and Social Structure

As the Romans became more and more powerful, they became more and more a military and political factor in the East. They conquered the Greek states, which had been under the rule of various Hellenistic kings descended from Alexander's successors, as had Egypt and Syria. In 146 B.C.E. the Romans destroyed Corinth. In 63 B.C.E. the Roman general Pompey intervened in an internal fight in Jerusalem over the priesthood and political power. The Romans were then in control of Judea from 63 B.C.E. on, although they periodically changed the form of government they used to rule it. As the Romans became more powerful in the East, they did little to "romanize" or "latinize" the East. Instead, as they moved into the eastern Mediterranean, they simply adopted the Greek system, the "Greek world," and did not attempt to make it non-Greek. The Greek language, Greek culture, religious practices, and education, and the polis structure all remained in the East throughout Roman rule there, all the way until it was ruled by the Christian Constantine, and beyond.

One thing the Romans made even more central to their system of law and culture than had the Greeks was the patron-client system.[16] The terms "patron" and "client" come from the Latin, and it is true that the "official" patron-client systems that were enshrined in Roman law were more developed and dominant than in surrounding cultures. For that reason, some people even want to restrict the term "patron-client" to discussions of Roman systems. But anthropologists have used "patron-client" language and models to describe structures and practices of many different peoples, and it must be admitted that the basic aspects of what anthropologists have labeled "patron-client systems" existed all around the Mediterranean, affecting the day-to-day activities of almost everyone to some extent.

As we will see, understanding the expectations that patrons had of their clients and clients had of their patrons will help make sense of many issues of unity and conflict in the New Testament and early Christianity, even though those expectations in early Christianity—unlike in Roman society—were not inscribed in law. And in order to understand the patron-client system, we must examine the ancient household.[17]

I use the term "household" here, rather than "family," for good reason. Today, by "family" we normally mean the biological family: father, mother, and children. We may broaden that term to include the "extended family" of grandparents, grandchildren, and others.[18] But we normally are picturing the nuclear family with perhaps some extension. Ironically, although the English word comes from the Latin *familia*, the Latin was not taken to refer to the father, mother, and children. The term was originally, and always to some extent, taken to designate the slaves of a household, sometimes including the freed slaves as well (the "freedmen" and "freedwomen"). Legally, therefore, the ones who truly belonged to the familia were the slaves, not the free members of the household. It thus is a bit less misleading to speak of the ancient household rather than the family.

Moreover, the household included other persons we in the modern world would not include in the family. The Roman household was constructed like a pyramid (see Fig. 3; although this mainly describes the Roman household, it holds true for others in the ancient Mediterranean to some extent). At the top was the *paterfamilias* ("father" of the "familia"), the oldest free man of the household, the father (or grandfather if he was still living). Under him were his sons and daughters. At the bottom of the household pyramid were the slaves. But above the slaves and below the free offspring of the paterfamilias were the freedpersons, former slaves who had been freed but were still considered part of the household and in Roman law were legally still part of the household and still owed the householder duties. In Roman law, the Latin word for "client" (*cliens*) refers to the freed slaves of a paterfamilias. Most households also included at least some free people who were unofficially connected to the paterfamilias and therefore were functionally also members of the household, although they were not legally part of it. They may have occupied an unofficial position of status above the freedmen and below the free children.

Notice that I have not mentioned the wife and mother yet.[19] Legally, most free wives of Roman citizens were not members of the household of

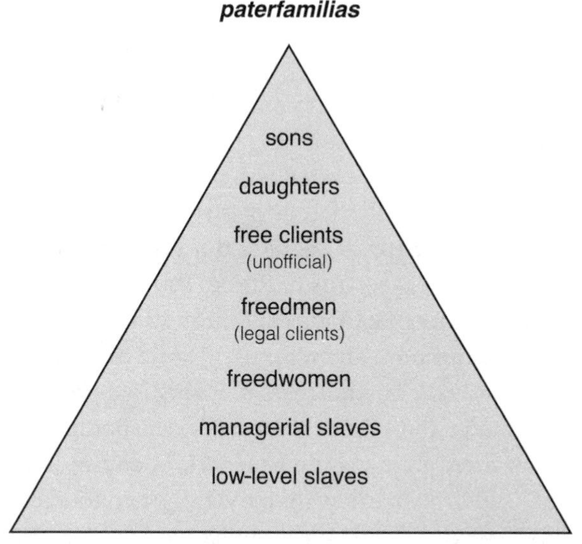

Fig. 3 Structure of a Patriarchal Greco-Roman Household

their husbands (and in Rome, women could be citizens also, although they lacked many of the rights and advantages of citizenship enjoyed by the men). They remained members of the household of their father. Legally, they were expected to be under the control and protection of their fathers, or perhaps brothers, or even grandfathers if they were still living. But because life expectancy in the ancient world was so much shorter than in ours, several generations were usually not still present in most households. People just died out sooner.

It is interesting and important that the Romans, unlike the Greeks and many other peoples of the time, did not allow the wife to become a member of the household of her husband. Wives even kept their own financial resources they had received from the households of their fathers. There were laws restricting gifts between husbands and wives precisely in order to keep riches from migrating too much from some households to others.

There were sensible reasons the Romans set things up this way. From the time of the republic and into the time of the empire, the ruling class of Rome was made up of many different households, important extended families. By keeping women under the household of the men of their original family, the upper-class Romans tried to maintain some balance in size and importance among these households. The ruling class cared little about the household arrangements of the much, much larger lower class. What it cared about was keeping the major elite families in balance. It did not want a king, or even a cabal of leaders, to be able to arise. It hoped to maintain a balance of power among the several major households of Rome, the "great" families of Rome.

Slaves were obviously members of the household of the paterfamilias. Unlike American slavery, in which the vast majority of slaves remained slaves all their lives and emancipation was rather rare and difficult, Roman slaves could often expect to be freed in their lifetimes if they lived long enough. Male slaves once freed, though, did not become "free" men but "freedmen"—an official legal status in Rome. They still owed certain duties to their paterfamilias. For example, a Roman man might put a slave in charge of a small business to run on his own, or he might employ a slave as a secretary, or a physician, or a business manager in a project controlled by the owner. Slaves were sometimes rented out as laborers to other people. Slaves would give their wages to their owners, of course, but usually they were allowed to keep some of them. Some slaves, therefore, especially those managing a business and turning a profit, could become financially independent, save enough money, and buy their freedom. The money did not legally belong to the slave; the slave and everything he might accumulate were legally the property of the owner. But practically speaking, and in some legal contexts, slaves had much control over at least some money and property, which were called the *peculium*.

Because slaves could not legally own property or sign contracts, it sometimes made sense for owners to free certain slaves so they could do those things. An owner might free a slave who had been working as his business manager so the slave could take on more responsibilities in his job, such as signing contracts, lending or borrowing money, or running another business, say, in another town. An owner who lived in Rome but owned an import-export business in the port at Ostia would probably want a dependable person to manage the business there legally. Whereas some such activities would be difficult for a slave to accomplish, a freedman would have no such legal impediments. Rich Romans often freed slaves, therefore, not out of altruism, but for the owner's financial gain.

It is also important to note that Rome was quite unusual in another aspect of emancipation. When a Roman citizen freed a slave (at least when the emancipation was done according to certain legally prescribed procedures), that former slave (male or female) became not just a freedperson but also a Roman citizen. Any children born to a freed citizen after his emancipation were born both "free" (they did not suffer from the lower status of "freed" as their father did) and Roman citizens. As odd as it seems to modern people, slavery provided one of the very rare means of upward social mobility in what was otherwise a rigid status hierarchy of Rome.[20]

Although sons and daughters were legally still part of the household of their father as long as he was alive, we need not imagine that they actually lived in the same house. They might well set up their own households, marry, and have children, slaves, and freedpersons of their own. So practically speaking, sons and daughters enjoyed freedom and controlled property, even though legally everything they had also belonged to the paterfamilias. Much the same was true for wives. Although they did not share in the legal ownership of their husband's property, we see them regularly "taking care of things" for their husbands and the household. So although the legal situation stipulated that the wife had her property and the husband his, things got more mixed up than that in everyday life.

We can see the importance of this household and patron-client system by noting how many aspects of everyday Roman life and politics it affected. Roman society, as I've already noted, was strictly and rigidly hierarchical. There was no illusion about democratic structures or equality—not, that is, across class and status lines. Social power was nakedly linked to wealth and status. The Roman legal system was even explicitly partial toward the wealthy and the upper class.[21] Judges were expected to side, most of the time, with the richer man rather than the poorer man. They seemed to have bought into a certain ideology that seems strange to us. Since the rich man is rich, he must have less incentive to cheat the poor man out of his pittance. But since the poor man has nothing, he has an incentive to try to cheat the rich man out of his money. The assumption, even explicitly expressed sometimes in the law, was that the richer man was more likely also the more honest man. Judges were therefore expected to favor other members of their own class.

Slaves, of course, had no legal standing to represent themselves or anyone else in a court of law, but freedmen could do so. But it might make much more sense for a freedman to be represented by his patron or by a lawyer hired by his patron. His patron enjoyed power and honor simply by being of higher economic and social status. A man needed someone of higher status than himself to function as his patron, certainly in court, but also in many other contexts. In court, as in society and politics more generally, it helped to have strong patrons. In fact, unless a man was himself near the top of the social hierarchy, it was necessary to have a powerful patron.

But patrons needed clients also. If a patron wanted to run for office, he needed the votes and the canvassing of his clients. Even if he needed only more prestige, he had to have a large entourage, which would be made up of his household, his clients, and his "friends" (a term that in Latin was often a code word for "clients" when it might be embarrassing to be called a "client"). Clients were expected to show up in the morning at the home of their patron, to greet him (the *salutatio*), and perhaps to accompany him around town that day as he attempted to make political deals. In return, patrons were expected to give gifts to their clients, often in the form of cash. In the Roman patron-client system, money was passed down the social scale in return for honor that was passed upward. As we will see, this becomes central for understanding early Christian churches and some of their conflicts.

The Rise of Julius Caesar and Octavian

The vast majority of Romans, even the free citizens, were poor people. For the most part, they had little or no access to the powerful households that ran the city. They had little or no access to powerful patrons. This was a "need" Julius Caesar set about to meet in his very person.

Roman politics in the late republic (including the first century B.C.E.) was dominated by two political parties: the *optimates*, meaning "the best," who tended to support the interests of the wealthy senators and the few wealthiest families; and the *populares*, that is, "of the people," who attempted to gain their political power by pushing for policies that were more beneficial to the lower classes. Julius Caesar came from a patrician family—that is, not only a family of the upper class, but also one that boasted an ancient aristocratic lineage. One would have expected him to side with the optimates, even though his family, though patrician, was not one of the wealthiest of Rome. But in the party politics of the Senate, Caesar began siding with the more populist faction. He had great birth credentials, and to those he attempted to add political power by making himself popular with the poor majority of the population.[22]

To become a truly successful Roman politician, it was almost necessary to serve as a general at some point. Julius Caesar capitalized on his role as general of a large army that was at the time winning battles in Gaul (modern France). Generals were often responsible for paying their soldiers, or at least for making sure they got paid. Caesar had a reputation for paying his soldiers well. In doing so, he was in a sense setting himself up as the "patron" (unofficial, of course) of his army, his soldiers. At one point, in fact, the Senate, nervous about Caesar's growing popularity and power, ordered some legions removed from his army in Gaul and transferred to Syria. The story goes that Caesar—out of his own pocket, although we must remember that his pockets were full of plundered war booty—gave each of his departing soldiers a year's pay. He was in a sense buying the ongoing loyalty of his separated soldiers. He was acting as their patron and making them his clients.

Back in Rome, Caesar gained more power and pushed policies that moderately helped the lower classes. He did not actually cancel debts (which the poor were always clamoring for and the wealthy always feared), but he mitigated debt problems. He advocated other policies that eased some of the strains on the poor in Rome and its environs. Conservative forces in the Senate feared that he was setting himself up to be dictator, as was doubtless the case. So on the famous Ides of March (March 15) in 44 B.C.E., he was stabbed by a gang of senators led by Brutus and Cassius.

Caesar's adopted son Octavian formed an alliance with Caesar's friend Mark Antony, along with a lesser-known figure named Lepidus. The three of them initially were successful in their battles against other forces of the Senate. In the end, however, Mark Antony and Octavian fought a civil war, which Octavian won, defeating Mark Antony and causing Cleopatra, by that time the lover of Mark Antony and mother of two children by him, to commit suicide. Octavian became sole ruler of Rome and its territories in 27 B.C.E.[23]

Octavian refused the title of "king" (as had Caesar before him) and instead assumed traditional republican titles. One of his propagandists said about him: "The pristine form of the Republic was recalled as of old."[24] Octavian himself, now known by his adopted title and name Augustus, said, "I transferred the Republic from my power to the dominion of the Senate and the people of Rome."[25] In other words, Augustus was insisting that he was no king, but just another senator, though perhaps the "first" (*princeps*) among a Senate of equals. Of course, all these are lies. Augustus did reconstitute the Senate, but it was precisely that: a Senate reconstituted by Augustus, who had become an emperor, that is, the one wielding ultimate power and authority. Certainly in his propaganda and, one could argue, at least to some extent in reality, he did set himself up, as had Caesar, as the "patron of all the people," the "patron of the patronless." The radical change effected by Augustus, who was following Caesar's aborted lead, was a change from an oligarchy of wealthy families exercised through an infighting and competitive Senate to the rule of one man and his household. Augustus became the paterfamilias of the entire new Roman Empire (see Fig. 4).

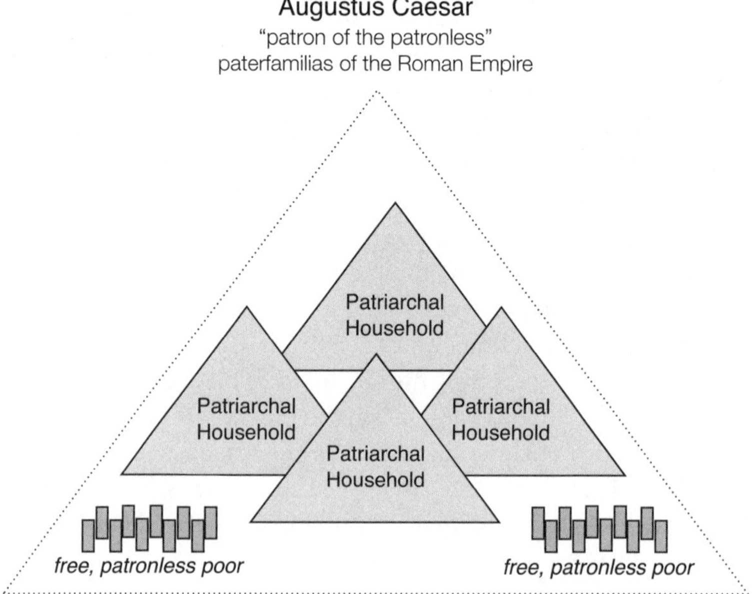

Fig. 4 Augustus as Paterfamilias of the Roman Empire

The Pax Romana

The reign of Augustus inaugurated what historians call the Roman Empire, as distinct from the previous Roman Republic. It also ushered in a period of two hundred years of the Pax Romana, the "Roman Peace." Rome had been wracked by civil wars and other conflicts during the previous hundred years, and although wars and smaller conflicts continued on the frontiers of the empire, within the center there was a notable period of peace.[26]

Historians have generally believed that this period was a good one in the ancient history of the world, dubbing especially the second century C.E. the "golden age" of Roman rule. It is debatable, though, whether it was that good for everyone. Non-Romans and poor people may have seen the Pax Romana as more oppressive than pleasant. After all, in our own time, the decade or so after the fall of the Soviet Union was dubbed the Pax Americana by many pundits. But what was seen as benign for humanity by most Americans and conservatives around the world was seen by many others as merely the triumph of turbo-capitalism, promoted for the benefit of large American and multinational corporations but to the detriment of the lower classes, who saw their well-being decline just as the wealth of the very wealthy skyrocketed. And the so-called Pax Americana was followed, of course, by the terrorist attacks and the subsequent American wars of choice of the early twenty-first century: over ten years of constant and expensive warfare. Similarly, although the lower classes of the Roman Empire have left no records by which we may judge their reactions to Roman rule, we must assume that it was not as favorable as many historians have made it out to be.

The Romans maintained a modicum of peace, for one thing, by leaving local populations pretty much alone with regard to local customs, religious practices, and living arrangements. When they thought it necessary, they maintained peace by destroying communities and forcibly moving populations. The Romans tried to do so, however, only when they believed that it was necessary to maintain absolute control.

Rome itself prospered by taxation. The Romans held censuses, though not universal ones as claimed in Luke 2:1–3. They did so in order to keep taxes high and fully paid.[27] The Romans themselves did not actually collect taxes in most of their territories. Rather, they depended on local, upper-class elites to do so. People in the provinces who were already at the high end of the social scale would bid for the right to collect local taxes, and of course, the Romans tended to take the highest bids. Those local elites would be in charge of tax collection, using their inferiors to collect enough to pass along to Rome, but keeping substantial amounts for themselves. The taxation system, therefore, tended toward thorough corruption, since the incentive of tax collectors was to collect as much as possible, and Rome had little incentive to police the practice.

This is why the epithet "tax collector" is coupled in the Gospels with "sinners." The local rich, some of whom would have bought the franchise for collecting taxes, may have profited by the "Roman peace." But the vast majority of inhabitants, who would have been the majority poor rural population combined with the poor in the cities, suffered from the system of taxation and thus blamed their fellow locals for being traitors to their own people for the benefit of themselves and Rome. Tax collectors were unpopular because they worked for the local wealthy, who were working for the Romans and usually impoverishing the poor. The Romans maintained their power, to a great extent, by keeping the poor poor. The Pax Romana probably did sound great to the Romans and the provincial elites, who tended to be their allies. It probably was a mixed blessing, if that, to the rest of the provincial population.

The Romans did make improvements, however, and one of the most significant was in travel.[28] Pompey had cleared the Mediterranean of pirates, which is something that our modern governments can't seem to do.[29] They built roads and maintained some communication. The Romans had a mail service, although it was for official use by the government only. This meant, in any case, that Roman officials, in Rome and throughout the empire, could have mail delivered fairly quickly by ancient standards. They even used a horseback relay that could travel one hundred kilometers per day. Soldiers were expected to be able to travel thirty kilometers per day with a full pack. That was possible only because the Romans maintained major roads, built by the army. These roads, of course, weren't built just for the good of the population. Just as the American interstate freeway system was originally designed and built to enable the rapid movement of the American army in the possible case of a major war (it was begun during the cold war), so the Romans built their road system primarily for their army.

But of course, others used the roads as well. The roads, combined with the sea lanes for passenger and shipping travel, rendered the ancient Mediterranean, including the land surrounding the water, much more accessible for all travelers. This is certainly one of the reasons Christianity spread so easily, and that Paul, for one, was able to travel several times around the eastern Mediterranean, from Syria to Jerusalem to Asia Minor to Greece, back to Judea, and eventually to Rome. Paul, like any ancient traveler, would have preferred to go by sea, which was still much faster than by land, but if necessary, he could also have traveled on the roads built and maintained by the Romans.

I have already mentioned that the Romans did not attempt to force Roman religious practices or gods onto the populations of the lands they conquered. Although it has been a popular Hollywood idea that the Romans oppressed other religions, or perhaps just the Christians, that is inaccurate.[30] The Romans actually tolerated local religions. They didn't care much what gods people worshiped. In fact, the Romans had a reputation, which they nourished among themselves, of being very pious in the sense that they believed that sacrifices and offerings should be made to the gods of whatever land they were in at the time. Different peoples were allowed, indeed encouraged, to use and care for their own gods.

Since at least the time of Julius Caesar, Jews had enjoyed certain privileges. They could observe the Sabbath. They weren't required to serve in the army. They weren't expected to sacrifice to the emperor, or to the goddess Roma, or to any other gods. They were allowed to circumcise their male boys, even though the practice was considered barbaric by the Romans and probably by most people except the Egyptians, who also practiced circumcision.[31]

The Romans were not tolerant, though, of practices, religious or otherwise, they feared would lead to insurrection or conflict. They would not tolerate any religious group or any club or voluntary organization at all that might be rebellious. The Romans, for example, regularly outlawed volunteer fire departments in local places out of fear that they might provide opportunities for the locals, especially the poor, to gather and begin gossiping about how to cause trouble for their Roman overlords. The Romans were concerned about religious practices only when they feared that those practices might cause political problems. They were not at all concerned about religious beliefs.[32]

As will be explored further in the next chapter, Jews fell into the system in many different ways. Sometimes they were relatively happy clients of the Romans. Sometimes they were subversive enemies of the Roman order. As I said, they were officially recognized by the Romans, but even this recognition sometimes caused problems for them. For example, in Alexandria, Jews were a dominant minority of the population. The population of Alexandria, a very "Greek" city, was divided into different groups with different civic privileges and recognition. The highest in status were the "Greeks," not necessarily people who came from ethnically Greek ancestry, but those who spoke Greek, lived like Greeks, and had, by that means, attained Alexandrian citizenship, wherever their forebears had originally come from. At the bottom of the scale were the native Egyptians. In between were the Jews.

The Jews were not "citizens" (unless they also enjoyed Alexandrian citizen status as "Greeks," which some did), but they were at least higher in both legal and unofficial status than the local Egyptians. The Egyptians therefore resented the Jews' special status as a privileged ethnos. This led to not-infrequent conflicts and even pogroms. The local elite, backed by the Romans, occasionally had to intervene on the side of the Jews or their enemies, according to the situation and the winds of politics.

To conclude: the fact that the Romans took over a "universal" empire originally created by Alexander, with a Greek veneer, and ruled it with some flexibility, but an iron fist nonetheless, enabled several centuries of something like a combined culture for the entire Mediterranean. The West remained Latin; the East remained Greek (again, in the form of a veneer over local differences). And the Romans were able to maintain the balance for centuries. This is doubtless a major reason Christianity was able to spread as it did, from the tiny following of an unknown, obscure, and executed Jewish prophet in Judea to Rome and "the ends of the earth," at least as they imagined it.

CHAPTER 4

Ancient Judaism

Overview: Of the kingdoms that arose from Alexander's empire after his death, those of the Seleucids and the Ptolemies are the most pertinent to an understanding of the New Testament. Especially important is the rule of Antiochus IV Epiphanes, who forced the issue of Hellenism in Jerusalem by profaning the temple. Jews reacted in several different ways to hellenization, but a revolt arose under the leadership of Mattathias and his sons, who would rule in the Hasmonean dynasty. After the spread of Roman rule, Judea was under client kings and procurators until the Jewish War and the destruction of the temple in 70 C.E. Revolt was only one Jewish response to foreign rule; another was apocalypticism, as we see in Daniel and also in Jesus' teaching and the early Christian movement.

After Alexander: The Seleucids and the Ptolemies

The chronological end of the Old Testament, generally, is the sixth century B.C.E., in the 500s.[1] I say "chronological end" to indicate that that is when the narrative of the history of Israel comes to a close. That is not actually the latest date of the writings of the Old Testament. As we will see, the book of Daniel was composed in the second century B.C.E., and its final form was written only around 164 B.C.E. But Daniel attempts to place itself chronologically centuries earlier: it claims to have been written by a wise man who was a Jew living in captivity in Babylon in the 500s, after Jerusalem had been captured and many Judeans had been exported to Babylon in 586 B.C.E. The latest writing of the Hebrew Bible, therefore, is Daniel, but that book claims to have been written in the sixth century.

As described in the last chapter, after the death of Alexander, his empire was divided into kingdoms ruled by his former generals and their descendants.[2] The two most important for us are the Greco-Syrian kingdom of the Seleucids and the Greco-Egyptian kingdom of the Ptolemies. For the purposes of ancient history in general, it is important that Antiochus II Gonatas would rule what had been Greece and Macedonia, and those areas had their own independence until the Romans defeated them in the second century B.C.E. For the purposes of the history of Judaism, the kingdoms of the Seleucids and the Ptolemies are more relevant.

Palestine lay on the border separating these two kingdoms and therefore was a constant bone of contention, passing sometimes into Seleucid and at other times into Ptolemaic control. Wars went on for many decades.[3] In 175 B.C.E., Antiochus IV Epiphanes ascended to the throne of the Seleucid kingdom and thus became the ruler also of Judea, which had been under Seleucid control since 198 B.C.E. The kings of the Seleucid dynasty tended to take either Seleucus or Antiochus as their names, and modern scholars differentiate them by numbers and sometimes nicknames or titles attached to their names. "Epiphanes" is Greek for "manifest," and thus Antiochus was probably claiming divine honors for himself by taking this title. His propaganda would therefore advertise him as "god manifest." As we have seen, this was not unusual for kings in the eastern part of the Mediterranean. Alexander had already appropriated divinity for himself, as had Persian rulers before him.

At this time, the highest leader of Jerusalem and Judea was the high priest. After many years of hellenization, Jerusalem, or at least the elite of the city, was already fairly hellenized. The high priest was Jason (note the Greek name), who had paid Antiochus large sums for the priesthood, a position appointed by the king, and for the "privilege" of establishing Jerusalem as a Greek *polis*, named Antioch at Jerusalem (in honor of the rulers named Antiochus).[4] We should note that at this point there is little evidence of a culture clash between Judaism and Hellenism. The inhabitants of Jerusalem, we must recall, had already experienced years of acculturation to Greek ways.

Trouble arose when a man named Menelaus attempted to buy the high priesthood for himself and displace Jason and his cohorts. Again, note that this Jewish claimant to the position of high priest bears a distinctly Greek name, demonstrating again the hellenization that had already taken place in Jerusalem. Menelaus's problem was that he had promised Antiochus more money for the position than he had on hand. He apparently attempted to pay off Antiochus with gold vessels plundered from the temple in Jerusalem.[5]

A violent conflict broke out between the forces of Jason and those of Menelaus over who could claim the high priesthood and therefore rulership of Judea, under permission of Antiochus, of course. Antiochus used the chaos as an opportunity to take more direct control of the city. He sent Syrian forces to take the city, and he apparently plundered the temple sometime around 168–167 B.C.E. Syrian forces were garrisoned in Jerusalem. The temple cult was in some way adjusted to accommodate the Syrian forces, and a cult to the god Zeus Olympius, who was probably thought to be the same god as the Syrian god Baal Shamem, was established in Jerusalem.

The Jews, Hellenization, and the Maccabean Revolt

It is sometimes popularly imagined that all ancient Jews worked hard to maintain their traditional practices and beliefs and resisted attempts by outsiders to "force" alien practices and beliefs on them. Doubtless, as we will see, there were Jews who resisted hellenization, although it was impossible for those living around the Mediterranean to avoid it completely. But there were other Jews who seem to have advocated Greek ways.

It is not hard to see why. Just as many people in other countries learn English, pay attention to American popular culture, and hope to send their children to be educated in American universities, so elite families in the ancient world adopted Greek ways to advance themselves in the urban culture of Mediterranean cities, which were all affected by hellenization to some extent. Just as modern people of many different cultures find it necessary to know some English, so peoples of all sorts of ethnicities in the ancient world learned enough Greek to get along in business and, if possible, educated their children extensively in Greek language and literature.[6]

Thus, as we have already seen, the two Jewish men vying to be high priests around 170 B.C.E. both bore clearly Greek names: Jason and Menelaus. Greek language and culture—and perhaps even religious practices—therefore must have been advocated not simply by Antiochus and his forces, but also by Jewish leaders. Besides paying Antiochus for allowing Jerusalem to declare itself a Greek polis, Jason had already in 175 B.C.E. established a Greek gymnasium to educate Jewish boys; he had established the "ephebate," which meant that Jewish boys would have to go through Greek education and passage as ephebes in order to become citizens of the city.[7]

Once Menelaus was in charge, Greek culture was advocated even to the extent of suppressing traditional Jewish practices. There is some uncertainty about the chief architects of the anti-Jewish laws, but they seem to have been put in place after 167 and before 164.[8] Circumcision was forbidden; people were told that they could not keep the Sabbath, and something happened in the holy of holies in the temple that offended many Jews. Perhaps an idol was set up, or even a pig was sacrificed. And as noted earlier, the temple was dedicated to Zeus Olympius.[9]

It is important to note, however, that some Jews went along with these changes with little or no objection. In fact, some Jewish leaders pressed hellenization on their fellow Jews.[10] It is not difficult to see things from their perspective. They were simply practicing the same kind of adjustment to hellenization and syncretism other peoples were. They probably did not see themselves as being disloyal to the God of Israel. They would have said that the same God worshiped by Israel was worshiped by Greeks, simply with the name of Zeus. So some Jews reacted to hellenization and syncretism by accepting them and accommodating themselves to the cultural changes that were taking place.

But there wasn't simply one way Jews reacted in this period. The Dead Sea Scrolls were first discovered sometime in or before 1947 but continued to come to light for many years thereafter.[11] These texts are mostly in Hebrew and Aramaic. They bring to light many different controversies among different groups of Jews, but they also represent a form of Judaism that resisted Hellenistic influences insofar as it was able. They appear to be, at least to some extent, a "sectarian" response both to other Jews (the Pharisees, for instance) and to "outsiders," such as Greeks and Romans. We are also told of groups of Jews called *hasidim* in our sources, who were Jews resisting Hellenism and advocating a strict form of Torah observance.[12] (These ancient hasidim should not be confused with modern movements that bear that name. The modern groups grew out of medieval and early modern forms of Judaism in eastern Europe and have no direct continuity with the groups of the same name in ancient texts.)

Then we have the reaction of Mattathias and his sons, who came to be known as "the Maccabees" (see 1 Macc 2). Mattathias was a priest from

Jerusalem who had settled in a village called Modein, in the hill country of Judea. The story goes that officers from the king arrived in the village with instructions to force the Jews to sacrifice (perhaps to Zeus Olympius, although the text does not make that explicit; 1 Macc 2:1–18). Mattathias, as a leading man of the village with several grown sons, was invited to be the first to sacrifice. He refused. Instead, when another Jew came forward to sacrifice, Mattathias killed him right on the altar. He also killed the king's representative and fled with his sons to the hills.

Mattathias and his sons led what today would probably look something like guerrilla warfare against Antiochus and any Jews siding with him. They tore down the altars that had been set up around the countryside; they forced uncircumcised males to be circumcised; and they did what they could to restore traditional Jewish practices. Before long, though, Mattathias died, and his son Judas took over the mantle of leadership (1 Macc 3:1). He earned the nickname "Maccabeus," which means "hammer," and we get the enduring name for the war and his family from that nickname: the Maccabees and the Maccabean War.

Against the odds, this ragtag bunch of basically guerrilla fighters, up against the far superior army of Antiochus IV Epiphanes, recaptured Jerusalem and took control of Judea.[13] In 164, they rededicated the temple in Jerusalem, an event still celebrated by Jews as Hanukkah (2 Macc 10:1–8).

Judas Maccabeus did not reign as official king at that point, but he did control Judea, and ongoing conflicts continued against the Greco-Syrian dynasty for years. After the death of Judas, rule passed to his various brothers, some of whom did eventually take the title "king." This dynasty takes its name from the family name, Hasmoneus, and has been known to history as the Hasmonean dynasty, which was in power from 165 to 60 B.C.E.[14]

The Prophecy of Daniel

Thus some Jews responded to hellenization by adopting it, with various degrees of enthusiasm. The Maccabean revolt, though, represented a different response: reaction, rebellion, and an attempt at restoration. Other Jews, however, didn't believe that armed reaction and war were the proper routes to take. They believed, instead, that they should be as loyal to the God of Israel and the Torah as possible, but keep their heads down and wait for God to intervene. They believed that God would somehow miraculously come from heaven or send an angel or messiah, fight Antiochus and his dynasty, defeat the oppressors of Israel, and usher in the new Kingdom of Israel, the

Kingdom of God, on earth. The book of Daniel derives from these kinds of Jews.

The book of Daniel divides basically into two parts. The first half, Daniel 1–6, contains stories of Daniel and three other young men of Judea's elite, taken as prisoners to Babylon. The stories are sometimes simply entertaining tales about the wisdom and talents of these young men. But some of them are also designed to teach Jews to be loyal to their own God and traditions even when they are in foreign lands or are confronted with foreign cultures. The part that concerns us here, though, is the second half, chapters 7–12, which narrates a series of visions and prophecies Daniel is said to have experienced. The visions are in code, with future rulers represented by different animals or persons, and they prophesy about important political and military events of the Hellenistic period.

The different visions constitute something like different cycles. Rather than chapters 7 through 12 narrating several centuries in a linear manner, the different visions often narrate, through varying symbols, the same historical events more than once. Historians of the Hellenistic eastern Mediterranean can identify which beasts or other symbols are supposed to represent which ruler, general, or member of their families. The author also tells us explicitly at times which empire or king his symbols refer to. The narrative setting of the book (not when it was actually written) has Daniel in captivity in Babylon. The Babylonian empire (Media) was eventually overtaken by Cyrus and his Persian empire. So the author of Daniel conveniently informs us of the historical referent meant by a ram he had seen in his vision. An angel gave him the interpretation: "As for the ram that you saw with the two horns, these are the kings of Media and Persia" (Dan 8:20). A male goat represents "the king of Greece" (8:21). "As for the horn that was broken, in place of which four others arose, four kingdoms shall arise from his nation but not with his power" (8:22). This is doubtless a reference to Alexander, his death, and the kingdoms that arose from his divided empire. Each chapter in this part of Daniel narrates the political history of the region through different symbols and images.

Chapter 11 begins with another prophecy of how Persia is defeated by Greece: "The fourth [king of Persia] shall be far richer than all of them, and when he has become strong through his riches, he shall stir up all against the kingdom of Greece" (Dan 11:2). This is a reference to Darius, the Persian emperor who overran Asia Minor and attempted to take Greece. "Then a warrior king shall arise, who shall rule with great dominion" (11:3). The author proceeds to describe Alexander's rule, his death, and the subsequent division of his empire: "His kingdom shall be broken and divided toward the four winds of heaven but not to his posterity" (11:4). As we know, Alexander did have one child, but his empire went not to his own child but to "the four winds of heaven."

With the next several verses, we enter the history of conflict between the Seleucids, called the "kings of the north," and the Ptolemies, the "kings of the south." The author usually just calls them by those terms even though he ends up talking about several different Seleucids and Ptolemies. With a good history book—or with an adequate study Bible with good notes—we can trace the political history of the period all the way from Alexander the Great to Antiochus IV, including politically strategic marriages. For example, Daniel 11:6 reads, "After some years they shall make an alliance, and the daughter of the king of the south shall come to the king of the north to ratify the agreement. But she shall not retain her power, and his offspring shall not endure." A good study Bible will often note that this is probably a reference to the marriage of Berenice, daughter of Ptolemy II Philadelphus, to Antiochus II, which took place in 252 B.C.E. Berenice and her child were killed.

Now we can skip down to the time of our immediate concern. The author later speaks of Antiochus IV Epiphanes: "At the time appointed he shall return and come into the south, but this time it shall not be as it was before. For ships of Kittim shall come against him, and he shall lose heart and withdraw" (11:29–30). "Kittim" is a code word in much Jewish apocalyptic writing of this time that represents a threatening foreign force, usually the Greeks or the Romans. Here it is a reference to Rome, and the event described is Antiochus IV's attempt to take control of Egypt. The Romans wanted to maintain some kind of balance of power between the Seleucids and the Ptolemies in order to avoid having to fight a more powerful opponent eventually on their eastern front. They intervened, therefore, in Antiochus's ambitions in 168 B.C.E. and forced him to leave Egypt and retreat to his own territories.

It was on his way back through Palestine that Antiochus now mounted an attack on the temple, probably for funds and booty to pay for his unsuccessful campaign in Egypt. This is described in the verses that follow: "He shall turn back and pay heed to those who forsake the holy covenant. Forces sent by him shall occupy and profane the temple and the fortress. They shall abolish the regular burnt offering and set up the abomination that makes desolate" (11:30–31). This term, sometimes translated "the abomination of desolation," occurs three times in Daniel and is later taken up in Christian apocalyptic texts (see, for example, Mark 13:14; Matt 24:15; and Chapter 6 in this book). This is therefore a reference to the desecration of the temple that happened in 168. The verse "He shall seduce with intrigue those who violate the covenant" (11:32) refers to those Jews who sided with Antiochus and the hellenizing program.

"But the people who are loyal to their God shall stand firm and take action. The wise among the people shall give understanding to many; for some days, however, they shall fall by sword and flame and suffer captivity and plunder" (11:32b–33). Who are the wise? The author of the book is certainly one of them. The first several chapters were moral tales about how "wise" Jews should live under pressures to adopt foreign practices. This author sees himself as one of the "wise" who don't openly fight the hellenizing forces, but who endure and teach other Jews to resist.

Some scholars believe that we may also have here a slight hint about the opposition of the Maccabeans: "When they fall victim, they shall receive a little help, and many shall join them insincerely" (11:34). The "little help" may be a reference to Judas Maccabeus and his forces. But if that is the case, it is notable that this author doesn't put much faith in Judas's efforts. He believes that Antiochus will be overthrown not by human armed forces alone, but by God.

The author, though, proceeds to prophesy about further activities of Antiochus. He predicts that Antiochus will arrogate divine honors to himself and in fact set himself up as the highest of the gods (11:36–38). But Antiochus, he says, will be attacked again by "the king of the south," which will prompt a counterattack on his part. He will again invade Judea: "He shall come into the beautiful land" (11:41); he will defeat all surrounding peoples; and he will even capture Egypt, Libya, and Ethiopia (11:43). Hearing rumors of threats from back east and north, however, he will return east: "He shall pitch his palatial tents between the sea and the beautiful holy mountain. Yet he shall come to his end, with no one to help him" (11:45). The author prophesies, that is, that Antiochus will make camp between "the sea," the Mediterranean, and "the holy mountain," a reference to Zion, the mount of Jerusalem. And he will die there.

Our "prophet" actually got his history remarkably right just up to the end here. He correctly "predicted" many battles, marriages, dynastic changes, and deaths. He saw correctly that Antiochus IV would attempt to take Egypt, only to be turned back by the Romans. He saw correctly that Antiochus and apostate Jews would desecrate the temple in Jerusalem. But Antiochus was not then attacked by Egypt, he did not invade through Judea in a counterattack, and he did not defeat Egypt and conquer the Libyans and Ethiopians. He did not then make camp in Palestine between Jerusalem and the sea. And he did not die there. Antiochus actually died of a disease in Persia in 164.

This is the way modern scholars date an ancient apocalyptic writing. We look to see where the "prophecy" goes awry. The "deceit" of many apocalypses from the ancient world is that they are written by someone famous from deep in the past.[15] They claim to be "foreseeing" events that actually have already happened at the time of writing. Often, the author then claims to have sealed up and hidden the document so that it will be discovered many centuries later and then published right at the time it is most needed. Of course, its time of publication is actually its time of writing, but the prophecies gain credence by correctly "predicting" all sorts of events that the reader knows have already occurred. In the case of Daniel, the author claims to be writing in the sixth century B.C.E., but he actually must be writing between 168 and 164. He knows about many of the exploits of Antiochus, up to his plundering and desecration of the temple. But he apparently does not know that Judas beat the Greco-Syrians and their Jewish allies, retook Jerusalem, and cleansed the temple in 164. And he does not know how Antiochus actually died later in 164. Thus he was writing probably just before 164.

And note the major event predicted by the author after his "historical" narrative comes to its end: the angel Michael, the "prince" of the nation of Israel, will arise, defeat the forces of evil, and deliver the righteous. The dead will be raised, some to everlasting life, others to "shame and everlasting contempt" (Dan 12:1–2). In other words, the climactic "end" promised by apocalyptic prophets is predicted to take place in the year 164 or immediately thereafter, just after the death of Antiochus. As we shall see throughout this book, the apocalypticism of Daniel came to inform the worldview and expectations of Jesus, Paul, and all of earliest Christianity to some extent. It was one Jewish way among several of responding to the world changed by hellenization and then by romanization.[16]

The Jewish War and the Destruction of the Temple

In 63 B.C.E., about one hundred years after the cleansing of the temple, the Roman general Pompey entered and took control of Jerusalem. As had Antiochus before him, Pompey took advantage of a conflict between two men and their factions who were fighting over who would control Judea. Pompey's entry into Jerusalem marks the beginning of direct Roman rule of Judea. Later in that century, Herod the Great was given the title of king by the Roman Senate. He ruled from 37 to 4 B.C.E. After Herod's death, his kingdom was split among his three sons, but Judea eventually was placed under direct Roman rule again in 6 C.E., under a series of different governors. Pilate was in that position, ruling Judea, when Jesus was crucified by the Romans.[17]

During the first century C.E., there were sporadic uprisings among the Jews, some drawing on apocalyptic ideology, others more like banditry. The Jewish historian Josephus, who himself led the Jewish forces in Galilee during the great Jewish War of 66–74, describes several eschatological prophets who led people to the Jordan or prophesied the destruction of Jerusalem or of the Roman oppressors.[18] Some of these seem to have fashioned themselves as messiahs, the "anointed one" expected to usher in the eschatological kingdom of God.[19] Of course, since it was considered an act of treason and rebellion for anyone in the Roman Empire to call himself a king without the title being conferred by the Senate, the Romans put down all such movements harshly.

The most important revolt of the Jewish people during this time began in the year 66 C.E.[20] Jews in both Judea and Galilee revolted against Rome. They drove the Roman squadron out of Jerusalem. In the year 70, the Romans finally retook Jerusalem after a very long siege. They destroyed the temple. The year 70, therefore, becomes a central and important year for dating events among Jews, as well as Christians. The destruction of the temple, which had been considered by many Jews the only legitimate place to sacrifice to God, meant the end of the Jewish sacrificial system for the most part. Thereafter, although there was a gradual and long period of change, Jews substituted other forms of piety for animal sacrifice: the study of the Torah, prayer, and meetings in synagogues. The end of the Jewish War was marked by the Roman capture a few years later of Herod's fortress at Masada, now an Israeli shrine and tourist destination.

The last of the ancient Jewish revolts occurred in 132–135 and is called the Bar Kokhba revolt after the name of the man who led it, who was himself thought by some to be the Messiah: Simon Bar Kokhba, Simon "son of a star." That revolt was also suppressed by the Romans, who then destroyed Jerusalem and rebuilt it as Aelia Capitolina, an obviously Roman name. For many years thereafter, Jews were not allowed in Jerusalem. In the centuries following, Jews turned from the older sacrificial, priestly system of the Jerusalem temple and developed the culture of bookish learning and commentary on the Torah we know as rabbinic Judaism.[21]

Concluding Lessons

The central lessons to take away from this historical overview are these. First, hellenization was supremely important for the birth and growth of Christianity because it united the eastern Mediterranean world in a way it had not been previously united. By Jesus' time, all of Palestine was hellenized to some extent, only to different degrees. If Jews lived in a village or the countryside, as the majority of the population did, they would have spoken Aramaic and perhaps used the older, more traditional Hebrew for certain occasions. But if one was an elite person among the upper class in the cities, one would be expected to speak Greek and have some exposure to Greek culture. Syncretism was also important. People were expected to mix gods, religious practices, assumptions, and beliefs from different sources and cultures.

Second, Judaism was an extremely varied ethnic and religious reality. The kind of rabbinic Judaism that later became "normative" Judaism did not exist in the same way in the first century. The majority of Jews lived outside Judea, even outside Palestine, and spoke Greek. There were many different ways of "being Jewish" at the time. In fact, some scholars use the term "Judaisms" to highlight that before 70 C.E., Jews believed many different things and practiced their ancestral traditions in many different ways—or not at all. Christianity first developed as just one more way of "being Jewish," and it could do so precisely because of the variety of kinds of Judaism already in existence.

Third, we must remind ourselves that Judea and Jerusalem were not as important in the ancient world as we tend to assume they must have been. Since that region was the cradle of Christianity and Judaism, we tend to imagine that it was important to ancient people also. But Judea was something of a backwater geographically and culturally to most of the inhabitants of the ancient Mediterranean. The Jews were also politically not usually of great import. The Jews were never truly independent and politically self-determining during Hellenistic and Roman times. They were always either directly subservient to greater powers—Egypt, Syria, Rome—or obliged to maintain careful awareness of them.

Fourth, in spite of being no great political power, the Jews owned an ideology that supported imperial pretensions. We may imagine, for example, a Jewish boy, perhaps resentful of the Roman soldiers who hit him and forced him to carry their bags, hearing the book of Psalms read. "Why do the nations conspire and the peoples plot in vain . . . against the Lord and his anointed [Messiah]? . . . He who sits in the heavens laughs. . . . 'I have set my king on Zion, my holy hill'" (Ps 2:1–6, excerpts). The boy had these prophetic psalms, as he may have taken them to be, promising that a Jewish king would overthrow the Romans and restore the great, wide, rich kingdom of David and Solomon. The Jews, or those inclined to read their scriptures this way, had an ideology of empire and world domination in their scriptures, but their social and political predicament was the opposite. It was in that potential maelstrom of Jewish ideology conflicting with Jewish reality that Jesus was born.

CHAPTER 5

The New Testament as a Historical Source: A Comparison of Acts and Paul's Letters

Overview: The accounts of Paul's travels in the Acts of the Apostles and Galatians seem to contradict each other at many points. Their descriptions of a meeting in Jerusalem—a major council in Acts versus a small, informal gathering in Galatians—also differ quite a bit. How do we understand these differences? A historical-critical reading of these accounts does not force these texts into a harmonious unity or accept them at face value. Instead, a critical reading carefully sifts through the details of the texts and asks which of them is more likely to reflect historical accuracy.

Faith and History

It is legitimate, of course, to read the New Testament for the purposes of faith. As discussed in Chapter 1, if someone takes the New Testament to be scripture, a theological reading of it is entirely appropriate—in fact, for that person, necessary. But this introduction to the New Testament does not attempt a Christian theological interpretation of the New Testament. Rather, in this book we read the text through the eyes of modern historical criticism, using the text as a source for what we may say about Jesus, early Christian churches, and early Christian beliefs and practices.

But one cannot take the narratives or claims of different New Testament documents uncritically as "history." The New Testament may be a fairly reliable historical resource for early Christian belief and practice, but it is not a reliable historical account of "what actually happened." The texts of the New Testament, that is, are in no way "historical accounts" of what Jesus said or did, or what early disciples said or did. This is true not because these texts are out to deceive or are simply "false," but because they were written long before the invention of modern historiography, and what I mean by "historical" (when one is speaking, say, of the historical Jesus or a historical account of Paul's journeys) is an account that "plays by the rules" of modern historiography. That means approaching these texts with an attitude of skepticism about what they claim "really happened" to whom, where, and when.

The documents of the New Testament actually do provide the best materials we have for doing much of the historical work of reconstructing early Christianity, including the historical Jesus or the historical Paul. Other than the *Gospel of Thomas*, which I will get to in a few more chapters, the best data we have for constructing a historical account of the life and teachings of Jesus are our four canonical Gospels. Many other gospels survive from the ancient world, but most scholars are convinced that they provide no data about Jesus that improve on or add to the data provided by the canonical Gospels and *Thomas*. And although we have other accounts about Paul and even other letters said to be by Paul from the ancient world, the materials of or about Paul in the New Testament provide the best historical material for constructing a probably historical account of him and his ministry. The best sources we have on both Jesus and Paul, as well as much else of the earliest forms of Christianity, then, are the documents of the New Testament.

To demonstrate some of the things we can and cannot discern about history from these texts, and to show how a proper historical skepticism should proceed, I offer here an in-depth comparison of the itinerary of Paul, where he went, when, and why, as found in the Acts of the Apostles and in his own letter to the Galatians. We need not be so skeptical that we say that the New Testament is nothing but later fabrications by pious Christians, but we must be skeptical enough not to take any of its narratives at face value.

Paul's Travels in the Acts of the Apostles

We first encounter Paul in Acts at the stoning of Stephen, although he is there identified by his "Jewish" name, Saul (Acts 7:58). This takes place in Jerusalem, and the idea we get is not that he has recently arrived, but that he has been living in Jerusalem for a long while. The author of Acts elsewhere informs us that Paul's hometown was Tarsus, in Cilicia (along the coast of what is now Turkey and Syria), but that he lived and studied in Jerusalem as a young man (22:3). In his first scene, he minds the cloaks of those who stone Stephen. He is briefly then described as persecuting the followers of Jesus in Jerusalem (8:3).

From Jerusalem, Paul journeys to Damascus, in Syria, in order to persecute and arrest Christians there (9:2). On the way, he experiences his famous "Damascus road" vision of Jesus. He goes on to Damascus to await further instructions from the Lord, and he remains in Damascus, blinded by his vision, for three days (9:9). After his conversion and baptism in Damascus, Paul remains there "for several days" arguing with other Jews (9:19). Then after "some time," and after Paul gets into trouble with the authorities, he is helped to escape from Damascus (9:23–25).[1]

He goes back to Jerusalem, but the disciples there refuse to receive him because they already know who he is and that he persecuted them previously. Barnabas, however, testifies to Paul's conversion and persuades the church to accept him. After that, Paul spends some time (we aren't told how much) in Jerusalem, debating again with other Jews (9:27–29). Eventually, he leaves Jerusalem for Caesarea, on the coast, and then goes to Tarsus, his hometown (9:30).

Some time later, Barnabas, now leading the church in Antioch in Syria, fetches Paul from Tarsus to Antioch, and Paul works with Barnabas in the church in Antioch (11:19–30). After some time, though, Barnabas and Paul go from Antioch to Jerusalem, bearing famine relief for the church there (11:30). We aren't told how long they remain in Jerusalem on this trip, but we are later told that they return from Jerusalem to Antioch (12:25).[2] The next movements of Paul constitute what is often called his "first missionary journey." With Barnabas, Paul (and here his name begins to be mentioned first rather than after that of Barnabas) travels through regions now part of southern Turkey (Antioch, Cyprus, Attalia, Perga, Derbe, and others) and then back to Antioch (Acts 13). Once back in Antioch, they are said to remain there "not a little time" (14:24–28; the literal translation of the Greek; often translated in English as something like "for some time").

After a controversy over circumcision erupts in Antioch, Paul and Barnabas are "appointed" by the church in Antioch to journey to Jerusalem to consult the leaders there (15:2). The so-called Jerusalem council takes place with Barnabas and Paul participating. After the agreement and conclusion of the council (the account of which I will examine more closely later), Paul and Barnabas return to Antioch (15:30–35). Paul and Barnabas agree to split up (again, the account and its historicity will be discussed later). Paul pairs up this time with Silas, and they journey from Antioch through various regions of Asia, Macedonia, and Greece in what is called Paul's "second missionary journey."

Paul's Travels in Galatians

Paul's geographic history according to Galatians can be covered much more quickly precisely because it is much simpler than that presented in Acts. Paul admits that before his vision and apostolic calling he was a persecutor of the church, but he says nothing of persecuting Christians in Jerusalem or Judea (1:13). We are not told explicitly where he was when he experienced his "call," but he does insist that he did not any time around that event go to Jerusalem. In fact, he says he first went to "Arabia," which probably refers to the region southeast from Syria, on the east side of the River Jordan, in the desert, and then he says he "returned to Damascus" (Gal 1:17)—all of which makes it sound as if Paul was simply living in Damascus at the time (not that he had merely traveled there from Jerusalem). It was there and perhaps other regions of Syria where he apparently had been persecuting followers of Jesus.

Paul says that he traveled to Jerusalem only three years later (we don't know whether it was three years after his "call" or after his return to Damascus). He stayed with Cephas (Peter) for fifteen days (1:18). Paul insists that at that time he saw no other apostle except James, Jesus' brother. He even swears that he is here telling the truth and leaving nothing out (1:19–21). In fact, he insists that none of the people of the churches of Judea at that time knew him by sight, only by reputation (1:22). He writes that he then went to Syria and Cilicia (1:21).

According to Paul, he did not travel to Jerusalem because he was "appointed" by the church in Antioch, but in response to a revelation he had. He does confirm that he traveled with Barnabas (and Titus; 2:1–2). Paul says this happened fourteen years "after"—meaning, I think, fourteen years after his first, fifteen-day visit to Jerusalem. The three men from Antioch had a "private meeting" with the leaders of the Jerusalem church, certainly including James (the brother of Jesus), Peter, and John (son of Zebedee), and perhaps a few others. We aren't told how long Paul remained in Jerusalem, but it is implied that he, Barnabas, and Titus returned to Antioch after the meeting.

The narrative resumes some time later when Cephas visits Antioch (2:11). A controversy over table fellowship erupts, with Barnabas and Peter taking one side, and Paul the other (2:11–14). This is apparently Paul's version of the event differently described in Acts 15:36–40, and it must be at this point that Paul split with Barnabas and left Antioch, although Paul does not narrate those events, perhaps, as I suggest later, for his own good reasons.

Although Christians have attempted to harmonize—explicitly in biased scholarship or merely in their own minds—these two different accounts of "what Paul did, when, and where," it should be obvious that these are two very different and irreconcilable accounts. In Acts, Paul is well known to the churches throughout Judea and especially in Jerusalem. Paul himself claims the opposite. In Acts, Paul spends much time in Jerusalem long before he goes to Damascus. In Galatians, Paul himself insists that is not true; he implies that he simply was already in Damascus. According to Paul, he was in Jerusalem only once before the "Jerusalem conference" (in Paul's narrative, it is hardly a "conference," but a "private meeting"). That visit took no more than fifteen days, and of the church leaders he saw only Peter and James.

According to Acts, Paul was in Jerusalem at the beginning, before he became a Christian (Acts 7–8). After his "conversion," he visited Jerusalem to seek acceptance by the church there (Acts 9:26). The second time he visited Jerusalem was with Barnabas to deliver famine relief (Acts 11:20). The third trip was for the "council" (Acts 15:2).

Note also that by Paul's numbers, seventeen years pass after his vision before he is seen by anyone in Jerusalem except Peter and James (adding the "three" of Gal 1:18 to the "fourteen" of 2:1, which is I think the best interpretation). That simply cannot be squared with the account in Acts of Paul's multiple appearances in Jerusalem, his persecution of the churches there, his arguments later with other Jews, and his other two visits there from Antioch. The two accounts contradict one another. In fact, Paul's account sounds almost like a self-conscious rejection of the narrative of Acts, although of course it is not, because at the time he wrote Galatians, Acts was not yet written.

The Meeting in Jerusalem and the Conflict in Antioch

More important, perhaps, than the geographic and chronological contradictions are different accounts of what actually happened in significant controversies. We have to remember that Paul wrote Galatians many years before Luke and Acts were written. We don't know precisely when Paul wrote, but most scholars would place the date within a few years before or after 50 C.E. Luke and Acts were certainly not written until several years after the destruction of the Jewish temple in 70, and scholars tend to date both to sometime in the 80s. Paul therefore did not have the Acts account available. Whether the author of Acts knew Paul's letters is debatable; he never mentions them.

According to Paul, about seventeen years after his vision and calling by Jesus, he and Barnabas, taking along Titus, went to Jerusalem to confer with the church's leaders there, in particular James, John, and Peter, whom Paul calls by the Aramaic version of his nickname, Cephas ("rock"). This James is doubtless the brother of Jesus, who was recognized as the main leader of the church in Jerusalem. Paul insists that it was a private meeting with a few of the leaders, though he admits that some "false brothers" "slipped in" (Gal 2:4). In the end, all the central characters agreed with what Paul and Barnabas had been teaching all along: that gentiles did not have to be circumcised when they joined the church. They agreed that Peter's mission would henceforth be among "the circumcised" and that Paul's would be among "the uncircumcised." The only stipulation they stressed was that Paul and Barnabas, in their missions among gentiles, would keep in mind the poorer disciples living in Judea (remember that many of these had been poor peasants from Galilee; they had little means of existence in Jerusalem), meaning that funds should be sent from the better-off gentile churches to the poorer Christians in Judea (2:9–10). This meeting hardly deserves the epithet "Jerusalem council."

The account of what must have been the same event in Acts is notably different. It is a large, open council, including "the apostles and the elders" (15:6). Peter gives a speech reiterating what had already been the decided policy of not requiring circumcision (see 11:1–18). The "whole assembly" listens to Barnabas and Paul's descriptions of their successful ministry among gentiles. James, who often seems to represent the more "conservative" side of the debate (see Gal 2:12), gives a speech in which he says that he has made a decision in favor of Barnabas and Paul (Acts 15:19). This decision is then ratified by "the apostles and the elders, with the consent of the whole church"

(15:22). The narrative describes even a larger meeting of the minds than "the apostles and the elders." They write an official letter to the church in Antioch making the decision public (15:22–29). They do add some new requirements: gentile converts are to be taught to abstain from food that has been sacrificed to idols, from blood, from anything that has been strangled, and from *porneia*, usually translated "fornication," although the Greek word when used by Jews of the period could refer to any sexual activity they considered sinful (15:29). This list seems to reflect traditional Jewish notions that God had, even at the time of Noah, given a few rules that were supposed to be followed universally, not just by the Jews (see Gen 9:4–6; Lev 17–18).

The differences in the narratives are striking. Who was present, who led the meeting (mainly James, according to Acts; not so for Paul), and what was decided? The one thing both accounts agree on is that gentiles were not to be required to be circumcised. But Paul seems to know nothing of the other four rules for gentiles. And as we will see in 1 Corinthians and Romans, Paul does not tell all gentiles they cannot eat "idol meat."

The differences between the accounts of disagreement between Paul and Barnabas are even starker. According to Acts, Paul and Barnabas have a slight disagreement about "personnel" for their second journey. Barnabas wants to take John Mark along again, but Paul objects because John Mark had left in the middle of their first journey (15:38; see 13:13). The disagreement is called "sharp" by the author of Acts, but Paul and Barnabas seem to part rather amicably, and Paul is sent off on his own journey by the Antioch church with apparently hearty commendation (15:40).

What Acts portrays as a disagreement about personnel for the second journey, Paul portrays as a substantial conflict that included not merely Barnabas, but also Peter and the entire church in Antioch, including some interlopers who had come "from James." For Paul, the issue is whether Jewish believers will continue table fellowship with gentile believers, and it is prompted by hypocritical—or at least vacillating—behavior on Peter's part. "Cephas" had been eating with gentile Christians on a visit to Antioch. Facing criticism from "people from James," he stopped. The "circumcision faction," as Paul calls it, won the day. Even Barnabas, Paul claims, was "led astray by their hypocrisy" (Gal 2:13). Paul publicly rebukes Peter, Barnabas sides with Peter, and Paul is apparently defeated.

It is not hard to see the issue from Barnabas and Peter's side. They may have simply felt that if eating with gentiles so offended more conservative Jewish believers, they would do so only when those believers were not present. When others visited, though, some accommodation could be made to preserve the unity of the church. Paul, however, obviously believed that such accommodation had already destroyed the unity of the church. Eating together in the ancient world was a central sign of community and acceptance, as it often is even today. That is often the very reason, sociologically speaking, for dietary restrictions in religious groups: to maintain visible social boundaries for the religious community. Paul took Peter's actions as already destroying the unity of the church, to the detriment mainly of the gentile believers.

Paul does not tell us how the affair ended, and I think that must mean he lost the fight. After all, in his letters—and those written by others in his name—we see the names of many people associated with Paul in his ministry, but never that of Barnabas. And after this incident, Paul is never again associated with the Antioch church; his base of operations may be in Ephesus, or Corinth, or other places, but never again Antioch. The split between Paul and Barnabas was obviously not as benign and amicable as Acts narrates it.

Which Account Is More Accurate Historically?

If a historian is to write a modern historical account of "what really happened," which source do we trust more, that of Acts or that of Paul? Was Paul really so active in and around Jerusalem for so much of his early life and ministry? Or was he active only in Syria and other places further north and east from Judea? Were the early decisions about circumcision made in a small, relatively private meeting or in an open, public council including the apostles, the elders, and most of the Jerusalem church? Did everybody agree, even at that early date, that gentiles should avoid eating anything that had been sacrificed to an idol, or was that an issue that continued to trouble churches for decades?

Many people are inclined to accept the Acts description as probably more historical. After all, they read it in a book that looks a bit more like history. The author tells us that he used sources, and they seem to have been both oral and written (Luke 1:1–4). Moreover, Paul's account is obviously driven by his own goals. He especially wants to prove that his own gospel was given to him directly by Jesus and that his apostleship and authority are completely independent from the Jerusalem leaders and church. Even Paul's urgent protestations that he is telling the truth (Gal 1:20: "I do not lie!") make it obvious that he has an agenda. Acts simply sounds more like history, and Paul sounds like a man with an agenda.

But Galatians is, after all, a firsthand account. The author of Acts was not present at the events he describes, and he wrote decades afterward. Paul was there, and it is quite probable that he writes not long after the events. We have to count back, but if Paul received his "call" around 34 C.E. (scholars agree that it was not many years after the death of Jesus, which we may place at or around 30), and we count fourteen to seventeen years after that, his meeting in Jerusalem with the leaders there must have taken place approximately between 47 and 52 C.E. Even if he is writing Galatians later than many scholars think, say around or after 55, he is writing only a few years after the events he describes. A firsthand account written a few years after the event must be historically preferable to one written decades later by someone not present.

And as we will see when we examine Luke and Acts, their author also has an agenda. He clearly goes out of his way to portray the early church with little or no internal conflict. He also wants the center and origin of all church missions and policies to proceed from Jerusalem outward (as will be shown in Chapters 9 and 10 in this book). And he wants to present Paul as of lower official "status" in the church than the twelve and James. As scholars recognize, the author of Acts had his own reasons for telling the story the way he did. He exaggerates Paul's presence in Jerusalem and Judea, and he exaggerates Paul's dependence on the Jerusalem apostles and church. He also minimizes conflict; thus his more "sanguine" version of the argument at Antioch.

Historical Criticism

For any historian, a good working motto is *de omnibus dubitandum*: doubt everything. That does not mean that historians reject all accounts in the end, just that we must begin with skepticism and test the sources we have, asking how they may be biased, where they got their information, and what their purposes in writing were. This is different from reading the New Testament as scripture with an attitude of faith. And that is not to say that one should not read it in faith as scripture, but only that the historical critic must not do so.[3] Like all ancient documents, the New Testament does not present us with simply "what really happened."

The exercise of this chapter can be duplicated for other issues of the New Testament. If one carefully compares the birth narratives presented by Matthew and Luke, one finds that it is next to impossible to harmonize them in any historically respectable way. Was Jesus' family from Nazareth, ending up in Bethlehem only because of a census (Luke), or was his family originally just from Bethlehem, moving to Nazareth only years later and after a sojourn in Egypt (Matthew)? Did they stay in Judea only a little over a month and then return immediately to Nazareth (Luke), or did they remain in Bethlehem for a period of up to two years and then spend additional time in Egypt before settling in Nazareth (Matthew)? Were there wise men who visited him (Matthew), or were there angels and shepherds (Luke)?

Similar contradictions occur when one compares the resurrection appearances of the different Gospels. Did all Jesus' appearances to his disciples take place only in and around Jerusalem (Luke), or did he appear to the eleven only later in Galilee (Matthew)? Did the appearances take place only over about a month's time (Luke), or did he appear both in Judea earlier and some time later in Galilee (John)? The different accounts can be harmonized only by gymnastics not permitted to reputable modern historians. That is fine because the New Testament need not be regarded as a history book. But using it as a resource for constructing a historical account of early Christianity necessitates reading it critically, not naively.

Gospels

CHAPTER 6
The Gospel of Mark

Overview: The Gospels of the New Testament are not biographies; they do not have the same interests we have when we pick up a modern biography. This chapter introduces what the ancient Gospels are and how to interpret them through a historical-critical lens. This means that the events they narrate are not taken at face value as historical. The Gospel of Mark illustrates how the Gospel writer skillfully crafts a narrative in order to deliver a message. It is a message that emphasizes a suffering Messiah and the necessity of suffering before glory. The Gospel's apocalyptic passages predict troubles for the Jewish temple and incorporate this prediction into its understanding of the future coming of the Son of Man.

Gospels and Biography

Popular opinion may think of the Gospels as biographies of Jesus, but they are not—at least not anything like modern biographies. We don't get a personal portrait of Jesus in the Gospels. We don't see how he developed over time. We don't know anything about how he may have changed from teenager to apocalyptic prophet. We are told next to nothing of his relationship with his parents, brothers, or sisters. One of the most important aspects of modern biography is tracing how personality and character develop over time. The main character's psychology is important. We get none of that in the Gospels. The Gospels are not biography.

Long ago a German scholar characterized the Gospel of Mark as "a passion narrative with an extended Introduction."[1] The designation is apt. A "passion narrative" is a narrative about the arrest, trial, and crucifixion of Jesus and sometimes includes resurrection stories. "Passion" comes from the Latin *passio*, which does have something to do with our word "passion," but it also means "suffering." For the ancients, indeed, passions and desires, even love, were emotional, psychological, but also physical states or conditions from which people "suffered." The story of Jesus' suffering occupies a large chunk of the Gospel of Mark.

Mark is the shortest Gospel in the Bible, with only sixteen chapters. One-third of Mark is a narrative of what took place only in the last week of Jesus' life. The flow of Mark, or, we may imagine, the "outline" of the Gospel, is already informative of its content. First is what for the ancient reader would be the title: "The beginning of the good news of Jesus Christ" (Mark 1:1). The word here translated as "good news" is *euangelion*, which is also translated as "gospel." Because the ancient reader did not have the text with the title "The Gospel According to Mark," this first line would have functioned as the title. From 1:2 to 1:13, we have a very brief initial introduction to Jesus. Then 1:14 to 9:50, nine chapters of the book, cover Jesus' entire Galilean ministry: healings, exorcisms, teaching, miracles, and travel mainly through Galilee, which is where he is from. Chapters 11 through 15 narrate merely the last week in Jerusalem. In 16:1–8, we have rumors of his resurrection.

And they are "rumors," not yet descriptions. Most modern publications of Mark have the Gospel ending at 16:8, with female disciples seeing the empty tomb and a "young man" who tells them that Jesus was raised and that the disciples should go to Galilee, where they will see him. The very last words just inform us that the women told no one, "for they were afraid." This is a strange way to end any book, but especially a Christian gospel. The ending is just as abrupt and strange in the original Greek.

Many editions of the Bible, therefore, include, either as a footnote or just after 16:8, another small paragraph often titled "The Shorter Ending of Mark": "And all that had been commanded them they told briefly to those around Peter. And afterward Jesus himself sent out through them, from east to west, the sacred and imperishable proclamation of eternal salvation." Some Bibles add even more to that, reflecting the fact that many ancient manuscripts of Mark actually have several different endings. Then there is the "Longer Ending of Mark," more familiar to most people because it was included in the King James Version and other older Bibles. On closer inspection, however, it is clear that the "Longer Ending" is actually a later invention, using resurrection appearances from the other Gospels and weaving together a more "satisfactory" ending to Mark. Modern scholars recognize all these alternative endings as later scribal inventions, and we simply accept that Mark probably did end at 16:8.

But that means we must attempt to explain why the author would end his Gospel that way (and for convenience I will continue to call him "Mark" even though we don't know who actually wrote the Gospel and are fairly certain that it wasn't John Mark). As discussed in the last chapter, historical criticism of the Bible sometimes concerns itself with "what really happened." But it also attempts to explain why an author would have written the way he did (and although we don't know who wrote many of these documents, we can be fairly sure they were most likely men). What points did the author want to get across, and to what kind of audience? Who were likely his first readers, and how did they understand his writing? In this case, we do not read the texts for what they tell us about events in the past. Rather, we read them as intentional communications written to convey a message in a particular social-historical situation.

We may, therefore, read the Gospels as ancient literary productions, examining their use of character, plot, and structure. In that case, the critic wants to read Mark as standing on its own, as its own literary unit. That means not reading Mark through the lens of the Jesus we may find in Matthew, Luke, or John, but looking only for the "Jesus" of Mark. One of the fundamental rules of modern historical criticism of the Bible is to avoid harmonizing the different documents. We take each Gospel individually, as making its own points and having its own aims. Furthermore, we want to avoid anachronism: we shouldn't attribute a meaning to the text that we can't show to be believable in its ancient context. We don't want to assign a motive or intention to the author that would be highly unlikely for its time of origination. So one way to approach this kind of interpretation is to imagine, taking the ending of Mark as an example: How would an ancient audience "hear" Mark's ending? What sense would they have made of it?

The Problem of the Messianic Secret

Before attempting a solution to the problem of Mark's ending, I turn to another perennial problem readers have long had with Mark's narrative. Again and again in Mark, Jesus heals someone or performs some other miracle and then tells the person not to tell anyone else about it. The first time Jesus tries to silence someone is at Mark 1:25, when Jesus rebukes an "unclean spirit" possessing a man. The spirit cries out, "What have you to do with us, Jesus of Nazareth? Have you come to destroy us? I know who you are, the Holy One of God." After forcing the spirit to be quiet, Jesus heals the man. A bit later in the same chapter, we are told, "And he cured many who were sick with various diseases, and cast out many demons; and he would not permit the demons to speak, because they knew him" (1:34). This is intriguing: Jesus does not silence them because they were saying false things about him; on the contrary, he did so "because they knew him."

After healing a leper, Jesus commands him also to keep it a secret: "After sternly warning him, he sent him away at once, saying to him, 'See that you say nothing to anyone; but go, show yourself to the priest, and offer for your cleansing what Moses commanded' " (1:43–44). Repeatedly in Mark, therefore, we get a pattern: Jesus performs some wonder, often healing or exorcizing someone; the people are amazed, but Jesus tells them all, the demons as well as the people, not to say anything to anyone about it. Usually, however, the persons can't keep the secret, and so fame about Jesus and his remarkable abilities spreads anyway (1:45, for example). This pattern does occur in other Gospels, but it is much more prominent in Mark, and since we are convinced that Matthew and Luke both used Mark as one of their sources, it is likely they got it from him. For Mark, though, it seems to be a significant repeated pattern in his Gospel.

An older hypothesis suggested that this did not reflect any actual event in Jesus' lifetime but was a literary device invented by the writer of Mark himself.[2] According to the scholar who promoted the theory, the author knew that Jesus did not openly proclaim himself to be the Messiah during his lifetime. That was something Jesus' followers came to believe about him only toward the end of his life or even after his death. Because Mark knew that Jesus was not "known" to be the Christ during his lifetime, but he himself did believe that Jesus was the Christ, he invented the literary device of having Jesus keep his true identity secret during his ministry.

The problem with this theory, as many people can recognize on a careful reading of the Gospel, is that even though Jesus commands people to silence, they proclaim the news anyway. Regularly in Mark, we are told that his fame spread because of news of his great deeds being broadcast. So the theory doesn't really make sense of the messianic-secret motif and its function in the Gospel. Another problem with that theory is that Jesus does, at least in one instance, command a healed person to tell the news: in the case of the man healed of a "legion" of demons (Mark 5:19–20). I will offer an explanation for the puzzle of the messianic secret after I glance at other problems our exegesis should try to solve.

The Problem of Misunderstanding

Mark emphasizes that even though the demons correctly know Jesus' true identity, most others in the story seem to misunderstand both his teachings and who he is. Even his closest disciples seem regularly puzzled and confused, leading Jesus to rebuke them repeatedly for their lack of understanding. After Jesus calms a storm on the Sea of Galilee, his disciples ask themselves, "Who then is this, that even the wind and the sea obey him?" (4:41). After the miracle of the multiplication of the food and a similar sea miracle, this time Jesus calming a sea storm after walking on the water, the author tells us, "And they were utterly astounded, for they did not understand about the loaves, but their hearts were hardened" (6:51b–52).

At one point, Jesus seems completely frustrated by the repeated obtuse lack of understanding on the part of his disciples. He has attempted to warn them about the plotting of his enemies by cautioning them about "the yeast of the Pharisees and yeast of Herod" (8:15). They take this as a veiled criticism of them for failing to bring bread along. Mark continues,

> Jesus said to them, "Why are you talking about having no bread? Do you still not perceive or understand? Are your hearts hardened? Do you have eyes, and fail to see? Do you have ears, and fail to hear? And do you not remember? When I broke the five loaves for the five thousand, how many baskets full of broken pieces did you collect?" They said to him, "Twelve." "And the seven for the four thousand, how many baskets full of broken pieces did you collect?" And they said to him, "Seven." Then he said to them, "Do you not yet understand?" (8:17–21)[3]

The theme extends up to the end of the Gospel, to Jesus' crucifixion. Mark tells us that as Jesus was dying, he let out a cry on the cross in Aramaic, "Eloi, Eloi, lema sabachthani?" Mark gives us the translation: "My God, my God, why have you forsaken me?" which is a quotation from Psalm 22:1 (although Mark does not tell us that). He does point out, though, that people surrounding the scene, who perhaps should have recognized the quotation, completely misunderstood Jesus, thinking instead that he was calling out for Elijah (Mark 15:34–36).

Now, it is no mystery to us readers who Jesus is. We are told at the beginning that he is "the son of God" (1:1). But most of the people, including his closest disciples, seem not to "get" who he is and fail repeatedly to understand his true identity—or perhaps just something about that identity. Indeed, it seems that the only ones who recognize Jesus rightly are the demons and unclean spirits and, in the end, the Roman centurion who has just crucified him. Just when Jesus dies, and the curtain of the temple is torn from top to bottom, the centurion says, "Truly this man was God's Son!" (15:39). It should come as no surprise, then, when we reach the end of the Gospel, and the women are said to have fled from the tomb, amazed, confused, and terrified. They understand so little about Jesus that they fail even to pass along to the disciples the message given to them by the "young man" at the tomb. The Gospel ends in confused silence.

A Critical Turning Point

Although there are many scholarly ways to make sense of these different "problems" in the Gospel of Mark—the messianic secret, the repeated misunderstandings, the confusing ending—I offer one. This explanation is not my invention, and I am not saying that it is the only legitimate hypothesis about how the Gospel all "works together." I believe that books of the New Testament, like all texts, are open to many different interpretations and that it is only foolishness that expects there to be just one "right" one. But the reading of Mark I offer here is one that is respectable and feasible, one among several probable suggestions for why the author wrote his Gospel the way he did. I can lay out my interpretation by concentrating on what I take to be a turning point of the Gospel as a whole, the events that are narrated from Mark 8:27 through 9:1.

The passage begins with Jesus asking his disciples, "Who do people say that I am?" (8:27–30). All the way through the book, the identity of Jesus has been a recurring issue: demons seem to know; other people ask, "What sort of man is this?", his own disciples seem confused. So an attentive reader should come to attention at Jesus' question. But we aren't given a completely open answer quite yet. "And they answered him, 'John the Baptist; and others, Elijah; and still others, one of the prophets.' He asked them, 'But who do you say that I am?'" And now we readers are on the edge of our seats: will the disciples get it right this time? "Peter answered him, 'You are the Messiah.'" Ah, now they get it. And of course, now Jesus will praise Peter and admit it all openly. But no. "He sternly ordered them not to tell anyone about him." The messianic secret again. Why has Jesus dropped the opportunity here to "come out" as the Messiah and acknowledge the correctness of Peter's confession? Jesus, at least in Mark, is apparently not a very good evangelist.

But the next sentence provides an important clue about what Jesus is doing. "Then he began to teach them." What? Only now has Jesus begun to teach? No, Jesus has been teaching throughout the first several chapters of Mark. But this is obviously a clue from the author that we are at some kind of turning point in Jesus' teaching and in the Gospel. "Then he began to teach them that the Son of Man must undergo great suffering, and be rejected by the elders, the chief priests, and the scribes, and be killed, and after three days rise again" (8:31).

Christians, and even other people who know anything about basic Christianity, simply assume that part of what it meant for Jesus to be "the Christ" was that he would suffer and die for the sins of humanity. But the Jewish concept of "messiah" in the ancient world did not include the idea that a messiah would suffer and die at all. The Messiah was expected to be a kingly figure, perhaps a priestly figure, or perhaps a combination of priest and king. Some people seem to have expected that he would be a human being; others, that he might be some kind of superhuman figure, much like an angel. But he was expected to arise from among the population or come on the clouds of heaven as a conquering commander of heavenly forces. He was never expected to suffer and die—especially not in a manner as humiliating and servile as Roman crucifixion, a despised, low form of punishment. It was illegal to crucify Roman citizens, precisely because that form of execution was considered to be so humiliating. If they were executed, it was by forced suicide at their own hands or perhaps by beheading. Crucifixion was reserved for the lowest. And Jews would never have expected such a thing to happen to a messiah. The word means "anointed," after all: the "anointed king," not a slave or manual laborer or criminal.

Christians have read into Jewish scriptures the combination of messiahship with suffering by taking passages that did refer to a chosen figure of suffering, most often as the prophet who endures suffering on behalf of the people, and combining those passages with different passages that were taken to refer to a messianic figure. So the "suffering servant" passages from Isaiah, which were not taken by Jews to refer to a messiah, were combined with passages from the Psalms, the prophets, and elsewhere that were taken as referring to a messiah.[4] Or psalms that depicted the righteous man who is unjustly tortured (for example, Psalm 22) were linked to psalms that were taken as speaking of a future king (for example, Psalm 2). The combination of these originally different "prophecies" into one prophecy about Jesus, the suffering Messiah, was a product of Christians who were trying to make sense of how Jesus could be both the Christ and a crucified man. It was a combination, moreover, that was not only an innovation; it was also anathema to Jews and laughable to the Romans and Greeks. As Paul said, reflecting real social and cultural realities, it was "a stumbling block to Jews and foolishness to Gentiles" (1 Cor 1:23). No Jew in the time of Jesus expected that the Messiah would be crucified. Messiahs don't suffer; messiahs aren't beaten; messiahs aren't crucified. This is the foolishness and stumbling block Mark's Gospel is designed to overcome.

Notice also the sentence after the passage I have just quoted, the passage where Jesus, for the first time in Mark, predicts his suffering: "He said all this quite openly" (8:32). The author of Mark, in spite of some rather inelegant Greek style, is a clever writer, after all. He regularly uses short, pithy sentences to jerk the reader's attention to an important point. We have just encountered the first "passion prediction" in Mark. That term is used by scholars to designate those passages in the Gospels, and each Gospel has some, where Jesus prophesies that he will suffer, be killed, and rise again. Mark 8:31 is the first "passion prediction" in this Gospel, although others will come later (see 9:31, 10:33–34). The author, therefore, draws the reader's attention to this as a central quotation by following it with a notation: reader, this is open teaching! "He said all this quite openly."

But Jesus is not allowed the last word here. Right at the point where Jesus says that he will suffer and die, Peter takes offense, and reasonably so, given what Jews expected of their messiahs at the time. We aren't told the content of Peter's "rebuke" of Jesus, but it doubtless was precisely that Jesus must be confused because messiahs don't suffer and die. They win, conquer, and liberate. But Jesus turns right around and rebukes Peter, and in the open. Note that Peter had disagreed with Jesus in private: he "took him aside" (8:32). Jesus, though, turns Peter back to the other disciples and rebukes him in front of them all, even calling him "Satan": "Get behind me, Satan! For you are setting your mind not on divine things but on human things" (8:33). A suffering messiah is not common sense at that time. It is not a "human thing." But it is a "divine thing," proving one more time that God does not believe in "common sense."

To drive the point home, the author then has Jesus address the entire crowd.

> He called the crowd with his disciples, and said to them, "If any want to become my followers, let them deny themselves and take up their cross and follow me. For those who want to save their life will lose it, and those who lose their life for my sake, and for the sake of the gospel, will save it. For what will it profit them to gain the whole world and forfeit their life? Indeed, what can they give in return for their life? Those who are ashamed of me and of my words in this adulterous and sinful generation, of them the Son of Man will also be ashamed when he comes in the glory of his Father with the holy angels." (8:34–38)

That is what messiahs were expected to do: come in glory with holy angels. Then Mark concludes the scene with an important prophecy: "And he said to them, 'Truly I tell you there are some standing here who will not taste death until they see that the kingdom of God has come with power'" (9:1).

In this passage, we have seen the full pattern that informs parts of Mark, as well as the entire Gospel: a correct identification of Jesus; a charge to secrecy; a correction of a misunderstanding about the necessity of suffering; and a promise of future, eschatological glory and reward. In fact, the author emphasizes Jesus' promise of future glory in 9:1 by immediately adding the story of Jesus' transfiguration on the mountain.

> Six days later, Jesus took with him Peter and James and John, and led them up to a high mountain apart, by themselves. And he was transfigured before them, and his clothes became dazzling white, such as no one on earth could bleach them. And there appeared to them Elijah with Moses, who were talking with Jesus. Then Peter said to Jesus, "Rabbi, it is good for us to be here; let us make three dwellings, one for you, one for Moses, and one for Elijah." He did not know what to say, for they were terrified. Then a cloud overshadowed them, and from the cloud there came a voice, "This is my Son, the Beloved; listen to him!" Suddenly when they looked around, they saw no one with them anymore but only Jesus. (9:2–8)

This story functions as a proleptic portrait of the way Jesus will appear after he goes through the suffering of crucifixion and burial. He will be transformed into glory in the resurrection. But that hasn't happened yet, so it makes perfect sense that the author immediately stresses the motif of secrecy: "As they were coming down the mountain, he ordered them to tell no one what they had seen, until the Son of Man had risen from the dead" (9:9). The emphasis is returned to the upcoming death of Jesus and the need for secrecy in the meantime.

It is as if Jesus must teach people a new and different notion of the relation between the Messiah and glory. They all think that the Messiah will simply come in glory, with his holy angels, and take rulership of the earth. What Jesus has to teach them is that the Messiah must first go through suffering and death and only afterward enjoy the rewards of glory. Jesus tells people to keep his identity a secret so he can teach them a new notion of what the Messiah will be and do. Once he has gone through death and suffering, there will be no more need for secrecy: they will have learned that a suffering messiah is possible after all.

The Apocalypse in Mark

Mark is an apocalyptic document: it fixes attention on the coming of the Messiah, on the imminent end of the current political and social world, on the coming judgment of human beings, and on the future establishment of the kingdom of God. Even the style of writing in Mark suggests the breathless pace leading up to the end of this world. Mark uses the word "immediately" so many times that his writing style would not pass muster in any college writing course, and he pushes the pace of his narrative to move quickly from one scene to another. The emphasis on suffering is also an aspect of ancient Jewish apocalyptic literature. Although the Messiah was not expected to suffer, righteous human beings were. Indeed, the genre of apocalyptic literature is devised to provide psychological and emotional relief to those unjustly experiencing persecution and suffering, as the later chapter on Revelation will make clear.

Although the Gospel of Mark does not belong to the genre of apocalyptic literature (which will be further explored in Chapter 23 in this book), it does contain its own "little apocalypse," as scholars call it, in chapter 13. As with most apocalypses, it begins with a narrative and moves to prediction, in this case Jesus' prediction of the destruction of the temple in Jerusalem:

> As he came out of the temple, one of his disciples said to Him, "Look, Teacher, what large stones and what large buildings!" Then Jesus asked him, "Do you see these great buildings? Not one stone will be left here upon another; all will be thrown down." When he was sitting on the Mount of Olives opposite the temple, Peter, James, John, and Andrew asked him privately, "Tell us, when will this be, and what will be the sign that all these things are to be accomplished?" Then Jesus began to say to them, "Beware that no one leads you astray. Many will come in my name and say, 'I am he!' and they will lead many astray. When you hear of wars and rumors of wars, do not be alarmed; this must take place, but the end is still to come." (13:1–7)

As is often the case in apocalyptic prophecies, a time line of catastrophic events is narrated: wars, rumors of wars, and false prophets. These do not constitute "the end" itself, but its precursors and warnings. Jesus continues, "For nation will rise against nation, kingdom against kingdom; there will be earthquakes in various places; there will be famines. This is but the beginning of the birth pangs. As for yourselves, beware; for they will hand you over to councils; and you will be beaten in synagogues" (13:8–9). Note that Jesus predicts suffering also for his followers. So Jesus is not the only one who must endure suffering in order to get to glory. His disciples also will follow his lead in that pattern.

Jesus goes on to predict that the good news of his message will go throughout the earth before the end. Families, however, will be divided by different loyalties; brothers will betray one another even to death; fathers will turn against children and children against parents. And Jesus' disciples will be universally hated. "But the one who endures to the end will be saved" (13:13). The last statement before Jesus turns to narrate the actual events of the "end" is one urging endurance in suffering.

But then Jesus gets to the end itself. "But when you see the desolating sacrilege set up where it ought not to be (let the reader understand), then those in Judea must flee to the mountains" (13:14). Again, the author inserts an aside—"let the reader understand"—jerking his readers' attention to this point: this is important; this is where you especially must pay attention. And that one thing is the setting up of the "desolating sacrilege" (the "abomination of desolation" in older translations) "where it ought not to be." Our author knows the book of Daniel, and on those prophecies he bases these (see Dan 9:27, 11:31, 12:11). The "desolating sacrilege" must be something terrible that will be placed in the temple in Jerusalem, probably an idol of a foreign god, the emperor himself, or some other "Antichrist."

Notice, though, that from this point on, we aren't given other predictions of "historical" events. Instead, there are just descriptions of those awful events of "the end" themselves and warnings: "Woe to those" (13:17). The next events are those of the end itself: the darkening of the sun and moon, stars falling from heaven, heavenly "powers" shaken (13:24–25). Next is the *parousia* itself, the "coming" of the Son of man on the clouds "with great power and glory." And then there is the prediction of the last event here narrated: "Then he will send out the angels, and gather his elect from the four winds, from the ends of the earth to the ends of heaven" (13:27). The wicked will have been destroyed in the eschatological catastrophes, and the formerly suffering righteous will be saved.

When is all this supposed to happen? We know one thing for certain: the author expects it to happen within one generation from when Jesus supposedly predicted it: "Truly I tell you, this generation will not pass away until all these things have taken place" (13:30). Although he proceeds to admit that no one except the Father knows the exact day and hour, neither the angels nor even the Son (13:32), he has given some clues. The clearest, and the one immediately preceding the final eschatological catastrophes and the coming of the Son of Man, is the setting up of the "abomination of desolation" in the temple.

Let's note also what Mark does not tell us. The author nowhere narrates the actual surrounding of Jerusalem by the Roman army, the destruction of the temple, the destruction of Jerusalem itself, and the carrying off of thousands of Jews into Roman slavery. We know that those things actually did happen in and just after 70 C.E. But the Gospel of Mark makes no mention of them. This is notable precisely because the version of this "little apocalypse" that occurs in the Gospel of Luke does predict those events (see Luke 21). As we know, the author of Luke used Mark as one of his sources, so Luke was written sometime after Mark. It is significant, I argue, that Luke gives details of events that took place after 70 C.E., whereas Mark does not. In fact, his apocalypse predicts the coming of the Son of Man just after the setting up of the "desolating sacrilege" in the temple.

We saw in Chapter 4 that apocalyptic writings can be dated by seeing where their "prophecy" no longer fits what we know of the events of "real history." Daniel was correct in many of his predictions about the wars and marriages and treaties of the Seleucids and Ptolemies. He was wrong, though, in his prediction about how Antiochus IV Epiphanes would die, and he seemed to know nothing about the victory of Judas Maccabeus. Thus we date the writing of Daniel, or at least the second half of it, the "apocalyptic" part, to sometime between 168 and 164 B.C.E. If we follow the same method for Mark, we should place its writing just before 70 C.E. or close enough following it that the destruction of the temple and Jerusalem had not had time to "sink in" yet. After all, the author portrays Jesus as predicting the destruction of the temple. But the author does not narrate it, or anything after that event either. Many scholars think this is good evidence that the Gospel of Mark can be dated just like many other apocalyptic writings: by where the "history" goes wrong.

Another clue to the situation of writing may be had by returning to the strange ending and its pointing to Galilee. Might that indicate that the author or his local church was located in Galilee or at least had a strong connection to it? We may imagine—and it is imagination—that "Mark" was a Christian living in Galilee just before or during the Roman war with Judea. Palestinian Jews revolted against Rome in 66 C.E. From then until 70, Roman legions made their way through Galilee, destroying cities and towns that had resisted them and rewarding the few that had sided with them. They soon surrounded Jerusalem and laid siege to it for many months. The author of the Gospel would have seen all this, perhaps himself experiencing the early parts of the war. If we may imagine him writing at this time, it would be understandable that he would expect that the Romans would win and that they would destroy the temple. He may have believed that the "desolating sacrilege" would be a Roman standard, a statue of the emperor, or perhaps even a Jewish messianic pretender. But, following the prophecies of Daniel and perhaps those of the historical Jesus himself, our author would have taken that event to signal the final end, after which it could not be long before the Son of Man would come in victory.

In this context, Mark writes his Gospel with this message: "Things are going to get a lot worse before they get better. Just as they got worse for Jesus before they got better for him, beginning with his resurrection and culminating in his future coming, they will also get worse for us before they get better. But they will get better. You must endure just as Jesus endured. You must suffer just as Jesus suffered. But if you think the Romans are going to win and we will all be destroyed or enslaved, you don't have the proper faith." The author takes the Jesus depicted in his Gospel as the model for the behavior he wants to emulate and to urge on his fellow Christians: suffering will be followed by glory. But the suffering is nonetheless necessary, for us as for him.

This also may make sense of the strange ending of the Gospel in its lack of actual resurrection appearances. The author may have left out any past resurrection appearances because he believed that the ultimate appearance was going to happen quite soon, and those Christians in Galilee would meet Jesus in Galilee just as the young man had told the women to tell the disciples. Perhaps that message didn't get through to them immediately, but the Gospel of Mark is now carrying it: go to Galilee; wait there; there you will see the risen and glorified Jesus. In a sense, the author is telling his readers, "All we have to do is stay here and wait. Jesus will come for us soon."

Of course, this is speculation.[5] Tradition has held that the Gospel of Mark was written in Rome, but we've already seen that the traditions linking Mark to Rome and Peter are questionable. At any rate, whether in Galilee or elsewhere, the Gospel of Mark, with its puzzles and problems, may be understood if it is read as a document written to teach endurance in the face of suffering by a promise of salvation and glory at the end of the Roman world.

CHAPTER 7
The Gospel of Matthew

Overview: The Gospel of Matthew contains some of the most famous passages that both Christians and non-Christians recognize. But Matthew presents itself paradoxically as preaching both a Torah-observant Christianity and a Christian mission to gentiles. The figure of Jesus in Matthew is as a teacher, the founder of the church, and the model for the apostles and Matthew's own community. Matthew is writing for a church community that needs encouragement to have faith in a time of trouble.

The Most Famous Gospel

The Gospel of Matthew, from the second century on, has been the most popular Gospel, which is probably why it ended up first in our Bibles. It is the Gospel most familiar to both Christians and non-Christians. If there is a story or saying that occurs in Matthew but also in Mark or Luke—and there are many—people usually know the version that appears in Matthew if they know it at all. Matthew's birth narrative, very different from Luke's, is one people can often recall: an angel appears to Joseph in a dream telling him not to send away his now mysteriously pregnant fiancée but to marry her anyway; wise men in the East see a new star and follow it to Judea; the scheming King Herod finds out the likely birthplace and time and has all infants under the age of two slaughtered; the holy family goes to Egypt to escape; following another instruction in a dream, Joseph later moves the family back, but ends up settling in Nazareth to escape the possible wrath of Herod's son, who now reigns in Judea.

People who may know little of the Bible know the "beatitudes," and they usually know the Matthean version rather than the wording found in Luke: "Blessed are the poor in spirit, for theirs is the kingdom of heaven. Blessed are those who mourn, for they will be comforted. Blessed are the meek, for they will inherit the earth" (Matt 5:3–5). A collection of these teachings, along with many others, is found in Matthew in what has come to be called "the Sermon on the Mount" (Matt 5–7). Most people know the sermon by that name, and they may not know that many of the same teachings are found in Luke, but in a sermon Jesus delivers on a plain, not a mountain (Luke 6:17–49).

In Matthew, the Pharisees repeatedly make important appearances, more than in the other Gospels, and they are regularly called "hypocrites." It is no accident, therefore, that in English the very word "pharisee" came to mean "hypocrite," as a quick look in almost any dictionary will confirm. This reflects, of course, the long tradition of Christian anti-Semitism. In the ancient world, Jews did not take Pharisees to be hypocrites any more than any other human being. The Pharisees of Jesus' day, in fact, were the precursors of the later rabbis. Gamaliel, considered by rabbinic Judaism to be one of its forefathers as a righteous rabbi himself, makes appearances in the Acts of the Apostles as a leading Pharisee (Acts 5:34). Paul, as depicted in Acts, even claims to have studied at his feet (Acts 22:3). The fact that the word "pharisee" could become synonymous with "hypocrite" in English is in great part due to the influence of the Gospel of Matthew.

Matthew ends with what has come to be called the "Great Commission." According to Matthew's account, Jesus appeared after his resurrection to the surviving eleven disciples in Galilee on a mountain (Judas Iscariot had by this time killed himself, according to Matthew's account). Matthew's Gospel ends with Jesus' words sending the disciples to evangelize the world: "All authority in heaven and on earth has been given to me. Go therefore and make disciples of all nations, baptizing them in the name of the Father and of the Son and of the Holy Spirit, and teaching them to obey everything that I have commanded you. And remember, I am with you always, to the end of the age" (Matt 28:18–20). This quotation is familiar to Christians, but often to others as well.

All these aspects of Matthew render it for many people the most familiar of our Gospels. But when it is read carefully, Matthew is also the most "Jewish" of the canonical Gospels. It is not actually the most Jewish of all gospels from the ancient world, because we do have references to others, and some that still survive, that teach an even more Jewish form of early Christianity. But of the four canonical Gospels, Matthew comes across, when carefully examined, as emphasizing Jewish piety and practice. For example, in the other Gospels there are some hints that Jesus was open to speaking with gentiles, and his disciples are sometimes depicted as having contacts with gentiles. But Matthew makes it very clear that in his opinion, Jesus carefully limited his ministry, and that of his disciples, to "the house of Israel" during his lifetime. When he sends out his twelve disciples in chapter 10, he explicitly forbids them to speak with gentiles or even Samaritans (Matt 10:5–6), unlike Jesus in John, for instance (see John 4:7–42). The other Gospels don't contain this limitation. Matthew uses the word "gentile" only for "outsiders," including Jewish members of the church who have been kicked out of the community (see Matt 18:17). This is true even though Matthew's church obviously included gentiles by the time he wrote his Gospel. Jesus, in Matthew, signals a "turn" to a gentile mission precisely in the Great Commission just quoted: "all the nations."

The Gospel of Matthew begins with unmistakable echoes of Jewish scripture. "The book of the genesis of Jesus the Messiah, son of David, son of Abraham" (Matt 1:1; my translation). The word "genesis" here is often translated as "genealogy," and it certainly does have that meaning. My translation "genesis," though, emphasizes that someone who was reading Matthew in Greek and knew Jewish scripture would immediately know that Matthew was beginning his book by alluding to the first book of the Jewish Torah, called Genesis ("beginning") in the Greek translation of the Hebrew Bible. In the Hebrew Bible, Genesis is not only the "beginning" of scripture, but also the beginning of the world, the entire earth, the beginning of history. Certainly Matthew uses the two Greek words *biblos geneseōs*, "the book of the beginning," quite consciously to begin his own book. It is appropriate, moreover, that they eventually became the first words of the New Testament.

A Jewish reader would also note that Matthew singles out David and Abraham as the most important forefathers of Jesus, David as the most important king of Israel, and Abraham as the father of the nation of Israel and all Jews. Then Matthew creates for Jesus a genealogy (it is not, of course, historical) that clearly imitates the "begats" so familiar to us from the book of Genesis: "Abraham begat Isaac, Isaac begat Jacob," and so on (Matt 1:2). It is also no accident that the author constructs his list in three segments of fourteen: fourteen generations from Abraham to David, fourteen from

David to the Babylonian exile, and fourteen from the exile to the Messiah (1:17). This has nothing to do with history, of course. But the numbers three and fourteen (twice seven) are significant in ancient numerology, including Jewish numerology.

Matthew also contains what we might call a Jewish *haggadah* on Moses. Rabbinic sources divide materials into *halakah*, which refers to the teachings about the Torah on how to live, that is, "legal" material, and *haggadah*, which is a Hebrew word used in rabbinic tradition to refer to stories that provide, usually, moral lessons or pious instruction. An haggadah is a "tale" or a "parable" told to illustrate some aspect of the Torah. Matthew provides an account of Jesus' birth and upbringing that looks a bit like a Jewish story depicting Jesus as Moses. A baby is born under extraordinary conditions; an evil king orders the slaughter of all infant boys of a certain area, but the baby escapes, survives, and eventually becomes the one who saves the people (Matt 2; compare Exod 1–2). By divine order, Jesus is taken for protection to Egypt, a movement that providentially fulfills the prophecy, "Out of Egypt I have called my son" (Matt 2:15; see Hosea 11:1). Jesus, like Moses, comes out of Egypt to save the people. Throughout the Gospel, Jesus is portrayed in ways that recall Moses or, at times, Joseph. It is quite possible that Matthew has Jesus deliver his new interpretation of the Torah, the law of Moses, on a mountain because Moses delivered his law from a mountain (Matt 5–7; Exod 19:3, 24:12, 24:15, and passim).

Before offering other observations about the structure of Matthew's Gospel, I must take a brief detour to introduce modern theories for solving the "synoptic problem." "Synoptic" means "seeing with" or "seen with." It is a technical term, borrowed from Greek, that is used to express how the first three Gospels, Matthew, Mark, and Luke, all seem to be telling much the same story, with similar or identical events and sayings, parables, and teachings, sometimes in identical wording. The three have much wording, as well as their basic outlines, alike. Why this is the case is called "the synoptic problem." There have been many different theories: Matthew was written first, Mark used Matthew but abbreviated it, and Luke used Matthew and Mark. Or perhaps Mark was the earliest, Matthew used Mark, and Luke used both Matthew and Mark. The hypothesis—and we must remember that it is only a hypothesis; we have no proof—accepted by most scholars today suggests that both Matthew and Luke used Mark, but independently of each other.

But Matthew and Luke both share other material, often in the same wording, that they cannot have found in Mark. Most scholars also believe, therefore, that there existed another written source we no longer possess, a source that consisted mainly of sayings of Jesus. They call that hypothetical document "Q," from the German word *Quelle*, "source" (the theory was developed by German scholars, and English speakers just adopted the name given it by Germans). Many scholars believe that Matthew and Luke each had access to this Q source and also Mark, and that both Matthew and Luke took the basic outlines for their Gospels and many of their events from Mark, and many of the sayings from Q (Fig. 5).

That hypothesis, or one like it, allows scholars to compare sayings and events as narrated in Mark, Luke, and Matthew to see how each author uses his "source" material (either Mark or the hypothetical Q) to construct his own account. We can observe, that is, the editorial activity of each author to discern what his particular interests and tendencies are—his particular "theology," if we may use the word in a rather loose sense. By doing this, we can see that Matthew takes different sayings of Jesus—some of which he got from Mark, some of which he got from another written source (say, Q), and some of which he may be getting from oral traditions or other sources he used but which are lost to us—and arranges them into individual speeches or "sermons" of Jesus. Thus sayings that occur in several different places in Luke (and therefore probably in Q) are grouped together in Matthew to form the Sermon on the Mount (Matt 5–7). Parables that occur in Mark and

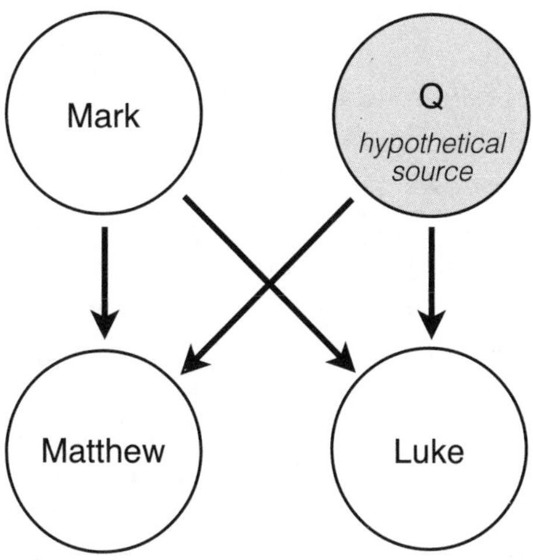

Fig. 5 A Solution to the Synoptic Problem

Luke in various places are grouped together in Matthew in one sermon of and about parables (Matt 13).

Some scholars have suggested that the author of Matthew intentionally arranged five separate sermons or speeches of Jesus, and that the number five was meant to parallel the "five books of Moses," the Pentateuch (from a Greek word) or Torah (from the Hebrew): Genesis, Exodus, Leviticus, Numbers, and Deuteronomy. As Moses gave Israel five books of the Torah, so Jesus gave Israel five sermons: Jesus' own version of the Pentateuch, the Torah.[1] The first of these is the Sermon on the Mount. The second is chapter 10, instructions Jesus gives to his disciples about the mission to Israel. The third is chapter 13, a sermon of parables. The fourth is chapter 18, which looks like a sermon of instructions about the makeup and behavior of the church. The fifth and last of these "books of the law of Jesus" is chapters 23–25, a very long speech that includes Matthew's own version of "the apocalypse" (Matt 24), with much taken from Mark 13, but also Jesus' condemnations of the scribes and Pharisees (Matt 23) and his instructions and warnings about being prepared (Matt 25). This suggestion—that the five main sermons of Matthew are intended to imitate the five books of Moses—is not accepted by everyone, but it is interesting in its own right, and if it is true, it emphasizes even more the intention of the author to portray Jesus as another, and perhaps superior, Moses.

I present one final point to demonstrate just how "Jewish" the Gospel of Matthew is. The author quite frequently interprets a saying or action of Jesus or others as fulfilling scripture, more so than the other Gospels. The birth of Jesus, Matthew believes, fulfills the prophecy of Isaiah 7:14. His birth in Bethlehem fulfills Micah 5:1–2. As already noted, his coming from Egypt fulfills Hosea 11:1. The slaughter of the innocents by Herod is said to fulfill Jeremiah 31:15. And the family's settling in Nazareth is said to fulfill a citation, "He will be called a Nazorean" (Matt 2:23; scholars are unable to find a corresponding scripture citation for this one). All these are found in just the first two chapters of the Gospel, but the theme of "fulfillment" continues throughout Matthew, tying his Gospel firmly to Jewish scripture before him.

It is highly ironic, though, that modern scholars stress how "Jewish" Matthew is, because Matthew has been used as a resource for some of the worst Christian anti-Semitism, perhaps more than any other Gospel (with the possible exception of John, which has traditionally been read in churches on Good Friday, including its strongly negative portrayal of "the Jews"). As I mentioned, it is in Matthew that the "scribes and Pharisees" are most loudly and most often condemned and repeatedly labeled "hypocrites." And one of the most anti-Semitic accusations—that the Jews are "Christ killers"—took its inspiration from the shout of the crowds at Jesus' trial as depicted in Matthew: "His blood be on us and on our children" (27:25).

In line with this history of Christian anti-Judaism, Jesus' comments in Matthew on the law of Moses have been taken as a Christian rejection of that law (which is a complete misreading of the Gospel, as we will see). Matthew's Jesus is read as substituting the "good" law of Christianity for the "bad" law of the Jews. Christians have traditionally taught that Christianity rejected the law as a rejection of Jewish "legalism." The Old Testament is stereotyped as representing the "God of wrath" and is contrasted with the "God of mercy" of the New Testament. The New Testament God is the loving father, full of grace; the Old Testament God is a God of judgment, full of condemnation. Thus the Matthean Jesus' words "You have heard it said . . . but I say to you" (Matt 5:21–48) have been interpreted as the rejection by Jesus of the legalism of the Jews and the replacement of Jewish law by a Christian law of love. This dualism has been so dominant in Christendom—part of Western "common sense"—that even people who know next to nothing about the Bible and are not religious still invoke the caricature of the "Old Testament God of law and judgment" contrasted with the "New Testament God of love." It is highly ironic that what modern scholars see as the most "Jewish" of the four Gospels has also functioned for many as an inspiration for anti-Jewish ideology and action.

Jesus and the Torah in Matthew

Most Christians have been taught, traditionally and at one time or another, that Christianity represents the supersession of Judaism. The thing that makes Christians and Jews alike is their worship of the same God. What separates them is that Christians need not follow Jewish law. It surprises people when they come to realize, as modern scholars have done, that this is not at all the attitude to the law in Matthew.

Jesus, in fact, is portrayed in Matthew as explicitly condemning any notion that he is rejecting the law or teaching his followers not to obey it:

> Do not think that I have come to abolish the law or the prophets; I have come not to abolish but to fulfill. For truly I tell you, until heaven and earth pass away, not one letter, not one stroke of a letter, will pass from the law until all is accomplished. Therefore,

> whoever breaks one of the least of these commandments, and teaches others to do the same, will be called least in the kingdom of heaven; but whoever does them and teaches them will be called great in the kingdom of heaven. For I tell you, unless your righteousness exceeds that of the scribes and Pharisees, you will never enter the kingdom of heaven. (Matt 5:17–20)

This would seem to be about as straightforward as one could wish: Matthew believes that Jesus insisted that all members of his community, which by this time certainly included gentile converts, were expected to obey the law of Moses strictly. Christians have been taught that the "fulfillment" of the "law and prophets" mentioned in the first sentence took place once and for all in Jesus himself. Christians need not obey the Mosaic law because it has been "fulfilled" by Jesus' obedience. But that is certainly an interpretation that the author of Matthew would have heatedly repudiated. Matthew believes that Jesus taught the continued necessity of the law "until heaven and earth pass away."

This can be borne out by a more careful look at those passages known to scholars as the Matthean "antitheses": "You have heard . . . but I say." Immediately after the passage just quoted on the enduring law, Jesus says, "You have heard that it was said to those in ancient times, 'You shall not murder' " (5:21). But Jesus does not quote the scripture in order then to say, "But I say to you, go ahead and murder. You will be covered by grace, and God will forgive you." Rather, he teaches that not only murder is wrong, but even being angry with another human being. He forbids people even from calling one another "fool!" (5:22). Jesus quotes the commandment not to commit adultery (5:27), but he does not follow it up by saying, "But I say to you, you may commit adultery." Instead, he says, "Everyone who looks at a woman with lust has already committed adultery with her in his heart" (5:28). In each of these cases, Jesus quotes a commandment of the Jewish law not to abrogate it, but to intensify it: to require something even more difficult and stringent. Jesus does not get rid of the commandments of Moses. He retains them but teaches that they must also be completely internalized. If killing is a temptation, how hard is it to avoid anger? If adultery is difficult to avoid, how much more so is lust?

Christians have also completely misunderstood the commandment "An eye for an eye, and a tooth for a tooth" (Exod 21:24; Lev 24:20). Rather than representing some kind of harsh system of retribution, it was an attempt to moderate retributive systems so that they did not spiral into even greater violence. The law was originally intended to say, "If you must retaliate, you may not retaliate to any extent greater than you have suffered." The law taught that members of one tribe could not slaughter ten people of another tribe in retaliation for the killing of one person of their own tribe. So even in the original, in the Hebrew Bible, the intent was to limit retribution, not command it.

Here again, Jesus makes the commandment even more demanding. He teaches that although the law allowed some retribution, his intensification of that law means that his followers must "turn the other cheek," give up an outer cloak after having been robbed of one's coat, and carry a soldier's pack two miles when the law requires only one (5:38–41). Throughout the Sermon on the Mount, Jesus does the opposite of what many Christians have thought he was doing: rather than abrogating the Jewish law and replacing it with something more "loving" or "merciful," he teaches that people should not only keep the Mosaic law but even go beyond it, go the second mile, internalize the intent of the law, obey the law and more.

There are a few passages that seem to suggest that Jesus was going against the Torah. In one, the Pharisees and scribes ask Jesus why his disciples "break the tradition" by not washing their hands before eating (15:1–20). But note that Matthew identifies this not as a commandment, but as a tradition. And it is important to see how Matthew, taking the story from Mark, alters Mark's text for his own version of the event. According to Mark, Jesus first condemns the Pharisees and scribes for their hypocrisy, but then also teaches that people are made "unclean" not by what goes into their mouths, but by what comes out (Mark 7:14–15). Jesus even repeats the point: "Do you not see that whatever goes into a person from outside cannot defile, since it enters, not the heart but the stomach, and goes out into the sewer?" (7:19). At this point, though, Mark interrupts his quotation of Jesus to add his own parenthetical aside, as Mark likes to do: "Thus he declared all foods clean" (7:19).

Now, it is not at all clear that Jesus, even in the story as told by Mark, was going so far as to get rid of kosher laws entirely. That is how Mark interprets the scene. Matthew, though, does not. Although Matthew takes the story and much of the actual wording from Mark, he leaves out Mark's parenthetical remark. Instead, Jesus simply does what many prophets of Israel had already done: he emphasizes that the ethical demands of the law are more important than its commandments about sacrifice or ritual: "For out of the heart come evil intentions, murder, adultery, fornication, theft, false witness, slander. These are what defile a person, but to eat with unwashed hands does not defile" (Matt 15:18–19). Matthew leaves out Mark's comment on the meaning of Jesus' teaching here because he does not believe that Jesus "declared all foods clean." On the contrary, Matthew establishes, first, that hand washing was tradition, not commandment, and second, that what goes on in the heart and mind of the person is more important than outward rituals. There is no breaking of the law here, or any teaching that lessens the commands of the law.

As odd as it may seem for Christians, the Gospel of Matthew does not conceive of a law-free form of loyalty to Jesus. Nowhere in Matthew's Gospel does Jesus or the author teach that Jesus' followers may make law observance optional. Although the author does not explicitly address the issue, I think it obvious that he would have expected gentiles also, upon conversion within his own church, to have been circumcised, to keep kosher, and to observe the Torah just like the Jews in the congregation. The Jesus of the Gospel of Matthew teaches the intensification of the Jewish law, not its abrogation. And that seems to be expected of all members of the community, including gentiles.[2]

Jesus as Church Founder

More than any other Gospel, Matthew portrays Jesus as the founder of the church. In fact, Matthew is the only Gospel that even uses the word "church." The word is not found in the other Gospels at all, and with good reason: the church did not exist in Jesus' time. It grew up only after his death and as a result of his death and a belief in his resurrection. But Matthew, unlike the other Gospels, portrays Jesus as self-consciously "founding" the church even during his lifetime. Matthew retrojects the founding of the church, and even discussion of rules for the church's life, into the mouth of Jesus.

In the previous chapter, we saw Mark's story about Peter's confession (Mark 8:27–33). Matthew takes over the story but changes it in ways that reveal his own interests and ideas. In Mark, Peter confesses that Jesus is the Messiah, and then Jesus tells the disciples to be quiet about that. Jesus predicts his upcoming suffering, Peter rebukes Jesus for saying such a thing, and then Jesus rebukes Peter, even calling him "Satan." The story is quite different in Matthew. After Peter's confession, "You are the Messiah, the Son of the living God," Jesus commends Peter: "Blessed are you, Simon son of Jonah! For flesh and blood has not revealed this to you, but my Father in heaven" (16:17). But Jesus then goes further and speaks of building his church: "And I tell you, you are Peter, and on this rock I will build my church, and the gates of Hades will not prevail against it. I will give you the keys of the kingdom of heaven, and whatever you bind on earth will be bound in heaven, and whatever you loose on earth will be loosed in heaven" (16:18–19). Jesus himself founded the church, even during his earthly ministry, according to Matthew.

Then in Matthew 18, as I've already noted, we find rules about how the church should run itself. If one believer sins against another believer, the offended person should first go to the offender himself. If the offender does not seek to reconcile, the other person should first take two or three other members of the community along when he confronts the offender. If that also does not work, the person is told to take the matter to the church, and if the offender will not listen to the whole church, he is to be expelled from the community altogether (18:15–17). Only Matthew tells these stories of Jesus founding the church and giving rules for its later behavior. These stories are certainly not "historical." That is, the historical Jesus almost certainly did not say these things about the church. They demonstrate, though, the interests of the author of the Gospel. They show that he was concerned for the life and behavior of his own community, his church.

Jesus as Model for the Disciples

Mark tells us that Jesus impressed people with his teaching (Mark 1:22), but he doesn't really pass along much of Jesus' teaching. Matthew does. As mentioned earlier, Matthew has gathered many of Jesus' parables into one section of his Gospel, now numbered as chapter 13. After several parables, Matthew closes the section with this quotation of Jesus: "Therefore every scribe who has been trained for the kingdom of heaven is like the master of a household who brings out of his treasure what is new and what is old" (13:52). Matthew has presented Jesus as just such a householder, taking the old from the law of Moses, the prophets, and Jewish scripture in general, but adding also what is "new," that is, his own interpretations and teachings. Moreover, Matthew is here saying that his own church must have its "scribes" who do the same. The members of Matthew's community are to imitate Jesus.

There is another aspect of Jesus' ministry that is initially a bit puzzling, but that I argue is meant also to be imitated by his followers: the tendency of Jesus in the Gospel of Matthew to "retreat" in the face of danger. This is a motif peculiar to Matthew's Gospel and is not found generally elsewhere: repeatedly Jesus is threatened by some force, and rather than meeting the danger, he retreats.

The first time Jesus does so could be considered the flight to Egypt by the holy family (Matt 2:13–15), but since Jesus is just an infant at that time, that action may be attributed by the reader more to the agency of Joseph. The motif becomes more obvious in Matthew 4:12: "Now when Jesus heard that John [the Baptist] had been arrested, he withdrew to Galilee." Up to this point, Jesus has been in Judea to be baptized by John (3:13–17). He has then been in "the wilderness" enduring temptation by the devil (4:1–11). But when he hears that John has been arrested, he "retreats" from the scene of action and goes to Galilee.[3] In fact, the Greek word here translated by the New Revised Standard Version (NRSV) as "withdraw" (*anachōreō*) is also the word used for a military retreat. Matthew uses it several times to characterize Jesus' first action when confronted with a threat. This is a puzzling way to depict one's hero: Jesus not as the savior on a white charger, but as the cautious man in "retreat." And Matthew repeats the pattern more than once.

In Matthew 12, we are told that Jesus humiliates the Pharisees by rebuking them and, in spite of their criticism, healing a man on the Sabbath. The Pharisees leave in order to plot Jesus' destruction (12:14). Matthew continues, "When Jesus became aware of this, he departed. Many crowds followed him, and he cured all of them, and he ordered them not to make him known" (12:15). The word here translated "departed" is the same as that used in 4:12: "retreat." Note that Matthew may be taking over the messianic-secret motif from Mark, but it sounds different in his hands. It here sounds as if Jesus has run away from the Pharisees because he has learned that they are conspiring for his death, and he tells the crowds to keep his activities secret, perhaps in order to avoid being caught.

In chapter 14, Matthew narrates the murder of John the Baptist by Herod Antipas. After John's disciples bury his body, they go and tell Jesus what happened. Again, Jesus retreats: "Now when Jesus heard this, he withdrew [the same word, "retreated"] from there in a boat to a deserted place by himself" (14:13). I find this a curious Matthean motif: regularly when faced with danger, Jesus is presented not in a heroic light as facing persecution and overcoming it, but as retreating from it. The word itself, along with the theme, seems to be favored by Matthew. It occurs once in Mark, once in John, and twice in Acts, but ten times in Matthew, usually describing the action of Jesus. What do we make of this "retreating Jesus"?

This pattern, however, includes more than just the "retreat." In Matthew 4:12–17, the first time we see the pattern clearly, Jesus retreats from a threat of danger, but he doesn't just hide someplace. He preaches: "From that time Jesus began to proclaim, 'Repent, for the kingdom of heaven has come near' " (4:17). In Matthew, this is the point at which Jesus begins his ministry. Jesus retreats from danger so that he can take his message elsewhere. The same happens in Matthew 12:15–23: Jesus retreats from the threat on his life by the Pharisees, but then he "cured all of them." His retreat is followed by intensified ministry. In Matthew 14:13–14, Jesus first hears of the death of John and then retreats, but in his retreat he also heals the sick and teaches the crowds. The retreat of Jesus regularly leads not to the end of his ministry but to its beginning or intensification. It is a tactical or strategic retreat.

In this, Matthew again holds up Jesus as a model for the later behavior of his followers. Matthew 10 is a full speech by Jesus to his disciples instructing them on how they should carry out their ministry of healing and proclamation. He also predicts that they will face persecution. They will be hauled before courts, threatened, and punished. But Jesus tells them also to retreat in the face of persecution. (Although the word here is not the same as elsewhere, it does mean "flee" from a threat: *pheugō*.) And Matthew makes sure we know that Jesus is telling his disciples to follow his example: "A disciple is not above the teacher, nor a slave above a master; it is enough for the disciple to be like the teacher, and the slave like the master. If they have called the master of the house Beelzebul, how much more will they malign those of his household!" (10:24–25). Matthew ends the speech with this emphasis on the disciples as the embodiment and representatives of Jesus: "Whoever welcomes you welcomes me, and whoever welcomes me welcomes the one who sent me" (10:40).

Matthew is telling members of his own community that they are to be "good scribes," just as Jesus was. As Jesus did, they will face threats, punishment, and persecution. Their response must be, yes, to endure the suffering. But more than that, they should follow Jesus' example (at least as depicted by Matthew): retreat in the face of danger, but retreat in order to carry out the ministry elsewhere. The "retreating Jesus" is a theme special to Matthew, but it makes sense, given his goals of modeling his community on what he sees as the example of Jesus.

The Stilling of the Storm in Matthew

As I have noted, we can learn a lot about a particular writer's agenda and goals in writing by comparing one account with a source the author used. Comparing Matthew's version of an event or saying with Mark's, from whom he likely got it, gives us important clues about his own purposes for his Gospel. I here adopt as an illustration of this practice a comparison of the "stilling of the storm" in Mark and Matthew, and I take the example from a famous essay published in 1948 by Günther Bornkamm.[4]

In Mark's version, the story is rather simple (Mark 6:45–52). Jesus sends his disciples across the Sea of Galilee in a boat while he stays behind to dismiss the crowd and to pray. The disciples are straining at the oars against a strong headwind when they see Jesus walking on the water, attempting to pass by them. They think they are seeing a ghost and cry out, at which time Jesus calms them and gets into the boat. The wind suddenly ceases.

Matthew adds several elements to the story and elaborates it (Matt 14:22–33). Instead of merely noting that there was a strong headwind, Matthew says that the boat was "battered by the waves" and was "far from the land," a more precarious scene than in Mark (Matt 14:24). Then Matthew adds an entirely new story. After the disciples discover that they are looking at Jesus himself, not a ghost, Peter asks to be allowed to come to Jesus on the water. Jesus says, "Come." But once Peter is out of the boat, he becomes terrified and begins to sink. He cries, "Lord, save me!" Jesus pulls him up, but admonishes him, "You of little faith, why did you doubt?" They both get into the boat, and the wind ceases. Matthew ends his version of the story not with the confusion and misunderstanding of the disciples, as in Mark, but quite differently: "And those in the boat worshiped him, saying, 'Truly you are the Son of God' " (14:33).

In Bornkamm's interpretation, Matthew has taken a rather simple "nature miracle" and turned it into something like an allegory for the church of his day. The church, as Matthew has already made clear, must experience persecution and opposition, represented by the "battering" of the boat by waves and wind. Christians, though, are to look to Jesus for their salvation, as Peter did: "Lord, save me!" Peter here represents "every Christian" who needs Jesus for salvation. But they are to attempt to turn their "little faith" into full faith. The idea that the church includes many people with "little faith" occurs repeatedly in Matthew. In fact, the term seems to be a favorite of the author to describe members of the church who have some, but not enough, trust in Jesus.[5] Finally, Matthew changes the ending he gets from Mark so that the disciples perform the action he expects of members of his own church: not confusion and misunderstanding, but worship of Jesus as Lord.

Bornkamm's essay, published in the middle of the twentieth century, was one of several early examples of what scholars call "redaction criticism." The word "redaction," of course, merely means "editing." In fact, we use "redaction" also in English—rather than the more colloquial "editorial criticism," which would mean the same thing—simply because English-language scholarship learned the method from German scholars, and *Redaktion* is the German word for "editing." The method examines how authors alter (edit or redact) stories or sayings they seem to have found in another source—in this case Mark, although scholars do the same thing when they speculate about how Matthew or Luke may have altered something they found in Q. By studying how the Gospel writer changed materials he got from someone else, we can better see his own intentions in writing.

In this case, we come up with interpretations of Matthew that help us imagine his setting: his church, his purpose in writing, and his intentions. "Matthew" (recall that I use the name only for convenience; we don't know the name of the actual author) is writing in a church that does include gentiles but that, in his opinion at least, must remain linked to Israel by obedience to the law of Moses. It seems that he expects the members of his church to keep kosher, to observe the Sabbath (though in a less strict way than some other Jews), and to continue circumcising male members of the church, probably both their male children and gentile converts. He sees himself and them as a community of teachers and scribes, passing along the teachings of Jesus and interpreting Jewish scripture rightly. They suffer persecution for following this crucified Messiah, and perhaps because of their own different interpretations of the law. But they are to endure, to follow and worship Jesus, and to flee from persecution when they can, but to use that retreat as an opportunity to evangelize further.

This is a version of Christianity quite unlike what most people today know about. It is hard for us to imagine a version of Christianity that takes Jesus to be the Messiah and accepts gentiles into the church but insists on the continuing observation of the law of Moses. But that is apparently what we see in the Gospel of Matthew. The author would certainly not believe that he was offering a different "religion" from Judaism. He sees himself rather as teaching the proper way to be "Israel." This Gospel was certainly written after 70 C.E., and no doubt before the end of the first century. Most scholars would date its composition to sometime around 85 C.E., but that is only a guess. Here, toward the end of the first century, we have a Jesus-believing, law-abiding sect of Judaism that calls itself "church."

CHAPTER 8

The *Gospel of Thomas*

Overview: The existence of the *Gospel of Thomas* had been known from ancient writers, but it was only after the discovery of the Nag Hammadi codices that the actual text became available. The *Gospel of Thomas* is basically a collection of sayings, or *logia*, that sometimes seem similar to, though perhaps more primitive than, sayings found in the canonical Gospels. Sometimes, however, the sayings seem better explained as reflecting a certain "Platonizing" understanding of the world similar to what would later be held by "Gnostics." This involves a rejection of the material world and a desire for *gnosis*, a secret knowledge, in order to escape the world and return to the divine being.

The Nag Hammadi Codices and Thomas Literature

Perhaps the single most persistent theme of this book is the diversity of early Christianity. In fact, scholars now can sometimes be heard talking about "early Christianities" to stress how varied the movement was in its early years, all the way through the second century. An excellent way to illustrate that variety is an examination of Christian documents that did not make it into the canon, that were not considered "orthodox" by later Christians, and that are therefore relatively unknown to modern people. The *Gospel*

According to Thomas (the title borne by the text in the manuscript, although there the title comes at the end of the book rather than at its beginning) has become one of the most famous of these hitherto lesser-known pieces of early Christian literature, and it provides a good example of a kind of Christianity different from that reflected in the New Testament.

According to some ancient traditions and the *Gospel of Thomas* itself, Thomas was the twin brother of Jesus. The word "Thomas" itself means "twin" in Aramaic or Syriac. Thomas is also identified as "the twin" in the Gospel of John (20:24, 21:2), although that source does not identify who the other twin is. The Greek word for twin is *didymos*. In the *Gospel of Thomas*, therefore, he is identified as "Didymus Jude Thomas" (prologue). ("Jude" is an anglicization of "Judas," which is the Greek form of the Hebrew name "Judah.") In the ancient world, he was sometimes also identified with the author of the New Testament letter of Jude. In traditions lively in ancient eastern Christianity (in Syria, Mesopotamia, and even India) and in some other documents relating his deeds and sayings, he is explicitly said to be the twin brother of Jesus.

A body of literature grew up connected to Thomas. Besides the Coptic *Gospel of Thomas*, which this chapter will analyze, we also have, among other writings about Thomas, *The Book of Thomas*, also among the Nag Hammadi documents, and *The Acts of Thomas*, which was an ascetic but rather erotic account popular among ancient Christians. Since this literature seems to have been especially popular in churches in Syria and Mesopotamia, it is often suggested that there existed something like a "school of St. Thomas" in those locations, perhaps in Edessa, Syria.[1] Even today, Christians in western India, sometimes called "Mar Thoma" (meaning "St. Thomas") Christians, trace the founding of their churches to the mission of St. Thomas.

Another popular book is known as *The Infancy Gospel of Thomas*. It describes not Thomas's life and ministry, but the early years of Jesus' childhood. It makes for entertaining reading still today.[2] In it, Jesus comes across as something like a little show-off and bully. When he is rebuked for making some clay pigeons on the Sabbath, he claps his hands and makes them fly away. He strikes one of his teachers dead for criticizing his schoolwork. When another child bumps into him on the street, he strikes the kid dead, although in the end he is persuaded to raise from the dead all those who made the mistake of crossing him.

Not all these writings associated with the name of Thomas come from the same kind of Christianity. Some are less theological than entertaining. Some teach a radical form of early Christian asceticism. And some show influence from certain philosophical sources later associated by scholars with Gnosticism.[3] This variety of documents illustrates the profusion of early Christian texts that sprang up during the second century. Although they were excluded from the New Testament, they bear witness to the diversity of forms of Christianity that existed in the second and third centuries, before the lines between what would later be called "orthodoxy" and "heresy" were firmly drawn and institutionally enforced. We have long known about much of this literature, and even of the existence of a *Gospel of Thomas*, but we had no more than a few fragments of the text until the complete *Gospel* was found in the middle of the twentieth century.

In 1945, near a town called Nag Hammadi along the Nile River in Egypt, an Egyptian digging for clay came across twelve large books, codices, along with fragments of a thirteenth. The documents survive in Coptic, the everyday language of that part of ancient Egypt in the Roman period, but they all seem to be translations from Greek originals. The date of writing of the different documents varies a good deal, with some scholars placing the composition of the *Gospel of Thomas* in the first century. But many of the Nag Hammadi texts seem to have been written in Greek in the second century. The Nag Hammadi codices themselves were manufactured just before 350 C.E. and were buried in a sealed pot probably not long after that. Scholars imagine that they may have been buried to keep more "orthodox" Christians from finding and destroying them, but that is no more than a possibility. We have no evidence for why they were buried, and why there, nor for whom they belonged to before burial.

Unlike the canonical Gospels—and many other noncanonical gospels—the *Gospel of Thomas* has no narrative structure to contain and contextualize its sayings. There are no stories of Jesus' ministry, healings, or activities other than talking to his disciples. There is no passion narrative, and there are no resurrection stories. The *Gospel of Thomas* is simply 114 sayings of Jesus (*logia* is the plural form in Greek, *logion* the singular).

Even if the *Gospel of Thomas* was compiled and written in the second century, that is not to say that some of its sayings don't go back to Jesus himself. Many of the sayings in *Thomas* look very much like similar sayings in the synoptic Gospels, and many scholars would argue that sometimes the form of a saying or parable in *Thomas* looks more "primitive" than the form of the saying or parable as preserved in the canonical Gospels. That is, *Thomas* may contain a saying that is closer to what the historical Jesus may have uttered than the form of that saying in our Bibles. So scholars who do research on "the historical Jesus" (see Chapter 13 in this book) use *Thomas* along with the four canonical Gospels to attempt to figure out what the historical Jesus "really said." There is no doubt that the discovery of the entire *Gospel of Thomas* has been hugely significant for the study of early Christianity and the quest for the historical Jesus.

The Sayings of the *Gospel of Thomas*

The *Gospel of Thomas* begins with a hint at the "obscurities" to come: "These are the obscure sayings that the living Jesus uttered and which Didymus Jude Thomas wrote down. And he said, 'Whoever finds the meaning of these sayings will not taste death'" (prologue and saying 1). The word translated here as "obscure" also means simply "hidden" or "secret."[4] It is a clue that we are entering self-consciously esoteric (hidden, available only to "insiders") early Christian literature. It also raises the question, if these sayings are being written and therefore "published" here, just how "hidden" can they be?

But that some of these sayings are "obscure," at least to us, is not in doubt. Even here at the beginning, we may wonder, why does Jesus teach obscurely to his disciples? Why does the reader have to "find the meaning" of the sayings? Why can't Jesus teach openly and plainly what people need to know for their salvation? So from the very beginning we are in a different kind of early Christian literature, one that depends on esoteric teaching, needs careful interpretation, and will puzzle those who don't have the proper hermeneutical keys.

As I noted already, there is no real narrative in the *Gospel of Thomas*, no passion story, no burial, and no resurrection. In fact, one may get the feeling that the Jesus who is speaking is already resurrected. Indeed, that is how many people read the Jesus of the *Gospel of Thomas*: he is a wise teacher passing along hidden knowledge in his resurrected form, already a "spiritual" being.

Some of the sayings of this Gospel, however, look little different from those found in the synoptic Gospels.

> Jesus said, "Listen, a sower came forth, took a handful, and cast. Now, some fell upon the path, and the birds came and picked them out. Others fell upon rock, and they did not take root in the soil, and did not send up ears. And others fell upon the thorns, and they choked the seed; and the grubs devoured them. And others fell upon good soil, and it sent up good crops and yielded sixty per measure and a hundred and twenty per measure. (9)

This saying is very like those found in our Bibles (Matt 13:3–9; Mark 4:3–9; Luke 8:5–8). In fact, the version of it provided here is simpler and more straightforward than those in the synoptic Gospels. That could make us think that it is more "primitive" than those versions. That is to say, the *Thomas* version is more like what Jesus may have actually said. After all, in the synoptic Gospels, the simple parable is followed by a rather complex interpretation, and many people have long noted that the interpretation doesn't seem to fit the parable very well. This leads some scholars to suggest that the historical Jesus may actually have told a parable like this, but that later Christians—or even our Gospel writers themselves—couldn't resist elaborating Jesus' simple parable with extensions and interpretations. In that case, the simpler version found today in *Thomas* might be an "earlier" version (closer to the version Jesus actually gave) than the more complicated versions found in our Bible. In any case, this is an example of a saying in *Thomas* that is scarcely different from the versions found in the synoptic Gospels.

Just before that saying is another that invites comparisons:

> What human beings resemble is an intelligent fisherman who, having cast his net into the sea, pulled the net up out of the sea full of little fish. The intelligent fisherman, upon finding among them a fine large fish, threw all the little fish back into the sea, choosing without any effort the big fish. Whoever has ears to hear should listen! (8)

In this case, we have a parable that is not found exactly like this in our Bibles, but seems to make the same point as other parables in our Bibles, stories in which a wise person casts away pearls of lesser value in order to keep one pearl of great value (Matt 13:45–46), or in which people sort through a catch of fish and put all the "good" fish into a basket but throw out the "bad" (Matt 13:47–50). But in Matthew, the point seems to be that the good and bad fish represent good and bad people, who will be separated and differently judged at "the end of the age." In *Thomas*, the point seems to be that only certain human beings have the "intelligence" to know what is of supreme value and to choose that over all other things. But although the parable is different from those in Matthew, it does close with a phrase identical to one with which we are familiar from our canonical Gospels: "Let those with ears, hear!" (see, for example, Matt 13:9, 43; Mark 4:23; Luke 8:8; and passim).

There are other sayings from *Thomas* that are harder to understand and sometimes inscrutable, at least to me. For example, "Jesus said, 'Where there are three divine beings they are divine. Where there are two or one, I myself dwell with that person'" (30). Although the last part of this sounds a bit like Matthew 18:20 ("Where two or three are gathered in my name, I am there among them"), it is clearly saying something different from that. Is the reference to the "three" to the Trinity? If so, that reference seems to relate not at all to the rest of the saying.

Here is another saying that sounds a bit like a synoptic saying: "Jesus said, 'Foxes have their dens and birds have their nests. But the son of man has nowhere to lay his head and gain repose'" (86). Until the last few words, it resembles a familiar saying from our biblical Gospels (Matt 8:20; Luke 9:58). But the part about "gaining repose" has a rather mystical air, or at least it is not obvious. Those words may have some kind of hidden or special meaning here.[5]

One way *Thomas* seems to be clearly different from our biblical Gospels is its lack of apocalypticism or even interest in a future "kingdom of God." This is borne out by the next-to-last saying, perhaps appropriately placed toward the end of the book to address questions of the end of this world and the coming of the kingdom. "His disciples said to him, 'When is the kingdom going to come?' [Jesus said,] 'It is not by being waited for that it is going to come. They are not going to say, "Here it is" or "There it is." Rather, the kingdom of the father is spread out over the earth, and people do not see it'" (113).[6] The kingdom is not something one can look to the future to provide (and note that it is called neither "of heaven," as in Matthew, nor "of God," as in Mark, Luke, John, and Paul). The kingdom is present and exists already all over the earth. Most people are just not able to recognize it. This is a radically noneschatological kingdom; it is a present kingdom.

Another peculiarity of the *Gospel of Thomas* is the special role it assigns to Thomas. Thomas is the only disciple who seems correctly to understand who and what Jesus is. He is the holder of hidden and special knowledge that Jesus will not share even with Peter, James, John, or any other disciple. This can be illustrated by another saying that closely resembles synoptic sayings up to a point, but radically diverges from them as the text continues:

> Jesus said to his disciples, "Compare me to something and tell me what I resemble." Simon Peter said to him, "A just angel is what you resemble." Matthew said to him, "An intelligent philosopher is what you resemble." Thomas said to him, "Teacher,

> my mouth utterly will not let me say what you resemble." Jesus said, "I am not your teacher [speaking only to Thomas here, as indicated by the singular form of "your"], for you have drunk and become intoxicated from the bubbling wellspring that I have personally measured out." And he took him, withdrew, and said three sayings to him. Now, when Thomas came to his companions they asked him, "What did Jesus say to you?" Thomas said to them, "If I say to you one of the sayings that he said to me, you will take stones and stone me, and fire will come out of the stones and burn you up." (13; my bracketed insertion)

Thomas's last words are something like an ancient version of "I'd answer your question, but then I'd have to kill you."

There are several interesting aspects of this quotation. The first is its setting up of Peter and Matthew as giving Jesus good but not great answers to his question. Only Thomas seems to have the answer Jesus is looking for. As I pointed out with my insertion in the quotation, from the Coptic we can see that Jesus uses a singular expression when he tells Thomas that he is not Thomas's teacher because Thomas (unlike the other disciples) has already drunk and become drunk on Jesus' knowledge. Then the passage leaves us with no knowledge about the three sayings Jesus gave Thomas in private. It withholds even from us readers the esoteric knowledge passed orally from Jesus to Thomas—and perhaps then orally from Thomas to only a select few Christians? In other words, we have here evidence of a two-tiered hierarchy of divine knowledge: that available textually and openly to all Christians, and that available orally and privately to select Christians.

There are many other mysterious sayings and puzzles in the *Gospel of Thomas*, some of which I think I can explain, some of which just leave me baffled. But in order to show how I explain those I believe I can, I must provide a detour to introduce the late ancient intellectual movement traditionally called "Gnosticism."

Proto-orthodoxy and Gnosticism

An important Greek word for "knowledge" (though not the only one) is *gnosis*. The word *gnostikos* was used for anyone "in the know," for someone who "knows," although it would have struck most Greek speakers as an odd use of the word. It became a special word used by some early Christians for people who were especially knowledgeable about things divine, even things hidden from most people and known only by secret passage of knowledge or revelation. Clement of Alexandria was a Christian author who wrote around 200 C.E. and is considered mainly orthodox by Christian tradition. He thought of himself as a "Gnostic" Christian. He held that there exists public knowledge that all Christians may and should have, but there exists also esoteric knowledge reserved for more advanced, philosophical, wise Christians. Thus the term "Gnostic" could be used in the second century even by completely orthodox Christians.

As I have already noted, in the second century, and even the third, the lines that would later divide "orthodox" from "heretical" Christians had not yet been clearly drawn and enforced. *Doxa* can mean "fame" in Greek, or "opinion," or other things, but here it means belief and knowledge. *Ortho* in Greek can mean "straight," but here it means "correct." In the earlier period of Christianity, what counted as correct Christian thinking was still too much debated to have settled what was orthodox and what was heterodox (thinking "other," the basic meaning of *hetero*). Some scholars therefore avoid the implied anachronism of using the term "orthodox" for this period by using "proto-orthodox" instead, which is simply taken to refer to those Christians and that kind of Christianity that later won out and became the "orthodox Christianity" reflected in the creeds and councils of the fourth and fifth centuries.

The term "Gnostic" later became a label that some Christians seem to have appropriated for themselves, but that other Christians used as a label for beliefs they viewed as heretical. So some church fathers call people "Gnostics" without intending a compliment. Scholarship in the past twenty years has experienced an energetic debate about whether we, as historians, should even use the term "Gnostic" for what may have been a wide-ranging spectrum of many different persons, groups, and beliefs. Some scholars question whether there ever was a delineable movement that can reasonably be identified by that term.[7] Clearly not all the books in the Nag Hammadi collection, for example, fit any one theological portrait. It is also clear now that there was no "church" in late antiquity that one could identify as "the Gnostic church" or a socially united version of "Gnosticism." Some scholars, persuaded that the large category "Gnosticism" was an invention of enemies and did not exist socially, urge that we dispense with the terminology completely and come up with other ways of talking about what they see as simply a wide variety of philosophically tinged late ancient Christianity.

Others scholars, and I include myself here, agree that there was not a "Gnostic church" or even a fully coherent movement, but we also believe that the term does usefully identify a constellation of assumptions, beliefs, and texts that have much in common theologically. Moreover, that constellation of beliefs set Christians who held those beliefs apart from others who would later represent "orthodox" theology. It is this imagined, loosely defined grouping of beliefs that I will describe here.

I believe there were early Christians who had been influenced by late ancient forms of philosophy, especially Platonism and Neoplatonism, but who also wanted to interpret the mythical stories of the Bible, such as the creation of Adam and Eve, and the person and work of Jesus in terms of those philosophical currents. They were reading Genesis, we might imagine, through the lens of Plato's *Timaeus*. They took sayings and writings about Jesus, but interpreted them so that they could fit with more "educated" notions of divinity and humanity. They interpreted Jewish scripture and Christian traditions about Jesus to fit what they considered a more "spiritual" or "philosophical" manner than the "literal" manner used by "ordinary" Christians in most churches.

One may even, although it is a stretch, think of Platonism as "proto-Gnosticism." Plato's writings put forth a philosophical theology that posited many gods but ultimately only one supreme divinity. That divine being was beyond anything we human beings can conceive, but even what we conceive, we do so only insofar as we share in the being and knowledge of that divinity. Platonism taught a dualism of body and soul and a hierarchy of the material universe. The reality of "matter" was dependent on but inferior to the reality of "idea" or "form," something that truly existed but was not composed of the lower, coarse stuff of "matter." Material substances change and therefore are inferior to immaterial entities, such as thoughts or god, which do not change. This hierarchy of matter and spirit, body and mind, informs everything we see about and in our world, according to Platonism.

What scholars have traditionally called Gnosticism takes over these and other Platonic notions and runs even further with them. For Plato, for instance, matter was inferior to mind or soul, but that did not mean that material substances in themselves were evil. Some Christians, though, later interpreted the inferior nature of matter to mean also that it was evil. They sought the escape of their souls from the prison house of the body. Salvation was then conceived as possessing the knowledge of how we human beings, who are essentially not our bodies but our minds or souls, may escape the imprisonment of materiality and embodiment in order to join the ultimate source of our minds or souls, which is the highest, ultimate god.

If God is complete goodness, and God is the source of all things, how did it come about that the purest of things derived from God, our souls or minds, became entrapped in the prison of materiality? In other words, if God is good and all-powerful, how can evil still exist? This theological problem, which goes by the technical term "theodicy," meaning the "justification of god," has vexed many human beings, whether Jewish, Christian, or Muslim, who believe in one God who is both pure goodness and the source of the world. Ancient Gnostics (or those authors of the texts I am here still identifying by that traditional term) suggested elaborate mythologies to explain the rise of evil and materiality.

According to much late ancient philosophy and theology, the supreme ultimate divine being is pure thought. That thought, however, thinks, and those thoughts of pure thought become "emanations." In essence, they become dependent but separate divinities. Other thoughts emanate from those lower thoughts to engender still lower divinities, and on and on until the universe is full of divinities of many different levels of both power and goodness.

According to one such myth, these divine beings eventually emanate in pairs of male and female, which need each other in order to produce still other divine emanations, new gods. At some point, though, the divine being Sophia ("wisdom") decided to attempt to emanate a new being without her male divine consort. She wanted, that is, to give birth without a male partner. The idea that females might be able to give birth without male involvement intrigued many ancient writers and horrified many ancient men.[8] A common belief was that females on occasion could do so, but the result would be some kind of monster rather than a "normal" offspring. This is what some texts say happened to Sophia: she did bring forth another god, but it turned out to be a monster god, incompetent, bungling, morally ambivalent, or even evil.

I will call this god Ialdabaoth because he is so named in *The Secret Book According to John*, another Nag Hammadi text, from which I am taking this version of one of these creation myths.[9] It is precisely that bumbling and even evil god who is depicted in Genesis as the creator of the material world. The world as we know it is so imperfect because it was made by an imperfect god. We experience evil and suffering because the material world was created by a god who seems to have been able to do no better. That god also created many other beings, filling the universe with all kinds of beings people would call angels, gods, demons, spirits, or whatever. Eventually, that god, aided by other heavenly beings, created Adam, blowing part of the spirit of his own mother into Adam's body to make it animate. For Gnostics, if human beings have any divine "spark" in them, it is because they possess a small bit of the good spirit or fire that originally came from the supreme God.

I could draw from many different myths and teachings to illustrate the wide variety of beliefs and texts scholars have called Gnostic, but for my purposes here—an interpretation of the puzzles of the *Gospel of Thomas*—I need provide only the most minimal, schematic account of the ancient Gnostic myth and theology, and I can do that by citing only a few texts. One is a poem attributed to a second-century writer named Theodotus and passed along to us by Clement of Alexandria. It may be interpreted as a poetic riddle that alludes to central aspects of the theology and mythology of a group of Christians sometimes called the "school of Valentinus."[10]

> Who we were, what we have become,
> Where we were, whither we were thrown,
> Whither we are hastening, from what we are redeemed,
> What birth is, what rebirth is.[11]

Interpreted, the poem provides a nutshell introduction to a basic myth of the origins and end of human nature. As Gnostics, before being entrapped in the materiality of the body, we may imagine we were sparks of divinity ourselves, pieces of the pure God beyond all materiality and limit. We have become, however, sparks trapped in our bodies, and bodies trapped in the world of matter. Where we were was with the Supreme Divinity; we were even part of that divinity. But we have been "thrown" into this world and body. Whither are we hastening? To return to the God above all. From what are we redeemed? From materiality and embodiment. From this world. Therefore, what is birth? Our physical birth was not the beginning of life, but of death. "Birth" was really death. And our death from this body will be rebirth.

The true self, at least of those human beings fortunate enough to be true Gnostics, is a spark of divine fire. Through physical birth, it became entrapped in materiality. If persons can learn the mysteries of this origin and true being, they may live in an informed way so as to learn the secrets that will take them back through the levels of the universe to the supreme perfection of true divinity. Gnostics also believed, though, that all those evil or jealous gods that had been created by the creator god (the lower bungling or evil god) were intent on keeping human beings in their lower position. Evil powers, therefore, exist in the heavens and fight against anyone attempting to pass through their ranks. They try to make our "sparks" sleepy or drunk so that we forget our true origin. They do this to keep human beings imprisoned. We need secret knowledge to know how to get through and around them to reach our true, divine home again.

This basic, simple narrative is illustrated also by *The Hymn of the Pearl*.[12] According to this little myth, now found embedded in the *Acts of Thomas*, a powerful king in the East sends his royal prince to Egypt to get a precious pearl that is guarded by a fierce dragon. The prince is poisoned or, perhaps more accurately translated, "drugged" and intoxicated by the Egyptians, but he is awakened by a message from the king. He arises, defeats the dragon by using the "name" of his father, and returns with the pearl to the East. He puts on a robe of gnosis, knowledge, and ascends to the king's palace, entering the realm of peace, where he lives happily ever after. The story is a way of illustrating the basic myth about the origins of true Gnostics or wise men: the fall of the spirit into materiality and forgetfulness, the necessity of special knowledge for salvation, the escape from the prison of matter and this world, and the return through special knowledge to our divine origins.

Many people will insist that even if there was such a thing as ancient Gnosticism, the *Gospel of Thomas* is not that, and they are certainly right on many accounts. One important aspect of much of the "Gnostic" literature of the Nag Hammadi documents, for instance, is an emphasis on many different gods and on evil, jealous gods in opposition to the true God, the father. The *Gospel of Thomas* does not mention any gods like that (although they may be represented symbolically here or there; see *Thomas* 21, quoted below). Neither does it identify the bungling junior god with the God of creation in Genesis. The *Gospel of Thomas* has none of the elaborate myths and strings of names and mystical terms we find in many of the Nag Hammadi texts. I am not trying to demonstrate that the *Gospel of Thomas* is a Gnostic text. I do believe, however, that if readers know those texts and myths, we can make sense of many of the sayings in *Thomas* that otherwise remain puzzling or even inscrutable.

For example:

> Mary said to Jesus, "What do your disciples resemble?" He said, "What they resemble is children living in a plot of land that is not theirs. When the owners of the land come they will say, 'Surrender our land to us.' They, for their part, strip naked in their presence, in order to give it back to them, and they give them their land." (21)

Although this saying has some resemblance to a few in the canonical Gospels, in which owners of land or vineyards force tenants to give up the land or produce, it is in the end quite different.[13] But it makes perfect sense in light of the myths and ideas we've just seen. It may even be read as an allegory. Who are the owners of the land? The evil powers that rule the earth because they created the earth. Who are the children? The true disciples of Jesus who have learned their true nature. They gladly strip themselves even of their bodies in order to return those to the gods of the world and return in their true selves to their true home.

Gnostic texts sometimes portray the true being of the wise person, the soul or mind, as a spark of fire, of light. This they originally received from the high God. Note, then, this saying from *Thomas*: "His disciples said, 'Show us the place where you are, for we must seek it.' He said to them, 'Whoever has ears should listen! There is light existing within a person of light. And it enlightens the whole world: if it does not enlighten, that person is darkness'" (24). Notice that the light may not exist in all human beings, but only in "persons of light." Many of these ancient "knowing" Christians believed that human beings existed in a hierarchy. Those most knowledgeable and superior were the Gnostics, who possessed true but secret knowledge. They were divine sparks of light that had emanated from the Divine. But not all human beings possessed these sparks. Many, if not most, were more like beasts than like God. They might experience some kind of salvation eventually, perhaps in the ordinary ranks of the church. But the "Gnostic" disciples were different: they did not need the "normal" teachings of the church; they already possessed the divine light within themselves.

As Jesus elsewhere puts it, "It is amazing if it was for the spirit that flesh came into existence. And it is amazing indeed if spirit (came into existence) for the sake of the body. But as for me I am amazed at how this great wealth has come to dwell in this poverty" (29).[14] The spirit does not exist for the sake of body or flesh. It merely lives in the body as "great wealth" dwelling in "poverty." In fact, the Jesus of *Thomas* urges his disciples to "strip" themselves of their bodies. "His disciples said, 'When will you be shown forth to us and when shall we behold you?' Jesus said, 'When you strip naked without being ashamed, and take your garments and put them under your feet like little children and tread upon them. Then you will see the child of the living. And you will not be afraid'" (37). Again, the body is mere clothing that can be stripped off and despised. True knowledge leads "knowing" Christians to be able to reject the body and materiality and learn their true nature as a spark of divine fire.

This is done only via gnosis, knowledge. The knowledge of our true origins and nature is what saves us: "When you become acquainted with yourselves, then you will be recognized. And you will understand that it is you who are children of the living father. But if you do not become acquainted with yourselves, then you are in poverty, and it is you who are the poverty" (3). Bentley Layton, whose translation I am citing, uses here, as in most cases in this translation, the English words "to become acquainted" rather than "to know" to stress that the kind of "knowledge" here celebrated is not mere book knowledge or knowledge of some fact. Rather, it is the full recognition of the secret truths Jesus passed on to Thomas, and Thomas to those select Christians endowed with special knowledge of their true origins, nature, and end. As Jesus again puts it (many examples are available because *Thomas* often repeats its central points), "Whoever has become acquainted with the world has found a corpse, and the world is not worthy of the one who has found the corpse" (56). Thomas teaches that even our living material body is nonetheless a corpse.

The *Gospel of Thomas*, in spite of sharing many similarities with our biblical Gospels, differs from them in significant ways. The New Testament Gospels believe not in the complete destruction of the body or flesh, but in its perfection through resurrection. They do not base salvation on correct knowledge secretly passed along that informs persons of their true origin and nature. For the canonical Gospels, salvation is gained by believing that Jesus is the Messiah of God. The New Testament Gospels do not look for the kingdom of God within persons but invisible all around them; rather, the canonical Gospels teach people to await an army of angels led by Jesus, who will sweep away the Romans and all opponents and establish an apocalyptic kingdom of God in the immediate future. They do not believe in escaping from the world, but in Jesus redeeming the world.

We need not settle the debate about whether the *Gospel of Thomas* is really "Gnostic," or even whether "ancient Gnosticism" refers to a "real thing" in antiquity. I argue, though, that some kind of constellation of ideas and myths that we find in a variety of early Christian sources and in the codices of Nag Hammadi is necessary for unraveling *Thomas*'s puzzles. And when we have done that, we witness in that text—and many others even more "Gnostic" than it—a form of Christianity quite different from the version that won the battles for "orthodoxy." We see a fascinating kind of early Christianity not available to us in our Bibles, but important for our history.

The Spread of Christianity

CHAPTER 9
The Gospel of Luke and the Acts of the Apostles, Part 1: Structure and Themes

Overview: Luke and Acts, two volumes of one work, are structured very carefully by the author to outline the ministry of Jesus and the spread of the gospel to the gentiles. The Gospel of Luke emphasizes the themes of Jesus' Jewish piety, his role as a rejected prophet, and the reversal of earthly status. The Gospel of Luke ends in Jerusalem, and the Acts of the Apostles begins there and then follows the spread of the movement to Samaria and the gentiles. By closely analyzing the Gospel of Luke and Acts, we see that the author was not concerned with historicity or chronological order. Rather, he writes his "orderly account" to illustrate the rejection of the gospel by most of the Jews and its consequent spread to the gentiles.

The Introduction to the Gospel

As with the other Gospels, we do not know who wrote Luke and Acts, although most scholars are convinced that the same author wrote both of them as two volumes of one work. I will call him "Luke" for convenience, but we must keep in mind that this was likely not the Luke said to be a physician and companion of Paul (see Philem 24; Col 4:14; 2 Tim 4:11). We can, though, suggest motivations and interests in his writing and even imagine the sort of early Christian context in which he wrote. We do that, as we have done for documents already examined, by analyzing the text itself. We have no information about the author or his context other than what is contained in these two books.

The author does not claim to have been an eyewitness of what he narrates, certainly not for the Gospel.[1] Indeed, he begins the Gospel with a description of his research:

> Since many have undertaken to set down an orderly account of the events that have been fulfilled among us, just as they were handed on to us by those who from the beginning were eyewitnesses and servants of the word, I too decided, after investigating everything carefully from the very first, to write an orderly account for you, most excellent Theophilus, so that you may know the truth concerning the things about which you have been instructed. (Luke 1:1–4)

This opening sets the Gospel of Luke apart from the other Gospels because it begins just as an educated ancient reader might expect a book to begin.

First, the author addresses his book to someone named Theophilus. The most common way to begin a work of literature was by a dedication, which often took the form of an address. The address did not mean that the work was really intended only for the person named. Rather, it was a literary form meant to honor a friend or patron. Thus I might begin a book, if I were an ancient author, like this: "My dear Mr. Snufflemoot, since you asked me, while we lunched recently at Mory's, to give you an account of my recent yearlong journey in Africa, I have put together this modest description. I hope you enjoy it, although it is but a humble scratch." By beginning his Gospel the way he has, the author lets us know that he is consciously composing a work of literature. Whereas the Acts of the Apostles would have looked to an ancient reader like historiography, the Gospel would likely have seemed to such a reader like a *bios* (a "life," though not a "biography" in the modern sense).

Since such dedications were a literary commonplace, we suspect that "Theophilus" may not have been a real person at all. If he was a real person, he was a man of high status, as is indicated by the author's epithet "most excellent," but also by the mere fact that he is addressed as a patron. But the name could be symbolic and fictional. *Theo* derives from the Greek word for "God," and *philos* is the Greek for "friend" or "lover." Luke may be using the name as a symbol for his "ideal reader": a "lover of God" or someone "beloved of God." Although we don't know whether "Theophilus" was real or a fictive conceit, his presence in the prologue is another indication of the literary pretensions of the author.

As I said, the prologue admits that the author was not an eyewitness of the events he narrates. In fact, he indicates that he used sources: "just as they were handed on to us." We know, as I've already explained in previous chapters, that the author of Luke used Mark as one of his sources. He also used the Q source—or if one does not accept the Q hypothesis, he must have used some version of Matthew. We know, though, that he used at least two written sources, and I believe more, as I hope to show in this and the next chapter. He likely also used traditions from oral stories and sayings passed around in early churches. He is, at any rate, not shy about admitting his use of sources.

It might be thought that the author is claiming superiority over Mark and other sources by stating that his goal was to write an "orderly account," that is, in correct chronological order. But that is probably not the best way to interpret those words. Indeed, we can tell that Luke actually altered the order of events he found in his sources for his own thematic and theological purposes. We can tell, that is, that he moves things around in his narrative not out of concern for proper historical chronology but for other reasons. What he means by "orderly account," therefore, more probably is that he thinks his narrative is constructed "accurately" for purposes of teaching the gospel.

The Structure of Luke and Acts

Important clues for the interpretation of Luke and Acts can be gained by noting a simple outline of the two books read together (see Fig. 6). After the prologue and dedication, the Gospel begins with stories of the births of John the Baptist and Jesus and a story of Jesus' childhood. Then chapter 3 provides a transition by narrating the baptism of Jesus by John, John's teachings, Jesus' genealogy (quite different from that in Matthew), and Jesus' endurance of the temptations of the devil in the desert, something of a preparation, testing, or initiation period before the beginning of his ministry. All that action takes place variously in Galilee and Judea, and it may be seen as a narrative of events before the Galilean ministry of Jesus.

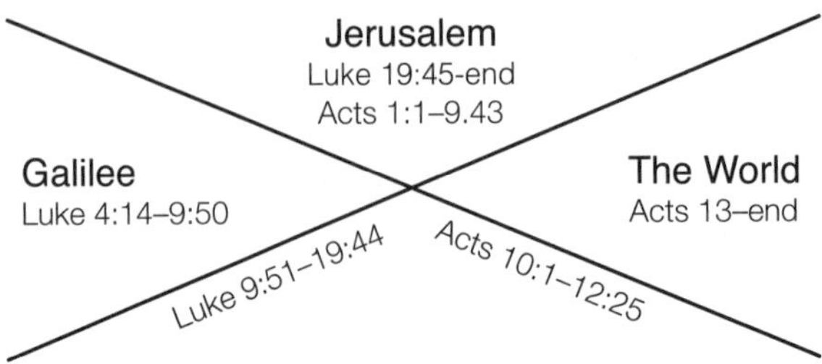

Fig. 6 Geographic Structure of Luke-Acts

Jesus' ministry in Galilee begins at 4:14 and continues until 9:50. Luke is quite clear that all these events take place in Galilee, a fact that seems to be important to him. In 9:51 Luke places an important indicator of a shift in his narrative, even providing a chronological marker: "When the days drew near for him to be taken up, he set his face to go to Jerusalem." What is meant by "taken up"? Does this refer to Jesus' crucifixion? In the Gospel of John, we will see that Jesus being "raised up" can refer to his crucifixion, but also to his exaltation in resurrection or ascension. But there is no sure indication that is the meaning of the words here in Luke. Do they refer to his ascension, to be narrated at Luke 24:51 and Acts 1:9? It is impossible to know. Perhaps they are intentionally ambiguous. In any case, as we will soon see, Luke places importance on Jesus' "day in Jerusalem" in his larger scheme of salvation history. This verse serves as a foreshadowing of what is to come in Jerusalem as a turning point in the history of the salvation of humankind. But it is also a turning point in Luke's narrative, for it is here that Luke ends Jesus' "Galilean ministry" proper and begins Jesus' long "journey to Jerusalem" that will occupy the next ten chapters of his Gospel.

Just before that turning point at 9:51, however, the author seems to have placed a transition section between the Galilean ministry and the journey to Jerusalem. Luke 9:1 begins with Jesus calling his twelve disciples together to give them power and instructions for their own ministries in his name. Indeed, we may read 9:1–50 as a section focusing on the theme of discipleship and turning the attention of the reader from the direct ministry of Jesus himself to the ministry that will follow as carried out by his disciples. Thus 9:1–50 intervenes between Jesus' Galilean ministry and his journey to Jerusalem to provide a grouping of teachings about discipleship.

Then the long section 9:51–19:44 comprises Jesus' activities as he travels from Galilee to Jerusalem. It is clear that the author has taken materials that occurred in different places in his sources and edited them by placing them in this "journey to Jerusalem" section he has artificially constructed. And throughout these chapters, Luke regularly brings the attention of the reader back to the fact that Jesus is on his way to Jerusalem, as if he is facing a cosmic-historical deadline and appointment there. Luke 10:1, for instance, notes that Jesus appointed seventy disciples and sent them ahead of him on the road. In 10:38, we are told that Jesus stopped by "a certain village" to visit Mary and Martha as he and his entourage were "on their way." In 13:22, the author notes that "Jesus went through one town and village after another, teaching as he made his way to Jerusalem." In 13:33, Jesus prophesies about his coming fate in Jerusalem, claiming, "It is impossible for a prophet to be killed outside Jerusalem." In 17:11, the author reminds us that Jesus is traveling "on the way to Jerusalem," passing now through the border region between Galilee and Samaria.

Each of the Gospels has "passion predictions," statements by Jesus in which he predicts his suffering and death, but Luke makes sure to note that Jesus emphasizes that these events must take place in Jerusalem. One such prediction occurs toward the end of the "journey to Jerusalem" section. "Then he took the twelve aside and said to them, 'See, we are going up to Jerusalem, and everything that is written about the Son of Man by the prophets will be accomplished. For he will be handed over to the gentiles; and he will be mocked and insulted and spat upon. After they have flogged him, they will kill him, and on the third day he will rise again'" (18:31–33).

The author then turns our attention a few more times to the fact that Jesus is journeying to Jerusalem. He finally concludes this section with Jesus coming near the city and weeping over it in 19:41–44. Jesus enters Jericho in 19:1. He tells a particular parable "because he was near Jerusalem" (19:11). Then, "after he had said this, he went on ahead, going up to Jerusalem" (19:28). He enters Bethphage and Bethany, two suburbs of Jerusalem, in 19:29.

The author of this Gospel has carefully constructed a large section of his work to emphasize Jesus' journey to Jerusalem. By comparing Luke with Mark and Matthew, we can see that its author took materials—sayings, stories of healings and other events, and parables—removed them from the chronological context in which he found them, and placed them in this ten-chapter section of his own work. It is as if he wanted to stretch out Jesus' trip to Jerusalem, and to do so he had to borrow materials he found embedded in other places in his sources and pad out this section so that he could emphasize Jesus' journey to Jerusalem. It is by comparing this editorial activity with that of the other Gospels that we can see that this must have been an important theme for this author; Jesus' journey to Jerusalem has special significance for him. Finally, at 19:45, Jesus is in Jerusalem, and from that point until the end of the Gospel of Luke, Jesus' every activity takes place in Jerusalem and its suburbs.

The Acts of the Apostles begins with Jesus and all his disciples in Jerusalem after his resurrection. Mark had hinted that Jesus would appear to his disciples in Galilee, not Jerusalem. Matthew explicitly tells us that according to his view, Jesus appeared to the eleven disciples only in Galilee (Matt 28:7–10, 28:16). According to the Gospel of John, Jesus first appeared to his disciples in and around Jerusalem, and sometime later in Galilee (John 20–21). Luke obviously knew these traditions and probably other traditions about resurrection appearances of Jesus. He certainly knew the Gospel of Mark and quite probably other traditions that told of Jesus appearing in Galilee. He intentionally, therefore, limits all resurrection appearances of Jesus to Jerusalem and its immediate environs. In fact, according to Acts, Jesus explicitly orders his disciples not to leave the area until after they receive the "baptism of the Holy Spirit," which takes place on Pentecost, about fifty days after his resurrection (Acts 1:4–5). So Luke, unlike the other Gospel writers and Paul, limits the resurrection appearances to Jerusalem or villages around it and to a chronological period of no more than fifty days. He keeps the attention of his readers fixed on Jerusalem and Judea both at the end of the Gospel and the beginning of Acts.

Acts can be divided into three major sections. Acts 1:1–9:43 narrates events that happen before the "gentile mission." The church is supposed to be all Jewish followers of Jesus, and the events first take place in and around Jerusalem. Beginning in chapter 8, the mission expands to include Samaria. Samaritans were considered close cousins, so to speak, of Jews since they were also loyal to Moses and had their own version of the law of Moses and the scriptures. So a Christian mission to the Samaritans is now one step outward from an exclusive mission to Jews. That first foray to Samaria is followed by a story in which Philip preaches and baptizes an Ethiopian eunuch, who is either Jewish by birth or an adherent of some sort to Judaism, because he is returning to Ethiopia from worshiping in Jerusalem and is found by Philip reading Jewish scripture (Acts 8:26–40).[2] This again represents something like a "step outward" from the exclusive mission within Judea. The first major section of Acts appropriately includes, toward its conclusion and transition section, the story of Paul's vision and baptism (9:1–31)—appropriately because although Paul himself is a Jew and even persecutes the church out of his zeal for Judaism, he will become the primary missionary to the gentiles in Acts.

From 10:1 to 12:25, we have a long transition section during which the Christian movement—often called "the Way" by the author of Acts—evolves from a purely Jewish movement to one including gentiles. This section begins with the conversion of the first gentile, Cornelius, and his household by Peter (Acts 10).[3] That event is followed by a debate about whether gentiles may be converted without circumcision, which is decided in the affirmative (11:1–18). Then at 11:19–20 we have a distinct turning point at which time the mission truly goes to the gentiles: "Now those who were scattered because of the persecution that took place over Stephen traveled as far as Phoenicia, Cyprus, and Antioch, and they spoke the word to no one except Jews. But among them were some men of Cyprus and Cyrene who, on coming to Antioch, spoke to the Greeks also, proclaiming the Lord Jesus" (11:19–20). After this, the author narrates the founding of the church in Antioch, which will end up being a central, predominantly gentile church, though including Jews, in Acts.

I have altered the NRSV quotation of Acts 11:20 slightly. That version, in place of "Greeks," has "Hellenists," indicating, probably, that the translators and editors took the reference to be not to gentiles but to Greek-speaking Jews. There are some ancient manuscripts, however, that have the word there as "Greeks."[4] I think that must have been what the author intended—or, as I will explain in the next chapter, what his source had. In other words, if the author of Acts wrote "Hellenists" and meant by that Greek-speaking Jews, I suggest he was using a source that originally had "Greeks." My reason is that the narrative here clearly depicts a shift of activity from a mission carefully kept exclusively to Jews to a mission that now includes gentiles. It would be nothing new to say that Jewish Christians were preaching the gospel to Greek-speaking Jews. They had been doing that not only from the event of Passover but also even in the Gospel of Luke. "Hellenists" had all along been members of the community (see Acts 6:1, 9:29). The names of the seven deacons selected in Acts 6:1–6 indicate that they were Greek-speaking Jews. Even the names of two of Jesus' closest disciples (Andrew and Philip; see Luke 6:14) suggest that Greek may have been their first language, although they obviously must have spoken Aramaic also. I take it that the more likely term used by the author of Acts 11:20—or if not him, his source—was "Greeks." He is, after all, telling his readers about something new that is happening in Acts 11, and that would be the mission expanding to include gentiles, "Greeks."

Acts 13:1 marks the beginning of the last major section of Acts and continues to the end of the document. From that point until we end with

Paul in Rome, the center of the world for Acts' ancient readers, we are in the part of this two-volume work dominated by the gentile expansion of the church, the time "after the entry of the gentiles," in my terminology.

The author of Luke-Acts has carefully constructed his work to place Jerusalem at the center. The overall narrative shape of Luke moves the attention of the reader from Galilee, the site of the beginning of Jesus' ministry, toward Jerusalem in a long journey by Jesus and his disciples and to the climactic events of the death and resurrection of Jesus. Acts takes up the narrative flow by concentrating on Jerusalem at the beginning and then moving through other regions of Judea and on to Samaria. It then transitions to the outside world and the gentile mission, moving to Antioch in Syria, to Asia Minor, and to Greece and Europe, eventually ending up at the center of the gentile world, Rome. As we will see in the next chapter, this is not really the way Christianity spread. It is a schematic arrangement meant to serve the purposes of the author of Luke-Acts. In order to see how that arrangement worked, we must analyze the major themes of the two volumes.

The Themes of Luke

Luke borrows much of the material from Mark, including some basic chronological structure, such as the exposition of a long ministry beginning in Galilee and culminating in Jerusalem only in the last week of Jesus' life. But Luke also changes things around from the order in which they occurred in Mark, as we saw already in Luke's elaborate construction of the journey to Jerusalem. A passage that excellently illustrates this tendency, as well as several of the central themes for Luke, is Luke 4:16–30, Jesus' sermon in his hometown of Nazareth.

In Mark, that incident comes further along in his narrative, at 6:1–6. According to Mark, Jesus goes from Galilee to the Jordan to be baptized by John, and we are probably to understand that this takes place in the part of the river closer to Judea (Mark 1:9). After his desert temptation (1:12–13), we are told that Jesus returned to Galilee (1:14). He travels around the Sea of Galilee and goes to Capernaum, where he performs healings, teaches, and appears to stay at the home of Peter and Andrew (1:29). He subsequently is shown traveling "throughout Galilee," preaching and casting out demons (1:39). He returns to Capernaum for several days, and we now learn that it has become his "home" (2:1). The narrative thereafter continues with many more travels around Galilee, and with Jesus sometimes returning "home" to Capernaum (for example, 3:19). He even travels on the other side of the Sea of Galilee, outside the region of Galilee itself (5:1). It is only after his move to Capernaum and further ministry in and outside Galilee that he visits Nazareth. There he teaches a bit in its synagogue and is rejected by the people in the village. Mark informs us, rather surprisingly, that Jesus was not able to perform many miracles there (6:1–6).

Luke does something completely different with the story. In the first place, he transfers the event from its occurrence in the middle of Jesus' Galilean ministry, as it occurs in Mark, to the very beginning of his ministry. In Luke, Jesus goes straight to Nazareth on his return to Galilee from the baptism and temptation (Luke 4:16). Luke knows from his sources that Jesus was supposed to have performed many miracles in Capernaum, as he lets slip in 4:23: "Do here also in your hometown the things that we have heard you did at Capernaum." But we readers haven't seen those events yet. Jesus moves to Capernaum, in Luke, only after this scene in Nazareth (4:31). So Luke has consciously moved the Nazareth incident to make it the inaugural event of Jesus' ministry. It is his inaugural address in Luke's Gospel.

And Luke has beefed up the story considerably, using it to foreshadow several themes he will elsewhere elaborate more fully in Luke and Acts. The first one appears at the very beginning of the passage: "When he came to Nazareth, where he had been brought up, he went to the synagogue on the sabbath day, as was his custom" (4:16). One of the themes Luke emphasizes is that Jews in the early Christian movement remain good, loyal, pious Jews. He will also eventually, in Acts, portray how the Christian movement becomes more and more gentile, and he will stress that gentiles need not observe Jewish laws or customs. But throughout both Luke and Acts, the Jews who follow Jesus remain good Jews. Even Paul, who takes the gospel to the gentiles more than anyone else in the narrative, nonetheless worships in the temple when he is in Jerusalem, takes a traditional Jewish vow, and insists throughout that he has remained a good Jew. He speaks Hebrew; he stresses that he studied with Gamaliel, the famous rabbi; and his arguments with other Jews are merely over proper interpretation of Jewish scriptures and doctrines (see Acts 21:26; 22:2–3; 23:6; the theme recurs several times elsewhere).

Only Luke among our Gospels stresses how carefully law abiding and pious Jesus' parents are. Mary is related to a priest, Zechariah (Luke 1:36), who, along with his wife Elizabeth, is depicted in ways reminiscent of Old Testament saints. Luke points out that Mary and Joseph have Jesus circumcised eight days after his birth, and that Mary presents herself and Jesus for purification in Jerusalem around a month later "according to the law of

Moses" (2:21–22). The remark that Jesus went to the synagogue "as was his custom" in 4:16 is one more expression of Luke's intention to present Jesus, and all the Jewish characters, as "good Jews."

The scripture Jesus is assigned to read by Luke also begins with a thematic emphasis of Luke: "The Spirit of the Lord is upon me" (4:18). The Holy Spirit, whether designated that way or simply with the term "spirit," is in fact the main actor of Acts and the agent who moves the narrative along repeatedly. Therefore, while Jesus is the main character in Luke, the Spirit has the leading role in Acts. It takes Jesus' place, in a way. It descends on the church at Pentecost (Acts 2:1–4) and descends on the first gentile converts (10:44). The Spirit strikes people dead when it is lied to (5:3–11) and participates as a main figure of authority in the "council of Jerusalem" (15:28). The author of Luke and Acts, therefore, reaches back to the prophet Isaiah in order to have Jesus begin his first sermon by invoking the Holy Spirit (Luke 4:18–29; Isaiah 61:1–2, 58:6).

The rest of that quotation from Isaiah is also thematically important for Luke. Jesus reads that he was anointed "to bring good news to the poor . . . to proclaim release to the captives and recovery of sight to the blind, to let the oppressed go free" (4:18–19). That Jesus' gospel is about salvation of the poor and liberation for the oppressed had already been emphasized earlier, being a major point made by Mary's song, known as the Magnificat. The song, following the model of and echoing Hannah's song in 1 Samuel 2:1–10, links the low status of Mary herself to all those who will be delivered from lowliness, humiliation, and oppression. More than that, the song prophesies not just the raising up of the lowly, but the bringing down of the high and mighty: "He has scattered the proud in the thoughts of their hearts. He has brought down the powerful from their thrones, and lifted up the lowly; he has filled the hungry with good things, and sent the rich away empty" (1:51–53).

The rich will be made poor, and the poor will be made rich. One of the passages that show this to be a special concern of Luke is his version of the "beatitudes" he shares with Matthew. Whereas Matthew had said, "Blessed are the poor in spirit" (Matt 5:3), Luke says simply, "Blessed are you who are poor" (Luke 6:20). Matthew's Jesus says, "Blessed are those who hunger and thirst for righteousness" (Matt 5:6); Luke's Jesus says, "Blessed are you who are hungry now, for you will be filled" (Luke 6:21).

In keeping with Mary's words in the Magnificat, Luke adds "woes" to his beatitudes, "woes" not found in Matthew's version of this material. And whereas Matthew did have "woes" to towns that had not received Jesus and to the scribes and Pharisees (Matt 23:13–36), Luke's are directed against the rich: "But woe to you who are rich. . . . Woe to you who are full now" (Luke 6:24–25). We cannot know whether Luke is quoting Q or some other source available to him, but since all this emphasis on the "reversal" of rich and poor, powerful and powerless, seems to recur so often, it seems more likely that he is including it precisely because it is a major concern of his own. We are probably seeing in these instances the editorial activity of the author. He signals this theme also in Jesus' first sermon.

Luke has the last line of Jesus' quotation of Isaiah as follows: "to proclaim the year of the Lord's favor" (Luke 4:19). The King James Version translates this as "the acceptable year of the Lord." This reflects another theme of interest to Luke. Later in the Gospel, when Jesus arrives at Jerusalem, he prophesies against Jerusalem, predicting its destruction. There he says that this will be punishment because the people of Jerusalem "did not recognize the time of your visitation" (Luke 19:44). For Luke, that "time" or the "acceptable year" is the time when Jesus is in Jerusalem and yet is rejected there, as he will be rejected here in Nazareth, by his own people. The "time" is whenever Jesus provides the message of salvation to his people, but they reject him. As he says later in the sermon, "Today this scripture has been fulfilled in your hearing" (4:21). That, in fact, is one of the reasons, as we will see further, that Luke makes Jerusalem so central for the Gospel and Acts. The central event that changed all history, past and future, was that "time" or "acceptable year of the Lord" when Jesus "visited" Jerusalem and was rejected.

The last theme of Luke and Acts I will illustrate with Jesus' sermon is that of the prophet rejected by his people, which leads to a turning of the prophet from the people of Israel to foreigners, and also leads to the persecution and death of the prophet. This comes not from the quotation from Isaiah with which Jesus begins his sermon, but from his invocation of two of the greatest Hebrew prophets, Elijah and Elisha (4:25–27). Note first, though, that before that invocation, the people respond positively to the beginning of Jesus' sermon. They do not reject him when he says, "Today this scripture has been fulfilled in your hearing." Rather, "All spoke well of him and were amazed at the gracious words that came from his mouth" (4:22). They turn on him only when he compares himself with Elijah and Elisha.

And it is not just the comparison with the great prophets that enrages them. They are angered when Jesus points out that Elijah helped no widows in Israel during a famine, but only a foreign widow (4:25–26). Elisha likewise bypassed many lepers he could have healed in Israel in order to heal a foreigner, the Syrian Naaman (4:27). What enrages the crowd is Jesus' citation of prophets taking their message to gentiles.

This theme will play itself out repeatedly in both Luke and Acts. Jesus is presented many ways in Luke and Acts, as Messiah, king, the Son of Man, son of God, and many others. But one way of presenting Jesus that Luke emphasizes more than the other Gospels is as the prototypical prophet who preaches to the Jews, is rejected by them and killed, and whose message eventually goes to the gentiles. The first prophet of Luke is John the Baptist, as his father styles him in his song (Luke 1:76). Jesus in his first sermon takes the mantle for himself also. "No prophet is accepted in the prophet's hometown" (4:24). The Jews themselves later recognize Jesus as "a great prophet" (7:16). Later still, Jesus says that he is going to Jerusalem "because it is impossible for a prophet to be killed outside of Jerusalem" (13:33). The theme appears repeatedly.

It continues in Acts. The first Christian martyr is Stephen, who recalls that Israel rejected the prophet Moses (Acts 7:35–43). Stephen seems to taunt the Jews into killing him also: "Which of the prophets did your ancestors not persecute? They killed those who foretold the coming of the Righteous One, and now you have become his betrayers and murderers" (7:52). It is to be expected, therefore, that they will kill Stephen.

This pattern is repeated over and over in the ministry of Paul as depicted in Acts. Paul's regular practice when entering a new town (remember, as depicted in Acts; Paul's letters seem to contradict this) is to go first to the synagogue. In case after case, most of the Jews reject the gospel, although Paul regularly wins over a handful of them. After his rejection by his own people, Paul leaves the synagogue and goes to the gentiles, where his preaching finally meets with success. This is a favorite theme of the author of Luke and Acts: those preaching the gospel are prophets rejected by their own people, the Jews; that rejection leads to taking the message to gentiles; and the mission to the gentiles leads to the persecution and often the death of the messengers.

All these themes we see recurring throughout Luke and Acts have been packed into this first sermon of Jesus, which the author has transposed from its place later in the narrative of Mark to the very beginning of Jesus' ministry. This demonstrates, for one thing, that when the author said he would be providing an "orderly account," he probably didn't mean to imply that he would tell the story in the order he found it, unless we take him to be simply dishonest. More likely, he knew that he was telling the story in the order he deemed best to give his message the greatest possible impact. He sacrificed historical chronology for theological message, and he then packed several of his favorite themes into the transposed story.

CHAPTER 10

The Gospel of Luke and the Acts of the Apostles, Part 2: Editing the Beginnings of Christianity

Overview: By analyzing how the author of Luke and Acts edits his sources to alter the chronological flow of events in Acts, as he also did in his Gospel, we can see that his theological interests trump the historical order of events. In Acts, he moves things around in order to present a more linear and schematic account of how the Christian movement spread from Jerusalem to the rest of the world. By noting how he uses the story of Stephen, the "first Christian martyr," we may discern some early Christian views on the temple and the law that are not, after all, the positions of the author of Luke and Acts himself. And by seeing how he edits the "little apocalypse" from Mark, we see him bringing Jesus' apocalyptic predictions up-to-date for the author's own time.

How Did Christianity Spread?

How did a ragtag bunch of peasant followers of a crucified Galilean Jewish prophet grow to be a movement that drew the attention of Roman rulers? How did the followers of Jesus, a Jew unnoticed by the rest of the world during his lifetime, end by establishing small cells, "house churches," in cities and towns around the ancient Mediterranean? How did that band of former fishermen, farmers, tax collectors, and possibly prostitutes come to have representatives in Rome, the capital of the world?

The actual historical answers to that question are hard to come by; that is, we don't have enough historically useful data to answer it in any really satisfactory way. At the end of this book, I will return to the question and attempt some answers. But we encounter in the book of Acts one early attempt, perhaps the first, to answer it. The author paints a portrait of how the early Jesus movement grew from Jerusalem to Judea, to Samaria, to the regions of the eastern Mediterranean, and eventually to Rome. In fact, the author gives his readers something of an outline for the work in Acts 1:8. Jesus, just before ascending to heaven after his resurrection, gathers his disciples and tells them to wait in Jerusalem for the time being. "But you will receive power when the Holy Spirit has come upon you; and you will be my witnesses in Jerusalem, in all Judea and Samaria, and to the ends of the earth."

That ends up being how the author constructs the narrative of Acts, in something like a series of concentric circles (see Fig. 7). The disciples begin their ministry by preaching and performing miracles in Jerusalem. They venture into the rest of Judea. Only later do they take the mission to

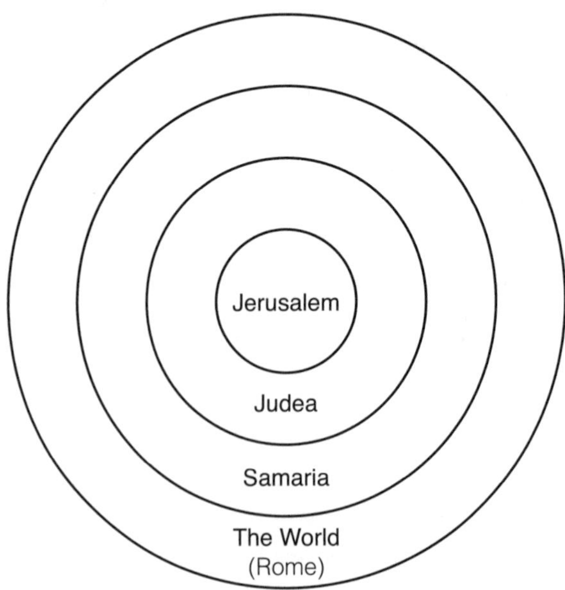

Fig. 7 Geographic Structure of Acts

Samaritans (Acts 8:1–25), to an Ethiopian (8:26–29), and to the predominantly gentile regions on the coast of Palestine (8:40). In Acts 10:1–11:18 we find the first mission to gentiles themselves. From Acts 13:1 until the end of the book, we have the gentile mission proper, led mainly by Paul. The book ends with Paul in house arrest in Rome, which was considered the center of the "known world," representing for our author the "ends of the earth."

That, at least, is the way the author of Acts wants us to believe Christianity spread. Historians, though, being a naturally skeptical lot, doubt that it happened that neatly and linearly. Remarkably, the author of Acts also leaves clues in his text that his version is more schematic than actually historical. By a careful examination of his text, noting how he seems to have taken over and edited other sources from early Christianity, we can see that the actual spread of Christianity was more spontaneous and messy than his schematic outline reveals on its surface. We can also, thereby, get an idea of how early Christian authors used the written and oral sources at their disposal.

Who First Preached to Gentiles?

For the first seven chapters of Acts, the focus of attention is firmly on Jerusalem. The disciples are all in Jerusalem. They pool their resources and, at least in the beginning, live communally, meeting in homes and in the temple. The church's leaders preach, perform miracles, and are persecuted to some extent by the Jerusalem authorities. That persecution comes to a head when a young Greek-speaking Jew named Stephen provokes the crowds and the authorities with his preaching that slights the law of Moses and even seems to attack the temple system, as I will demonstrate later. As a consequence, he is stoned and killed.

The killing of Stephen serves as the catalyst for most of the followers of Jesus to leave Jerusalem: "That day a severe persecution began against the church in Jerusalem, and all except the apostles were scattered throughout the countryside of Judea and Samaria" (8:1). A few verses later, we are told that these people did not just settle somewhere else, but rather traveled around, taking with them the message of Jesus: "Now those who were scattered went from place to place, proclaiming the word" (8:4). Several other events follow in the next few chapters that describe the spread of Christianity in Samaria and the conversion of the Ethiopian eunuch; then the conversion of Saul/Paul; some other activities of Peter in Judea and Palestine; the conversion of Cornelius and his household, the first gentiles to join the movement; and the acceptance of the gentiles by the church back in Jerusalem (8:5–11:18).

Just after that, we come to 11:19, and a careful reader will notice that the wording of that verse, and those immediately following, seems like a continuation of the narrative begun previously in 8:1–4. If we cut out 8:5–11:18 and connect 11:19 back to 8:4, the result actually flows together:

> That day a severe persecution began against the church in Jerusalem, and all except the apostles were scattered throughout the countryside of Judea and Samaria (8:1). . . . Now those who were scattered went from place to place, proclaiming the word (8:4). . . . Now those who were scattered because of the persecution that took place over Stephen traveled as far as Phoenicia, Cyprus, and Antioch, and they spoke the word to no one except Jews. But among them were some men of Cyprus and Cyrene who, on coming to Antioch, spoke to the [Greeks] also, proclaiming the Lord Jesus. The hand of the Lord was with them, and a great number became believers and turned to the Lord. (11:19–21)

As I explained in the previous chapter, I have altered the NRSV translation to say that these men spoke here to "Greeks," that is, to gentiles. Many English translations have the word there as "Hellenists," meaning Greek-speaking Jews, and that is the word in many ancient Greek manuscripts. It may indeed be what the author of Acts wrote. But if so, I believe he was changing the wording of a source he was using. If he actually wrote "Hellenists" rather than "Greeks" (the difference is a very few letters in Greek), he did so to reflect his desire to portray the general mission to the gentiles as happening only at this point in his narrative and not before.

What I am arguing is that the author of Acts had before him a written source much like what I quote above. He cut it into pieces, so to speak, placed the beginning of the paragraph (8:1–4) just after the death of Stephen, and saved the rest of the paragraph to add to his narrative only later, at 11:19. Between 8:4 and 11:19, he placed other events and materials before taking up again the story about the spread of the gospel to the gentiles in 11:19. That is, he spliced the various stories that now make up 8:5–11:18 into what was a previously unified narration about how the gospel was spread to the gentiles. Why did he do this?

The answer is obvious. The author of Acts wants to portray the spread of Christianity not only in a schematic manner (Jerusalem, Judea, Samaria, the rest of the world) but also as coming out of Jerusalem, the center of Judaism. He also wants to give the impression that the move of the gospel from a Jewish beginning to a gentile audience was God's will all along. He wants to depict as inevitable and divine the decision to invite gentiles into the church without imposing Jewish laws or circumcision on them. In order to stress how there was no "break" between Jewish and gentile versions of "the Way," he tells the story as if Peter, the central apostle and most important of the original twelve, was the very first apostle to preach to gentiles, convert them, and baptize them.

So the various stories gathered between 8:4 and 11:19 show the progression, through divine command and leading of the Holy Spirit, from a Jewish to a gentile mission. First, there is the mission by Philip in Samaria (8:5–25). Then there is the story of Philip converting an Ethiopian follower of Judaism (perhaps a man born Jewish but enslaved in Ethiopia, or perhaps an "adherent" to Judaism without becoming a full proselyte; 8:26–39) and then preaching along the coast to Caesarea (8:40). The various stories about the conversion of Saul/Paul and his eventual acceptance in the church back in Jerusalem come next (9:1–31). The author then tells stories that put Peter in place for the upcoming account of his conversion of the first gentile (9:32–43). Peter is reluctant to take such a controversial step, so he must be almost coerced by a threefold vision and the command of "the Lord" himself (10:11–16). Then the Holy Spirit intervenes to insist that Peter go to the house of Cornelius (10:19–20).

After Peter's activities, including witnessing the descent of the Holy Spirit on the gentiles and their speaking in tongues, the entire event is narrated again, this time by Peter to the church in Jerusalem, which unanimously confirms that "God has given even to the gentiles the repentance that leads to life" (11:18). Only after all those divinely ordained moments of transition, from an exclusively Jewish church to what is now a united Jewish-gentile church, does the author turn to Antioch, Paul, and his fuller mission to the gentile world.

Without all that intervening material from 8:5 to 11:18, we would get the impression that the first believers to preach to gentiles were simply anonymous Hellenistic Jewish followers of Jesus from Cyprus and Cyrene: "But among them were some men of Cyprus and Cyrene who, on coming to Antioch, spoke to the Greeks also" (11:20). Even now, by reading the text critically, we can tell that this was the message of Luke's source. The events he is there narrating, after all, were those that occurred just after the stoning of Stephen. He does not edit his source thoroughly enough to completely wash out the narrative detail that anonymous Christians first preached to "Greeks." But by slicing it apart from 8:4 and placing it only after the preaching of Peter to the gentiles, the author gives the impression that Peter actually was the first to preach to gentiles, as divinely ordained and compelled.

And of the two possibilities—who were the first followers of Jesus to preach to gentiles? Peter or those whose names are lost to history?—the latter is clearly the better historical account. It seems that the message of the Christian gospel spread by means of the usual messiness of most history. People whose names we do not know, no doubt Greek-speaking Jewish followers of Jesus, were the first to preach the gospel to gentiles. Luke's account is composed not in accordance with the strictures of modern historiography, but in order to have a united Jewish-gentile church that followed the commands of God and the leading of the Holy Spirit in its mission to the gentiles and its decision not to require those gentiles to follow the law of Moses. The author of Acts, as he did in Luke 4, shifts around the events as he found them in his sources so that they better fit his intended story and theology.

The Speech of Stephen

The long section in which Acts introduces us to Stephen and tells of his arrest and trial, his speech of defense—which actually becomes a sermon—and his subsequent execution by stoning provides us another opportunity to see how the author uses his sources (Acts 6:8–7:60). The author of Luke-Acts himself may have composed some of this material, but I will argue that key points in it, as well as the gist of Stephen's speech, must have been taken over from an earlier source. The author left several clues, however, in his edited version that give us some idea of the nature of his original source. First, we must note that the charge against Stephen was that he had said that Jesus would destroy the temple and "change the customs" Moses had given (Acts 6:14). Although these are said to be the accusations of "false witnesses" (Acts 6:13), it is not at all clear that Stephen wasn't guilty as charged.

In the Gospel of Mark (14:55–58; taken over by Matthew also; see Matt 26:59–61), Jesus is charged with saying, "I will destroy this temple that is made with hands, and in three days I will build another, not made with hands." Although Luke uses Mark as a source, he omits that charge from his own version of Jesus' trial. Rather than dispensing with it entirely, however, he transfers it to the trial of Stephen. It should also be noted that although this is called a "false" charge in Mark, as well as in Matthew and Luke, it is not clear that it actually would have been. After all, in Mark, Jesus had prophesied the destruction of the temple (Mark 13:1–2), a prophecy that Luke takes over from Mark and actually expands and emphasizes (Luke 21:5–6, 21:20–24). (John 2:19 contains the prophecy in a form that almost exactly matches the "false" charge of Mark, Matthew, and Luke, and it is put in the mouth of Jesus himself.) In Palestine of Jesus' time, even prophesying the destruction of Jerusalem or the temple could be considered treasonous.[1] Therefore, the clear prophecies of Jesus of the temple's destruction would have justified, in many people's minds, a charge of impiety against the temple.

Stephen's speech also shows evidence of opposition both to the temple and to the Mosaic law. It begins with a review of the history of Israel from the wanderings of Abraham, including the covenant of circumcision made by God with Abraham (Acts 7:2–8). A large section follows that narrates the slavery of Israel in Egypt, the raising up of Moses as deliverer and leader, the rejection of Moses, the incident of the golden calf, and the making of the "tent of testimony" as the divinely instructed edifice for the meeting place of God with Moses (7:9–45). Up to this point, Stephen has not explicitly attacked his audience; the story has been told fairly straightforwardly and with little emotion, mainly following the flow of Jewish scripture.

But then Stephen jumps ahead centuries to David, noting that before David, the people and God had all seemed happy with the tabernacle—the "tent of testimony"—as God's "place." David is singled out as the first to wish to build a "house" for God. He was not able. "But," Stephen continues, "it was Solomon who built a house for him" (7:47). And here the entire tone of the speech changes from historical narration to harangue, and highly impassioned harangue at that. Stephen begins by quoting Isaiah 66:1–2, in which God insists that he never needed or wanted a house, since heaven is his throne and the earth his footstool. This is where Stephen turns to invective:

> You stiff-necked people, uncircumcised in heart and ears, you are forever opposing the Holy Spirit, just as your ancestors used to do. Which of the prophets did your ancestors not persecute? They killed those who foretold the coming of the Righteous One, and now you have become his betrayers and murderers. You are the ones that received the law as ordained by angels, and yet you have not kept it. (7:51–53)

It is no surprise that with this sudden turn in the tone and content of his defense speech, the people become furious and rise up against Stephen.

It should be obvious that Stephen's speech actually does represent an attack on the temple and its institutions. There had always been a tension in the Hebrew Bible with regard to the Jerusalem temple and its cult. This is reflected in those several texts where David or Solomon wants to build a great temple and God refuses. It is reflected in many prophetic texts, similar to the one from Isaiah quoted by Stephen, that insist that God does not live in a "house made by human hands."[2] There were conflicting dual traditions in Judaism, one that enthusiastically supported the temple and its institutions and priests, and another that held it all in suspicion, if not real disdain and rejection. Stephen's speech comes from the latter tradition within Judaism: a Jewish attack on the Jewish temple.

We should also note the odd phrase that calls the law something "ordained by angels." According to most scripture, the law was given to Moses directly by God on Sinai, but there developed at some point a belief that God had not given the law directly to Moses but only through the mediation of angels. We find this tradition in Paul as well, as we will see in Chapter 16 of this book.[3] Indeed, it seems that some ancient Jews believed that angels had a large part in the actual writing of the law.[4] Stephen's few words here indicate that his speech comes from a branch of ancient Judaism or Christianity that demoted the law by linking it to angels rather than directly to God.

Thus Stephen's speech expresses two sentiments we know were held by other ancient Jews and Christians, sentiments different from a more dominant theology or ideology in Jerusalem. The first was a critique of the temple cult or perhaps a complete rejection of it. The second was a demotion of the law of Moses to something like an angelic document. It is not at all impossible that the historical Jesus may have held similar views about the temple. His "cleansing" of the temple may have actually been a prophetic prediction of its destruction, with his approval. Stephen's speech could in that way be closer to what Jesus taught about the temple than we now find to be the case even in Luke.

This is where I believe we have evidence that Stephen's speech was taken by the author from a prior source. Stephen's speech is an attack on the temple, and it does challenge the "customs delivered by Moses" (as the accusation in Acts 6:14 puts it). But the author of Luke-Acts shared neither of those sentiments. In other words, he did not edit the speech thoroughly enough to remove from it theological views he himself did not really share.

In regard to the temple, the author of Luke-Acts repeatedly portrays a reverence and piety for the temple on the part of his characters. The temple is central to the narrative, and usually in a positive way. Only Luke portrays the presentation of the infant Jesus in the temple, complete with traditional, Jewish-style prayers and praise given by Simeon and "the prophet Anna," both of whom lend their piety to the temple and have it returned to them by the temple (Luke 2:22–38). Only Luke provides us with the story of the twelve-year-old Jesus lingering in the temple, which he calls "my Father's house" (2:41–51).

In Acts, much of the activity of the fledgling community of believers takes place in and around the temple. "Day by day," we are told, "they spent much time together in the temple" (Acts 2:46). Peter and John, like the pious Jews they are, go to the temple at the designated times to pray (3:1). Peter preaches to the people in a part of the temple enclosure called Solomon's Portico (3:11), which the growing community continues to use as a meeting place (5:12). Paul also, even long after he has become the main missionary to the gentiles, visits the temple with reverence when he returns to Jerusalem. He pays for the shaving of the heads of four Jews who have taken a vow, has himself purified along with them, and goes to the temple with them to await the seven days of purification, after which they would complete the ritual with a sacrifice (21:24–26). Later, when Paul is on trial, he insists that all his conduct in the temple was perfectly decent and reflected the proper Jewish piety toward the temple and its cult (24:17–18; see also 22:17, 24:18, 25:8).

For the author of Luke-Acts, the Jerusalem temple is the natural center of Jewish piety, revered by the family of Jesus, Jesus himself, the early disciples and church, and Paul. None of this sounds like Stephen. That, I argue, is good evidence that the author of Acts took the speech from a prior source and placed it in his narrative depicting the "first Christian martyr" in Acts, but neglected to scrub it of an earlier anti-temple version of Judaism and early Christianity.

Luke and the Law

So Stephen represents a segment of early Christianity that demoted the law of Moses just a bit by insisting that it had been given to Moses not by God himself, but by angels. As I pointed out, this was not an unknown view at the time, but was it the view of the law held by the author of Luke-Acts? I don't think so. The author certainly believes that gentiles are not to be bound by the law. They are not required to be circumcised, and the only "rules" they are to obey that derive from previous covenants are those rules of the covenant God was thought to have made with Noah (see Acts 15:20, 15:29, 21:25; Lev 17:8–16; Gen 9). Other than that, Luke believes that the law of Moses constitutes the ethnic laws and customs of the Jews. Jews may well observe them—indeed, perhaps should observe them as pious Jews—but they are as irrelevant for gentile converts as the laws and customs of Egyptians, Lydians, Greeks, or any other ethnic people.

Throughout Greek historiography, geography, and "science," it was assumed that the world's population was divided into different peoples, different *ethnē* (the singular is *ethnos*). Greeks recognized that Romans, Egyptians, Scythians, Persians, and other peoples had their own languages, gods, familial structures, and customs surrounding all aspects of life. The word *nomos*, which in most places in our Bibles is translated "law," could also be translated "customs," since it need not refer to any actual written or oral "law," but just to the customary, received practices of different peoples. Ancient people recognized that different ethnic groups had their own laws and customs. That is precisely how Luke portrays the law of Moses and its relevance for Christians: Jews, even in the church, likely would continue to observe it; gentiles would not.

But that does not imply any negative evaluation of the Jewish law. In fact, Jews in the narrative of Luke and Acts are portrayed as pious and law abiding. Luke is the only evangelist to point out explicitly that Jesus' parents had him circumcised on the eighth day, precisely as required by the law (Luke 2:21). He portrays Joseph and Mary as fulfilling the law's requirement for the temple presentation of the infant about a month later, including the offering of a sacrifice of two turtledoves or pigeons (2:22–24). The family observes Passover every year, even with a long trek to Jerusalem (2:41). Jesus and his family are portrayed throughout as pious Jews who follow the law.

As was the case with piety toward the temple, Jewish Christians in Acts pointedly continue to observe the law. There is no hint that the Jewish believers do anything but continue to follow the law of Moses, keeping kosher themselves while they do not require it of gentile converts. Perhaps surprisingly, given his reputation for advocating a "law-free gospel," it is Paul who is used by the author to emphasize the continued law-abiding practices of Jewish believers. Throughout his travels, Paul always goes first to the synagogue in every city he visits, and he leaves the synagogue only when his message is rejected by "the Jews," as it almost always is. Back in Jerusalem, Paul stays in the temple for seven days, at the end of which he is intending to offer sacrifice (Acts 21:26; that plan is interrupted by his arrest). Paul insists that he was educated "according to our ancestral law" (22:3). The adjective highlights the idea that the law of Moses is the traditional, ethnic law of the Jews, as the laws of Solon were for Athens. Even when Paul is struck for calling the high priest a hypocrite, which according to the narrative he clearly is, Paul apologizes, saying that he didn't know that he was speaking to the high priest and admitting that the law forbids speaking against him (23:5, quoting Exod 22:28). Then Paul notes that he is a completely pious Jew, even a Pharisee (23:6). Note that Paul does not say that he was a Pharisee, but that he is one. According to Acts, Paul never ceased to belong to the famously law-zealous party.

Later, as Paul is being sent for protection to the Roman governor in Caesaria, the tribune informs the governor that Paul is innocent, as far as he can tell, of anything but disagreement about "questions of their law" (23:29). Again, the presence of "their" shows that the author is taking the Mosaic law to be precisely like Roman law or Greek law: ethnic laws and customs. In his hearing before Felix, Paul insists that he is still a believer in the law and the prophets (24:14). At still another hearing, Paul insists, "I have in no way committed an offense against the law of the Jews, or against the temple, or against the emperor" (25:8). Note that in that statement, Paul uses the term "law of the Jews" rather than "law of Moses." Finally, making his case to the Jews of Rome, Paul protests that he has done "nothing against our people or the customs of our ancestors" (28:17). Since the author of Acts takes the law of Moses to be precisely the ancestral customs of the Jewish people, he could just as well have said "law" there (the change would be *nomos* in place of the word *ethos* that occurs here).

Another sign of Luke's respect for the Jewish law, traditions, and customs is the way he styles his Gospel to look like "rewritten scripture." He imitates the content and style of the Greek version of the Hebrew Bible. After his introductory prologue, which is intended to imitate the style of the beginnings of Greek historiographical writings, the author begins, "In the days of King Herod of Judea, there was a priest named Zechariah, who belonged to the priestly order of Abijah. His wife was a descendant of Aaron, and her name was Elizabeth. Both of them were righteous before God, living blamelessly according to all the commandments and regulations of the Lord. But they had no children, because Elizabeth was barren, and both were getting on in years" (Luke 1:5–7). Not only does this sound like Jewish scripture, but it clearly recalls famous stories about pious but barren women, such as Abraham's wife Sarah or Hannah, the mother of Samuel.

As mentioned in the last chapter, Mary's song, the Magnificat (Luke 1:46–55), imitates, in style as well as content, the song of Hannah in 1 Samuel 2:1–10. But it, along with the song given to Zechariah (Luke 1:68–79), traditionally known as the Benedictus, also resembles many prayers or psalms of thanksgiving from the Bible. The prophecy of Simeon, when he sees the infant Jesus presented in the temple, recalls Old Testament prophecies (2:29–32). And the appearance of the elderly female prophet Anna recalls pious elderly women from the Bible (2:36–38). All these details of content and style show that the author of Luke intentionally modeled his work so that it would read like Jewish scripture in Greek translation.

We must admit that there is nothing in the speech of Stephen that directly contradicts any of this. But the clear critique of the temple in his speech and its demotion of the law of Moses as having been given by angels demonstrate that when the author of Acts was writing his account of the trial and speech of Stephen, he was using a source available to him but lost to us. He puts it into his text for his own purposes, even though he neglects to edit out its anti-temple message, which does not agree with his own. That, though, is fortunate for us because it allows us to see him in the process of editing his sources, as was the case with the sermon of Jesus in Nazareth, discussed in the previous chapter, and the account of the first evangelists to the gentiles discussed earlier.

It also allows us a glimpse into yet another—and different—way early Christians dealt with the Jewish law. Mark simply declared that Jesus had taught that "all foods are clean." Since Mark never gives us any other indication, he probably believed that the law was simply not binding on members of his church. They need not keep the Sabbath, and they need not observe Jewish food laws. And although he does not address the issue, he probably assumed that gentile believers need not be circumcised. For Mark, the law is a thing of the past.

For Matthew, in diametric opposition, the Jewish law seems to be still binding, certainly for Jewish believers, and probably also for gentiles, as I argued in Chapter 7. I think we must suppose that Matthew simply expected members of his church, including gentile converts, to keep the Sabbath, to keep kosher, and to be circumcised. There is absolutely no indication otherwise.

With Luke we have still another interpretation of the Jewish law. The author of Luke-Acts views the law of Moses as the legitimate, ethnic representation of the laws and customs of the Jewish people. For them, it has not been abrogated at all. Pious Jewish believers, such as Paul, will continue to observe it carefully. But it is not binding on gentile converts precisely because they are not Jews. Their entry into the church does not make them Jewish, and therefore, Jewish laws and customs are irrelevant for them.

But we have still another early Christian attitude to the law and the temple reflected in Stephen's speech and not completely hidden by the author's editing. That is the idea that the law was never supposed to be so important even for Jews. Sure, it was given by Moses, but Moses got it not from God but from angels. This position probably assumed that the most pious Jews had all along exaggerated the importance of the law. It is quite likely that some early Christians had a more negative view of the temple than did the author of Acts. They drew from a long tradition of Israelite prophets in emphasizing that the building of the temple by Solomon was a mistake in the first place. The true God of Israel needed no home but heaven and earth and refused to live in a "house made with human hands."

Although we haven't yet arrived at Paul's letters, therefore, we already have what may be three or four different early Christian attitudes toward the temple and the law. The early Christian movement was diverse even in its early stages.

Luke's Edited Apocalypse

As we have seen, Luke knew the Gospel of Mark and apparently had a copy of it before him as he wrote his own Gospel. We surmise this because he shares so much of his exact wording with Mark. By comparing what we have in Mark with the same or similar sayings in Luke, we can sketch out those theological concerns special to Luke. The best way to do this is to use some edition of a "gospel parallels," books that print the different Gospels in columns side by side for exact and easy comparison.[5] Otherwise, one must flip back and forth between the two Gospels.

If we compare Mark's "little apocalypse" in Mark 13 with Luke's version in Luke 21, we find some fascinating differences. As we saw in Chapter 6, the time line of the end-time in Mark includes a series of catastrophes, such as wars, earthquakes, and famines. Jesus there predicts that his disciples will be persecuted and hauled before courts. The good news will be preached throughout the world. Then, after those events, the "desolating sacrilege" will be "set up where it ought not to be" (Mark 13:14). That is to be the sign that the end is really upon them. They should pay no attention to any possible "false messiahs" about whom there are rumors at that time. Then, Jesus says, a series of cosmic events—the sun and moon darkening, stars falling—will herald the coming of the Son of Man, who will immediately bring about salvation for the faithful (13:24–27). The last "historical" event before the coming of the Son of Man is the setting up of the "desolating sacrilege."

Luke follows these events up to the point where Mark has the setting up of the "desolating sacrilege" (Luke 21:1–19). But just at that point, Luke adds new "historical" material, that is, events that we know actually happened. He says that Jerusalem will be surrounded by armies (21:20), and the people will "fall by the edge of the sword and be taken away as captives among all nations." Finally, "Jerusalem will be trampled on by the gentiles, until the times of the gentiles are fulfilled" (21:24). In other words, Jesus in Luke predicts not just the setting up of the abomination of desolation but also the surrounding of Jerusalem by armies (and doubtless these are meant to be the armies of Rome), the defeat of the rebellious Jews and even innocent noncombatants, the enslavement of Jews and their deportation to other countries, and the total domination of Jerusalem by gentiles. All these things happened, of course, during and after the Jewish War with Rome. Jerusalem was destroyed and occupied by the Romans, and the entire land was subdued by 74 C.E.

It is only after this period, which Luke calls the "times of the Gentiles," that the author comes to the "end" itself. There he adds some signs: signs in the sun, moon, and stars, but also in the sea (21:25). Then the Son of Man comes "in a cloud with power and great glory" (21:27). We should also note that the "desolating sacrilege" that was rather obscurely prophesied in Mark makes no appearance in Luke. Mark was unclear about precisely where it would be "set up," although he may have thought it would be in the temple, following Daniel. But Luke has left that event out of his account, although it is a key sign for Mark. This may be because the author of Luke, obviously writing several years after the destruction of Jerusalem and the temple (the "times of the Gentiles" having intervened), knows of no such action on the part of the Romans. He may assume that the temple was simply destroyed before a false god could be set up there. At any rate, the author of Luke is writing long enough after the end of the war that he can bring Mark's account up-to-date for his own time. The Son of Man in Luke's apocalyptic prophecy does not come during the war, as he apparently did in Mark, but several years after it. Here again, the author of Luke-Acts has altered his source, in this case Mark, to make points important to him and his version of Christianity.

That brings us back to the centrality of Jerusalem and geography for the composition of Luke and Acts. The author has carefully constructed his account to place Jerusalem at the center of his story. Christianity grows from its beginnings in Jerusalem and Judaism to its expansion to the "ends of the earth." Jesus "visited" Jerusalem at the appropriate time appointed by God. His own countrymen treated him the way they had all the prophets of God. But God vindicated Jesus by raising him from the dead. Then the gospel of Jesus spread under divine providence and the leading of the Holy Spirit from Jerusalem to Judea, to Samaria, and to Rome, the "ends of the earth." The author has constructed a theological message by means of geographic and theological editing of his sources, and by embedding them in a schematic narrative of his own making.

CHAPTER 11

The Gospel of John

Overview: The Gospel of John is dramatically different from the synoptic Gospels. It is full of long dialogues, it speaks of "signs" rather than exorcisms or miracles, and its narrative differs at many points from the Synoptics. Themes in the Gospel of John are also repeated throughout—themes such as ascending and descending, light and darkness, and seeing and knowing. Johannine literature presents a high Christology that equates Jesus with God. The Gospel also reflects the sectarian nature of the community to which the author belonged.[1]

A Different World

"In the beginning was the Word, and the Word was with God, and the Word was God. He was in the beginning with God. All things came into being through him, and without him not one thing came into being. What has come into being in him was life, and the life was the light of all people. The light shines in the darkness, and the darkness did not overcome it" (John 1:1–5). From the very beginning of the Gospel of John, we sense that we are in a different world. This doesn't sound like the synoptic Gospels. And even though the *Gospel of Thomas* was very different from the three synoptic Gospels—having no narrative, only sayings, and presenting a very different theology and worldview—*Thomas* at least had many sayings reminiscent of the Synoptics. But John sounds different even from *Thomas*.

In fact, this beginning sounds like philosophy or real theology; the emphasis on "being" sounds almost like the German philosophy of Hegel or the like. "In the beginning" obviously recalls the beginning of Genesis, but what follows is not a narrative of divine events, as in Genesis, but statements about how things came into existence in a rather abstract way: "through him." Traditional classical Greek philosophy, as in Plato's *Timaeus*, was concerned with questions of "being," but we have seen nothing like this so far in the early Christian texts we have examined.

A bit further into the Gospel, we read: "And the Word became flesh and lived among us, and we have seen his glory, the glory as of a father's only son, full of grace and truth" (1:14). This is downright theological, much more than we find explicitly stated in the other Gospels. It sounds much like a Christian creed. This is not like Matthew, Mark, Luke, or even *Thomas*.

Besides the content of the statements, the style of writing in John is also quite different. For one thing, there is a lot of repetition. Even in the few verses I've quoted already, there is repetition of a kind that would never be permitted in a decent undergraduate paper. "In the beginning was the Word, and the Word was with God, and the Word was God. He was in the beginning with God." Just after that, the words "come into being" are repeated three times. This is not an oddity only of this prologue to the Gospel; it recurs throughout the book.

Readers quickly notice also that there is much more talking in the Gospel of John than in the other Gospels. Mark tells us that Jesus was a great teacher, but he gives us surprisingly little actual teaching in his Gospel, compared with the others. Matthew and Luke have long stretches of Jesus' teaching, but they don't have anything like the extended sermons and dialogues that go on for chapter after chapter in John. Even *Thomas*, which consists almost entirely of teaching and includes almost no narrative, has nothing like the sermons or dialogues of John. We can, though, flip open the Gospel of John at almost any point and find similar scenes: Jesus begins with some teaching, often in conversation with a person or group of people; a few sayings of Jesus that don't make obvious sense to his dialogue partners provoke a conflict; Jesus goes into long monologues, sometimes interrupted by the frustrated comments of the people; and the scene often ends either in confusion or in outright eruption of conflict or attempted violence. All these elements of the writing of the Gospel of John—repetitions, philosophical-sounding discussions and statements, scenes of failed dialogue, long stretches of Jesus' teaching—set the Fourth Gospel apart from the others. It has its own distinct theology and style.

Differences in the Narrative

There are also significant differences in what happens when and where in John. For one thing, it is often noticed that the characters with whom Jesus interacts in John seem a bit more lifelike than characters in the other Gospels, who seem a bit flat, like simple cutout figures placed in the story to provide a foil for Jesus' words and actions. They rarely have more than a few lines, compared with Jesus' longer stretches of speech. We see them as "a tax collector," "a sinner," "a Pharisee," "a young man," and little else. They seldom have names or fuller identities. In John, on the contrary, we feel that we are getting to know some of these people. There is almost a whole chapter depicting Jesus' conversation with Nicodemus (John 3:1–21; it rather degenerates into a monologue, but at least it begins as a dialogue). And we learn that Nicodemus is a Pharisee, a Jewish leader, a "teacher" (3:10). He appears later in the narrative to prepare Jesus' body for burial (19:39). And with his several questions to Jesus, we get the idea that he has a real personality. He seems truly to want to know what Jesus is talking about.

That scene is followed in John 4 by a long dialogue that Jesus conducts with a Samaritan woman. Although we never learn her name, we do learn that she has had five husbands and is now living with a man to whom she is not legally married (John 4:18). She is treated quite sympathetically, both by the narrator and by Jesus. She persuades the rest of her village to welcome Jesus (4:39–42). The villagers even urge Jesus to stay with them. We end up knowing more about Nicodemus and this Samaritan woman than just about any character in the other Gospels. So we've already seen two substantial narratological differences John offers, compared with the other Gospels: the prologue provides quite a different beginning to the Gospel, and the presence of more fully sketched characters stands out.[2]

There are also substantial theological differences in John. For one thing, as seen already in the prologue, the writer tells us of Jesus' preexistence. Modern persons may not immediately notice this as unusual because we, even people who don't believe in Jesus or God, know that Jesus is supposed to be divine and to have existed before his human birth. But we would not get that idea from the other Gospels, with the possible exception of *Thomas*. For the others, Jesus simply is born. In John, on the contrary, Jesus was always a divine being who simply "came into the world" at his birth.

John is full of other distinct themes. For example, the emphasis on light and darkness is regularly repeated. Jesus comes from light into darkness, but the darkness rejects him (1:4–5, 3:19). The darkness also represents "the world," but this is not simply the physical world we might conceive; it is the "cosmos," the universe that stands over against God, Jesus, and eventually the community of the author himself. The cosmos is a dark region Jesus must invade. The cosmos hated Jesus and so will hate his true disciples. But true believers are different because they are "born" from God and the Spirit (see especially John 3:3–7). This spiritual birth is completely different from the birth of the "flesh" (3:6). Another theme is the close identity of Jesus with the Father. This is something we can see from the other Gospels, but it is raised to a new height of concern in John.

With the other Gospels, we are introduced to John the Baptist with more or less elaboration: less elaboration in Mark, much more in Luke. In the Gospel of John, though, the Baptist is introduced suddenly and in a rather confusing way, as if we are supposed to know who he is already: "There was a man sent from God, whose name was John. He came as a witness to testify to the light, so that all might believe through him. He himself was not the light, but he came to testify to the light" (1:6–8). But although his introduction is sudden and not totally informative, John the Baptist plays a larger role in the Fourth Gospel than in the others. We are told in no uncertain terms that he is inferior to Jesus (1:15), but he continues carrying on his own ministry even after his first introduction. In fact, the author of this Gospel hints that he knows narratives about events surrounding the baptism of Jesus by John and has John mention that he "saw the Spirit descending from heaven like a dove" (1:32), but he does not actually narrate the baptism in his Gospel.

Moreover, unlike all the other Gospels, in John, Jesus begins his own ministry while John is still conducting his. In the Synoptics—and in this case Matthew and Luke may be simply following Mark's lead—Jesus does not begin his own ministry until after the arrest of John the Baptist. One might get the idea (which I will pursue a bit in Chapter 13 on the historical Jesus) that Jesus was a disciple of John until the arrest of the Baptist, at which time he began his own ministry of healing, exorcising, and teaching. But the Gospel of John tells a completely different story. John the Baptist openly testifies that Jesus is the "Lamb of God who takes away the sin of the world" (1:29, 1:36). Jesus welcomes some of the followers of John the Baptist to be his own disciples (1:37–42). Jesus and his disciples even conduct their own "baptizing" ministry in Judea at the same time John is continuing his baptizing activity in the region (3:22–24). And John's disciples have debates with Jesus' disciples about purification (3:25–30). There is an overlap of the ministries of the Baptist and Jesus in John of which we see nothing elsewhere.

In fact, what I have been talking about—the overlapping baptism ministries of Jesus and John—brings up another big difference between the narrative of John and the Synoptics. Matthew, Mark, and Luke all supply a story in which Jesus begins his ministry in Galilee, going to Judea only toward the very end of his life. Luke does place Jesus in Judea for his birth and for visits as a boy to the temple in Jerusalem, and he implies that Jesus is baptized by John in Judea or close thereby. But Jesus' ministry takes place first only in Galilee. Jesus ends up in Jerusalem basically for just the last week of his life.

John, on the contrary, has Jesus and his disciples in the "countryside of Judea," noting that he and his disciples were baptizing people there (3:22–23). According to John's account, Jesus and his disciples move back and forth between Galilee and Judea several times in the narrative—sometimes abruptly. They are in Judea in chapter 3, in Samaria in chapter 4, and in Galilee later in chapter 4. They are at a festival in Jerusalem at the beginning of John 5. Confusingly, Jesus seems to go from there straight to "the other side of the Sea of Galilee" (John 6:1). Next, Jesus first says that he will not go to Jerusalem with his brothers for a festival (7:6–9), but then he goes "not publicly but as it were in secret" (7:10). Jesus is back and forth between Galilee and Judea many more times in the Gospel of John, and this has led some scholars to suggest that the author mixed sources at his disposal in ways that are more confusing than intentionally constructed.

In fact, even since ancient times readers have puzzled about why John has the incident of the cleansing of the temple at the beginning of his Gospel instead of at the end, just after Jesus' first arrival in Jerusalem a week before his crucifixion (John 2:13; compare Mark 11:15–19; Matt 21:12–17; Luke 19:45–48). Some conservative Christians, insistent that the Bible can have no contradictions or errors of historical fact, suggest that Jesus must have performed the activity twice in his lifetime. Critical scholars suggest that the author of John must have placed the event where he did for his own purposes, even if we can no longer divine them.

The length of Jesus' ministry is likewise presented differently. In much popular opinion, Jesus was thirty years old when he began his ministry, and that ministry lasted about three years, making him about thirty-three when he was crucified. But this rather traditional notion is not found in any of our sources. Christians have arrived at the idea by taking Jesus' age at the beginning of his ministry from Luke 3:23 ("Jesus was about thirty years old when he began his work"), but the idea of three years' duration for that ministry comes from the Gospel of John—and then only because John apparently mentions three different Passovers during Jesus' ministry (John 2:13, 6:4, 12:1). If all we had were the synoptic Gospels, we would probably assume that Jesus' entire ministry took place during only one year, since there is no implication otherwise. And if we had only the Gospel of John, we might surmise that his ministry lasted about three years, but that he might have been as old as forty-five or so at the time (since people remark in John 8:57 that he is "not yet fifty years old"). Christians, as is often the case, have come up with the traditional age of Jesus and the length of his ministry by taking one detail from one Gospel and other details from another Gospel and harmonizing them to come up with an account that is true to neither Gospel and has little historical probability.

And where was Jesus' family originally from? According to Luke, Jesus' parents were from Nazareth, in Galilee. They journeyed to Bethlehem, supposedly the ancestral home of Joseph, for a "census," stayed a little over a month, and returned to their home in Nazareth (Luke 1:26–2:39). According to Matthew, they simply are at home in Bethlehem at the beginning; they live in Judea (Matt 2:1–11; see also 2:23). They flee to Egypt for at least a couple of years (see Matt 2:13–15). They intend to return "home" to Bethlehem, but Joseph decides, warned in a dream, to move the family to Nazareth in Galilee instead (Matt 2:19–23).

If all we had as a source were the Gospel of John, however, we would assume that Jesus' family simply was from Galilee and that he was the son of both Mary and Joseph. The Jews say they know his father is Joseph (John 6:42), and that he is from Galilee and therefore cannot be the Messiah (7:41, 7:52). The author shows that he knows that some people believed a certain prophecy that the Messiah would come from Bethlehem, the village of David (7:42). His bringing up of the prophecy could serve as a fine opportunity for him to mention that Jesus was, after all, born in Bethlehem and that his family came originally from Judea. He does not do so, and rather than supposing that he just let the opportunity slip, it is better to take that as an indication that he believed those Jews were simply wrong, and that for some reason they interpreted the prophecy wrongly, or they didn't understand where Jesus truly was "from"—that is, from heaven or the Father—and that his earthly birthplace didn't matter. At any rate, this is one more significant difference among the Gospels: the original home of his family.

More significant from a theological perspective is the fact that there is no institution of the Lord's Supper in the Gospel of John (called the Mass, Eucharist, or Communion in different branches of Christianity today). Scholars debate whether there is a reference to it in John 6:54–58, where Jesus does talk of eating his flesh and drinking his blood. But if that serves as a reference to the Lord's Supper, it is remarkable that the author does not narrate the actual establishment of the ritual by Jesus in his observance of his last Passover with his disciples. Instead, the author replaces the institution of the Lord's Supper with a different meal accompanied by a foot washing. During his last supper with his disciples on the night he is betrayed, Jesus washes the feet of his disciples, like a slave. Christians through the centuries have added this ritual to the Eucharist on the Thursday before Good Friday, the last Friday before Easter. In English, this day is called "Maundy Thursday" in some churches, a name that likely derives from the Middle English version of the Latin *mandatum* ("commandment"), the first word in Latin of the sentence translated "a new commandment I have given to you" (John 13:34). So in the Gospel of John we have a Maundy Thursday service in place of a Eucharist on Jesus' last night with his disciples.

The arrest of Jesus in John is also narrated quite differently. Instead of a rather quick arrest, Jesus has something like a conversation with the soldiers sent to arrest him. When they tell him they are looking for Jesus of Nazareth, he answers, "I am he," and they all fall back on the ground. They get up and rehearse the whole interchange again, but when Jesus answers this time, they seem able to remain on their feet (John 18:1–12). It is all, though, a rather strange scene.

There are also big differences in how John narrates the crucifixion of Jesus. According to all three synoptic Gospels, for instance, the crucifixion takes place on the first day of Passover. The Last Supper in the Synoptics is a Passover meal itself. According to Jewish reckoning, the beginning of a day was at sunset of what we would consider the previous day. So after sundown on what we would call Thursday, Jesus ate a Passover meal at the beginning of Passover, and he was crucified on Friday, the first day of Passover. John provides a completely different account. In John, the Last Supper is not a Passover seder. Instead, Jesus is executed on the "day of Preparation," that is, the day before Passover when people are having their Passover lambs slaughtered and sacrificed before they then eat the lambs along with the rest of the seder that evening (John 19:14, 19:31, 19:42). This may be symbolically significant for the author since he has already told us that Jesus is the "Lamb of God who takes away the sin of the world" (1:29, 1:36). At any rate, it is a significant departure from the account of the Synoptics.

There are many other differences in the narrative and style of the Gospel of John, but the last I mention is perhaps one of the most notable. Only in the Gospel of John are we told about "the beloved disciple," a disciple never named but whom Jesus is said especially to love. We first encounter him at the Last Supper, reclining next to Jesus (13:23; the author depicts Jesus and the disciples "reclining" at dinner, as was customary for some cultures of the ancient Mediterranean, especially Greeks and Romans). He is also one of the few people present at the cross when Jesus dies (19:26–27). He is said to be one of the first witnesses of the empty tomb (20:2–9). He is present with other disciples when the resurrected Jesus appears to them at the Sea of Galilee (21:7; called the "Sea of Tiberias" here in John; see also 6:1). And he is said to be the author of the Gospel (21:24).

Christian tradition has claimed that this was John, son of Zebedee and brother of James, thus the author of the "Gospel of John." And in Christian art, John has most often been depicted as very young, beautiful, and even girlish in appearance, as male artists probably would have imagined Jesus' especially beloved disciple to look. Legends therefore had him quite young during Jesus' lifetime, living a very long time, and composing "his" Gospel late in life as a supplement to the three synoptic Gospels. But there are no good historical reasons to accept any of this. We simply have no idea whom the author meant by "the beloved disciple," and it may have been a pure invention by the author himself or the Christian community of which he was a part. It is, though, one of the delightful puzzles of this very puzzling Gospel.

Major Themes of the Gospel of John

In pointing out major themes of the Fourth Gospel, we must resign ourselves to some limitation. The Gospel is so rich with so many different thematic elements, and those themes repeat themselves so often throughout the Gospel and then often recur in the letters of John, that we could get carried away into more detail than is advisable here. What follows, therefore, is only a listing of some of the most notable themes.[3] The reader can easily supplement these by simply taking a concordance (a book that lists all the words in the Bible, or the New Testament, and provides citations of verses where they occur) and looking up recurring words in John, such as "light," "to see," "to know," and so on. These themes, in any case, come up repeatedly in different parts of the Gospel, almost like bells struck again and again.

Throughout the Gospel of John we find emphasis on movement up and down. Jesus, in fact, is the descending and ascending redeemer. Jesus prophesies that his disciples will see "heaven opened and the angels of God ascending and descending upon the Son of Man" (John 1:51). But Jesus also moves in this way: "No one has ascended into heaven except the one who descended from heaven, the Son of Man" (3:13). This fits with a contrast between heaven and this earth: "The one who comes from above is above all; the one who is of the earth belongs to the earth and speaks about earthly things" (3:31). Jesus has "come down from heaven" to do God's will (6:38). He is the "bread that came down from heaven" (6:41; see also 6:58). And after his resurrection, Jesus has to ascend back to the Father (20:17).

Similar to this is the Johannine theme of being "lifted up." "Just as Moses lifted up the serpent in the wilderness, so must the Son of Man be lifted up" (John 3:14). But what does this refer to? The ascension of Jesus to the Father? Jesus says that this "lifting up" is something that the Jews themselves will do: "When you have lifted up the Son of Man, then you will realize that I am he" (8:28). We get one good clue later in the Gospel: "Now is the judgment of this world; now the ruler of this world will be driven out. And I, when I am lifted up from the earth, will draw all people to myself" (12:31–32). At that point, we may still be confused about what precise event is meant by the "lifting up from the earth," although it certainly does sound like the ascension. But the author then provides this commentary: "He said this to indicate the kind of death he was to die" (12:33). So we now know that at least sometimes the "lifting up" refers to the crucifixion, when Jesus is "lifted up" on the cross. In many cases, however, it is probably not wise to attempt to fix the meaning of the theme too rigidly. Like many other themes and aspects, the Gospel of John suggests layers on layers of meaning, with some things obviously meaning more than one thing at a time and inviting theological interpretation at many levels.

Thus also the relation of "seeing" to "knowing", both of which recur throughout the Gospel, is not always clear. In 1:18, we're told that "no one has ever seen God. It is God the only Son who is close to the Father's heart who has made him known." Here, seeing and knowing are joined together. Sometimes it seems as if Jesus is advocating a rather "empirical" way to find the truth. John the Baptist testifies about Jesus by invoking his own seeing: "And I myself have seen and have testified that this is the Son of God" (1:34).

Jesus invites those questioning him to "Come and see" (1:39). Jesus insists that he has seen and therefore knows: "Very truly, I tell you, we speak of what we know and testify to what we have seen" (3:11). So we get the idea that "seeing" is a perfectly acceptable, even necessary, way to come to true knowledge about Jesus.

But there are a few puzzling statements here or there that may suggest something else. In spite of sometimes inviting people to "see" and therefore to "know," Jesus also says that "the world," the cosmos, cannot receive the "spirit of truth" because "it neither sees him nor knows him" (14:17). In other words, "the world" doesn't have the ability to "see" and "know" even if it wants to. And toward the end of the Gospel, Jesus implies that believing without "seeing" is even better. Once "doubting Thomas" comes to believe in the resurrection of Jesus, which he does only when he sees Jesus, Jesus seems to chide him: "Have you believed because you have seen me? Blessed are those who have not seen and yet have come to believe" (20:29).

A final theme I will mention relates to this "seeing." Jesus doesn't perform nearly as many miracles in John as in the Synoptics. In fact, he performs no exorcisms at all, which is remarkable, given how dominant they are in the other Gospels. But another curiosity of the Fourth Gospel is that the author calls the miracles Jesus does perform "signs." The most famous of these is the turning of water into wine Jesus accomplishes at a wedding (John 2:1–11). At the end of the story, the narrator notes that this was "the first of his signs" (2:11). Some scholars have suggested that the way the author numbers a few of the signs indicates that he was using a written "signs source" that gave a narrated listing of miracles performed by Jesus. If so, he got mixed up in his numbering, because he later identifies a healing as Jesus' "second sign" (4:54) even though he has by that time told us about other "signs" Jesus had performed in the meantime (see 2:23, 3:2). But it may also be just that the final version of the Gospel we possess has been edited, perhaps more than once, and the order of events has been moved around, which would also make sense of the rapid back-and-forth movements between Judea and Galilee.

Usually, "signs" seem to be presented as a perfectly legitimate way to come to faith in Jesus (3:2, 6:14, 6:26, 6:30, 7:31, 9:16, 10:41, 11:47, 12:18, 12:37). But some ambiguity lingers. Once, Jesus seems explicitly to rebuke the need for "signs" as a means to faith (4:48). But again, John is full of puzzles and ambiguities, and those surrounding the meaning and value of "signs" may just remain ones.

Johannine Sectarianism

When I use the terms "sect" and "sectarian," I do not mean them in the pejorative sense often implied in popular speech. I am simply appropriating the terms from the sociology of religion. A "sect" is a group that maintains firm social boundaries between itself and the surrounding culture. It sees itself as "set apart" from the world around it. It may have a strong sense of "insiders" and "outsiders." It may indeed believe that its own members are the chosen people or the "saved," and others outside its group are the "damned" or are simply excluded from its benefits. Over the centuries, there have been many different Christian groups that have separated themselves not only from "the world" but even from other Christians. Many Christian churches consider themselves a "denomination" but not the "only church." That is, they are happy being, let's say, Presbyterian but make no attempt to deny that Baptists, Methodists, Roman Catholics, or members of many other organizations are also Christians. A "sect," on the other hand, may well deny that any other Christians are true Christians. The difference, in sociological terms, between a "sect" and a "denomination" is the degree of separation of the group from other religious groups or persons. It is a matter of how firm the boundaries are between it and other groups and human beings.

Scholars have come to believe that the Gospel of John arose out of a sectarian form of early Christianity that had arisen from Judaism but had separated itself from surrounding Judaism and even some other forms of Christianity, at least by the time of the writing of the three letters of John that we will examine in the next chapter. Some of the interpretive conundrums of the Fourth Gospel can be understood by recognizing the sectarian nature of the community that is reflected in the Gospel and the letters of John.[4]

Several of the themes I mentioned in the previous section show evidence of this sectarian nature. The stark divisions between the dark and the light, the fact that some people are children of God and others children of the devil, the radical difference between the "spirit" and the "flesh"—all these themes and others demonstrate a robust sense of boundaries between the community and "the world." The church of the author of this Gospel is "in the world but not of the world."

Several of the long scenes in John's Gospel enact this separation and sectarian point of view by narrating a long discourse of Jesus that degenerates into an argument between the people and Jesus. The people ask Jesus questions, and he seems never to give a straightforward answer. Instead, he answers by saying something that seems off the subject. When the people object, Jesus accuses them of hypocrisy or stubbornness or sinfulness. They end up rejecting him and threatening to kill him. This narrative pattern repeats itself so often (for example, in John 6 and 8) that it must be one expression of the sectarian worldview held by the author and probably his church as well.

One place where this becomes especially clear is in the long story of the healing of the blind man in John 9. I will go through it more carefully than usual in order to see how the narrative works to communicate a point not explicitly made in the text: that becoming and remaining a member of the church involve a separation from the world, even from one's family—a separation that may be painful but is nonetheless necessary. As I used the story of the stilling of the storm in Matthew to show that it can be read almost as an allegory of Matthew's church, so the healing of the blind man and its aftermath described in John 9 can be read as being more about John's church than about just Jesus or the blind man. We will see that many of the details of the story may be read symbolically as well.

The story of the healing is told in a rather simple way. Jesus points out that the man was born blind not as some kind of punishment of either him or his parents, but to show the glory of God in Jesus. Jesus is the "light of the world" that will open the eyes of the blind. Jesus spits and makes mud, which he rubs on the man's eyes, and then sends him to wash himself in the pool of Siloam, which the author tells us means "sent" (John 9:1–7). Asked to explain what happened, the man just says that a man called Jesus did it, and he tells how it happened. Other than that, he says that he doesn't know anything about Jesus or where he is (9:8–12).

The people then take the man to the Pharisees. We aren't told why, but the detail is necessary for how the story proceeds. There has to be a conflict, and in order to have that conflict, only now are we told that it was the Sabbath when Jesus performed the healing (9:13–15). The Pharisees say that Jesus cannot be from God because he broke the Sabbath with the healing. This causes a debate among the people, though, and the formerly blind man closes that piece of the scene by confessing that he thinks Jesus is "a prophet" (9:16–17).

In order to confirm that the man was born blind, "the Jews" call the man's parents, who confirm that the man is their son and that he was born blind (note that in the Gospel of John, "the Jews" come to be a character in themselves, in opposition to Jesus and his disciples, even though the author certainly knows that they were Jews as well). Then we get another new piece of information from the author that helps heighten the conflict aspect of the story: he now tells us that the parents are afraid "of the Jews" because "the Jews had already agreed that anyone who confessed Jesus to be the Messiah would be put out of the synagogue" (9:18–23).

More debate breaks out, with "the Jews" arguing that Jesus cannot be a prophet or a divine messenger because he is "a sinner," and the man repeatedly pointing to the miracle as proof that Jesus is "from God" (9:24–34). Eventually, Jesus is brought back into the scene after the man is driven out of the synagogue. Jesus asks if the man believes in the "Son of Man," the man asks who the Son of Man is, and Jesus answers that it is he himself. The man then makes a Christian "confession," "Lord, I believe," and worships Jesus (9:35–38).

The story ends with one further conflict between Jesus and the Pharisees. Jesus says that he "came into the world" so that those who do not see may see, and those who see may "become blind." The Pharisees ask if Jesus is saying that they are "blind." And Jesus, again as usual in John not exactly answering their question, concludes the entire story by saying, "If you were blind, you would not have sin. But now that you say, 'We see,' your sin remains" (9:39–41).

Scholars have pointed out that the story cannot possibly be any kind of accurate narration of an event that occurred in Jesus' life. Much of the story hinges on the claim that "the Jews" had decided and even publicized their decision to expel anyone from "the synagogue" who confessed Jesus to be the Messiah. This simply could not have happened during Jesus' lifetime. For one thing, all the evidence suggests that Jesus was not proclaiming openly in his lifetime that he was the Messiah. Most scholars believe that belief arose either secretly among his closest disciples late in Jesus' life or only after his death. Furthermore, although we do have some evidence that believing in Jesus might much later have caused someone to be banned from the synagogue, that was not certainly not happening during Jesus' lifetime. In fact, it was possible only several decades after his death. The entire story is premised on anachronisms.

Nonetheless, the episode reads very well as a symbolic story illustrating the life of a church many decades later, perhaps as late as the end of the first century C.E. For one thing, the man does not represent merely a blind man. He represents the "blindness" of persons before they know Christ. When his eyes are opened by Jesus (an event related to the Gospel's themes of "seeing" and "knowing"), he sees the light (the theme of light and darkness). His washing is probably meant to symbolize baptism, or it is at least perfectly permissible to take it as such. Even better, he is "baptized" in a body of water that is named "sent," because he will soon be sent to bear witness of Jesus and his own recent salvation by Jesus. "The Jews" and the Pharisees represent those Jews who reject the Christians' claims about Jesus being the Christ sent from God. The parents represent Jews who might like to become followers of Jesus but hold back out of fear of being excommunicated by the larger Jewish community. The proper response, though, would be for them, like their son, to move from believing that Jesus is "just a prophet" to accepting that he is the Christ and Son of Man. They should, like him, make the proper Christian confession, "Lord, I believe," and worship Jesus as divine.

Like many of the other discourses between Jesus and "the Jews" in the Gospel of John, this one ends in a division. Most of the people reject Jesus' claims. A few accept him, worship him, and become his followers. But it is necessary for them in their turn to be rejected by their countrymen and even their own households at times. The stories narrate a split, a division, with firm boundaries that came about not in Jesus' lifetime, but in the decades experienced by Christian Jews and gentiles in the last part of the first century and throughout the second century. This story, like many others in John, reflects the experiences of a sectarian group of followers of Jesus, cut off from other Jews and other human society because of their loyalty to Jesus.

Johannine Christology

But John's Jesus is not just any "Jesus." The Jesus of the Gospel of John, even more than the Jesus of the other canonical Gospels, is one of very "high" Christology. "Christology" refers to theories or teachings about the nature of Jesus. Even someone who believes that Jesus was not at all divine, but was just a human being, has a "Christology"; it is just a very "low" one. As we will see throughout many parts of this book, there was a great spectrum of different kinds of Christology in early Christianity, even within the New Testament. Some followers of Jesus doubtless saw him as a great man, but no more than that. Others accepted him as a "son of God," but did not take that as meaning that Jesus himself was divine in the sense that God is. Some early Christians thought Jesus was divine, but of a more junior divine status than God the Father. Only eventually, through much theological debate and conflict, did the Christian Church come to believe that in order to be "orthodox," one had to believe that Jesus was fully divine, of equal divine status with God the Father. The Gospel of John is remarkable when compared with other New Testament documents in its very "high" Christology, and this seems to have been the focus of most of the conflicts reflected in the Gospel and later in the letters.

Regularly in the Fourth Gospel, the debates concern Jesus' own nature more than any other issue. He is certainly presented as a prophet, as a teacher, as a healer, and as the "Son of Man." But the conflicts come to a head often, and the people around him become furious and want to kill him, when he makes claims to be equal to God. In chapter 5, the conflict begins, again, with a healing on the Sabbath, but it escalates when Jesus says, "My Father is still working, and I also am working" (5:17). That is not explicitly a claim by Jesus that he is equal with God the Father. Not all sons are their father's equal, of course. But the narrator makes the point for Jesus in this case by actually saying that this was a conclusion made by "the Jews" themselves: "For this reason the Jews were seeking all the more to kill him, because he was not only breaking the sabbath, but was also calling God his own Father, thereby making himself equal to God" (5:18). Note that the last phrase need not automatically and necessarily follow from the former claim. But it does for the author, and this is the crux of the conflict between the author and his community, on one side, and everyone else, on the other. Here, the opponents are represented as "the Jews." In the later letters, we will see that the opposition will include other Christians who did not share the precise Christology of our author.

The point is made again later in John 8, although it takes just a bit of reading between the lines to make this clear. John 8:12 begins the scene with Jesus, as usual, teaching about who he is. (Most of Jesus' teachings in John are not about how to live or behave, or even about the "kingdom of God," as they are in the other Gospels; rather, they are focused on Jesus' identity, which is not nearly as much the issue in the other Gospels.) As usual in John, Jesus makes some inscrutable claims, such as this one: "I am going away, and you will search for me, but you will die in your sin" (8:21). The people do not understand and even ask Jesus for clarification. Jesus answers with even more inscrutable (to them, anyway) sayings and proceeds to insults (8:22–30).

The rest of the chapter, though, is even more remarkable in its portrayal of the division Jesus' teachings inevitably cause among people. We are told that Jesus now turns his attention "to the Jews who had believed in him" (8:31). The discussion, though, again escalates into a hot argument, with name-calling on both sides. Jesus insists that the people (remember, these were his followers) are trying to kill him, implies that they are bastards (8:41), and finally says that they are children of the devil himself. "The

Jews" return the favor, calling Jesus a "Samaritan" and saying that he is possessed by a demon (8:48). The author, though, has not yet arrived at the very height of the conflict. That happens only when the Jews say that Jesus cannot have seen Abraham since he is "not yet fifty years old," and Jesus answers by saying, "Before Abraham was, I am." It is only then that they actually take up stones in an attempt to kill Jesus (8:58–59). And remember, we were told that these are people who had believed in him.

The climax of the scene, therefore, comes when Jesus uses the words "I am" to claim divine status. We are meant to recognize this as the name God used of himself when he spoke to Moses out of the burning bush (Exod 3:14–15). God's name is "I am." By using the "I am" title for himself, Jesus is claiming preexistence for himself and equality with the God of Israel and Moses. That is what prompts the people to reject the message and to attempt to kill him. The high Christology of the Gospel of John is the key to its sectarian stance vis-à-vis "the Jews" and all other peoples.

The Fourth Gospel contains a more radical claim about Jesus than we have seen in the other Gospels and will see in Paul's letters or many other early Christian documents. It took a while—from the beginnings of the Jesus movement to its growth into the Christian church—for this kind of high Christology to develop, which is another reason most scholars date the Fourth Gospel to the end of the first or the beginning of the second century. We need time to see such a high Christology gain a firm foothold in an early Christian community. As we will see in the next chapter, that Christology developed even more in later years of the Johannine community. We can trace that development by comparing the Gospel with the other documents from Johannine Christianity, the three letters of John.

CHAPTER 12
The Letters of John and the Spread of Christianity

Overview: The focus of the Gospel of John is on Christology. In the Gospel, Jesus is divine. In 1 John, many of the themes of the Gospel are echoed. The three letters of John possibly present us with correspondence of the Johannine community, a sectarian group insisting on the divinity and humanity of Jesus, against the Docetists and other differing forms of early Christianity. Comparing the kind of Christology we find in the Johannine literature with what we have seen elsewhere demonstrates again the diversity of different forms of early Christianity and how it spread.

Different Christologies

What kind of teaching about the nature of Jesus, what different "Christologies," do we find in early Christian texts? According to the Gospel of Mark, Jesus is certainly the Son of God (Mark 15:39). He is also known in Mark as the Son of Man and by other titles as well. Moreover, in Mark, Jesus is especially the suffering Son of God whose death is understood as "a ransom for many" (Mark 10:45; taken over also by Matt 20:28).

Whereas Matthew follows Mark in taking the death of Jesus to be a ransom sacrifice, Luke does not. Although we have seen that Luke takes over much he finds in Mark, he does not copy Mark 10:45, and the reason he does not is that he does not agree with that Christology: Luke does not interpret the death of Jesus as an atoning sacrifice. We can see this in several ways, as in Luke's omission of Mark 10:45. Another is how Luke changes what he gets from Mark elsewhere. For example, Mark portrays Jesus as silent and in anguish before and at the time of his death, even asking God why God has abandoned him (Mark 15:34). Luke leaves out that saying of Jesus from his crucifixion scene. In Luke, Jesus goes to his death with full confidence and knowledge. Where Mark has the cry of lamentation on the lips of Jesus on the cross, Luke instead depicts Jesus as calmly and voluntarily giving up his spirit: "Father, into your hands I commend my spirit" (Luke 23:46). Mark depicts the veil of the temple being torn just at the time of Jesus' death (Mark 15:38); this is probably meant to signify that Jesus' atoning death has now enabled humankind to gain access to the holy of holies, to God, by virtue of Jesus' death as "ransom." Luke moves the tearing of the veil to before the death of Jesus, probably precisely because he does not see Jesus' death as an atoning sacrifice. On the contrary, as we saw in the previous chapters on Luke and Acts, Jesus' death is the martyrdom of a righteous prophet, which is then reenacted in the death of Stephen and the sufferings of Paul and other Christian "witnesses" (remember that "martyr" simply comes from the Greek word for "witness"). This all reflects two different Christologies: the atoning, sacrificed Son of God in Mark and the exemplary martyr-prophet of Luke.

As we have also seen, there is no death of Jesus at all in the *Gospel of Thomas*. Jesus' death seems not to matter at all for that writer. Rather, Jesus is the divine revealer of secret *gnosis* that awakens the spark of knowledge and life in those destined to be saved and to return to their home with God. There is no interest in suffering in *Thomas* at all, except the attempt to escape the realm of suffering by the knowledge of the true nature of those who "know."

For the author of the Gospel of John, Jesus is fully equal to the Father; he is fully God. He is the "I am" who spoke to Moses out of the burning bush. He is also the descending and ascending redeemer, the bringer of light and knowledge and salvation. But unlike Luke and *Thomas*, John certainly does depict the death of Jesus as a sacrifice that takes away the "sin of the world." Jesus is the Lamb of God who is killed precisely at the time of the slaughter of the Passover lambs on the day of Preparation. John's Gospel contains the highest Christology we have thus far seen. (It is a bit unclear whether the author of the *Gospel of Thomas* took Jesus to be fully equal to the highest God;

perhaps he did, but at least this is not explicitly stated.) Matthew, Mark, and Luke could all be read to present Jesus as the Son of God, but not necessarily as fully equal to the Father. That equation is explicitly made in John.

What is considered by most churches to be orthodox Christology was not really fully formed and enforced until the fourth century. The emperor Constantine, attempting to bring unity to the squabbling churches, monks, and bishops, called a general council that met in Nicea in 325 C.E. The eventual result (to simplify what was actually a more drawn-out and complicated history) was the Nicene Creed, still recited in churches throughout the world.[1] According to the Nicene Creed, Jesus is "God from God, Light from Light, true God from true God."[2] Jesus was not created; he was "begotten, not made." But that begetting did not take place in time, because Jesus simply always was. Jesus is "one Being with the Father." Orthodox Christology was later reinforced (and elaborated somewhat) by the Council of Chalcedon in 451.[3]

It took years and years to get from understandings of Jesus' nature that were held by his followers in the year 30, probably the year of his execution, to those of "orthodox Christianity." But many of the elements of what would later come to be orthodoxy can be found in the Gospel of John, the most "orthodox" of the canonical Gospels. According to John, Jesus is fully God, coequal with the Father. He preexisted his earthly life. He is the descending and ascending redeemer. He is the Lamb of God sacrificed for the people. He is the expression of the love of God for the world, and in his death, his sacrifice, he takes away the sin of the world. To be saved, people must believe in him and hold correct beliefs about his nature. All these elements, much later to be defined as "orthodox," can be found in the Gospel of John, though not in many other branches of early Christianity.

The First Letter of John

The First Letter of John shares many themes with the Gospel of John. It even sounds like the style of the Gospel. Its beginning, for instance, recalls the prologue of the Gospel: "We declare to you what was from the beginning, what we have heard, what we have seen with our eyes, what we have looked at and touched with our hands, concerning the word of life" (1 John 1:1). We see references to "the beginning" and to themes of "seeing" and "hearing." Even the reference to "touch" may recall the famous scene in which Thomas insists that he must touch Jesus' resurrected body before believing, a scene found only in the Gospel of John (20:27).

"This life was revealed, and we have seen it and testify to it" (1 John 1:2). We recall the themes of testimony and witnessing, as well as revelation, from the Gospel. "And declare to you the eternal life." Eternal life was also a recurring motif in the Gospel. "We declare to you what we have seen and heard so that you also may have fellowship with us; and truly our fellowship is with the Father and with his Son Jesus Christ" (1:3). Just a bit later, we encounter references to light and darkness (1:5–6). We see that the "blood" of Jesus cleanses (1:7; recall the blood that flows from Jesus on the cross: John 19:34). Further still is a reference to being "born" of God (or Jesus; the reference is not clear; 1 John 2:29). The language, the style, and the echoes of certain terms and themes all show that this letter (although it reads more like a sermon than a letter; note that there is no epistolary opening or greeting) comes from the same general community as the Gospel does.

There are, though, interesting problems within the text of the letter, and some statements that seem to be contradictions of what we have in the Gospel. Toward the beginning, for example, we are told that we are all sinners: "If we say that we have no sin, we deceive ourselves, and the truth is not in us. If we confess our sins, he who is faithful and just will forgive us our sins and cleanse us from all unrighteousness. If we say that we have not sinned, we make him a liar, and his word is not in us" (1 John 1:8–10). This sounds like a straightforward insistence that "we" are sinners, but we can be forgiven if we acknowledge our sins.

Later, however, we come across what seem, at least on initial reading, to be contradictions:

> Everyone who commits sin is guilty of lawlessness; sin is lawlessness. You know that he was revealed to take away sins, and in him there is no sin. No one who abides in him sins; no one who sins has either seen him or known him. . . . Everyone who commits sin is a child of the devil; for the devil has been sinning from the beginning. . . . Those who have been born of God do not sin, because God's seed abides in them; they cannot sin, because they have been born of God. (1 John 3:4–9)

That section seems to deny what we read at the beginning. It clearly proposes a very sectarian either-or: one is a child either of God or of the devil; those who are of the devil sin; those who are of God do not. The writer earlier said that we "lie" if we say that "we have no sin." Here, he says that "we" "do not sin." Perhaps if questioned, the author could explain how there is no contradiction here. (Perhaps earlier he meant that we "had" sin, but no longer "have" it.) But unfortunately, we don't have the author to question, and there certainly appears to be a remaining problem in the text.

There are other problematic passages. There is certainly an emphasis on love in 1 John, just as we saw statements about love in the Gospel as well. But is this author talking about the same thing as the author of the Gospel when he talks about love? (Here are some of the first hints that we may have different authors for the letter and the Gospel.) The letter writer says, "Whoever loves a brother lives in the light" (2:10).[4] Later, he says, "For this is the message you have heard from the beginning, that we should love one another" (3:11). There are many such sayings in the letter. "We know that we have passed from death to life because we love one another" (3:14). "And this is his commandment, that we should believe in the name of his Son Jesus Christ and love one another, just as he has commanded us" (3:23). "Beloved, let us love one another, because love is from God; everyone who loves is born of God and knows God" (4:7). "Beloved, since God loved us so much, we also ought to love one another. No one has ever seen God; if we love one another, God lives in us, and his love is perfected in us" (4:11–12).

Strikingly, however, all these sayings are about loving "one another," that is, members of the same community. In what is perhaps the most famous verse in the New Testament, the Gospel of John proclaimed the love of God for the world. The King James Version of that verse, memorized by millions of Christians, reads: "For God so loved the world, that he gave his only begotten Son, that whosoever believeth in him should not perish, but have everlasting life" (John 3:16). The author of 1 John, on the other hand, says, "Do not love the world or the things in the world. The love of the Father is not in those who love the world" (1 John 2:15). We saw sectarianism in the Gospel of John also, and statements that emphasized the enmity between "the world" and Jesus and his disciples (see 15:18–19, for example). That is also manifested, and perhaps even exaggerated, in 1 John: "The world hates you" (3:13). And whereas God seems motivated in John 3:16 to save the world, the author of the letter, in a verse that seems to echo John 3:16, but only to an extent, says, "God sent his only Son into the world." But note how the sentence ends: In order to save the world? No: "So that *we* might live through him" (4:9; my emphasis).

Nowhere in 1 John are its readers told to love the world or anyone "in" the world. All commandments to love are for "one another." All the love talked about in the letter is centered only on the community of believers. It is an "internal" love, "brotherly" love. The author repeatedly commands his readers to love others within the community, but never those outside the community. The sectarianism of the Gospel is, if anything, strengthened in the letter.

A Splintering Church

As was the case with the Gospel of John, 1 John reflects a sectarian group, and its boundaries—determining who is in and who is out—are again greatly determined by Christology. Its "enemies" are even "antichrists."

> Children, it is the last hour! As you have heard that antichrist is coming, so now many antichrists have come. From this we know that it is the last hour. They went out from us, but they did not belong to us; for if they had belonged to us, they would have remained with us. But by going out they made it plain that none of them belongs to us. (1 John 2:18–19)

The community has already experienced serious division, and the people condemned by the author are, by his own admission, former members of the community. According to the sectarian worldview of the author, those people must not truly have been members of the community, though, precisely because they have now separated.

And what caused the separation? "Who is the liar but the one who denies that Jesus is the Christ? This is the antichrist, the one who denies the Father and the Son. No one who denies the Son has the Father also; everyone who confesses the Son has the Father also" (2:22–23). It would be odd if such people had belonged to the same community that produced and welcomed the Gospel of John if they actually did deny the title of Messiah, Christ, Anointed, to Jesus, or denied completely that Jesus was the Son of God. I think it likely, therefore, that the author is exaggerating somewhat. The other people may simply not have maintained quite as "high" a Christology as the author wanted. Or perhaps their beliefs about Jesus' nature just did not agree completely with that of this author in some other way. At any rate, what they believed about Jesus is certainly central to the disagreement here.

Later in the letter, however, we find another clue:

> By this you know the Spirit of God: every spirit that confesses that Jesus Christ has come in the flesh is from God, and every spirit that does not confess Jesus is not from God. And this is the spirit of the antichrist, of which you have heard that it is coming; and now it is already in the world. (4:2–3)

This indicates that perhaps the people who had left the community denied that Jesus was "flesh." After all, since "flesh" has such a negative meaning in the Gospel of John, it would make sense to believe that if Jesus is truly divine, he must not actually have been "flesh."

We know that there were early Christians who did not believe that the Christ was actually composed of flesh and blood. They insisted that Jesus had only appeared to be a fleshly human being, but was actually a spirit. He could walk on water, after all, and that is something a spirit could do, but not flesh and blood. He moved through walls and doors (see John 20:19, 20:26). Following the lead of ancient "heresiologists" (those Christians who wrote works against other Christians they considered "heretics"), modern scholars use the term "Docetism" to describe this Christology, and "Docetics" for those Christians who believed it: Christians who denied that Jesus Christ possessed a real flesh-and-blood body and held that he only "seemed" to have one (the word "docetic" comes from the Greek word that means "to seem" or "to appear").

We have early Christian writings that come from such Christians. The second-century *Gospel of Peter*, for instance, was accused of having Docetic passages, although the fragments of it we now possess don't contain any really explicit Docetic teachings.[5] We do know, though, that there were such Christians who believed that Jesus was divine, but not flesh and blood, and we may be seeing an early form of such teachings in the Christians here attacked by the author of 1 John. That may be behind the puzzling statement of our author when he writes, "There are three that testify: the Spirit and the water and the blood, and these three agree" (1 John 5:7–8).

It seems clear that 1 John was written sometime after the Gospel of John. Whereas "the Jews" are depicted as the main opponents in the Gospel, they make no appearance in 1 John at all. Instead, the opponents are former members of the same community, Christians who hold a different Christology. They may be denying Jesus full divine honors. They certainly seem to be denying that Jesus was embodied with flesh and blood. It is also probable that the author of 1 John was a different person from the one who wrote the Gospel.

He is, though, a member of the same community. In fact, although his views do not exactly match those of the Gospel of John, they are similar, and even the writing style echoes that of the Gospel. Scholars, therefore, often speak of a Johannine "school," an association of early Christians, at least some of whom were fairly well educated, who worshiped together, produced literary works together, and struggled to promote their own "brand" of Christianity and oppose others. As we have already seen, they continued over time, perhaps experiencing growth but certainly also change. By the time of the writing of 1 John, moreover, they were firmly committed to a theology that stressed both the divinity of Christ and his humanity as possessing real flesh and blood.

The Changing Community of 2 and 3 John

Although we can't say whether the last two letters of the Johannine corpus were written by the same person who wrote 1 John, we feel certain that we can assign them also to this Johannine circle or school. The author of 2 John gives us no name (the authors of the Gospel and 1 John, remember, are likewise never named). He calls himself "the elder." He writes to "the elect lady and her children." Most scholars believe that the "elect lady" need not be an actual woman, but may be a symbolic address meant to represent the church, and that "her children" refers to the members of the church.

The author praises the faith and beliefs of these Christians. "I was overjoyed to find some of your children walking in the truth" (2 John 4). We then see a rehearsal of the command of love that was so prominent in 1 John (5–6). But then he gets to what must be the main point of the letter: a warning about the "deceivers" and "antichrists," "those who do not confess that Jesus Christ has come in the flesh" (7). We know, therefore, that this author is confronting the same opponents attacked in 1 John (by himself, if he is actually the same author). And his main reason for writing is to tell the members of the other church not to receive anyone who teaches the doctrine he considers false: "Do not receive into the house or welcome anyone who comes to you and does not bring this teaching; for to welcome is to participate in the evil deeds of such a person" (10–11). He notes that he himself may come visit them, and he closes with greetings from his own church: "The children of your elect sister send you their greetings" (13).

To understand what is going on here, it is helpful to know something about ancient travel. People traveling for business or for whatever reason couldn't rely on the availability of hotels or guesthouses along the way.

There were, of course, taverns and places people could stay, but they were usually awful and often expensive, and many such places had bad reputations as the kind of place frequented by prostitutes and thieves. So early Christians, who did travel quite a lot, as we have seen from Acts and will see from Paul's letters, almost always relied on a network of Christian house churches in different areas where they could stay. It was also customary for local churches to provide funds or food for traveling preachers. When a text speaks of "sending" someone "along on their way," it often means just that: supplying some financial aid for the road.

The "elder," therefore, is writing to prepare another church for a possible visit from him, but also to instruct those Christians to close their doors to his theological opponents. He is warning the church that former members, perhaps of his own church, are now espousing wrong views about Jesus, and that they may be traveling around spreading their message. If they do show up, the other church must not welcome them or provide any assistance to them.

In a fascinating turnaround, 3 John provides a glimpse of just the opposite situation. In 3 John, "the elder" writes to an individual, Gaius, not to a church. Gaius was a common Latin name, and we have no more information about him, nor can we identify him with any particular ancient figure. There is obviously a close relationship between the elder and Gaius; the elder praises him fulsomely. One of his reasons for writing, apparently, is precisely to thank Gaius for receiving some traveling "brothers." In fact, these "brothers" may even be traveling as emissaries of "the elder" and his church. They are "strangers" to Gaius, but he welcomed them anyway, probably to his home. The elder then asks Gaius to "send them on in a manner worthy of God" (3 John 6).

In this case, it is clear that actual financial assistance is what he means. These Christian travelers can expect "no support from non-believers" (7; the Greek is "gentiles," but it doubtless refers simply to non-Christians), and therefore "we ought to support such people" (8). One of the reasons for the letter is to nurture precisely the network of support necessary for Christians to travel from town to town and church to church.

But there is another reason for writing. The elder continues:

> I have written something to the church; but Diotrephes, who likes to put himself first, does not acknowledge our authority. So if I come, I will call attention to what he is doing in spreading false charges against us. And not content with those charges, he

> refuses to welcome the brothers, and even prevents those who want to do so and expels them from the church." (9–10; I have altered the NRSV to replace its "friends" with "brothers," as in the Greek)

We have no idea who this Diotrephes actually was, but he was obviously a leader of a house church to which the elder had written a letter. Diotrephes had refused to receive the emissaries sent by the elder. He may have refused to allow the elder's letter to be read to the group. And he even expelled from his own house church members who had, against his orders, received the men sent from the elder.

In other words, Diotrephes had done precisely what the elder asked the other church to do: he had refused hospitality to certain Christian travelers and emissaries. But rather than refusing to receive the elder's opponents (the "deceivers" and "antichrists"), Diotrephes refused to receive the elder's own emissaries.

It may well be that the two letters, 2 and 3 John, were written about completely different situations: different house churches in different cities at different times. But it is intriguing, though pure speculation, to imagine that the letters are more closely connected than that. We may imagine that the elder first wrote 2 John and sent it with his emissaries—those who shared his theological views—around to other churches or even just to one other church, which he designates as "the elect lady and her children." Let us also imagine that Diotrephes is the main leader in that church. But since he does not agree with the views of the elder, he refuses to receive the elder's emissaries and turns them and their letter away.

The elder then has to write not to the church itself but to an individual he knows in the same region or city and ask him to receive his emissaries and support them also as they leave for another destination. The elder had a taste of his own tactics at the hands of Diotrephes: his letter and friends were turned away by the leader of the church. The third letter of John could be a letter written later by the same man, and perhaps even to the same city, but now addressed to an individual he hopes he can depend on better than he could Diotrephes and the house church he leads.

As I said, this is speculation. But if it is what happened, we would be seeing a community of Christians—Johannine Christianity—at four different stages of development and four different documents from generally the same community, but at four different times in its history. The Gospel of John was written at a time when the church was still struggling with its connection to Judaism. It was struggling to promote its own brand of high Christology over those Jews and Christians who were not willing to make Jesus as fully divine as—and in equal status to—the Father. The community at that stage was still seething somewhat from its expulsion from "the synagogue."

The First Letter of John comes from a later time in the life of the same movement. Now the church had experienced schisms, again over the central issue of Christology. But this time the problem was not with "the Jews" or Judaism. This division had come about because some of the "Johannine" Christians did not want to admit the full humanity of Jesus. They may have continued to believe that he was divine, but that meant for them, logically, that he therefore could not be "flesh and blood." They left the church of the author of 1 John, maybe even voluntarily, and the author wrote 1 John to make his side of the debate better known and more compelling.

That same author, or another one with similar views and writing style, later wrote to a specific church warning of the "schismatics" and asking that they not be received or supported by that church. The elder might himself be visiting, so he wrote to prepare the way for himself and to close the door for his opponents.

But then the leader of that church refused to receive the friends of the elder, so he had to write again, this time to an individual he knew in the same area. Here he turned against Diotrephes and asked support from Gaius—and also attempted to swing Gaius to his side. If this admittedly speculative time line can be granted, we have a fascinating portrait of a church changing and developing over time.

When I was growing up in Texas, we had a smart-alecky saying: "Let's make like a Baptist church and split." Churches where I lived were constantly dividing over all sorts of issues: doctrinal, personal, or whatever. It was fairly easy to get some people to split off from one church and form a new one. It was, in fact, the way some people made their living. This was also happening even in the first several decades of the Christian movement. A gradually developing "orthodoxy" also created, something like a byproduct, the forming and re-forming of many different Christian groups. Social fragmentation was the detritus of developing "orthodoxy." The Gospel and the three letters of John show this happening.

CHAPTER 13

The Historical Jesus

Overview: It is obvious that certain narratives in the New Testament contradict one another and cannot be woven into a historically coherent whole. How, then, do scholars construct who the "historical Jesus" was? There are several principles that historical Jesus researchers follow, which include considering data that (1) have multiple attestations and (2) are dissimilar to a text's theological tendencies as more likely to be historical. Using the modern methods of historical research, it is possible to construct a "historical Jesus."

Contrary Accounts in the New Testament

We've already seen that the New Testament contains contradictory historical accounts of various parts of early Christianity. The geographic and chronological account of Paul's activities as told in the Acts of the Apostles cannot be respectably harmonized with Paul's own narration in Galatians. The account of the birth of Jesus and the origins of his family provided by Matthew is totally different from that in Luke, and any harmonization cannot stand up to the standards of modern historiography. The different narratives of his resurrection appearances—who of his disciples claimed they had seen him, when, and where?—in Mark, Matthew, Luke, John, and Paul contradict one another. The New Testament is simply not a reliable source for the history of Jesus or early Christianity when taken at face value.

There have sometimes been people who have used these historical observations to make the extreme argument that Jesus of Nazareth never existed at all but is a figment of the pious imagination of early Christians. No reputable scholar, to my knowledge, today makes such an argument. There is a spectrum of opinion about whether we can say much of anything historically about Jesus, with some scholars more skeptical than others. But most of us believe that if we use our sources with care, we can say a few things about Jesus of Nazareth that are defensible from the point of view of modern historiography. This chapter attempts merely to introduce the problem and offer a few suggestions for solutions. A really adequate treatment of the subject would necessitate a book of its own.[1]

The Trial of Jesus

To demonstrate the difficulty in constructing a historical Jesus, we may take an issue one would assume was an important historical event about which we would love to know the facts: the trial of Jesus. Even for something so important, we have no reliable information. According to the Gospel of Mark, our earliest source of any such information, Jesus was tried first before "the high priest and all the chief priests, the elders, and the scribes" (Mark 14:53). Some people were brought forward to give what Mark calls "false testimony," mainly accusing Jesus of talking about the destruction of the temple, which he claimed he could rebuild in three days without human hands (14:48). Even this, which seems on the surface not a punishable offense, is depicted as being delivered by conflicting and false testimony. When the high priest asked Jesus if he was the Messiah, Jesus answered only, "I am. And you will see the Son of Man seated at the right hand of the Power and coming with the clouds of heaven," echoing the book of Daniel (Mark 14:62; cf. Dan 7:13 and also Ps 110:1).

Mark claims that the "chief priests" consulted with "the elders and scribes and the whole council" before then turning Jesus over to Pilate. The "trial" before Pilate, according to Mark, consisted of nothing more than Pilate asking Jesus, "Are you the King of the Jews?" and Jesus answering with the enigmatic words "You say so" (Mark 15:1–2; it is not clear, even with the help of the Greek, what that is supposed to mean). Mark then tells us that the "chief priests" accused Jesus of "many things," but that Jesus said no more, even after Pilate asked him, "Have you no answer?" (15:3–5). So according to the Gospel of Mark, the only thing Jesus said at either trial was the "I am" statement to the chief priest and "You say so" to Pilate.

The Gospels of Matthew and Luke add material to Mark's when they produce their versions of the trials. But the greatest difference from Mark's version is found in that of John. Whereas both trials in Mark, before the Jewish leaders and then before Pilate, take only a few verses, the much more elaborate scenes narrated in John take up a good part of two chapters. Jesus appears before Annas, who is said to be the father-in-law of the high priest, Caiaphas (John 18:13), and then before Caiaphas himself (18:24). At Pilate's headquarters, we have first a conversation between Pilate and the Jewish leaders (18:29–32), and then a much longer exchange between Pilate and Jesus, culminating in Pilate's famous dramatic question to Jesus, "What is truth?" (18:33–38). Then follows an exchange between Pilate and the people (18:38–40), the torture of Jesus, the presentation of him before the people, and another exchange between Pilate and the people (19:1–7). Then follows still another exchange between Pilate and Jesus (19:8–11), another between Pilate and the people (19:12), and finally, the last presentation of Jesus to the people, a bit more back-and-forth, and the handing over of Jesus for execution (19:16).

In Mark, Jesus says almost nothing. In John, he carries on a theological and philosophical dialogue with Pilate for verse after verse. In the Gospel of Luke, we find the addition of another entire hearing before Herod (the son of Herod the Great and ruler, at the time, of Galilee; Luke 23:6–12), none of which is even hinted at in any other Gospel. What, if anything, in all this is historical?

Probably nothing. In fact, it is quite probable that there never was a trial of Jesus at all. Jesus was executed by crucifixion, which was a common method of torture and execution used by the Romans. The usual manner of execution among the Jews was stoning. So the execution of Jesus was a Roman affair, possibly with the cooperation of the Jewish leadership in Jerusalem. The Romans did not need to try a troublesome Jewish peasant in order to kill him. They tortured and crucified nameless lower-class people all the time. In order to get rid of Jesus, who had caused a disturbance in the temple, had made radical-sounding pronouncements and prophecies, and was rumored to have aspirations to kingship, the Romans would have simply taken him by force and crucified him the next day along with a few others they were getting rid of. There was no need for any trial, much less two or more before different "courts." It would have been more trouble than a Roman governor needed for the desired result.

Moreover, even if there were some kind of trial of Jesus, there is no way information about it would have survived to be transmitted to his disciples, who could then pass the stories along so that they could eventually be recorded in our Gospels. By most of the evidence, Jesus' disciples scattered when he was arrested. Even if Peter tried to follow and observe a trial, as the Gospels suggest, there is no way he, a lower-class, uneducated peasant from Galilee without significant connections among the elite in Jerusalem, could have gained access to any actual hearings. If any such hearings took place, they did so behind closed doors, without stenographers or note takers, and with no one to report later to the disciples what had happened. Given the realities of how the Romans governed their provinces, and the social status of Jesus and his immediate disciples, there is simply no way any real information about any such trials could have made it back to the followers of Jesus.

Any narrative of any such trial is purely the product of later Christian imagination, which thought that since Jesus was the most important man in history, there "must have been" significant trials before his execution. The fact is that in all probability, no trial even took place, and if it did, we have no historical record of it. I will note later that we probably can be certain of what Jesus was executed for, but we have no reliable evidence that any real hearing or trial was ever conducted before his execution.

So for significant events about which we wish we knew something historical, we have no reliable data. We have only conflicting accounts of Jesus' birth and family backgrounds; we have contradictory accounts of resurrection appearances; and we have no good information on whether he was tried, and if so, what happened. None of the materials we have on those issues rises to the level of history.

What Is "History," and Is It Essential?

Before getting to what we can say about "the historical Jesus," I need to address a few theoretical and theological questions about the topic. First, we must be clear that when we put forward a "historical Jesus," that is not the same as "the Jesus who actually existed in the past." The "past" does not exist, at least not in any way that is accessible to any human being.[2] Historians sometimes speak in a confusing way when they say that they are "reconstructing" a historical event. They actually are not "reconstructing" it; they are simply "constructing" a historiographical account of something that happened in the past. So any "historical Jesus" offered by a modern historian is not a reconstruction of the Jesus of the past, but a construction produced by that historian.

As I have explained more fully elsewhere, philosophers of history sometimes make this point by differentiating "history" from "the past."[3] The "past" refers to what actually happened—say, the Civil War. The "history" of the Civil War refers more particularly to some account of the Civil War: how a historian may depict or narrate "what happened" in a linguistic account. In the same way, when I refer here to "the historical Jesus," I do not mean "Jesus of Nazareth as he really was." That Jesus is not accessible to us in any way. By "the historical Jesus," I mean an account of Jesus constructed using the normal methods of modern historiography. The "historical Jesus" must not be confused with "the real Jesus" or "Jesus as he really was."

We must also be clear that the historical Jesus is in no way necessary for Christian faith. Christian faith is based on beliefs about what Jesus of Nazareth means theologically. When I say "Christian faith," I realize that I am evoking a debatable entity, but for the purposes of this book, I am not concerned about delineating a particular kind of Christianity. I am referring to the central, general doctrines held by almost all people who call themselves Christians, which are variously defined in traditional creeds, publications of different churches, and common ways Christians have read and do read the Bible. For my purposes here, Christian faith need be no more than the belief that Jesus Christ is the Son of God who saves humanity.

Christian faith says, among other things, that "God was in Christ reconciling the world to himself," to cite one Pauline summation of the gospel (2 Cor 5:19). Such a statement can be neither confirmed nor denied by modern historiography. In other words, a historian can confirm the probability, using regular historical methods, that a man named Jesus lived and died in the first century. But the historian cannot confirm—or deny—that "God" had anything to do with that fact. God is not one of those things that are subject to modern historical analysis. The theological Jesus is just not the same as the historical Jesus. The theological Jesus—the full Christ who inspires and grounds Christian faith and doctrine—is a product of concern for theologians and Christians. The historical Jesus is one constructed by the rules of modern historiography.[4]

These are not points that are true only for Jesus. I may want to talk about who George Washington is for popular American piety. In that case, telling the story of George Washington as a boy chopping down a cherry tree and then confessing the deed to his father may be indispensable for the "full" George Washington important in American patriotic lore. But the story is not true for the "historical" George Washington; just about all historians agree that it was circulated by a popular biographer of Washington, Mason Weems, because it was just too good a tale to ignore.[5] But it did not happen. The "Socrates" we see in Plato's dialogues is hugely important for philosophy and the history of Western culture, but we must not confuse that "Socrates" with either "Socrates as he actually lived" or "the historical Socrates," that is, a Socrates constructed by modern historiographical methods. Plato gave us his own, rather fictional, portrait of Socrates, not "the historical Socrates," but his portrait is still quite important for the later history of "Socrates" in Western culture.

These are perhaps theoretically (or theologically) confusing points, but they must be kept in mind. The historical Jesus is an account of Jesus constructed by modern historians playing by the rules of modern historiography. And the historical Jesus is not a necessary foundation for or component of Christian faith or theology. In fact, the historical Jesus is radically unacceptable for Christian faith precisely because no historical Jesus can be divine.

Methods of Historical Jesus Research

In the twentieth century, scholars developed a few methods for deciding what in the Gospels can be said to go back to the historical Jesus and what cannot. Scholars continue to debate whether these methods render reliable results, and I have no interest in adjudicating that debate and proposing definitive solutions. But making one's methods explicit at least has the benefit of raising to consciousness our own biases and predispositions. Laying out the criteria used for arguing for or against the historicity of any particular saying or event is useful in itself.

The first and perhaps most important such methodological rule or guideline is the criterion of multiple attestation. An event or saying—or perhaps simply a hypothesis of what Jesus was like—that is found in more than one of our independent witnesses has a better chance of representing the historical Jesus. The occurrence in that sentence of "independent" is important. We have seen that the Gospels of Matthew and Luke both used Mark as one of their sources, so finding a saying, even word for word, in Mark, Matthew, and Luke would not count as evidence from three different sources, but only one: Mark provides the tradition, and Matthew and Luke repeat it from him. But if one form of a parable occurs in Mark, and a different form of the same parable is found in Matthew and Luke together, we would then have two sources: Mark passes along the parable, and Matthew and Luke got a different form from the Q source they both used independently. Or, if the theory of Q is rejected, as some scholars insist, we may suppose that Luke got his version from Matthew. I will work here, though, on the assumption that the Q hypothesis is the most plausible solution to the synoptic problem.

Scholars debate whether the author of the Gospel of John had access to any or all of the synoptic Gospels. For the purpose of most historical Jesus research, however, John has usually been considered an independent source. We therefore have several sources that pass along material about Jesus: the synoptic Gospels, Q, John, the *Gospel of Thomas* (which many, though not all, scholars take to be an independent source), and Paul (Paul has few sayings of Jesus, but he does provide some).

The second most important methodological rule is known as the criterion of dissimilarity. Once we have ascertained the thematic and theological tendency of the writing itself, a saying or event that seems to go against that tendency—or against the general beliefs or assumptions of early Christianity more generally—has a better likelihood of being historical. The reasoning here is rather plain and commonsense. We know that each of our writers used materials gathered from sources he had available to him, both oral and written. We have also seen, especially in the chapters on Luke and Acts, that the authors did not always edit their sources so that they completely reflected only their own views. Authors regularly leave some details or elements of their sources in their text that do not completely match their own views or tendencies. A saying or event that reflects views different from those of the author or other early Christians therefore represents views that predate them. If a saying goes against the author's own agenda, it may constitute material surviving from before their writing. It may even have come originally from Jesus himself.

I can illustrate the use of both of these criteria with a few examples. According to all four canonical Gospels, the charge against Jesus—the legal reason he was executed—was written on a plaque attached to his cross. The actual wording differs somewhat. According to Mark, it read simply, "The King of the Jews" (Mark 15:26), which Luke changes very slightly to "This is the King of the Jews" (23:39), and Matthew changes to "This is Jesus, the King of the Jews" (27:37). We can count all three, however, as only one source, since Matthew and Luke may have merely gotten the idea from Mark. The Gospel of John has a more elaborate version, saying that Pilate put the inscription in Hebrew, Latin, and Greek, and that there was an argument between "the

Jews" and Pilate about the wording. But the wording is similar: "Jesus of Nazareth, the King of the Jews" (John 19:19).

We thus have what many scholars would count as "multiple attestation" that Jesus was executed on the charge of pretensions to the throne of Judea, which was for the Romans an offense punishable by death. It is attested in Mark and John, two of what we may consider independent witnesses.

The detail also passes the test of the criterion of dissimilarity. Early Christians and all our Gospel writers have several different titles for Jesus. "The Christ," of course, is one. So are "Lord," "Son of Man," "Son of God," "Rabbi," "Holy One of Israel," "Prophet," and many others. But early Christians seem not to have used the title "King of the Jews" in their worship of Jesus. It is not, that is, a common Christological title for Jesus, either in our Gospels or in early Christianity more generally. It has been argued, therefore, that it was not an invention of early Christians or the Gospel writers, but was really the charge the Romans used to condemn and punish Jesus. That Jesus was executed because he or someone else was claiming that he was the king of the Jews seems to be historically accurate.[6]

Another example is provided by the story that Jesus was baptized by John the Baptist. It is multiply attested: different versions are told in each of the synoptic Gospels. Although the Gospel of John does not narrate the actual event, there are clear indications that its author knows of the tradition (see John 1:29–34, for example). There are "Baptist" traditions apparently also in the Q material, showing some independent testimony of the importance of John the Baptist for the Jesus movement that Luke and Matthew share and that they did not get from Mark (see Matt 3:7–10=Luke 3:7–9; Matt 11:2–19=Luke 7:18–28, 31–35; 16:16). So we are safe in saying that the baptism of Jesus by John is multiply attested.

It is also clearly something early followers of Jesus did not invent. If Jesus was baptized by John, that could be taken to mean that Jesus was a disciple of John and therefore his inferior. Indeed, all our sources sense this, and so they go out of their way to demonstrate, in various ways, that Jesus was not inferior to John even though he was baptized by him. In Mark, John explicitly proclaims the superiority of Jesus even before the baptism (Mark 1:7–8). Matthew adds that John attempted to avoid baptizing Jesus (Matt 3:14). And as we have seen, John avoids narrating the baptism itself, although he certainly knows about it. All these were attempts to downplay the fact that Jesus was baptized by John. As I will note later, historians take that fact as historical and as an indication that Jesus began as a disciple of

John the Baptist. There was no reason for later Christian writers to invent the baptism by John, and they went out of their way to explain it away to some extent. It could even be seen as something of an embarrassment or detraction from Jesus' superior status. It therefore is almost certainly historical. It passes both the criterion of multiple attestation and the criterion of dissimilarity.

A third example of how these criteria work concerns the question, what, if anything, did Jesus teach about divorce and remarriage? That Jesus taught something seems evident because we have several references to the topic. In Mark 10:1–12 and Matthew 19:1–12, we have a story about a confrontation between Jesus and "some Pharisees." The wording is somewhat different in the two accounts, but they both agree that Jesus taught that divorce was forbidden: "What God has joined together, let no man put asunder." A different version of a similar prohibition is found in Matthew 5:32 and Luke 16:18 (in the method I am using here, a Q saying). The wording in Luke (a bit simpler than Matthew's wording) is as follows: "Every man who divorces his wife and marries another commits adultery, and whoever marries a woman who has been divorced by her husband commits adultery." So we have two independent witnesses—Mark and Q—that Jesus forbade divorce and remarriage, and two different forms of the tradition survive.

But we have another from Paul. In 1 Corinthians 7:10–11, Paul strongly urges couples not to divorce, and he claims to be passing along a command of Jesus: "To those who are married I command—not I but the Lord—that the woman must not separate from her husband (if indeed she does separate, let her remain unmarried or be reconciled to her husband), and a man must not put away his wife" (my translation). The wording here is obviously Paul's, but Paul wrote long before the publication of any of our Gospels, so he provides an independent, and much earlier, witness to the tradition.

Not only is the prohibition of divorce by Jesus multiply attested (by three sources: Paul, Mark, and Q), but it also passes the criterion of dissimilarity. A complete prohibition of divorce was almost unthinkable in Judaism of the time. Divorce was generally accepted and was expected in certain cases.[7] Divorce was permitted by the law of Moses, as Jesus and the Gospel writers know (they refer to Deut 24:1). And the complete prohibition of divorce we find on the lips of Jesus in these cases was so radical that even our authors who pass it along seem pressed to come up with exceptions or a more lenient position. To the straightforward prohibition he finds in Mark, Matthew adds some "exceptions" (Matt 5:32, 19:9). Paul also makes some exceptions (1 Cor 7:10–16). Throughout Christian history, churches have struggled to find some ways to allow for divorce and remarriage for Christians. Absolute prohibition of divorce is so radical that Christians have never really lived up to it. There is all the more reason to believe, therefore, that the command was not invented by early Christians but goes back to the historical Jesus.

Another example in which it seems clear that early Christians would not have invented a detail from Jesus' life is the tradition that at least one, two, or maybe more of his closest disciples were armed at his arrest. According to Mark 14:47, an unnamed companion of Jesus draws a sword and cuts off the ear of a slave of the high priest. The story is followed by Matthew and Luke, with interesting differences I will examine below. John 18:10–11 says that it was Peter who did the cutting, and he helpfully names the slave.

Again, not only is the story multiply attested (Mark and John), it clearly runs counter to all our Gospel writers'—and just about all early Christianity's—tendency to insist that Jesus' movement was peaceful and never intended to mount any kind of armed resistance or rebellion. Each of the writers also tries to play down the incident or give it some kind of proper motivation. After borrowing the basic account from Mark, Matthew has Jesus rebuke the disciple and even add some comments rejecting armed violence for the cause (Matt 26:52). Luke also has Jesus rebuke the disciple, but then he goes further and has Jesus heal the wounded man (22:50–51). In addition, Luke explains that only two disciples were armed, and only to fulfill a scripture (the scripture quoted, incidentally, says nothing about swords or arms at all: Luke 22:37–38; cf. Isa 53:12). John also depicts Jesus as rebuking Peter for the action (John 18:10–11). All the authors pass along the "fact" that Jesus' disciples were armed even though they are obviously uncomfortable with the detail. (It is customary to say that only one or two disciples were armed, but none of the sources except Luke add that detail; the others can be read as implying merely that some of Jesus' companions were armed.) The "fact" goes so clearly against the authors' interests in depicting Jesus and his movement as innocent that it cannot have been invented by them.[8]

The examples I have given thus far to illustrate the use of the criteria of multiple attestation and dissimilarity have lived up to the demands of both criteria. There is one passage, however, that I believe provides a good example of passing only the criterion of dissimilarity, but that I would argue does go back to the historical Jesus. In Mark 10:17–18, a man asks Jesus, "Good Teacher, what must I do to inherit eternal life?" Jesus answers, "Why do you call me good? No one is good but God alone." Although Jesus proceeds to answer the man, that first response is rather shocking. A Christian Gospel denying that Jesus is good? And further implying that he is not God? The saying has no multiple attestation (Matthew and Luke seem merely to follow Mark here), but I think it very unlikely that any Christian writer would have invented a saying in which Jesus seems to deny both that he is good and that he is God. I would argue, therefore, that Jesus must have said this or something very like it, and I would make that argument on the basis of the criterion of dissimilarity alone.

Besides these two criteria, scholars sometimes list others as well. One is simply the insistence that something cannot go back to the historical Jesus if it does not fit what we know of the social-historical context of his life in Palestine in the first part of the first century. This is sometimes called the criterion of social-historical context, but it is really just the common historical goal of avoiding anachronism. For example, when Matthew has Jesus talk about "the church" in Matthew 18:17, we may be certain that the historical Jesus did not make those statements. The church did not exist in his lifetime, and by all the evidence, as I will urge later, the historical Jesus was expecting the kingdom of God, not the founding of the Christian Church. We may be certain that Jesus did not make the kinds of "I am" statements from the Fourth Gospel we analyzed in the last chapter. It is very unlikely that any pious Jew would claim the divine name for himself at the time of Jesus. And it took years for Christology to develop so that such things could be said even by Christians about Jesus.

Also in John, Jesus is depicted as using certain puns, as playing on language, in a way possible only in Greek. When Jesus speaks with Nicodemus about being born "again" or "from above" (John 3:3; the Greek can be translated either way), the play of language makes sense only in Greek. The sayings, therefore, could not go back to the historical Jesus, who probably did not speak Greek but taught instead in Aramaic. Each of these is an example of something we find in our Gospels that cannot be attributed to the historical Jesus, simply on the basis of the limits of his time and place.

Some scholars add another criterion to those I have already mentioned: a criterion of coherence. This states that if something can be established about the historical Jesus on the basis of the other, more demanding criteria, something else in the tradition that seems "coherent" with it may also be historical. For example, if we can establish by means of the criteria of multiple attestation and dissimilarity that Jesus was not an ascetic with regard to diet—that he did not teach the avoidance of feasting or drinking wine—then we might argue that he was probably not an ascetic with regard to sexuality either, since both usually went together in the Judaism of his day. This is a rather weak criterion, however, because it builds speculation on speculation. The other criteria are, after all, to a great extent guesswork. To add even more speculation on top of that guesswork, merely on the argument that some saying or event "coheres" well with it, sounds to many historians like a weak argument.

Recently, it has been argued that all these criteria are not very reliable for constructing the historical Jesus, and that we should simply look for those aspects of his life and ministry for which we can find much evidence in different sources. Even if, for example, we question the historicity of any particular apocalyptic statement by or about Jesus, preaching about the kingdom of God and its imminence is simply so abundant in our sources that the historical Jesus must have held those views.[9] Therefore, in contrast to the common criteria developed in the twentieth century, more recent suggestions have insisted that we would do better in building a general portrait of the historical Jesus simply by noting what aspects of his life and ministry are most fully attested across our different sources.

A final note on method. The best scholarship on the historical Jesus admits that all such constructions are provisional and imperfect. We can never say for certain that we know that the historical Jesus said or did anything in particular. We should rather think of the conclusions of such historical research as ending up at some point on a scale of probability. Thus, instead of deciding that something "definitely did" or "did not" happen, we should use a scale something like (1) almost certainly historical; (2) probably historical; (3) could go either way; (4) probably not historical; and (5) almost certainly not historical.[10] Constructions of historical Jesuses, in spite of the sometimes overly confident tone of the writings of modern scholars, are hypothetical; they are depictions of what scholars think the historical Jesus probably did or did not do and say based on the necessarily flawed and provisional methods of modern historiography.[11]

Jesus as Apocalyptic Jewish Prophet

With all those methodological caveats in mind, I close this chapter with a brief section suggesting my own views about what we may say about the historical Jesus. Some of what follows is controversial, but I believe it represents a fair consensus of at least many modern critical scholars. I think it best to view the historical Jesus mainly as a Jewish prophet in the long tradition of prophets of Israel, but one who was influenced by forms of Jewish apocalyptic thought and expectation that had arisen and pervaded some segments of Judaism since at least the writing of the book of Daniel in the second century B.C.E. Jesus was a traveling healer, exorcist, and teacher who preached the imminent arrival of a kingdom of God that would overthrow and replace the current political orders with the direct reign of God, accomplished through a heavenly agent in the form of a messiah or "Son of Man."

The idea that Jesus was an eschatological prophet was very common, especially in German and American scholarship, throughout much of the twentieth century. It was challenged by a group of scholars known as the Jesus Seminar in the last part of that century.[12] Those scholars claimed that Jesus himself was not an apocalypticist, and that an apocalyptic strain of Christianity arose only after his death, leading to the apocalyptic nature of much of our surviving literature. Such scholars argue that the imminent apocalypse of Mark 13, for instance, was added to Jesus' own words and deeds and did not reflect the actual reality of the historical Jesus. I believe that challenge, by what I take to be a minority of biblical scholars, has failed. I and many other critical scholars continue to insist that the best construction of the historical Jesus is as an apocalyptic Jewish prophet.[13]

Two historical facts that are about as firmly established as a historical "fact" from the ancient world can be anchor this thesis. The first is the recognition, as already noted, that Jesus began as a follower of John the Baptist. Jesus was certainly baptized by John, and he seems not to have begun his own ministry until after the arrest of the Baptist. That all suggests that he was in the beginning a disciple of the Baptist. All our evidence about John the Baptist indicates that he was a prophet attempting to prepare the Jewish people for some urgent, imminent apocalyptic event, probably the arrival of the "reign of God." So Jesus began as an adherent of an apocalyptic movement.

The second fact is the obvious presence of apocalypticism in the earliest forms of Christianity we can discern. The letters of Paul, for instance, are imbued with apocalyptic expectations, as we will see in later chapters. Our earliest surviving Christian writing, according to most scholarly opinion, is Paul's First Letter to the Thessalonians, dated by most scholars to around 50 C.E. It is ample evidence that Paul was looking for the return of Jesus (the *parousia*, or "coming" of the Messiah in glory) very soon. Paul seems not to have expected that he would die before the event. All other evidence from the earliest strata of Christianity—Mark, Matthew, Luke, and their sources—shows apocalyptic expectations.

Furthermore, as argued earlier, one of the most secure things we can say about Jesus historically is that he was executed by the Romans on a charge of political sedition. He was killed either for claiming that he was the Messiah, the king of the Jews, or because others made the claim about him. We cannot know whether Jesus made such claims about himself in his lifetime. If he did, it is hard to understand why we don't have more evidence for such claims in the synoptic Gospels. But the Romans, for whatever reason, believed that Jesus was a messianic figure, in other words, a pretender to the throne of Judea. That would have been treasonous in the eyes of Rome and would have merited crucifixion. And the very idea that Jesus could have been seen as a messianic figure puts us again into the world of first-century Jewish apocalypticism.

Another event that took place at the very end of Jesus' life also frames the story in apocalypticism: the prophetic activity he carried out in the Jerusalem temple. There is much debate about what exactly Jesus said and did in the temple in the last few days of his life. I would argue, in any case, that his disciples had no reason to invent the story. They were going out of their way to paint him as peaceful and innocent of any possible charge of violence or sedition. They would have no reason to come up with such a story. In fact, I believe, along with many other scholars, that they played down any possible revolutionary interpretation of the event by portraying it as a "cleansing" of the temple. It is much more likely, in my view, that Jesus conducted there some kind of traditional prophetic "street politics" in a symbolic destruction of the temple rather than merely its "cleansing." Following other scholars, I believe that Jesus acted out a symbolic prophecy of the destruction of the temple and its cult. That also would have caused the leaders in Jerusalem to work for his arrest and destruction.[14] And again, the proper context in which to imagine such prophetic activity in the Judaism of the day was apocalyptic judgment and expectation.

The events that surround Jesus' ministry, therefore, that frame his ministry at its beginning and conclusion, are apocalyptic. He begins as a disciple of an apocalyptic Jewish prophet, he is executed as an apocalyptic messianic figure, and his followers later continue in a community infused with apocalyptic expectations. It is, in my view, impossible to make sense of the beginning and ending of his ministry as apocalyptic if Jesus eschewed apocalypticism himself. He was, if nothing else, an apocalyptic Jewish prophet.

In our sources, Jesus' sayings are more about the kingdom of God (or "heaven" in Matthew, doubtless reflecting Matthew's own editing activity) than they are about anything else. Jesus talks much less than most people popularly think about his own person or nature, or even about "ethics" and "morality." Even Paul, who does not talk extensively about the kingdom of God (preferring other language), nonetheless knows such language and assumes it. Again, the most natural source and home for such language in first-century Judaism was apocalypticism, and the most natural way to take such language is not the "spiritualized" meaning of later Christianity but the very "physical" and "political" meaning it would have had for most Jews of the time: Jesus was preaching about an imminent breaking into history by God and his agents that would overthrow the rule of the Romans and their upper-class Jewish surrogates and establish an eternal and universal reign under divine authority and power, headed by a king, a messiah, appointed and protected by God and his angelic armies. That would be the future government of the world: a universal, Jewish empire.

Beyond that general picture, we can say a few more things about the historical Jesus, most of which I cannot defend here because doing so would merit a book of its own. Jesus was a lower-class Jewish peasant from Nazareth, a small village in Galilee. There is no reason to believe the later legends that he was born in Bethlehem. He grew up probably in a family of hand laborers. He had brothers and probably sisters. His mother was named Mary, and his father, Joseph. Since we hear nothing of Joseph's activities from Jesus' adulthood, he likely was dead by the time Jesus began his preaching. His mother, though, and at least his brother James later were figures in the movement after Jesus' death, with James ending up as the main leader of the Jewish church in Jerusalem. Jesus certainly spoke Aramaic as his first language. If he spoke Greek at all, it was only enough to get by in bilingual situations. He probably could not write, and if he could read, it was only minimally.

Jesus did gather followers around him, some of whom were certainly women in central positions. Mary Magdalene was doubtless a close follower, later respected by the community after Jesus' death. Jesus also appointed twelve male disciples, doubtless as an eschatological symbol for the messianic reconstitution of the twelve tribes of Israel. He probably expected that these twelve men would be heads of the miraculously reconstituted twelve tribes in the eschatological world.

Jesus himself respected and followed the law of Moses. I think that he advocated a rather more relaxed enforcement of that law, allowing for more activities on the Sabbath than stricter Jews would have preferred and allowing a bit more lax observation of certain traditions, such as hand washings and associations with people of low repute. Jesus never rejected the Jewish law nor taught its abrogation at any point, but he may have taught a more "liberal" or relaxed interpretation of many of its requirements and other Jewish traditions.

As I argued earlier, I do think the historical Jesus taught that divorce and remarriage should be forbidden in all circumstances. This was actually a more restrictive command than anything in the Jewish law, and that may mean that Jesus was something of an ascetic when it came to sexual activities and the family. The common view in the ancient world was that one would get a divorce in order to marry someone else. Divorce was seen as accompanying sexual license. So the forbidding of divorce could be understood as part of an ascetic agenda with regard to sex.

But I also think Jesus taught against the traditional household and formed, in its place, a band of men and women separated from their traditional households and families and bound to one another as a new, eschatological household of God. There are few aspects of Jesus' ministry more certain to be historical than that he called people away from their families for the sake of the coming kingdom of God. The historical Jesus, therefore, was certainly not a "family man" in any way advocated by modern Christianity or ancient household ethics.

In spite of the possibility that Jesus was something of an ascetic with regard to marriage and family, he was not one with regard to eating and drinking. In fact, one of the things that may have differentiated the ministry of Jesus from that of John the Baptist, his early teacher, and other Jewish ascetics was that he and his followers did not follow an ascetic agenda with regard to food and drink. I think it is historical that he was rumored to be a man who enjoyed feasting and drinking when the rare opportunity arose for someone so poor, and that he kept the company of tax collectors, prostitutes, and other disreputable persons.

Did Jesus think he was the Messiah? This is, in my mind, highly debatable. He certainly was executed, as I argued, on the charge of claiming to be a king, but there are not many open teachings in which he makes such claims in the best of our surviving evidence. If he did teach that he was the Messiah, I think he must have done so secretly among his closest disciples. But then again, it may have been something Jesus did not believe about himself, but that others announced about him. Some of his sayings in our Gospels make it sound as if Jesus was expecting someone else to be the expected "Son of Man."[15] And Jesus almost exclusively, in the synoptic Gospels, speaks of any messiah figure in the third person.[16] At any rate, he was certainly taken by the Romans to be a messianic pretender.

One thing we can say for certain from a historical point of view: the historical Jesus was not the "founder" of a "new religion" called "Christianity." The historical Jesus expected the kingdom of God, not the Roman Catholic or any other church. Jesus of Nazareth preached the imminent breaking into history of God's agency to establish a new realm of divine rule on earth, not the establishment of anything like what we call a "religion." That is as certain a historical fact as can be established by any historian about anyone.

The Jesus of History and the Christ of Faith

As I said in the first part of this chapter, we must not confuse the historical Jesus with the Jesus Christ who is the basis and inspiration for Christian faith and practice. The historical Jesus is a construction of modern historians. It is always provisional, open to new revision and reconstruction. There are almost as many historical Jesuses as there are scholars interested in the cottage industry of that topic. The Christ confessed by Christians must be other than that. The Christ of faith is the Christ of the New Testament, the Christ of Christian creeds and confessions, and the Christ of the Christian liturgy and history, even as these present differing versions of "Jesus." The historical Jesus is neither necessary nor sufficient for Christian faith. But the topic is one of importance to historians of early Christianity and, used properly, could be of some interest even in theological reflections on the Christ of Christianity. But that is not the topic of this book.

Paul and Paulinism

CHAPTER 14

Paul as Missionary: 1 Thessalonians

Overview: The New Testament and other texts provide us with many accounts of the apostle Paul, some of which contradict one another. Throughout the history of Christianity, Paul has assumed many different roles for different people. For the early Christians, he was primarily a martyr. For St. Augustine and, later, Martin Luther, he was a man interpreting the gospel through his psychological struggle with guilt. The historical Paul seems to have been a man preaching an apocalyptic message to the gentiles.

Paul, the Protean Apostle

Just as one must read the Bible and other texts critically to find the historical Jesus as distinct from the Jesus of Christian faith, so we have to sift our sources to construct the historical Paul. For Paul, admittedly, there is much more to go on. He is a star character in the first "history" of early Christianity, the Acts of the Apostles, although, as we have already seen and will see further below, the Acts account of Paul is not very reliable as history. But we have seven letters from Paul's own hand and several other letters written by his later followers in his name. We have nothing comparable for Jesus himself or for any other first-generation follower of Jesus, that is, for any of his other apostles or first disciples. Paul ends up being central for the history of early Christianity simply because we have more to work with for him.

Paul, though, has throughout the centuries been many things for many people. Paul himself said that he was a changeable figure. "I have become all things to all people," he writes to the Corinthians (1 Cor 9:22), and some apparently held him at fault for that. Wayne Meeks, in a now-classic anthology of Paul's writings, called Paul "the Protean Apostle," invoking Proteus, the Homeric sea god who could change his shape miraculously to become any number of beasts or things.[1]

For much of history and for many people, Paul is thought to have been one of the "founders of Christianity," if not *the* founder. He is thought to have been the first missionary, for example, to take the gospel to Europe. In the ancient world, there was debate about whether Peter or Paul was to be honored as the first apostle of Rome, although gradually Peter won that competition. But many people, as we will see, insist that Paul rather than Jesus must be considered the "real" founder of Christianity, whether they appreciate the fact or bemoan it. Paul is popularly thought to be not only the first Christian missionary to the gentiles, but also the church's first theologian and creator of doctrines and dogma. All these things, in some people's minds, make Paul the real founder of Christianity, rather than Jesus.

As we have already seen in the chapter on Acts, that is an exaggeration encouraged to some extent by the book of Acts itself. The first followers of Jesus to evangelize Jews and gentiles, in Palestine and outside it, were doubtless people whose identities are lost to us, people who told their friends and families about their enthusiasm for a crucified Jewish messiah. And Paul looks more important in the grand scheme of early Christian history than he likely was simply because we have more information from and about him than from and about others, not necessarily because he was truly the most important evangelist of the first generation of the movement. We need not exaggerate Paul's importance for the founding, growth, or character of Christianity in order to appreciate him as a central and still-fascinating figure.

The early church, in fact, seems to have revered Paul not so much as the great and first theologian, but as a great martyr. In Christian art, he is often portrayed with a scroll in his hand (and usually as bald because of some ancient traditions), which is meant to depict his letter-writing apostleship. But he is also often depicted with a sword, referring to the tradition that he was martyred by beheading in Rome under Nero. So for much of Christian tradition, Paul was more the martyr than the theologian.[2]

Saint Augustine and Martin Luther, following Augustine many centuries later, took Paul to be the kind of person they saw themselves to be: an anguished soul worried about personal guilt and struggling with great difficulties to find peace and forgiveness from God. They interpreted Paul's words in Romans 7:19 to be an autobiographical description of his experience of guilt, attempting to be righteous by force of will and failing: "For I do not do the good I want, but the evil I do not want is what I do."

Luther, as an Augustinian Roman Catholic monk, worried about the state of his soul. He tried to live up to all the requirements of the church and his religious order but found himself crushed repeatedly under doctrine, requirements, and rules. We are all sinners and cannot save ourselves. Luther came to believe, reading Galatians and Romans, that Paul was the one who correctly taught that justification was of sinners through grace gained by faith, not by works of the Jewish law or the Catholic Church. This idea that Paul engaged in a psychological struggle to be righteous but constantly fell short, a struggle experienced also by Augustine and Luther, has been a reigning understanding of Paul throughout the modern world. This is, though, simply the great Lutheran, Protestant Paul. We will see that there are good reasons in Paul's letters to question this view.[3]

Many people have believed that Paul supplanted the "religion of Jesus" with a "religion about Jesus." Certainly, when we read the words of Jesus in our Gospels, they don't sound like Paul for the most part. Jesus says things like "Consider the lilies of the field"; he tells us not to worry because God will clothe and feed us as surely as he does the flowers and the birds. Jesus proclaims the coming of the kingdom of God, in which everyone will be blessed, peace will reign, the last will be first, the first will be last, and the poor will be rich and happy. Paul, on the other hand, talks about Jesus himself, and not necessarily as a "normal man" but as the Christ sacrificed for us, through whom we gain reconciliation with God. Paul talks not about the peace of flowers and birds, and not much about the kingdom of God, but about "justification by grace through faith" in Christ. As others have said, in the preaching of Paul, "the proclaimer" becomes "the proclaimed." Jesus, the one proclaiming the coming kingdom, becomes the Christ, the one in whom we must believe. And some people have sorely faulted Paul for this.

Friedrich Nietzsche, for instance, was no great fan of Jesus, but he really hated Paul and the kind of Christianity he believed Paul preached. This is Paul as the corrupter of the simple religion of Jesus. As Nietzsche wrote, "The 'glad tidings' were followed closely by the absolutely *worst* tidings—those of St. Paul. Paul is the incarnation of a type which is the reverse of that of the Saviour; he is the genius in hatred, in the standpoint of hatred, and in the relentless logic of hatred."[4] Paul made the cross the center of Christianity and turned it even more into a "slave religion." Salvation by the cross was Paul's invention, and that is what is wrong with Christianity.

Similarly, George Bernard Shaw said this about Paul: "No sooner had Jesus knocked over the dragon of superstition than Paul boldly set it up on its legs again in the name of Jesus."[5] Or elsewhere: Paul "is the true head and founder of our Reformed Church, as Peter is of the Roman Church. The followers of Paul and Peter made Christendom, whilst the Nazarenes were wiped out."[6] The religion of Jesus, according to Shaw, disappeared from the earth, and all we have left is this shell called Christendom.

Who Is the Historical Paul?

As dramatic and juicy as all that sounds, it isn't really true. Obviously, the Christianity that developed after the death of Jesus was something completely new and unlike either the faith of the historical Jesus or even much of his teachings. We have already seen that there is much distance between the historical Jesus and the Jesus of the Fourth Gospel. But those changes began happening immediately after the death of Jesus, once some of his disciples came to believe that they had seen him alive again, even before Paul became a follower of the movement. And although the letters of Paul are certainly central for later Christianity, it is much too easy to exaggerate that importance. What became orthodox Christianity—to say nothing of "Christendom"—took centuries to develop and, of course, is still developing. To put it all on Paul is completely inaccurate. It is bad history.

We can say some things about the historical Paul with some confidence, although uncertainties will remain, as in any historiographical endeavor. The best place to begin, however, is not with the misleading and unhistorical portrait of Paul in the Acts of the Apostles but with his own letters.

First, I must lay out the scholarly consensus on which of Paul's letters were actually written by him. Seven of the thirteen letters in the New Testament that bear Paul's name are almost certainly by him. Scholars therefore often call these the "undisputed letters," meaning that scholars feel little need to have arguments about their authenticity: Romans, 1 Corinthians, 2 Corinthians, Galatians, Philippians, 1 Thessalonians, and Philemon. The great majority of critical scholars believe that three of the remaining letters, 1 Timothy, 2 Timothy, and Titus, are pseudepigrapha, written by some follower of Paul long after his death but published in his name.[7] We call these the "Pastoral Letters" (or "Pastoral Epistles") because they show Paul setting up Timothy and Titus as "pastors" over churches.

Between these two groups of almost unanimously accepted Pauline letters and mostly rejected pseudepigrapha lie three letters about which scholars have more lively debates. I give them here in what I take to be an order of descending acceptance among scholars. Second Thessalonians is accepted by many scholars as authentically Pauline, but rejected (and perhaps increasingly so) by others. Colossians is accepted by some scholars as Pauline, but rejected by many others. Still fewer scholars accept the authenticity of Ephesians. I will call these three letters the "disputed letters," although other scholars call them the "deutero-Paulines." Figure 8 shows the division of the thirteen letters attributed to Paul into these three groups.

Using only the undisputed letters, what can we glean about Paul's life? In Philippians 3:5–6, Paul tells us that he was of the tribe of Benjamin, so he knows not only that he is a Jew, but which tribe he is supposed to be from. He also tells us that he is a Pharisee. This is interesting because Paul never says that he was a Pharisee. When he talks about being a Pharisee, he does not put it in the past tense. This is true also of Paul in Acts, where even after his conversion he speaks of himself as a Pharisee (Acts 23:6). This is significant because we don't have much historical material on the Pharisees before the destruction of Jerusalem in 70 C.E. In fact, Paul's letters are rare firsthand surviving documents from the hand of a Pharisee before 70.

Paul also says that he was "zealous" for the Jewish law; in fact, he brings up his persecution of the church before his calling as an apostle as evidence of his zeal for the law. In Galatians 5:11, Paul insists that he is not "still preaching

Canonical			Noncanonical
Undisputed	Disputed	Pseudonymous	(Pseudonymous)
Romans	Ephesians	1 Timothy	Laodiceans
1 Corinthians	Colossians	2 Timothy	Correspondence of Paul and Seneca
2 Corinthians	2 Thessalonians	Titus	
Galatians			
Philippians			
1 Thessalonians			
Philemon			

Fig. 8 Pauline Epistles

circumcision." He doesn't say much more than that, and he never explains this strange phrase, but it suggests that before becoming an apostle (and maybe even for a while afterward?), Paul was a preacher of circumcision. In fact, these different hints from Paul suggest that the reason he persecuted the Jesus movement in its early days was because it, or part of it, was teaching a gospel that did not advocate conformity to the law.

Acts portrays Paul's visionary experience more as a conversion to "the Way" than a call to apostleship. But that is not how Paul saw it. In the one place we hear Paul's own description of his experience, Paul speaks of it not as a "conversion" from one religion to another, or even from one sect of Judaism to another. Rather, he uses images and language like the descriptions of the calling of a prophet in the Old Testament. "But when God, who had set me apart before I was born and called me through his grace, was pleased to reveal his Son to me, so that I might proclaim him among the Gentiles, I did not confer with any human being" (Gal 1:15–16). This sounds like Isaiah 49:1: "The Lord called me before I was born, while I was in my mother's womb he named me." Or Jeremiah 1:5: "Before I formed you in the womb I knew you, and before you were born I consecrated you; I appointed you a prophet to the nations." Remember that the Greek word "nations" is the same word we translate in the New Testament as "gentiles." Paul obviously saw himself in this self-description of Jeremiah: a prophet to the nations. Paul did not see the experience as a conversion from one religion to another, but as a divine calling to take the true form of the worship of the God of Israel to the rest of the nations.

We can glean only a few facts about Paul's life and identity from his letters. In the next few chapters, I will add more to the portrait. But I must also point out that many ideas people have about Paul, many things they believe about his "biography," come only from the accounts about him in Acts, and I have already noted the dangers of using Acts for the "historical Paul." Much of what one might find, for example, in a popular bookstore account of Paul is overly dependent on Acts and so is historically questionable. Acts, for instance, portrays Paul as having grown up and been educated in Jerusalem, even at the feet of Gamaliel, a famous first-century rabbi and Pharisee (Acts 22:3). That is very unlikely. Paul never mentions it, even when it could have been useful for him, as in the Philippians passage I cited earlier. Paul also speaks fluent Hebrew in Acts.[8] But Paul never gives any indication in his letters that he read Hebrew or spoke or read Aramaic. To judge by his writing style and the fact that the version of Jewish scripture he used was Greek, and by the apparent fact that he grew up in an urban environment in the Roman East, Paul's first language was probably Greek. (That he was from Tarsus is found only in Acts and may or may not reflect actual history.) We have no reason to suppose that he spoke or read Hebrew. Many urban Jews outside Palestine did not.

According to Acts, Paul also was known as "Saul." Paul himself never mentions that. It could be that this is also part of the author's plan in Acts to portray Paul as a pious Jew, as being from a famous city (Tarsus), as having been educated by a famous rabbi (Gamaliel), and as an apostle who began his ministry in Jerusalem and Judea, as did all the apostles and disciples. Of course, Greek-speaking Jews might have had a "Jewish" name in addition to their "Greek" name, as is sometimes the case for Jews in the United States today, but we can't say for certain that Paul did so.

Is it also to burnish Paul's image that the author of Acts makes him a Roman citizen?[9] Paul never mentions anything like this in his letters. His name, Paulus in Latin, was a good Roman name. But it probably would have been a feather in his cap when he wrote to Rome if he could claim to be a Roman citizen—and one with the added honor of having been born a citizen (see Acts 22:28), which would mean that his father had also been a citizen, though not necessarily by birth. Roman citizenship would not have been an easy thing for a Jew to come by in the early first century in the East. It could have happened if one had been enslaved to a Roman citizen and later freed, which brought citizenship with it if the manumission was done in a prescribed way. But I believe we must use caution about claiming confidently that Paul was a Roman citizen. It fits too well the tendency of the author of Acts and is never hinted at by Paul.

Another significant difference between the Acts account and that of Paul's letters lies in how they portray his conduct of his ministry in each city. According to Acts, fitting with that author's theme "to the Jew first, and then to the gentiles," Paul goes first to the synagogue in every city containing one. If there is no synagogue, he goes to whatever place Jews or "god fearers" (Acts 13:16, 26; 16:14) of the city are likely to be found (as at a riverside in Philippi; Acts 16:12–15). Repeatedly, Paul leaves the synagogue and preaches to gentiles only after his message is rejected by the majority of the Jews in a city. This is, therefore, just what happens, according to Acts, in Thessalonica. Arriving in Thessalonica, Paul, "as was his custom," attended the synagogue for three weeks, attempting to persuade the Jews that Jesus was the Messiah (Acts 17:1–3). Some were persuaded, but others became jealous of Paul's success. They attempted to attack Paul and Silas, but not finding them, they attacked others who had become believers. In fact, we are not told that Paul preached his message to gentiles in Thessalonica, or that any gentiles were converted. Paul and Silas were forced to flee to Beroea, where the pattern was repeated (Acts 17:10–15).

We get an entirely different idea of how the church began in Thessalonica from Paul's letter to the church there, written, most scholars think, not long after he first established the church there and then left. Paul never addresses Jews in 1 Thessalonians. The recipients of the letter are clearly gentiles, and only gentiles. Paul tells them, "For the people of those regions [that is, Macedonia, the area of Thessalonica itself, and Achaia, the region south of it, including Greece proper] report about us what kind of welcome we had among you, and how you turned to God from idols, to serve a living and true God, and to wait for his Son from heaven, whom he raised from the dead—Jesus, who rescues us from the wrath that is coming" (1 Thess 1:9–10). These are former polytheists: gentiles, not Jews.

Another indication is provided in 2:14: "For you, brothers, became imitators of the churches of God in Christ Jesus that are in Judea, for you suffered the same things from your own compatriots as they did from the Jews."[10] These Thessalonian "brothers" are gentiles, former idolaters, in Paul's view. Paul commends them for enduring opposition. Note that any persecution they have faced (and we have no idea of the extent or degree of it) has been at the hands not of Jews (as the account from Acts states) but from other Thessalonians, other Macedonians, "your own compatriots." We have direct contradictions, therefore, of the Acts account. We have absolutely no record of any Jews in the Thessalonian church.

In fact, Paul, by his own words, considered himself a missionary not to Jews, but to gentiles (Gal 2:2, 2:8–9). True to his word, he apparently converted only gentiles in Thessalonica. According to Acts, it was "jealous Jews" who persecuted the believers in Thessalonica, meaning that Paul and Silas had to leave quickly. To judge from 1 Thessalonians, Paul and his companions were able to remain there long enough (surely more than a bit over three weeks) to convert a number of gentiles, establish a church, and make it strong enough that it survived persecution. And those converts were persecuted not by Jews but by fellow gentiles.

We also get an idea of what Paul preached to those Greeks when he first arrived in a city—and, as we will see later, what he apparently did not teach them that we might think is important. Paul told them that (1) the God of Israel was the only "true and living God," a typical Jewish claim against Greek and Roman gods; (2) Jesus was the Son of God (in other words, the Emperor was not, nor did any others exist); (3) God was angry with the world because of its sins and practices of idolatry; (4) Jesus had been crucified and raised from the dead by God; and (5) Jesus would be returning to rescue those loyal to him from the divine wrath that was on its way soon. This seems to have been something like the kernel of Paul's basic message—quite suitable for gentiles, but not so much for Jews. The main message is a basic narrative of what God has done through Jesus and the need to reject polytheism and the traditional gods and religious practices of their own ethnic group and to believe in Jesus, who is coming soon to rescue them from the impending wrath of the God of Israel.

Paul, Apostle to the Gentiles

First Thessalonians is valuable for what it shows us, though sometimes only through hints, about Paul's ministry in what seems to have been an early period. For example, although Paul may well have been from an upper-class background—though certainly not from the highest elite class of the provinces of the Roman Empire—he tended to support himself usually not by contributions from his converts and churches but by manual labor. He reminds the Thessalonians, "You remember our labor and toil, brothers; we worked night and day, so that we might not burden any of you while we proclaimed to you the gospel of God" (1 Thess 2:9). The reference "night and day" is not an exaggeration. Manual laborers, even skilled laborers, usually had to work from dawn to dusk just to earn enough for a subsistence living for themselves and a small household. If Paul, Timothy, and Silvanus (a Latin version of the name Silas, as he is called in Acts) were going to preach, teach, and train these new converts, and yet had to work in workshops or homes all day to earn a living, they would have been working night and day.

I mentioned that I believe that Paul was not originally from the working class. This is a supposition based on a couple of observations. First, the level of Paul's literacy and knowledge demonstrates that he had a good, though not a very top, education. Literacy levels were so low in the Roman Empire of this time that it has been estimated that not more than 10 percent of people, and probably fewer, could read and write. Many people may have been able to read a bit, but not write, the two skills being quite different. Then, as always, writing required much more education than simple reading.[11] Moreover, Paul's writing shows a level of education that must have included rhetoric, and rhetorical education came at the secondary level, a level usually attained by boys only at what would be for us high school and early college. Very few people could afford to have their sons educated at that level. That Paul's education must have included a fairly advanced level of Greek education is one indication that his family was probably not expecting him to become a manual laborer.

Second, when Paul talks about his manual labor, he speaks of it not as a manual laborer would but as someone who probably didn't expect to do it. He speaks of it as humbling and degrading. Actual manual laborers tended not to speak of their work in such terms. We sometimes get a glimpse of how they thought of their labor when they mention it on a tombstone. If anything, they seem proud of it. Paul, though, portrays his taking on of manual labor as enslavement and self-lowering he engaged in for a few reasons: to enable his mission to proceed independently; to be able to appeal in his message to those of lower social status; and to provide an example for his lower-class converts to continue working.[12] Thus later in 1 Thessalonians, Paul tells these manual laborers to continue "to work with your hands, as we directed you, so that you may behave properly toward outsiders and be dependent on no one" (1 Thess 4:11–12).

Acts, in the traditional translation, tells us that Paul was a "tentmaker" (Acts 18:3; see also 20:34, where Paul is made to point out that he supported himself and his companions by his labor). There weren't a lot of large "tents" in a city, of course, and the Greek can be translated more as "leather worker" or something of the sort. It has been suggested that if Paul were such a worker, he would have made the kinds of awnings that would be plentiful in front of shops and businesses in a Mediterranean city.[13] But since this detail of the precise nature of his manual labor comes only from Acts, we should be cautious about believing it with great confidence. At any rate, Paul did take on, apparently voluntarily and intentionally, manual labor as a means of self-support, but also apparently as a strategy for his mission. Working with and among people could provide one way into their confidence and a door for persuasion. We should, therefore, imagine Paul, Silvanus, and Timothy working with their hands day after day in workshops, shops, and homes as they spread their word.

One of the messages Paul and his companions seem to have emphasized was a new sexual ethic for his converts. Paul regularly warns his followers about avoiding *porneia*. It comes up as an issue here also. First Thessalonians 4:1–8 explicitly addresses the issue, although we get no hint that Paul is here correcting misbehavior but rather warning against it. The word *porneia* is not easy to translate into English. It is, of course, the Greek word from which we derive "pornography." For most Greeks, it was just the word for sexual intercourse, or almost any sexual activity. The simplest word for "prostitute" was *pornē*, a "sex worker."

Jews, however, used the word for any and all kinds of erotic activity they considered wrong. Thus when Jews condemned porneia, they could mean fornication, adultery, any form of oral sex, homosexual sex, allowing the woman to be "on top" or penetrating a man, or a man being penetrated in any way by either a man or a woman. Most Jews seem to have included even masturbation in their condemnations of porneia. As Paul's language shows, Jews tended to link sexual immorality especially to "gentiles" and the "gentile world"—and remember, that could include many things we would not include in "fornication."

For Paul, even the experience of sexual desire and passion was something he expected from "the gentiles," and that also he tried to preclude from Christian experience, even in the experience of sex itself.[14] Thus here in 1 Thessalonians, Paul instructs these former idolaters not to have "lustful passion" even for their wives, "like the gentiles who do not know God" (4:5). Paul does not consider these people, who are certainly gentiles ethnically, actually to be "gentiles" any longer. Rather, they are members of the household of Christ, the son of the God of Israel. Thus they also, as Paul expected would be the case with good Jews, must avoid porneia completely.

This is a point at which it is important to insist that the addition of "and sisters" to Paul's text misleads. First Thessalonians 4:1–8 is clearly addressed to men, not to women. That fact requires that I provide my own translation this time, although I will concentrate only on verses 3–7:

> For this is God's will, your sanctification; keep yourselves away from porneia. Each of you should know how to control his own vessel [or "thing"] in holiness and honor, not in the passion of desire, like gentiles who do not know God. Let no one take advantage or cheat his brother in this matter, because the Lord is the avenger concerning all these things, just as we told you before and bore witness. For God did not call you to uncleanness, but in holiness.

Paul begins 3:1 by addressing the "brothers," and he seems not to be thinking of any women who may be in the church except as "vessels" for the overflow of their men's sexual needs.

Paul addresses the men, and he tells each man to "control his own thing." The Greek here is ambiguous. It could refer to the man's sexual organ, or to his wife. If it refers to the latter, however, it is shocking to see Paul refer to the women as seeming to "belong" to the men. And note that the "wrong" committed by the man is not against any woman, but against the man whose woman is the object of another's lust. Paul is concerned about men "cheating" the other men of the community. The language used is that of finances and property.

One scholar has argued that since one can find women in no part of 1 Thessalonians, there must have been no women in the community, or at least not in Paul's mind.[15] As far as we can tell, Paul never addresses women in this letter. Many people will object and point out that in Greek, as in English until recently, the word "brothers" could be taken as including women in the audience. But elsewhere in the letter, as in this passage, it is clear that Paul is addressing only the men. He does not talk to the women because he either does not believe that there are any in the church or considers them to be not quite "real" members of the church—perhaps in the way that only men could be citizens in a Greek *polis*. Even if women were in the room, they didn't "count." This suggestion is even more convincing when we notice that in his other letters Paul quite readily addresses both men and women, even by name. When Paul gives instructions to married Christians in 1 Corinthians 7, for instance, he balances his instructions to both the woman and the man, addressing each in turn. This makes his statements in 1 Thessalonians 4:1–8 stand out all the more as addressed only to the men.

So here Paul shows a traditional Jewish abhorrence of porneia, a linking of it to idolatry and the gentile world "out there," and he attempts to guard against it by insisting that the men of the church use only their own women for their sexual needs. This must have constituted one of the most important and recurring tasks Paul gave himself: to turn these "former gentiles" and idolaters into sanctified people of the God of Israel. Moreover, that meant teaching them to avoid idolatry and all sorts of behaviors Jews had traditionally associated with idolatry, including the many kinds of sexual activities they included in the category of porneia.

The *Parousia*

Up to this point in 1 Thessalonians, Paul seems to be reminding the men in this church of things he has already taught them (and remember, I am assuming that Paul takes it to be a church of men). At 4:13, however, Paul clearly turns his attention to a matter about which they need new instruction and new information. Apparently, since Paul has left Thessalonica, some members of the community have died. Those still living seem to have taken this as a surprise, and they are worried that their dead loved ones have therefore missed out on the "festivities" Paul has promised after the coming of Jesus on the clouds. In other words, Paul had apparently told them nothing about any afterlife experience or future benefits to be expected for those who die before the coming of Jesus.

Now Paul explains that the dead will not miss out on future salvation. In fact, he says that they will precede the living in meeting Jesus. "For since we believe that Jesus died and rose again, even so, through Jesus, God will bring with him those who have died. For this we declare to you by the word of the Lord, that we who are alive, who are left until the coming of the Lord, will by no means precede those who have died" (4:14–15). Paul continues with something like a timetable of events, which he apparently had not taught them before. "For the Lord himself, with a cry of command, with the archangel's call and with the sound of God's trumpet, will descend from heaven, and the dead in Christ will rise first. Then we who are alive, who are left, will be caught up in the clouds together with them to meet the Lord in the air; and so we will be with the Lord forever. Therefore encourage one another with these words" (4:16–18).[16]

From our modern point of view, it is remarkable that Paul tells them all this only now. Modern people tend to assume that Christianity, and indeed all religions, make some kind of afterlife a primary reward for being religious in the first place. The Thessalonians had certainly been promised some reward for believing in Christ. They were told they would be "rescued" from the apocalyptic wrath of God directed at idolaters and sinners. They were probably also told something about the "kingdom of God" and what their place might be in it. They may have been promised "glory." But Paul hadn't said anything about the afterlife for anyone who died in the meantime. They had become Christians without any promise, necessarily, of what would happen to them after death. Paul, therefore, gives them this description of what will happen, blow by blow, so they need not worry about their dead loved ones.

The next section of the letter returns to material Paul had already told them, so Paul introduces the topic of the sudden *parousia* (the coming or arrival of Jesus) by saying, "You do not need to have anything written to you" (5:1). Paul simply reminds them that the "day of the Lord" will be soon, will be sudden, and will occur when the rest of the world least expects it. He reminds them, however, that they should not be surprised, but ready, and thus remain faithful and live productive and moral lives.

If 1 Thessalonians really is the earliest letter from Paul we have, it provides interesting hints about how he conducted his ministry, what he typically taught to recent converts, and why he sometimes felt the need to write later with new teaching or reminders and exhortation. Paul arrived in a city and looked for Jews or gentiles who had attached themselves less formally to Judaism, people sometimes called "god fearers." Paul seems to have looked first for some place where he could work and live, and he may have attempted to connect himself and his companions to people who practiced the same trade as he did or something similar.

Mainly while working and through informal contacts—rather than preaching openly on a soapbox, as we might otherwise imagine—Paul told these Greeks and members of other ethnic groups living in Greek cities about a Jewish prophet who had been executed by the Romans but had been raised from the dead by God. Jesus Christ was expected to return with an angelic army to rescue all those who put their trust in him from the destruction that God had promised was imminent. But if Greeks joined his other followers in these new "churches," "town assemblies," as they were called, they had to reject their traditional gods, stop offering them sacrifices or anything else, including prayers, give up their traditional sexual practices, sleep chastely only with their wives, and worship only the God of Israel and Jesus, God's son and representative. If they did so, they would also share in the glory of the new, coming kingdom that was just around the corner. They would be rich and famous (the main meaning of *doxa*, often translated "glory") instead of poor manual laborers. That seems to have been Paul's method and message. To me, at any rate, it is surprising that Paul succeeded with it at all. He must have been persuasive.

He obviously was persuasive enough that in a few years he established a small network of such churches in western Asia Minor, Macedonia, and Greece. Other churches may have begun as did this one in Thessalonica: a male club of Greek-speaking gentile manual laborers, recently initiated by water into a new group that demanded adherence and loyalty to the God of the Jews and an expected Jewish king—an apocalyptic, Jewish sect of gentiles.

CHAPTER 15
Paul as Pastor: Philemon and 1 and 2 Corinthians

Overview: Philemon, 1 Corinthians, and 2 Corinthians give us several indications of how Paul attempted to manage those churches he founded. They show us his leadership styles and his pastoral practices. In Philemon, a very short letter, we see how the rather informal dynamics of a house church may have worked, with none of the institutional structures of the later church. In 1 Corinthians, Paul is concerned with controversies that have been dividing the church, most probably along social status lines. Second Corinthians shows that some of these issues seem to have been resolved, but 2 Corinthians 10–13 (probably a separate letter) presents Paul in a defensive posture, struggling to justify his position over and against the new "super-apostles" who have infiltrated the Corinthian church.

Philemon and Paul's Apostolic Authority

Philemon is the shortest of Paul's surviving letters. Paul writes it from prison, although we don't know from which city. He addresses it to a man, a woman, and another man—Philemon, Apphia, and Archippus—who may be members of one household and, indeed, the leaders of a church that meets in their house. What is more curious, as we will see later, is that although Paul is writing to ask a favor of Philemon (probably, since he is named first), Paul also addresses the letter to "the church in your house" (Philem 2). In other words, we can assume that Paul expected the letter to be read out loud in a meeting of the house church, even though Paul is actually asking only Philemon for something.

Paul's wording in the letter is ambiguous, probably intentionally so. Therefore, it is impossible to be certain even about the circumstances, much less about what exactly Paul is asking from Philemon. Most scholars believe that Onesimus was a slave of Philemon who had run away or left the household for some reason and had gone to Paul for protection. Paul is therefore pleading with Philemon on behalf of Onesimus. The main options that have often been suggested are three: (1) Paul is asking Philemon to accept Onesimus back as a slave, but without punishing him for whatever wrong he had committed, including running away (see 17–18). (2) Paul is asking Philemon to forgive Onesimus for any wrongdoing and allow Onesimus to remain with Paul to serve him while he is in prison (see 13–14). (3) Paul is asking Philemon to free Onesimus (see 16 and 21). It is impossible to know for sure which of these is the case, if any. Paul seems intentionally to veil his language in ambiguity in order not to appear to be "ordering" Philemon to do anything, but to allow Philemon to retain his own status as a leader and to act, if at all, magnanimously.

As I mentioned in Chapter 3, slaves sometimes served their owners as business managers or skilled accountants. They could travel on business for their owners or even live in other cities, managing affairs for their owners elsewhere. Onesimus may have been just such a managerial slave. Perhaps he has mismanaged a business venture or even done something dishonest with regard to Philemon's business affairs. If so, he could well have gone to Paul, knowing that Paul was an important friend of his owner, and asked Paul to intercede for him with the owner. This was not unusual in the Roman world: friends of slave owners interceded on behalf of their slaves or freedmen. That very well could explain the situation. But that is still only speculation. We have only Paul's words to go on, and they are not at all clear about the actual situation.

What is clear is Paul's skillful use of rhetoric to attempt to persuade Philemon to act without even spelling out very clearly how he wants Philemon to act. This also would not be unusual. Ancient letters were not normally sent through a postal service. They were carried by representatives from the writer to the recipient.[1] The bearers of the letter were therefore usually friends or acquaintances of the writer. They were often also expected to add oral communication to the written text; they could enlarge on the contents of the letter, explain it, add other information, and give the addressees more information about the writer and his or her wishes. We don't know who carried this letter to Philemon from Paul. It may have been Onesimus himself, since the letter reads almost like a "recommendation letter" for Onesimus, and such letters were often sent along with the person being recommended. At any rate, we may be certain that Philemon and the "church in his house" knew much better than we what Paul was really asking for.

Here is where we can see Paul's rhetorical sophistication—indeed, his attempt even to manipulate Philemon. Paul first really lays it on, stressing his close relationship with Philemon and praising him. "I have indeed received much joy and encouragement from your love, because the hearts of the saints have been refreshed through you, my brother" (7). But then Paul hints at his own authority, implying that had he wanted to, he could have "commanded" Philemon to obey (8). Paul is an "old man," a "prisoner of Christ Jesus," which, far from being shameful, as it would normally be in the ancient world, carries honor in the subculture of Christianity. Paul is clearly imitating, as an apostle, the sufferings of Christ (9). Paul again hints that he could, if he wished, "force" Philemon's compliance, but he prefers Philemon's actions to be "voluntary" (14). He hints that Philemon should treat Onesimus exactly as he would Paul himself (17). But Paul skillfully slips in a comment that Philemon owes Paul his very life, probably indicating that Paul was the one who converted Philemon (19). Paul then returns to allowing Philemon the magnanimous role as Paul's benefactor (20). Finally, Paul says that he is confident that Philemon will do even more than Paul asks, perhaps another hint at the manumission of Onesimus (21). Just before the close of the letter, Paul says that he hopes to use Philemon's guest room in a future visit (22).

The elaborate back-and-forth of different rhetorical moves is remarkable. Paul wants to communicate his superiority to Philemon as an "old man," as a witness of Christ Jesus in his sufferings, and as the one who converted Philemon and thus "saved his life." Obviously, although Paul does not use the word in this letter, he is playing the role of an apostle. But he also allows a few superior positions to Philemon: as the householder who has been the gracious host of Paul in the past and will be in the future, as a central leader and inspiration to the churches, and as the "patron" and "benefactor" to Paul's "client" status. Paul walks a very tight line between making himself a debtor to Philemon and reminding Philemon of his debts to Paul. These are all clear indicators of social status, higher and lower, and Paul manipulates them magisterially.

Even more than that, Paul seems to manipulate also the fact that this letter will be read out loud in a gathering of the house church, and not privately by Philemon himself. The second-person possessive pronoun in Greek translated at the beginning ("to the church in *your* house"; 2) is singular, probably indicating that Paul is here addressing Philemon directly as the host of the church. But the second-person pronoun in verse 3 is plural, indicating that here Paul addresses the entire church: "Grace to *you* [plural] and peace from God our father and the Lord Jesus Christ" (3). From that point until the very last word of the very last verse, however, all the occurrences of "you" are singular, whether they are pronouns or other grammatical forms. Also, the addressee is consistently called "brother" (7, 20). Finally, though, the last sentence is again addressed to the whole church, and in the Greek, the very last word of the letter is the plural "your": "The grace of the Lord Jesus Christ be with *your* [plural] spirit" (25).

In other words, Paul frames all his requests to Philemon in the larger rhetorical context of an address to the whole house church. He knows the letter will be read aloud in the whole church, probably by his emissary who can also then serve as a commentator on it. I have no doubt that this was part of Paul's strategy to get more than he was explicitly asking for. We must imagine the social makeup of the church. It did contain a few people of higher social status, including someone with enough resources to have a house large enough to accommodate the gathering of the church in some larger room. That householder obviously had slaves, which, though not necessarily indicating that he was rich, does suggest that he was not of the lowest class. But there are obviously other people in the house church who are from the lower class. There are probably other slaves and freedpersons in the church, as we can tell was the case in other churches of Paul. And there were probably manual laborers living at only a subsistence level. In fact, doubtless the majority of the members of the church were very poor people: slaves, freedpersons, and free persons living in poverty.

Thus we may wonder whether the fact that most of the people in the church were more like Onesimus than Philemon would have anything to do with how Paul's letter was heard in church. Would Paul's requests for leniency, and perhaps even manumission, for Onesimus have a better chance if they were read out loud in a gathering of mainly lower-class persons?

Would Philemon have felt any social pressure to be more magnanimous than Paul explicitly asked him to be if he heard Paul's words while sitting among the entire house church, with many members just at the poverty line? It is intriguing to imagine.

The letter is also a clear indicator that the church, the Christian movement, has attained nowhere near the institutional development it will achieve even in the second century, much less the fourth and fifth centuries. There are no "priests" with clearly ordained positions of authority. There are no bishops or even deacons in any kind of official position. Even Paul's authority is more a "charismatic" one, in which he must carefully employ rhetoric to get his way. If he makes an "order" at all, it must be as an imprisoned apostle who was given authority by a revelation from Christ he received privately, not by any official action of the church as an institution. Paul says that he could command Philemon to do as he wishes, but there was no institutional structure to back him up if Philemon refused. So Paul must exercise leadership carefully and through persuasion rather than through the kinds of institutional offices and structures that will develop later. The Letter to Philemon shows Paul doing precisely that as best he could. It would be fascinating to know, although we cannot, how the drama played out.

First Corinthians

Paul's correspondence with the church he founded in Corinth also shows him attempting to bring order to a potentially chaotic and divided church—and to do so without the benefit of institutional backing or authority.[2] If 1 Thessalonians showed us a church in infancy, the Corinthian letters show us one in adolescence. Here is a church that has been around for a while, long enough for factions to develop. As I will demonstrate, it likely contained people of different social statuses, with a minority of people enjoying at least a bit of financial and social stability among a majority who were certainly from the lower class. It contained slaves and freedpersons as well as free people, perhaps even some Roman citizens. That there are several issues about which the Corinthians are divided shows a church beyond its beginnings and attempting to come to terms with disagreements about how to live this new life.

A comparison with the church in Thessalonica can be clearly made by analyzing 1 Corinthians 15, in which Paul faces essentially the same problem as he did in 1 Thessalonians: What happens to Christians after death? In what form will Christians enjoy an afterlife? Whereas Paul apparently had not told the Thessalonian converts much of anything about that issue, and thus they were dismayed when members of their church suddenly died before the *parousia*, Paul has obviously taught the Corinthians about the Christian hope (shared with many Jews, of course) of the resurrection of the body. The problem that has arisen at Corinth, however, is not whether there will be an afterlife existence for Christians, but what its precise form will be.

This is made clear by Paul's rhetorical questions that no doubt echo some of the Corinthians themselves: "How are the dead raised? With what kind of body do they come?" (1 Cor 15:35). Although Paul has spent much time up to this point in the chapter arguing simply for the resurrection, this verse indicates that the central issue has not been a Corinthian denial of the afterlife itself. They may very well have believed in the immortality of the soul, a doctrine that would be much more in line with philosophical Greek ideas. What these Corinthian skeptics were questioning was the resurrection of the body, a skepticism that would be completely understandable in a Greek context informed by any amount of Greek philosophy or learning.

Greek philosophy of many different schools would have long ago pointed out that the human body is made of changeable, malleable matter. Anyone could see that bodies buried in the ground fairly quickly rotted, and that the flesh and even the bones eventually turned into other kinds of matter. How would a resurrected body even be able to exist with all the flesh and organs rotted away? And what of those bodies lost at sea and devoured by fish? The matter of those bodies would have become assimilated to the matter of the fish, which would have been eaten by other fish that perhaps then were eaten by human beings. The different pieces of matter, the "atoms" or whatever fundamental substances made up the body, would have been absorbed and assimilated to new bodies and new chunks of matter. When Greeks mocked the notion of the resurrection of the body—which they did when they heard about it in the second century and later—they raised precisely these kinds of questions. It just seemed obvious, especially to any educated Greek, that any notion of a resurrection of bodies was crass and ridiculous, a notion not worthy of belief for anyone with the least amount of education.

Thus in 1 Corinthians 15, Paul defends not just the Christian preaching of the afterlife, but the specific doctrine of the resurrection of the body. The way he does so shows that he is sensitive to ideas that the matter of the universe is constructed on a cosmic and material hierarchy, and that any body that could be resurrected must not be constituted of the crass flesh and blood of current human bodies. He argues, therefore, for a transformation of the flesh-and-blood body into a "pneumatic body," a body composed not of flesh and blood but of the higher substance of *pneuma*, a word that is often translated "spirit," but that in the ancient Greek world referred to a rarefied "stuff" that made up the substance of air and breath. Pneuma was the refined material substance that gave life and thought to human beings. Paul constructs an elaborate argument to demonstrate that the resurrected body he has preached will be able to be "raised" and live eternally, but only because it will be composed not of flesh and blood but of pneuma.

Paul constructs this argument by first arguing that any resurrected body will not be exactly the same constructed body that is buried in the ground. It will be a transformed body, the way a flower has continuity with the seed but doesn't look anything like the seed that was buried (15:36–37). In the same way, God has given different kinds of "bodies" to different beings at different locations in the hierarchy of the cosmos. There are different "fleshes" for human beings, animals, birds, and fish (15:39). Paul and his audience would have recognized this list as a descending hierarchy. Paul then changes his term from "flesh" to "body" because the next hierarchy he lists is of bodies that are not fleshly bodies, but bodies nonetheless: sun, moon, and stars, with even the stars having different levels of "glory" in their bodies (15:40–41).

In the same way, the human body that will be buried ("sown") is perishable, in dishonor, in weakness. The body that will be raised will be imperishable and will be raised in glory and power (15:42–43). For the next verses, though, I must question the translations provided by the NRSV and just about all other English Bibles. The NRSV says that the human body is sown a "physical body" and raised a "spiritual body" (15:44). It later says that "it is not the spiritual that is first, but the physical, and then the spiritual" (15:46). This is an inaccurate and misleading translation. The word translated here as "physical" is not the one derived from the Greek word for "physical" or "natural" (*physis*, nature). It is the word more regularly translated as "soul" or "life" (*psychē*, or the adjective *psychikos*). Paul is not making a distinction of material versus immaterial here, but one between a body that is "merely alive," that is, in a normal, "natural" state, and a body that has been miraculously transformed into one entirely composed of the material of pneuma.

According to ancient Greek notions, including quite scientific and philosophical ones, the stuff that races through human bodies to cause movement to limbs, to cause pain to be felt, and to give the power of both life and thought was pneuma. It was not, though, an "immaterial substance," as modern theology would say, but a very refined form of matter itself. It was refined air or breath. It was something like our concept of oxygen, or even electricity. But it was "stuff."

That will be for Paul the "stuff" of the transformed and resurrected body. That is why he says explicitly, agreeing with his more "sophisticated" hearers who had objected to their own notion of a resurrected body of flesh and blood: "Flesh and blood is not able to inherit the kingdom of God; the mortal is not able to inherit immortality" (15:50). Paul admits that flesh and blood are mortal and cannot last into eternity. But God takes care of that problem by transforming the flesh and blood body into a body made of pneuma, something, we may imagine, like a body made completely of oxygen or electricity, an "electric body." And this was a kind of "body" that even educated Greeks might be persuaded to accept as being raised and "inheriting the kingdom of God."[3]

This controversy and Paul's attempted solution to it (we don't know whether he convinced everyone in Corinth, as we will see later) suggest that the Corinthian church may have been split along social class lines. People with little exposure to Greek education would probably have had no trouble accepting a belief in resurrected bodies. After all, Greek myths and tales also sometimes told about dead bodies coming back to life and walking around, and ghosts were considered embodied in some sense. But more educated Greeks scoffed at such stories. It was therefore quite probably those more educated converts who had doubted any teaching about a resurrected body. Paul's redefinition of what would constitute the substance of a resurrected body would have gone a long way toward allaying philosophical objections. I take it that this issue and how it seems to have divided the church are also some indications that the different issues addressed in 1 Corinthians seem to have divided the church along the lines of higher versus lower social classes, as I will illustrate with other examples.

The Historical and Social Context of the Church in Corinth

Corinth was an important and relatively wealthy city in the first century. The ancient city sat right at the narrow strip of land, the isthmus, that connected Achaia, the Greek area just to its north, and the Peloponnese, the large peninsula of southern Greece. All overland trade had to pass through this city and the surrounding land it controlled. The isthmus also stood between the Corinthian Gulf and the Saronic Gulf. To avoid shipping and traveling all around the coast of southern Greece, a long and dangerous trip, goods were carried overland from one gulf to the other, traversing the Isthmus of Corinth. Lying thus right at this narrow crossroads of trade and travel—both north to south and east to west—Corinth had always been an important city.

In 146 B.C.E., Corinth was sacked and destroyed after a battle with the Romans. Julius Caesar refounded the city as a Roman colony in 44 B.C.E. and gave it a Latin, Roman name. It seems that veterans and Roman freedmen settled there, and Latin was the language found on most inscriptions until the time of the emperor Hadrian (117–138 C.E.). At the time of the founding of the church in Corinth, it was a bustling, important city with people from many lands and ethnic groups, and with a long Greek history and now a Roman upper-class veneer.

Paul writes to the church in Corinth from Ephesus (1 Cor 16:8). This is not the first letter Paul has sent to the church. He mentions a previous one in 1 Corinthians 5:9, which we unfortunately do not possess. At the time of writing of 1 Corinthians, in any case, the church seems now to be made up of at least two different house churches. Paul has heard news of the church there from different sources. One of those he calls "Chloe's people" (1:11). The Greek suggests that these are people who belong to the household of a woman named Chloe. The term could include free "clients" of Chloe (even if they were not legally so under Roman law), but it more likely means that these were slaves and freedpersons. As I have noted, both slaves and freedpersons could travel and conduct business for an owner, and that seems to be what is going on here. Paul does not say that Chloe herself is a member of the church, but I think that since he mentions her name at all, she probably is. Thus one of Paul's sources of information is members of the household of a woman. Having a household like this, probably with slaves and freed "clients," would indicate that Chloe is likely of higher status than most people of the society, although it need not mean she is among the true elite or wealthy of the city.

In 1 Corinthians 7:1, Paul mentions at least one letter he has received from the Corinthians, or perhaps from just one of their factions: "Now concerning the matters about which you wrote." Paul introduces several of the following topics he will address with this same opening, "Now concerning," and it may be that this is a list of issues brought up in that letter. Toward the end of 1 Corinthians, Paul expresses joy that three men from the church in Corinth have come to visit him in Ephesus: Stephanas, Fortunatus, and Achaicus (16:17). Their names are interesting. Stephanas is a regular Greek name, meaning "crown." Achaicus would have meant "someone from Achaia" (probably taken by Paul to be much of central Greece; see 1 Cor 16:15). The name Fortunatus, though, is Latin, and means something like "lucky." It would not be surprising if he was a freedman of a Roman and thus had been given the kind of name one might give a slave. If he was a freedman of a Roman citizen, he might now have enjoyed Roman citizenship. These three men may have been the ones who brought the letter to Paul from Corinth. Whether or not that is so, they obviously were another source of information.

Then Paul mentions "our brother Apollos" (1 Cor 16:12) as being with him in Ephesus at the time. Paul had even asked Apollos to go to Corinth, but he had refused for the time being. We know, though, not only from Acts but also from 1 Corinthians 1:12 and elsewhere in the letter that Apollos was considered a central figure among the Christians at Corinth, and thus he may have sometimes also provided Paul with information about the church there. Paul clearly, though, treats Apollos more as an equal than as his assistant, as he seems to treat Timothy (see 16:10).

Of Stephanas, Paul also says that the members of his household were the "first converts in Achaia" (16:15). I take this to indicate that one of the house churches in Corinth met in the home of Stephanas. If Chloe is also a member of the church, perhaps another met in her home. If, as seems to be the case, there were a few different house churches, all considered by themselves and Paul to be the general "church in Corinth," that could explain how easily the church became so divided over so many different issues.

Following other scholars, I have argued that on most of these issues, the church was split along lines of social class and status, with those of lower status and no education taking one side of many of the issues, and those of higher status, with some education, and their dependents and associates taking the other side.[4] That the church in Corinth included both higher-status and lower-status people seems clear even from the beginning, where Paul says, "Consider your call, brothers; not many of you were wise by human standards, not many were powerful, not many were of noble birth" (1 Cor 1:26). This line has sometimes been taken to support the rather Hollywood and popular idea that early Christians were all from the lower classes: slaves, peasants, and poor people. But many scholars point out that Paul says "not many," implying that at least there were some Corinthian Christians who precisely were "wise," "powerful," and of "noble birth."

The term "wise" here does not mean simply inherent smarts or wisdom. It indicates education, probably rhetorical education, which meant training at least to the secondary level. "Noble birth" should not be taken literally here to mean actual aristocracy. It is almost certain that none of the earliest Christians were from any of the older "aristocratic" families of either Greece or Rome. The term probably means for Paul simply people born into well-heeled local families of Corinth, or perhaps those whose father was a Roman citizen at the time of their birth, making them Roman citizens as well. But these words indicate that a small minority of the Corinthian Christians were not of the lowest social strata of the city.

We are so accustomed to reading the New Testament as saying something only about theology that scholars have, until recently, mostly ignored this kind of indication of the social realities experienced by the first Christians. But 1 Corinthians, especially in the past thirty years or so, has served as a mine of information about the social history of the first churches. And most scholars have come to believe that many of these churches were not necessarily homogeneous in social status level and class. I have argued extensively elsewhere that conflicts that appear to us to have been theological were also about social conflict and social power.[5] Although I cannot demonstrate here how that reading would work for all of 1 Corinthians, I provide a few examples.

Issues of Controversy in the Corinthian Church

The letter Paul writes to the church in Corinth addresses several different issues, far too many for me to discuss in this chapter. The different Christians, perhaps even different house churches, are claiming their "favorite" apostles: Paul, Apollos, or Cephas; some are just claiming to be "special" followers of Christ (1 Cor 1:11–12, 3:1–9, 4:6–7). Some of the Corinthians especially value "wisdom" and "speech," referring to philosophy and rhetoric (2:1–13). One man is sleeping with his stepmother, and apparently at least some of the Corinthians are not inclined to care (5:1–2). At least one other man seems to be taking another Christian, or Christians, to court and suing him or them (6:1–8). Some of the men are using prostitutes (6:12–20). Others have questions about marriage and sex: should, or even may, Christians abstain from sex with their spouses (chapter 7)? Some Christians have no objections to eating food that has previously been offered to an idol, while others are worried about the practice (8:1–11:1). There is a controversy about women praying and prophesying in church (11:2–16). There is much division over the Lord's Supper (11:17–34) and over "speaking in tongues" (chapters 12–14). And we have already seen how Paul deals with a church divided over the issue of the resurrection.

To begin, let's analyze the conflict over the Lord's Supper and Paul's attempts to solve the problem. Ancient dinner parties were generally conducted in ways that emphasized social status differences. Those of higher status could expect to be given better seats, closer to the head of the table. Different kinds of food and a different quality of wine would be served to different groups of people: the "friends" of the host, those more his "equals," might be served better dishes and wine, the "clients" of the host something else, and those even further down the social pyramid would get food and drink of still worse quality. None of this was considered even remarkable to most people of a Greek or Roman city. They expected it.

This seems to be something of what is happening in Corinth. First, we must understand that the Lord's Supper in the beginning of the Christian movement was not the sharing of only a tiny morsel of bread and a sip of wine. We can tell from what Paul says in 1 Corinthians 11:17–34 that it was a full meal, in the midst of which, perhaps, the "words of institution" from Jesus would be quoted and some prayers offered, followed by the distribution and sharing of bread and wine. But that ritual was surrounded with a full meal that seems to have been something of a potluck, or at least with the richer Christians expected to provide most of the food and drink.

Thus Paul complains that different groups in Corinth, even when the church is gathered for the Lord's Supper, are eating and drinking their own, private dinners: "Each of you goes ahead with your own supper, and one goes hungry and another becomes drunk" (11:21). Those not having enough food are not only "going hungry"; they are also thereby being humiliated (11:22). It is easy, once we know how ancient dinner parties were experienced, to imagine what was happening.

Most laborers in an ancient city, both working slaves and other manual and skilled laborers, owed their full days to their employers. Most of the time, they could not have attended a church meeting until the sun went down unless it happened to fall on a holiday. Paul is describing a situation, therefore, where the wealthier Christians, who enjoyed more leisure and freedom, were arriving early at the church meeting. They also likely brought food and drink for themselves, their households, and their friends. The poorer people, unless they were members of the household of a richer church member, were arriving late at the meetings, after others had begun to eat and were even tipsy. One of Paul's solutions to the problem, therefore, is simply to tell those who are able to arrive early to "wait for" the rest (11:33).

Moreover, those members of higher status must be the ones Paul is especially addressing with his rebukes. After all, if Paul asked the poorer members, "Do you not have houses to eat and drink in?" (11:22; I have altered the NRSV "homes" to "houses" as better reflecting the Greek and the context), most of the poorer members would have had to say no. They slept perhaps in the hallway upstairs from a shop where they worked, or with many other people in a crowded tenement, or some similar place. Most of them did not have their own houses.

Paul's main objection to the way the Corinthians are observing the Lord's Supper is that they are doing so divided by class and privilege. The haves are ignoring or despising the have-nots. So when Paul says that they must "discern the body" before they eat and drink, he is not referring primarily to the host of the body of Jesus in the bread. Rather, he is referring to the entire church as the "body of Christ," as he terms it elsewhere in 1 Corinthians (for example, 6:15–20, 12:12–31). Paul says that those who have been slighting and humiliating the poor by showing no concern for their desire to eat and drink have thereby been despising the body of Christ himself.

It is not likely that the haves saw things this way at all. They were, after all, behaving just as people were expected to behave in their society. Those of higher status enjoyed the privileges of higher status. It had always been so. The poor should be satisfied that they got anything at all. They should not expect to be "equal." Paul is therefore turning the status expectations of the Greek city—or at least those of its upper-class members—on their heads. He insists that the have-nots be treated with special regard and honor, precisely because God himself "chose what is low and despised in the world, things that are not, to reduce to nothing the things that are" (1 Cor 1:28).

Paul follows precisely the same strategy in dealing with the problem of eating food sacrificed to idols. Meat was a precious and rare commodity in an ancient city. Most people could not afford to buy it in the market. The main time they would eat meat would be at a sacrificial festival provided either by the city or more often by a wealthy individual who paid for the festival and its expenses out of his own pocket in return for the honor he and his family would then gain. The sacrifices would be made, some of the materials would be burned for the god, some would be given to the priests or other officials of the cult, and then the rest would be distributed to the people for their own feasting with their families and friends. But of course, any participation in these activities was precisely what Jews and early Christians considered idolatry.

The poor Christians at Corinth would have had to attend a sacrificial setting in order to eat meat, and it would have been meat that had been sacrificed to a deity. The more "superstitious" Christians, no doubt, probably believed that the god, perhaps in the form of a "demon," could have "possessed" the meat, and that by eating it, they could endanger themselves with demonic possession. They did believe, in at least some contexts and in some sense, that when they ate the "body and blood" of Christ in the Lord's Supper, they were ingesting Christ himself. Why wouldn't a similar process take place if they ate the sacrificial foods of Apollo or Aphrodite, two of the most important and powerful gods of Corinth?

Even meat sold in a marketplace likely would have come from some kind of sacrificial practice. The officials or priests who were given portions of the sacrificed animal—often choice portions—had the liberty of making a bit of money by selling their portions to a butcher, who would then process the meat and resell it to people. In other words, unless one were rich enough to buy an animal and have it butchered and prepared, one could scarcely avoid eating meat that had been part of a sacrifice. The poor could hardly do so if they ate meat at all.

So this topic was dividing the church at Corinth. Some people were pointing out that "all of us possess knowledge." That is, we who have some learning know that the idols are not real gods, or even demons. They are "nothings." There is only one God, and one Lord Jesus Christ (8:1–6). Food is just food. Eating will not bring us closer to any god, nor will avoiding food help us (8:8).

Paul responds rather lengthily (chapters 8–10) by basically agreeing with these Christians who say they "know" what realities will or will not harm them. Paul agrees that if someone has the proper "knowledge," then eating meat that has been sacrificed to idols will not harm that person. But Paul believes that if a person without that "knowledge" eats such meat, it may well harm that person, or at least his "conscience" (10:27–33). The Corinthian Christians should, Paul says, alter their behavior, again, out of deference for the good of the other person. If my eating meat harms my brother or sister, I should refrain, at least when I'm in their presence.

But note how this issue also seems to have status relevance, which becomes obvious only when we know the social realities of ancient practices of meat eating and ancient philosophical teachings about the realities of gods. Those exposed to ancient intellectual culture would have learned that it was "superstitious" to believe that gods or demons caused disease and harmed people. If you were not a Jew or Christian, but were somewhat educated, you might well have believed that gods and demons did exist, but they were benign beings, and they would never harm people. If you were someone who had become a Christian, but still had the advantage of some education, you would probably have come to the conclusion that the gods and demons simply didn't exist and that there was "only one God." In any case, the slogans Paul quotes in this context sound like slogans familiar to us from contemporary popular philosophy, often associated with Cynics or Stoics: "All of us possess knowledge"; "All things are lawful for the free man" (8:1; see also 10:23).

Several scholars therefore have pointed to the debate over food offered to idols as one issue that divided the church along the lines of social status. Those more likely to boast of their "knowledge" were those better-off Christians; and their slogans Paul quotes back to them sound like slogans of contemporary philosophy, which they were not likely to have picked up if they were members of the poor working class. Moreover, those people probably most afraid of the gods and demons surrounding them were those who had had little exposure to ancient philosophy, which had taught for centuries that such fears were "superstitious."[6]

Again, therefore, Paul meets the higher-status Christians part way. He agrees with them that they are right in their "knowledge," and that he shares it. But he wants them, nonetheless, to modify their behavior for the sake of those less well-off Christians who may be more tempted to eat meat sacrificed to idols because that would be the only meat they would likely be able to get. They lack the "knowledge" necessary to protect their fragile, weak consciences, but they may face even more temptations to eat sacrificial meat. Paul again attempts to modify the behavior of the "strong" to accommodate the problems faced by the "weak."[7]

Throughout 1 Corinthians, Paul attempts to bring unity to a divided church. In fact, 1 Corinthians may be called a *homonoia* letter.[8] The word means "concord" or "harmony," and the term denotes a genre of political and public speeches common in the Greek and Roman worlds. Although 1 Corinthians is a letter rather than a speech, it contains many of the commonplaces of such speeches on unity. The glaring exception to the rest of the genre that Paul's homonoia letter makes is his use of status-role reversal as the strategy for promoting unity. Just about all such speeches we have from the ancient world urge unity by insisting that those of lower social status remain contentedly in their place. The rich should remain rich without oppressing the poor, and the poor should remain poor without seething with jealousy of the rich. Hierarchy maintenance is the hallmark of ancient homonoia speeches.

Paul's strategy in 1 Corinthians goes directly against that tide. Once we know about other such speeches and letters, we can recognize how odd it would have seemed for Paul to urge unity by advocating a reversal of normal statuses. Paul asks those of higher status to give up their own interests and privileges for the sake of those Christians of lower status. Following the logic of Paul's "crucified Messiah," the world is turned upside down in order to maintain the unity of the body of Christ.

Second Corinthians

It is impossible to gauge fully how successful 1 Corinthians was, but we do have later correspondence in the form of 2 Corinthians. With a brief look at that document, we can make guesses about what happened next.

What is now called 2 Corinthians in our Bibles is almost certainly a later edited document containing fragments of what were previously at least two different letters, and some would argue as many as four or five. Some scholars believe that chapters 8 and 9 were originally two different letters related to the collection of funds Paul was taking up from his various Gentile churches to take to the church in Jerusalem. That may be true, although if I were pressed, I would argue that 2 Corinthians 1–9 may be read as one letter. It seems to me certain, however, that 2 Corinthians 10–13 must have originally belonged to a different letter and different circumstances entirely.

Paul does not bring up most of the issues that had occupied him in 1 Corinthians. Perhaps his argument for the resurrection of the body, to cite only one issue, was successful after all. The main issue dealt with in the different parts of 2 Corinthians is not so much any particular theological topic as it is the relationship between Paul and the church itself. There had obviously been a huge blowup, with Paul visiting the church only to be humiliated and possibly experiencing a painful break with an individual or part of the church (2 Cor 2:5–6; and for the "painful visit," 2:1, 7:2). At some point, Paul wrote the members of the church what he calls a "letter of tears" (2:4, 7:8). But chapters 1–7 seem to reflect a time when Paul and at least most of the church have reconciled.

Some scholars believe that 2 Corinthians 10–13 is precisely the "letter of tears" Paul mentions in 2:4 and 7:8. If so, chapters 10–13 would be from a letter Paul wrote before later reconciling with the church and then sending chapters 1–7. This hypothesis is not without merit precisely because the tone of 2 Corinthians 10–13 is so radically different from that in the rest of 2 Corinthians. Apparently a group of Jews (see 11:22) calling themselves apostles, but whom Paul sarcastically calls "superapostles" (2 Cor 11:5), had arrived in

Corinth. They must have emphasized their own power, rhetorical sophistication, and perhaps even miracle working. They denigrated Paul, claiming that he was "strong in his letters" but weak in his "bodily presence" (10:10). This is doubtless a criticism of Paul's speaking style. We have seen that Paul does show sophisticated use of Greek rhetoric in his letters. Scholars, therefore, have guessed that perhaps Paul had some kind of physical disfigurement, illness, or bodily weakness that made his personal presence, and therefore his public speaking, much less powerful than his writing.

There must be some truth in the criticism because Paul cannot simply refute it directly. He mounts a complicated defense of himself, emphasizing that he is truly an apostle—in fact, *the* apostle for the Corinthians. He insists that he was the founder of the Corinthian church and that these others are interlopers (10:14–18). He boasts, but only of the hardships and humiliations he has endured, which he turns into a sign of his true apostleship (11:7–33). He relates a revelation and a trip to the third heaven he was given "in Christ" (12:1–7). He even mentions a "thorn in the flesh" given him by God to keep him humble (12:7–9; a reference to a physical malady or deformity?). He admits that he "humbled" himself before the Corinthians, but that should not be taken as proof of his weakness as much as evidence that God works power through weakness (12:9–10). He threatens the "superapostles" and even members of the church that they will soon enough experience his "power" if they are not careful (13:2–3). But Paul also emphasizes his love for the Corinthians and his commitment to them, begging them, even while threatening, not to break off their special relationship with him or to allow others to take his place (11:11, 12:15).

This is Paul in a completely different mood. Chapters 10–13 of 2 Corinthians show Paul having to defend himself against charges that he is uneducated, weak, and powerless, and therefore not much of an apostle. It seems obvious to most scholars that these chapters cannot originally have been part of the same letter as 2 Corinthians 1–9, if those chapters are themselves a unity, which is also debated. Whether 2 Corinthians 10–13 was the "tearful letter" mentioned elsewhere in 2 Corinthians, or whether it was a later letter still, when relations between Paul and the Corinthians had once again deteriorated, we cannot know for certain. If 2 Corinthians 10–13 was the "tearful letter," then apparently it worked, Paul and the Corinthians reconciled, and they chose Paul over the "superapostles" after all. If 2 Corinthians 10–13 is to be dated after the rest of 2 Corinthians, it suggests further conflicts, and we do not know whether Paul's blazing defense worked in the end.

We do have a reference to the Corinthian church much later (the late 90s or thereabouts) in a letter known now as *1 Clement*, which is itself another homonoia letter, this time claiming to be from the church in Rome to the Corinthian church, but dealing with what is apparently a new series of conflicts and schisms. It provides no real evidence for what followed the exchange of letters between Paul and the Corinthians. We may suppose that Paul's rhetoric and skill (not to mention wonder-working and power) succeeded, but we cannot know for sure. The series of correspondence that now makes up the First and Second Letters of Paul to the Corinthians, in any case, provides fascinating glimpses of this powerful apostle and his attempts to be a successful pastor.

CHAPTER 16

Paul as Jewish Theologian: Galatians and Romans

Overview: The apostle Paul's description of the Jewish law in his letter to the Galatians ends up sounding very negative. Paul is careful to nuance this position, however, in his letter to the Romans. In Romans, it seems that Paul is defending himself against charges of being antinomian (opposed to law itself). Perhaps Paul treads carefully in order to ensure that his deliverance of a donation to the Jerusalem church from the gentile churches is received in a spirit of church unity.

Paul on Jewish Law in Galatians

Paul founded several house churches, probably small ones, in the area of Galatia. Although there is some uncertainty about exactly what region Paul means by "Galatia," it is certainly a region in what is now central Turkey, between what is now the modern city of Ancyra and Cappadocia. It was called "Galatia" because at some time the ethnic tribes known as the "Gauls" lived there. At the time Paul was writing, the Gauls occupied western and northern regions of Europe. Julius Caesar, for instance, had fought them in what is now France in the previous century. Ancestors of those Gauls, though, had moved as far east as Asia Minor, and thus this region was named for them. Paul's letter "to the Galatians," therefore, is apparently not addressed to just one church or town, but to several churches in the region.

After establishing those churches, Paul moved on. Another group of traveling Christian preachers, probably though not certainly Jews, must have arrived later, bearing their own version of the gospel and promoting it as a better one than Paul's. They must have pointed out to the Galatian converts—who were all gentiles and former idolaters—that since they now worshiped the God of Israel, prayed to a Jewish messiah, and counted themselves even as children of Abraham, the father of the Jews, they should go "all the way" and follow Jewish law also. As I pointed out in Chapter 10 on Acts, everyone knew that different ethnic groups had their own laws. If the Galatians had given up the gods and customs of their previous ethnic group and taken on those of "Israel," they should also follow Jewish law.

These other teachers no doubt pointed out that Abraham had been chosen by God, and that the promises to Abraham were made also to his descendants. But the covenant God made with Abraham was sealed with circumcision. Since the Galatian Christians now counted themselves among those descendants of Abraham, their men naturally should circumcise themselves also. All true "sons of Abraham" were circumcised. These teachers apparently told the Galatians that Paul had given them some good information, and that their baptism, probably by him or his companions, was certainly valid. But their full inclusion in the family of Abraham, Christ, and God could be completed only by becoming observers of the law of Moses. Or at least they told them that being circumcised was a necessary step toward full membership in the family. This is all perfectly natural reasoning, and we can easily imagine how the Galatians would have found the arguments compelling.

The traveling preachers of circumcision apparently informed the Galatians that Paul was certainly a good fellow, but that he was not actually one of the "real" apostles. The "pillars of the church" in Jerusalem were men who had been Jesus' disciples during his lifetime and had continued nurturing the community after Jesus' death. Who could be closer to Jesus than Peter, John, and James, the very brother of the Lord? The traveling preachers insisted that they, rather than Paul, were the true representatives of the Jerusalem leadership, and what they were offering was a legitimate supplement to Paul's gospel, which had gotten the Galatians started, but not fully "up to speed." Paul perhaps was an apostle of sorts, but a secondary one who had received even his gospel from the Jerusalem "pillars."

Once Paul gets wind of all this, he goes ballistic. We have no other letter from Paul in which the writing is as white-hot as that in Galatians. Unlike Paul's other letters, he does not begin this one with a thanksgiving, with compliments, or with assurances of love and solidarity. Rather, he begins in anger and disbelief: "I am astonished that you are so quickly deserting the one who called you in the grace of Christ and are turning to a different gospel!" Throughout Galatians, Paul writes as if he is spitting the words out.

As we saw in Chapter 5, the first part of Galatians consists of Paul telling how he was called by Christ and given his apostolic commission. Throughout that narrative, Paul insists that he got his gospel not from Peter, John, James, or anyone else, but directly from a revelation from Christ. He insists that he had long been serving as an apostle, preaching his gospel, before he ever even visited the others in Jerusalem. Paul insists so much on his independence from Peter, James, and every "pillar of the church" in Jerusalem and Judea in order to undermine any accusation that he got his message from Jerusalem. Paul tells of the meetings he later had in Jerusalem only to insist that even those Jewish leaders in Jerusalem agreed with him that gentiles need not be circumcised or keep Jewish law in order to be full members in good standing in the church. Much of the beginning of Galatians is taken up with Paul's defense of himself and his message by citing his own history.

But much of the rest of the letter consists of Paul's attempt to explain to the Galatians what the role of the Jewish law has been in history and what it should be for them. Here, Paul begins to sound very radical, at least when we remember that he was still a Jew and that he had earlier been a zealous advocate of law observance and circumcision. Paul notes that he said at one point to Peter, "We ourselves are Jews by birth and not gentile sinners" (Gal 2:15). As I have indicated already, the term "gentile sinners" was practically a redundancy for Jews like Paul. So although Paul was the apostle to the gentiles and founded churches of gentiles, he still uses the term "gentile sinners" as if the two words are synonymous.

Then Paul continues:

> Yet we know that a person is justified not by the works of the law but through faith in Jesus Christ. And we have come to believe in Jesus Christ, so that we might be justified by faith in Christ, and not by doing the works of the law, because no one will be justified by the works of the law. But if, in our effort to be justified in

> Christ, we ourselves have been found to be sinners, is Christ then a servant of sin? Certainly not! But if I build up again the very things that I once tore down, then I demonstrate that I am a transgressor. For through the law I died to the law, so that I might live to God. I have been crucified with Christ; and it is no longer I who live, but it is Christ who lives in me. And the life I now live in the flesh I live by faith in the Son of God, who loved me and gave himself for me. I do not nullify the grace of God; for if justification comes through the law, then Christ died for nothing. (Gal 2:16–21)

That is a pretty stark statement: if the law has anything at all to do with your justification, Christ died for no reason.

Later, Paul again drives a wedge between the law and faith: "The Law does not rest on faith; on the contrary, 'Whoever does the works of the law will live by them'" (3:12, quoting Lev 18:5). This division between faith and law would have sounded crazy to a Jew, as it still does for many Jews today. Most Jews would assume that the Jewish customs and laws were a sign of their faith, not the opposite of it. They kept kosher to live out their covenant with God and their faith in his trustworthiness. The opposition of faith to the law may sound natural to people today: even non-Christians are usually familiar with the Protestant commonplaces of "faith versus law" or "grace versus works." So perhaps we should remind ourselves how strange it would have sounded to any Jew in Paul's day to say that one must have either faith or works of law, and that no one could have both.

Paul goes on to say, "Brothers, I give an example from daily life: once a person's will has been ratified, no one adds to it or annuls it. Now the promises were made to Abraham and to his offspring; it does not say, 'And to offsprings,' as of many; but it says, 'And to your offspring,' that is, to one person, who is Christ" (3:15–16).[1] Paul is conducting a bit of fancy footwork in his exegesis. The Greek word translated here as "offspring" could also be translated "seed." Paul is insisting that the quotation of the promise in the singular must mean that the reference is not to the Jews, because that would necessitate the plural "seeds." The alternative Paul offers is that "offspring" must refer to Christ, the singular seed of Abraham. Anyone who is "in Christ" is also "in" the "seed of Abraham," including the Galatian gentiles.

Paul then points out that the law of Moses came about some 430 years after the covenant with Abraham (3:17–18). If observation of the law is what will supply "the inheritance" of Abraham, then how is it that the law did not arrive until long after the covenant was actually made? The law, therefore, must be, according to Paul's reasoning, irrelevant to the covenant of Abraham. The law was a latecomer, perhaps an afterthought. Or it had some other purpose than to seal the covenant, which had already been done by Abraham's faith. Again Paul does something counterintuitive to most Jews. He has separated the law from faith, and now he separates the law from the covenant and the promise. The law, according to Paul, was a much later addition to the scene, not a real "player."

The next few sentences are at first puzzling. Now that Paul has made the law irrelevant for justification, the covenant, and the promise, why did God add it at all? "Why then the law? It was added because of transgressions" (3:19). The Greek here is unclear, and most Christians have read this to say that God gave the law in order to keep people from sinning. The law was intended to help people avoid "transgressions." But the language could just as easily be read to say that God gave the law of Moses to cause people to "transgress." God gave the law to increase sin and transgressions.

I believe that is what Paul must have meant. That actually, as we will see, makes more sense in the context of Paul's whole theology of the law. But it is also supported by a passage in Romans, written almost certainly after Galatians. There Paul says, "The law slipped in so that transgression would increase" (5:20; my translation).[2] There, it is obvious that Paul believed that the purpose and result of the law of Moses was to increase sin in the world. This is truly a bizarre notion, but it does seem to be what Paul is arguing.

But let's finish the verse in Galatians. Paul continues by saying that the law was added "because of transgressions, until the offspring would come to whom the promise had been made; and it was ordained through angels by a mediator. Now a mediator involves more than one party; but God is one" (Gal 3:19–20). This is confusing, but I believe a solution is possible. We have seen that the "offspring" is Christ. Between the time of the covenant and the coming of Christ, who will become the means for the fulfillment of the covenant and promise, the law of Moses was "slipped into" history. But Paul is now suggesting that Moses did not receive the law directly from God, as an innocent reading of Exodus would suggest. Rather, Moses received the law from angels. We have seen this odd belief in the discussion of Stephen's speech in Chapter 10 of this book. Paul also believes it, as did some other Jews of the time.

Paul, though, reinforces the idea by pointing out that Moses served the role of "mediator" of the law, and this, for Paul, means that Moses could not have received the law from God, because God is one person, and mediators are not needed except when an agreement is necessary between two groups of people. Paul seems to be assuming some kind of ancient legal notion that held that when a contract was made between two individuals, no mediator was needed because each person simply represented himself. When a group wanted a contract with an individual, a mediator was not needed then either: the individual represented himself, and the group chose one of its own to finalize the deal. But when two groups needed to make a contract with each other, they had to choose a mediator, someone who was neutral for both parties. Paul uses this apparently legal notion to "prove" that Moses could not have received the law from God, since we all know that he was a mediator for the people of Israel. There must, therefore, have been a group on the other side of Moses, and for Paul that was the angels. The angels, not God, gave the law to Moses. This seems like a clear demotion of the law in importance, and at least something of a distancing of it from God.

But Paul is not done with the law yet. He then says, "Now before faith came, we were imprisoned and guarded under the law until faith would be revealed" (3:23). The law is depicted here as a prison guard. Paul is at least saying that the law "imprisoned" the Jews for all those years. As will become clearer in Romans, Paul actually believed, I think, that the law served to imprison all of humanity until the coming of Christ, although it is never clear how Paul imagined that functioning for gentiles. It is certainly not a flattering portrait of the law.

Then Paul compares the law to a slave pedagogue: "Therefore the law was our disciplinarian until Christ came. . . . But now that faith has come, we are no longer subject to a disciplinarian" (3:24–25). The word here translated "disciplinarian" is *paidagōgos*. It did not mean "pedagogue" in the modern English sense, and it did not refer mainly to a teacher. It referred to the male slave who took care of young boys (it means literally "a leader of a boy"), making sure they got to and from school, protecting them from sexual advances, and carrying their school supplies. These were often old slaves who were no longer capable of heavier work and who could be better depended on not to take sexual advantage of their charges. In art of the period, they are often depicted as ugly, and they sometimes were portrayed as cruel, beating boys unnecessarily. Paul is not comparing the law to anything good here. He is picturing it as the old, ugly, mean-spirited slaves many boys despised and feared.

But Paul is still not done with the law. Continuing the analogy of children under care, Paul points out that legally underage "heirs" are no better than slaves in a household. Even if they are the "owners" of the property, they can't take advantage of it until they come to maturity. In the meantime, they are under the charge of guardians. "So with us; while we were minors, we were enslaved to the elemental spirits of the world" (4:3). "Elemental spirits" here translates *stoicheia*. The word meant many different things in Greek. It literally meant "rows" or "ranks." It could be used of the different letters of the alphabet (imagine them in rows), or of ranks of soldiers. It also was used of the "elements of the universe," something like what we mean when we teach the chemical elements of the periodic table. So some ancient science suggested that air, fire, water, and earth were the fundamental "elements" out of which all material things were constructed.

But in much ancient Greek thought and culture, those material elements were also divine. In popular thought (though not necessarily among philosophers), "air" was not only an abstract divinity, but even Hera herself. The basic, fundamental building blocks of the entire cosmos were material divinities that could take on personal traits. Even in later Christian, Gnostic mythology, the word *stoicheia* referred to the ranks upon ranks of those demonic divine beings who lived in the atmosphere above the earth. They were jealous of human beings and attempted to keep them down. "Salvation" for this kind of religion means escaping the earth by defeating or deceiving these elemental divine beings in order to get to the true heaven and the highest God.

That is the way Paul is using the word here. Just as he argued that people were "imprisoned" by the law, so here he says that all people were enslaved to the stoicheia, and these he depicts as demonic, superhuman beings. The coming of Jesus, however, allowed escape from enslavement to the stoicheia. Those who before were "under the law" were "adopted" as children of God (4:4–5). "No longer a slave but a child, and if a child then also an heir, through God" (4:7).

But then Paul makes another of his remarkable claims. He points out that the Galatians in their previous lives were gentiles and therefore did not "know God." Now that they do know God, he asks, why would they want to return to being enslaved again? "How can you turn back again to the weak and beggarly elemental spirits [*stoicheia*]? How can you want to be enslaved to them again? You are observing special days, and months, and seasons, and years. I am afraid that my work for you may have been wasted" (4:9–11). Paul's way of describing their situation must have surprised them. They were certainly not intending to return to their previous idolatry. They were simply supplementing their baptism with some observation of Jewish laws and customs.

It is Paul who makes the alarming association of the law of Moses with the elemental spirits that the Galatians used to worship in the form of their gods. If they take up the law, Paul says, that will be precisely the same as if they began all over again with sacrifices and prayers to the Greek and local gods, who were, in Paul's view (which he would have shared with many Jews) actually demonic beings. Zeus was not, for Paul, a god at all, but a demon. That is not what is surprising. Most Jews believed this. What is surprising, and most likely shocking to his audience, is that Paul says that their acceptance of any observation of Jewish law is the same thing as a return to idolatry, a return to slavery to the stoicheia.

Paul has made some amazing statements about the law. It is not, in his view, at least here in Galatians, a guide for moral behavior. It is not a guard against sin. At best, the law of Moses was a latecomer in salvation history. It is the opposite of faith and the promise. It slipped into history to increase sin. It was the prison guard of humanity, the cruel and ugly pedagogue. It was given to Moses by angels, not by God. It was and is the tool of the demonic beings who enslaved humanity and still attempt to keep people from God. What could possess the Galatians to make them want any part of it?

To drive his points home, Paul turns again to scripture and constructs an elaborate allegorical exegesis of the story of Sarah and Hagar, the wife and the slave concubine of Abraham (4:21–5:1). Paul notes that Abraham had two sons: Isaac with his free wife and Ishmael with the slave Hagar. But then he makes each woman an allegorical type for two covenants. We would expect Sarah, as the mother of the Jews, to represent the covenant "from Mount Sinai," the site where Moses received the law of the Jews. And we would expect Hagar, as the mother of the Arabs, to represent the gentile nations. But Paul takes his allegory in surprising directions.

He says that Sinai is "in Arabia," but that it represents "the present Jerusalem, for she is in slavery with her children" (4:25). Sarah, though, does not represent the Jews, but "the Jerusalem above." Indeed, "she is free, and she is our mother" (4:26). Paul's allegory is confusing. We would expect Sarah to represent the Jews. She could symbolize either Sinai, the mountain on which Moses received the law, or Zion, the mountain of Jerusalem. But Paul equates Hagar with Sinai, with the law, with slavery, and with all those Jews who do not believe in Christ. Sarah represents all those people, Jew or gentile, who now constitute the community of faith in Christ, the true children of Abraham, the true "Israel."

Paul then reinforces his allegory by insisting that just as Ishmael persecuted Isaac in the story of scripture, "so it is now also" (4:29). We don't know of any real persecution gentile Christians were suffering at the hands of Jews at this time. But Paul implies that it is going on, and that is one more sign, in his mind, that he and other believers, gentile and Jew, are the true "Isaac," and not the unbelieving Jews who still follow the law. But for the Galatians to accept any of that law for themselves would be to "submit again to a yoke of slavery" (5:1).

Paul even tells the Galatians that if they allow themselves to be circumcised, they will be damned. "Christ will be of no benefit to you" (5:2). They will be "cut off from Christ" and will have "fallen from grace" (5:4). As we have seen, at least some early Christians believed that gentiles should accept the laws of Israel if they wanted to be included with the people of Israel. Other Christians apparently believed that observation of the law of the Jews was not necessary but could be optional. That would be a most natural point of view: it is not necessary for salvation, but what could it hurt? And perhaps it might help. Paul takes a more radical view. We don't know what exactly he believed about Jewish believers in Christ; I think he probably thought that it was acceptable for them to continue observing the law of Moses. But for former gentiles, Paul believed that any keeping of that law was absolutely forbidden. By doing so, they would cut themselves off from Christ and be damned. In Paul's mind, the law was not an option for the gentiles he converted. And that is nowhere clearer than in Galatians.

We don't know what happened in the Galatian churches after Paul sent his letter. Were his converts in Galatia convinced by his letter? Did they turn away from their infatuation with the other traveling preachers and the Jewish law and accept Paul's correction? We cannot know for certain. We have no "Second Letter of Paul to the Galatians." If Paul never again mentioned the churches in Galatia, we might suppose that he lost the debate and cut off his ties with those churches. But Paul does mention them in 1 Corinthians 16:1, telling the church in Corinth that it should follow the same instructions he had previously given the churches in Galatia about collecting money for the fund he wants to take to the church in Jerusalem. So at least at the time of his writing 1 Corinthians, Paul was on good terms with the Galatian churches. (This assumes that his letter to the Galatians was written earlier than 1 Corinthians, as I think probably is the case.)[3] That suggests, I think, that his rather radical and even stinging letter to them did its work, and they submitted again to Paul's authority as "their" apostle.

Paul Nuances His Position in Romans

Paul's letter to the Roman church is written in a very different situation, although it deals with many of the same issues as Galatians. First, we need to note that this is a rare example of Paul writing to a church he did not found. He seems to have intentionally restricted his apostolic activity to those regions where he had established churches himself. But he does write to Rome, intending to travel there, even though he did not establish that church.

Paul is concerned, though, about his reputation in the church in Rome. Romans is written, at least in part, to repair any possible damage to his reputation he may have suffered because of rumors about what he was saying about the Jewish law. And rumors were circulating. Not far into the letter, Paul quotes one. After laying out his message that people, both Jews and gentiles, are justified by grace through faith in Jesus Christ, and not by works of the law, Paul raises the question whether this means that God is unjust. If God justifies sinners, why not just continue sinning? "And why not say (as some people slander us by saying that we say), 'Let us do evil so that good may come'?" It does sound like a logical consequence of Paul's preaching. But he rejects it: "Their condemnation is deserved!" (Rom 3:8). Paul is bringing up rumors in order to refute them, and to a church he did not himself found. He seems to be in damage-control mode.

Besides laying out his "law-free" gospel, Paul goes out of his way several times to make it clear that he is not really "antinomian." He is not against the law itself, nor does he really believe that the law is bad. After explaining his views that righteousness, justification, and human reconciliation with God are a "free gift," he explains that the "law slipped in so that transgression would increase [my translation]; but where sin increased, grace abounded all the more, so that, just as sin exercised dominion in death, so grace might also exercise dominion through justification leading to eternal life through Jesus Christ our Lord" (Rom 5:20–21).

Paul wants to dispel any notion that he encourages sinning: "What then are we to say? Should we continue in sin in order that grace may abound?" (6:1). This is a logical question, given what he has said so far. So Paul answers firmly, "By no means! How can we who died to sin go on living in it? Do you not know that all of us who have been baptized into Christ Jesus were baptized into his death? Therefore we have been buried with him by baptism into death, so that, just as Christ was raised from the dead by the glory of the Father, so we too might walk in newness of life" (6:2–4). Paul answers the logical accusation that his gospel should lead to more sinning if the increase of sin caused by the law led to justification by grace in Jesus Christ. But he answers by saying basically that Christians are now in such a different "state," a different manner of being, that it would be inconceivable for them to sin. They are "in Christ" and so simply must not sin.

Paul has to keep coming back to this point. Later in the same chapter, he again raises the question: "What then? Should we sin because we are not under law but under grace? By no means!" (6:15). In Romans, Paul pursues a rhetorical and theological strategy unlike that of Galatians. In the first place, he explicitly addresses rumors that his gospel encouraged sinning. He also admits some explicitly positive functions of the law. He says that we know what sin is through the law: "Through the law comes the knowledge of sin" (3:20). He insists that rather than denigrating the law, as he could appear to have done in Galatians, his gospel actually "upholds the law" (3:31). Apparently, he believes that his more nuanced position as laid out in Romans "upholds the law" by noting its rightful place in the history of God's plan of salvation. He later comes out firmly to say that the law itself is not "sin" (7:7), although he still insists that it increased sin. And toward the conclusion of this long discourse on the law, Paul gets as explicit in his approval of the law as he can: "So the law is holy, and the commandment is holy and just and good" (7:12).

Paul in Galatians had portrayed the Jewish law as part of God's plan, but it comes across there as having just about only negative meanings and functions. In Romans, Paul takes the time to explain his views more clearly (or perhaps to state his altered views), and in doing so he backs away from the more negative things he had said about the law in Galatians. Now, not only does the law have the functions of causing sin and keeping human beings imprisoned in sin until the coming of Christ, but it also has brought valuable knowledge of sin. The law is in itself good and holy, although Paul still wants to emphasize that it never could bring justification before God. Only faith can do that, as the story of Abraham proves. Now, with the coming of Christ, however, even the limited historical usefulness of the law is past. The law is not evil, nor is it sin. It is, though, since the coming of Christ, a thing of the past.

The Social Context of the Letter to the Romans

The change in Paul's rhetoric in Romans from what we found in Galatians can be explained by examining the likely social reality of the church in Rome and Paul's relationship to it. According to tradition, the apostle Peter founded the church in Rome, but that is not historical. It is almost certain that the first followers of Jesus in Rome arrived there some time after the crucifixion of Jesus. They may have come from Palestine itself, or perhaps from earlier churches in the East. But the founding of Christianity in Rome was no doubt due to the travels of followers of Jesus whose names are forever lost to us. They are the same kinds of anonymous Christians who were the first to spread the message about Jesus throughout the East and to gentiles there.

The earliest house churches in Rome were probably either completely or predominantly Jewish. There was a large Jewish community in Rome in the first century, and it was probably among those Jews that Jesus' followers mingled and passed around their message about him. Fairly quickly, the Christian community drew gentiles also, and by the time Paul wrote to the Romans, the church in Rome was almost certainly predominantly gentile, with some Jews still active. In fact, at the end of the letter, Paul greets many people he must have known in the East who are now in Rome, and many of them are obviously Jews.[4] But I think Romans is evidence that the Jews are now in the minority of the Roman church.

We must also remember that we are talking about what were probably several house churches. Rome was the largest city in the empire, with perhaps as many as one million inhabitants. We may imagine that the Christians in Rome concentrated themselves in different house churches in different neighborhoods. It is entirely possible that some of them were more Jewish and others less so.

Paul writes to all these house churches as one church, a church he did not establish, for several different reasons. For one thing, Paul is planning a mission trip farther to the west of Rome, all the way to Spain. And he wants support—both financial and moral—from the Christians in Rome. In fact, he claims that his mission in the East has been so successful that he has no more work there to do. "But now, with no further place for me in these regions, I desire, as I have for many years, to come to you when I go to Spain" (15:23–24). Paul is exaggerating. At this time in his life, he can certainly point to accomplishments, but scarcely the evangelization of the entire eastern Mediterranean. He has planted a few house churches of gentile Christians in some of the major cities and towns in Asia Minor, Macedonia, and Greece. But in his mind, apparently, that is all he can do in the East. He seems to think that once he has merely planted a few "cells" of Christians in a few cities, his job there is done. So he plans to pursue the same kind of work in the western half of the empire.

He is here asking for future financial support. "For I do hope to see you on my journey and to be sent on by you, once I have enjoyed your company for a little while" (15:24). As I explained when I was discussing the Johannine letters, this is the language not only of moral support but also of material support. "Sending someone along" was one way of politely referring to material support for traveling preachers.

First, though, Paul wants and needs to go to Jerusalem, as he then explains. "At present, however, I am going to Jerusalem in a ministry to the saints; for Macedonia and Achaia have been pleased to share their resources with the poor among the saints at Jerusalem" (15:25–26). This refers to the collection Paul has been gathering from his gentile churches as a gift to the poorer Jewish church in Jerusalem. He is now at the point where he is preparing to take the money to Jerusalem.[5]

The collection had more than monetary meaning. I have brought up the patron-client structure several times already, and here we see it expressed again in Paul's view of the collection. Giving and taking in the Greco-Roman world were always expected to be reciprocal. Patrons gave money or other "gifts" to their clients in return for honor and deference, and even clients were sometimes expected to give "gifts" to their patrons. But reciprocity was always important.

Thus Paul describes the collection as the "payback" for the gift of the gospel the gentiles enjoyed from the first disciples of Jesus, Jews. "They [the gentile churches] were pleased to do this, and indeed they owe it to them; for if the gentiles have come to share in their spiritual blessings, they ought also to be of service to them in material things. So, when I have completed this, and have delivered to them what has been collected, I will set out by way of you to Spain; and I know that when I come to you, I will come in the fullness of the blessing of Christ" (15:27–29). The collection was significant for Paul not just because of its financial importance, although it does seem that the Christians in Jerusalem were poor and in need of help. Paul also sees the exchange, and it was in his mind an exchange, as joining the gentile churches he has established to the "mother church" of Jews in Jerusalem.

Paul's entire apostleship was an attempt to bring an originally Jewish gospel to the gentile world, but the church needed to remain united, with both gentiles and Jews in its ranks. That was part of Paul's apocalyptic vision: a worldwide "Israel" that included "the nations" along with the Jews. The collection was Paul's way of attempting to cement that unity.

But it was also a bit dangerous. If the Jewish believers accepted the gift from the gentile churches, that action could be interpreted as a sign of inferiority. Remember, more often money was passed downward in the social scale in exchange for honor being passed upward. Paul was doubtless concerned that the Jews in Jerusalem would not accept the gift because doing so could imply their inferiority.

Accepting the gift could also be taken to mean that the Jewish Christians completely approved of Paul's mission and even agreed with his "law-free" gospel. There were doubtless many believers in Jerusalem who did not. Paul knows that there will be some pressure on the leaders of the Jerusalem church to reject his gift because they did not want to signal an approval of his views about the law and gentiles.

Aware of these possible threats to his plan, Paul wrote to the Roman church, as an important and now-central church of the growing Christian movement in the capital city, in order to enlist its support in his upcoming journey to Jerusalem. We don't know exactly what Paul wanted the Roman Christians to do. Write a letter to Jerusalem? Send an emissary to support Paul? But I believe one reason Paul writes to them is that he is nervous about whether he and his gentile gift will be accepted by the church in Jerusalem, especially after its members hear the rumors about his view of the law. Paul nuances his earlier, more radical statements about the law. He calls it "holy" and "good." It served a good role in God's plan of salvation for the world. If Paul can convince the church in Rome, which comprises both gentiles and Jews, that his gospel is acceptable, he may have a better chance of succeeding in his trip to Jerusalem.

We don't know the outcome of Paul's trip to Jerusalem. Acts leads us to believe that Paul was warmly received by the Jerusalem church leaders, and that he was arrested in Jerusalem only because of false accusations against him by unbelieving Jews. But Acts never mentions Paul's collection, in spite of the fact we glean from his letters that it was hugely important for him and even helped define his mission. Is it possible that the author of Acts knew of the collection but refrained from mentioning it because he also knew that the money was rejected by the Jerusalem church? That would not fit his story about a completely unified Jewish-gentile church and complete unity between Paul and James, the leader of the Jewish church in Jerusalem. It is just possible that Paul's gift was not accepted, or at least not enthusiastically by the whole church. If it was not, his reputation as "antinomian," which he struggles to refute in Romans, could have been a reason.

The New "Center" for the Letter to the Romans

For many years, influenced by Protestant theology, most scholars considered the first several chapters of Romans the most significant part. It is there that Paul argues most explicitly for his doctrine of justification by grace through faith apart from works of the law. As I have been telling the story, that doctrine is still part of the picture, but even more central to the letter is the relationship between gentiles and Jews in the early church. Indeed, this reflects a shift in scholarship on Romans more widely. Many scholars, myself included, now tend to place Romans 9–11 at the center of the letter's concerns.

If, as I have suggested, Paul is anxious about the relationship between his gentile churches and the Jewish church in Jerusalem, and if the church in Rome went from being mainly Jewish to being predominantly gentile, then we may look at Romans 9–11 as providing Paul's way of dealing with both those issues. According to apocalyptic expectations held by many Jews of the time, and by Paul as well, the "end-time," the messianic time, would see the inclusion of the world's nations also in the kingdom of God. Paul quotes the prophet Hosea as predicting this: those who were "not my people" will become the children of God (Rom 9:25–26; Hosea 2:23, 1:10). According to this eschatology, after the Messiah arrives, all the nations of the earth will be brought in and offered salvation also. This is precisely the way Paul saw his mission to the gentiles. Since the Messiah has come in the person of Jesus, and since the church represents at least the "first fruits" of the coming reign of God, it is Paul's job as the apostle to the gentiles to bring them into the church in anticipation of their inclusion in God's eschatological reign.

In preparation for that, by divine providence, most of the Jews have not accepted the gospel about Jesus. Paul insists, though, that their rejection of the gospel was necessary so that the gospel would be taken to the gentiles. But once the "full number" of the gentiles has been drawn into the church, the divine "hardening" that has come upon the unbelieving Jews will be lifted, and those Jews will also be brought back in. "And so all Israel will be saved" (Rom 11:25–26). The crucifixion of Jesus, his resurrection as the Messiah, the rejection of the message by the majority of Jews, and the mission to the gentiles have all been events orchestrated by God so that when Jesus comes back, this time in victory, he will be able to reign over a kingdom that unites Israel with all the nations in a unified and now-redeemed and re-created world. The boundaries of Israel will be worldwide; indeed, they will encompass the entire cosmos.

One of the main reasons for writing Romans 9–11, therefore, was to tell the gentile Christians in Rome that even though they are now the majority of the church, they should not "lord it over" their Jewish brothers and sisters. Yes, there has been a "hardening" of the Jews who do not believe in Christ, but that will soon be softened, and Jews themselves will be brought back into the "people of God." The Jews, Paul reminds his gentile hearers, were the first "people of God." The gentiles should respect them, not dismiss them or look down on them. Even Jewish unbelief is part of God's plan. Romans 9–11 shows that one of the main reasons Paul wrote Romans was to show that he was still a loyal Jew who respected his fellow Jews and insisted that gentile Christians do so also.

Paul never saw himself as the founder of Christianity. He was not out to establish a "new religion." In fact, Paul never uses the word "Christian." He may not have known the term. If he did, I think he likely would have rejected it if it was taken to refer to a "new" religion, distinct from the faith of Abraham and the Jewish people. Paul's expectations were for a united people of God, Jews and gentiles, including the final salvation of "all Israel." If Paul knew the word "Christianity," he likely would not have approved of it either. It is important, I believe, that those words are never used in his letters. That would imply that Paul was out to start a new religion, and he clearly was not.

In this new vision of Romans and Paul, the letter and Paul's mission are not about individual salvation or any abstract doctrine of justification by faith. Romans is about the expansion of the nation of Israel to include the world. It is about the eventual salvation of the entire world and all peoples in the eschatological Israel of God. Paul was not necessarily the first Christian theologian. He may well have been, though, one of the most radical Jewish theologians.

CHAPTER 17
Colossians and Ephesians

Overview: In ancient times, documents that were falsely attributed to an author, called pseudepigrapha, were a common phenomenon. The letters to the Colossians and Ephesians are most likely pseudonymous works attributed to the apostle Paul. The writer of Colossians assures his readers that they already possess all the benefits of salvation and do not need to observe rules concerning feast days, Sabbaths, and worship of angels. Ephesians is based on Colossians, although it reads more like a theological or moral treatise. Both letters differ from Paul's theology in their realized eschatology and high Christology.

Ancient Pseudepigraphy

King Abgar of Edessa in eastern Syria wrote a letter to Jesus of Nazareth. Abgar says that he has heard of the worldwide fame of Jesus, especially his miraculous healings. Abgar himself is ill, he says, and since the Jews are not particularly friendly to Jesus, Abgar invites him to his kingdom in Edessa. He asks Jesus to come heal him, and he promises to provide a better welcome for Jesus than he is receiving among the Jews.

Jesus writes back:

> Happy are you who believe in me without having seen me! For it is written of me that those who have seen me will not believe in me, and that those who have not seen will believe and live. As to your request that I should come to you, I must complete all that I was sent to do here, and on completing it must at once be taken up to the One who sent me. When I have been taken up I will send you one of my disciples to cure your disorder and bring life to you and those with you.[1]

As it turns out, Jesus seems to be quite an eloquent letter writer.

Of course, none of this happened. Both letters were forged, maybe in the third century or early fourth. They are included in the *Ecclesiastical History* of Eusebius, who wrote in the fourth century. No modern scholar believes they are authentic. In fact, even ancient scholars pointed out that Jesus left nothing in writing.[2]

It is easy to imagine why some early Christian would have forged them. Jesus was later considered the most important human being in history. Surely he must have been world-famous in his lifetime. And a Syriac Christian may have wanted to promote the idea that his own church was ancient and even established by a disciple sent personally by Jesus. What better way to make the point than to "discover" a couple of letters documenting the fact? So the letters were forged. We do not know how Eusebius knew about them, but he did quote them in his *Ecclesiastical History.*

Even novice students can suggest reasons to doubt the authenticity of these letters. They will note, for example, that the letters are in Greek, and that Jesus likely did not use Greek—or at least that he could almost certainly not compose Greek, or even Aramaic or Syriac, in the high style of the letters. Even in English translation, the prose comes across as elaborate and fine style, judged, that is, by ancient standards of what counted as "fine style." The letters also show knowledge of the Gospel of John. The rejection of Jesus by the Jews, mentioned in Abgar's letter, is a predominant theme of the Fourth Gospel. And as we saw in Chapter 11, the themes of believing and seeing seem to come straight from John (see John 20:29). Even amateur "historians" can tell that these are forgeries.

There are many such forgeries from the ancient world, both Christian and non-Christian. The more polite term for them may be "pseudonymous writings," and biblical scholars are usually hesitant to call them "forgeries."

But a thorough study of the ancient practice demonstrates that ancient people themselves considered pseudonymous writings to be dishonest and immoral attempts to deceive an audience with a false ascription of authorship—unless they themselves were the ones producing the forgery, perhaps.[3] People tended to believe that falsely attributed works were actually written by the person the work claimed was the author. When they found out otherwise, they condemned the practice and the forger. So the idea that ancient people considered pseudonymity simply an acceptable part of their culture is a modern myth.

There were several reasons that someone would publish a pseudonymous work. One was money. Some of the kings of the Hellenistic empires attempted to build up huge libraries for themselves and their resident scholars. The library of Pergamum was famous; that of Alexandria in Egypt was even more so. To expand their libraries, rulers would pay good money for books, copies, say, of the works of Homer, the dialogues of Plato, the histories of Herodotus, or whatever. A pseudepigrapher could make very good money by forging a "newly discovered," previously unknown play by Euripides or letter of Plato and selling it as authentic. Galen, the second-century physician and prolific medical writer, complained about finding works forged in his name in bookshops. Someone was doubtless trying to make money by forging medical writings and selling them to booksellers.

The dominant reason people published pseudonymous works in early Christianity seems to have been to propagate their own theological points of view and oppose others. They did so by writing letters, gospels, and acts in the name of the apostles or other famous figures of the past. So we have fragments of a *Gospel of Peter* that no one believes Peter actually wrote. We have visions allegedly recorded by the very ancient Enoch or Ezra, which again no one believes they actually wrote. And, as here seen, we even have a letter allegedly written by Jesus himself to a king of Edessa. We have letters purporting to be a correspondence between Paul and the famous Stoic philosopher and adviser to the emperor Nero, Seneca. After all, if Paul was a great theologian, why should he not have corresponded with one of the most famous philosophers of the first century? But no one believes that any of these are authentic. They are forgeries. There are hundreds and hundreds of them, Greek, Latin, Jewish, and Christian.

None of this is very controversial. The controversy arises only when critical scholars suggest that several of the writings of the New Testament were also forgeries. In fact, of the New Testament documents, only eight were certainly written by the person claiming to be their author: the seven "undisputed letters" of Paul, as I have called them, and the Revelation of John, which was written by someone named "John," though not the apostle John, the son of Zebedee. The four Gospels are not pseudonymous because the texts themselves (not counting their "titles," which were added by scribes later) make no claim about authorship, except that the Fourth Gospel claims to have been written by the "beloved disciple," although he is not named. So the canonical Gospels are not pseudonymously but merely anonymously authored.

As we will see in future chapters, the Letter to the Hebrews is anonymously authored, although a few scholars have argued that the author at least implied that he was Paul.[4] The text, though, makes no explicit claim about authorship. The three letters of "John" also make no claim that they were written by John. The author of the last two of them just designates himself "the elder," as we have seen. But critical scholars are convinced that the letters claiming to be from the pen of James, Peter, and Jude are all pseudonymous, written in the names of those famous disciples by others many years after their deaths. Of the twenty-seven documents that make up the New Testament, only eight were certainly written by the person claiming to be the author, nine were anonymously published, and ten, I would argue, are pseudonymous, forged by Christians in the names of famous fathers of the church of previous years.

Colossians

The Letter to the Colossians comes after that to the Ephesians in the canon, but it was almost certainly written before Ephesians. The order of the letters of Paul in the canon seems to be a reflection of their length. They were probably placed in the canon in the order of longest to shortest, with some exceptions to keep pairs of letters together (Thessalonians; the Pastoral Epistles). But there are good reasons to believe that Ephesians was written after Colossians. Indeed, I will argue later that the author of Ephesians used Colossians as a model, taking ideas, words, and phrases from it. But the author of Ephesians was not the same person as the author of Colossians. So we have one admirer of Paul forging a letter in his name, and then another admirer of Paul, no doubt assuming that Colossians was actually authentic, using it to forge his own letter in Paul's name—one pseudonymous letter serving as the model for another.

The two main reasons scholars believe Colossians was not written by Paul are its writing style and its theology. The style of writing is very different from Paul's, as can be noticed by a careful reader even in English translation. But all English translations have "cleaned up" the style so that it sounds more like proper modern English style than it would be if the translation followed the Greek syntax more literally. Translated literally to reflect the Greek syntax, Colossians 1:3–8 reads like this:

> We give thanks to God the father of our Lord Jesus Christ always for you when we pray, hearing of your faithfulness in Christ Jesus and the love which you have toward all the holy ones [or "saints"] because of the hope laid in store for you in the heavens, which hope you heard about before in the word of the truth of the gospel that came to you, just as also in all the cosmos it is bearing fruit and growing just as also among you, from which day you heard and recognized the grace of God in truth, just as you learned from Epaphras, our beloved co-slave, who is your trustworthy servant of Christ, and who also made clear to us your love in the spirit.

This is all one sentence. In order to mimic the Greek style, I had to use all sorts of English connector words, such as "which," "who," and "from which," and lots of "ing" words, participles, because the Greek uses a lot of them. All those grammatical forms allowed the writer in Greek to string together very complicated sentences and go on for line after line without a full stop. Greek syntax allows that sort of thing.

Although that would be unacceptable style for modern American writing, it was perfectly acceptable for educated speakers of Greek of the first century. Indeed, people were taught to write, at least sometimes, in this flowery and flowing style. This kind of sentence is called "periodic," which means that several different dependent clauses, and clauses within clauses, phrases within phrases, are folded into and among one another and then made dependent on one or a few independent clauses. Periodic sentences are common in ancient Greek and Latin and in fact were imitated in nineteenth-century German academic writing, along with some other modern languages. They have been less popular in modern American writing.

There is, therefore, nothing wrong with this style of writing. The author is probably "showing off" a bit right here at the beginning of the letter in order to impress the reader with his ability to write fine and complex Greek. The point, though, is that this is just not the way Paul wrote. We do have, we believe, seven letters of his, and there is nothing anywhere in any of his letters that comes close to this style. Paul is capable of writing long sentences, of course, but he generally does not. Other scholars have published works that thoroughly compare Paul's seven letters with the language of Colossians on other aspects as well—vocabulary, syntax, grammar—and the reader may wish to follow the arguments further there.[5] For my purposes, this brief example will have to suffice. In terms of words, syntax, and all other issues of style, the author of Colossians had a distinctive style much unlike Paul's.

The author of Ephesians knows the letter to the Colossians and seems to have wanted to imitate it even in this style of writing. Here is an example of just one of his very long sentences, the first sentence after the salutation:

> Blessed be the God and father of our Lord Jesus Christ, who blessed us with every spiritual blessing in the heavenlies in Christ, just as he chose us in him before the foundation of the cosmos that we might be holy and blameless in his presence in love, having foreordained us for sonship [i.e., adoption] through Jesus Christ for himself, according to the pleasure of his will, for the praise of the glory of his grace which he granted us in the one he loves, in whom we have the washing through his blood, the forgiveness of transgressions, according to the riches of his grace which he lavished on us, in all wisdom and prudence, making known to us the mystery of his will, according to his pleasure which he set forth previously in him until the building up of the fullness of the times, recapitulating everything in Christ, things in the heavens and on the earth in him, in whom also we have become heirs, foreordained according to the plan of the one who accomplishes everything according to the plan of his will, so that we might exist for the praise of his glory, we who were the first to hope in Christ, in whom also you, hearing the word of truth, the good news of your salvation, and in whom also you believed, you were sealed with the promised holy spirit, which is the seal of our inheritance, for the washing of the possession, for the praise of his glory. (Eph 1:3–14)

Yes, this is one very long periodic sentence. It is, at least according to one count, 201 words in Greek.[6] It took me 250 English words to translate it as a periodic sentence in English. This kind of analysis is unfortunately lost on modern readers who cannot consult the Greek. But when Colossians and

Ephesians are read in the Greek, they simply look so different from Paul's style that it seems clear to many scholars that Paul simply did not write either of them.

This is not to say that Paul could not have written in that style; it is only to say that as far as we know, he did not. Paul writes fairly straightforward sentences. Sometimes they have grammatical problems. The sentences may start and stop, or they may interrupt themselves. That is perhaps just one indication that Paul dictated his letters to scribal assistants (see Rom 16:22). Paul also alternates between longer and shorter sentences, even exclamations of only two or three words at times ("By no means!" Rom 6:2, 7:7). We can imagine that the authors of Colossians and Ephesians considered Paul a model. They therefore began their letters in a high style they no doubt considered appropriate for their hero. But in doing so, they lost the advantage of verisimilitude: they did not, in fact, imitate him well, at least in writing style.

The Occasion of the Writing of Colossians

Colossians seems to have been written to counter a kind of theology and practice that perhaps claimed a Pauline pedigree but that this author considered totally illegitimate. We can get an idea of what he opposes by looking at a rather long quotation.

> Therefore do not let anyone condemn you in matters of food and drink or of observing festivals, new moons, or Sabbaths. These are only a shadow of what is to come, but the substance belongs to Christ. Do not let anyone disqualify you, insisting on self-abasement and worship of angels, dwelling on visions, puffed up without cause by a human way of thinking, and not holding fast to the head, from whom the whole body, nourished and held together by its ligaments and sinews, grows with a growth that is from God. If with Christ you died to the elemental spirits of the universe, why do you live as if you still belong to the world? Why do you submit to regulations, "Do not handle, Do not taste, Do not touch"? All these regulations refer to things that perish with use; they are simply human commands and teachings. These have indeed an appearance of wisdom in promoting self-imposed piety, humility, and severe treatment of the body, but they are of no value in checking self-indulgence. (Col 2:16–23)

There are many fascinating aspects of this quotation, and several things about it remain unclear even to experts. For instance, scholars cannot agree on what is meant by "worship of angels." Is he referring to people who are worshiping angels? Or do such people think that when they worship God or Christ, they are joining in with angels in their worship? From this distance, it is impossible to be certain about whom exactly the author had in mind, whether they were Jewish or gentile Christians, whether the rules and special days they wanted to observe came from Jewish scripture or elsewhere, and many other questions.

It seems clear, at any rate, that the author is opposing some kind of early Christian asceticism, the control of the body. The people the author is here condemning are urging practices such as observing certain holy days (festivals, new moons, Sabbaths) and avoiding foods and perhaps wine. They are doing so out of an attempt to produce a special holiness by practices of humility and self-abasement that this author insists were never taught by Paul.

Indeed, I believe that the "worship of angels" probably meant that these people were worshiping angels in an attempt to please God also. After all, the author brings up the "elemental spirits of the universe." These are the *stoicheia* we have seen Paul complaining about in Galatians, angelic- or demonic-type beings thought by some to rule the universe by occupying its atmosphere. The author of Colossians insists that there is no need for his hearers to "abase themselves" or worship these angelic-like stoicheia because Christians have already overcome them by being "in Christ" or having "died with Christ" (2:20). So the author is opposing a kind of early Christian asceticism that seems to have practiced aspects, probably, of Jewish piety (Sabbaths, food restrictions) in an attempt to placate angelic stoicheia they believed stood between themselves and God.

The way our author opposes such beliefs and practices is to insist that Christians already possess all the blessings of Christ. Christians need no "extra" asceticism, food restrictions, or observance of special holy days because they already have what God promises in Christ. First, the author elevates Christ to the highest possible level. Christ is "the image of the invisible God" (1:15). Any possible angels or stoicheia are no threat because "all things in heaven and on earth were created" in Christ. "Things visible and invisible, whether thrones or dominions or rulers or powers—all things have been created through him and for him" (1:16). There is no part of God the Father that is not available through Christ. "For in him all the fullness of God was pleased to dwell, and through him God was pleased to reconcile to himself all things, whether on earth or in heaven, by making peace through the blood of his cross" (1:19–20; see also 2:10).

Christians, the author insists, already enjoy all available blessings because they have died and risen with Christ, probably a reference to baptism (see 2:12).

> So if you have been raised with Christ, seek the things that are above, where Christ is, seated at the right hand of God. Set your minds on things that are above, not on things that are on earth, for you have died, and your life is hidden with Christ in God. When Christ who is your life is revealed, then you also will be revealed with him in glory. (Col 3:1–4)

The author is saying that the Colossians already have everything they could possibly possess because in their baptism they have already experienced death and resurrection with Christ. Because Christ "disarmed" all those heavenly powers in his death (2:15), the Colossians are already victors over them also and need do nothing to appease those powers. The only thing they await is the unveiling, the revealing, of the "glory" they essentially already possess. They will experience that glory when Christ is revealed at the end-time.

This may have been a great strategy for the author to persuade people to give up the unnecessary asceticism and special rituals he found offensive, but neither of these theological proposals fits Paul's theology. Paul's theology contains what we would call a "reserved eschatology." He taught that Christians had been "justified," but they had to await "salvation." Therefore, although he repeatedly puts "justification" in the past, he almost never says that Christians have been "saved."[7] He says that Christians "have been justified," and so they "will be saved" (Rom 5:9). For Paul, "salvation" is something that is "near" but has not yet arrived (Rom 13:11). "Salvation" is something for which Christians "hope" (1 Thess 5:8). These are just a few citations. Paul many times speaks of "salvation," but he conceives of it as still in the future.

Paul also conceives of Christian baptism as sharing in the death of Christ, but he never says that Christians "have been raised" with Christ. Thus in Romans, he says, "For if we have been united with him in a death like his, we *will* certainly be united with him in a resurrection like his" (Rom 6:5; emphasis added). Indeed, Paul spent much time in 1 Corinthians arguing against what seems to have been something like a "realized eschatology."

That is, some of the Corinthians were claiming already to be experiencing the wisdom, spiritual blessings, and power Paul believed were reserved for the time after the *eschaton*, the "end" of this world and the beginning of the next. Paul simply would not have said that the Colossians already possessed everything promised them "in the heavens," and he would not have taught them, if his other letters are any indication, that they had already been raised with Christ.

It is important for Paul's theology that Christians are living in an in-between time. According to traditional Jewish apocalypticism, there is the "before time," before the arrival of the Messiah, or the Son of Man, or the kingdom of God, and the "after time," after the coming of the expected event. At the point of the coming of the Messiah, the righteous dead will be raised, the world and its inhabitants will be judged, and the righteous will be rewarded and the evil damned. But note that the end of the "before time," the coming of the Messiah, and the resurrection of the dead all happen at the same time (see Fig. 9).

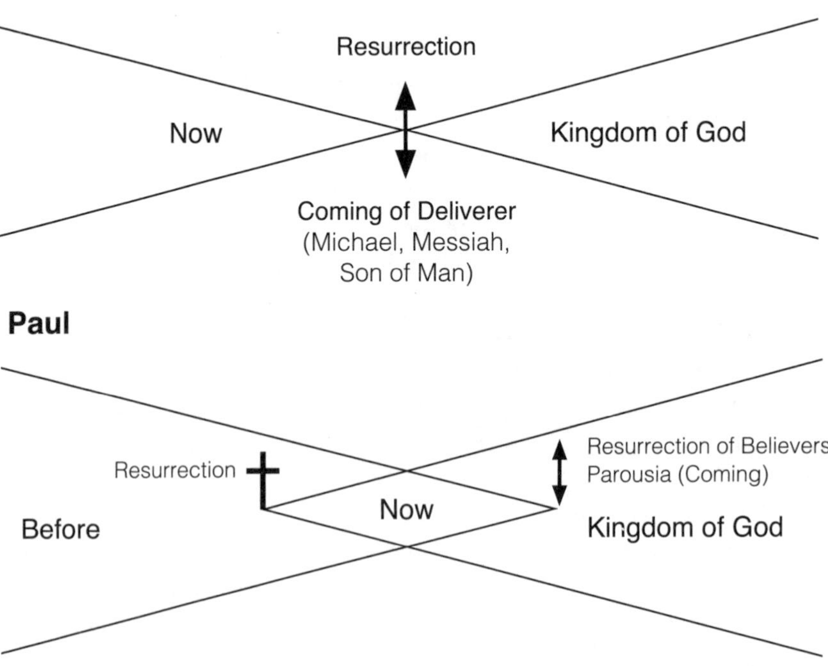

Fig. 9 Apocalyptic Time Lines

Early Christians had to adjust this traditional scenario because they believed that Jesus had already come and that he was the Messiah. They also believed that he had been raised from the dead. If all that is so, the kingdom should already be here. But Christians knew that evil still existed, the righteous dead had not yet been raised, and the Messiah had not yet come "in power and glory." So they changed the traditional time line so that they were living in a time between the "first resurrection," that is, of Jesus, the "first fruits of those who have died" (1 Cor 15:20), and the future general resurrection, that of their own loved ones and possibly themselves. For Paul, the full blessings of the resurrection, salvation, and heaven were still to be expected soon, but they were still in the future. In place of Paul's "reserved eschatology," the author of Colossians placed his own "realized eschatology." It would not have fit Paul's theology.

The high Christology of Colossians also clashes with Paul's Christology. Paul certainly believed that Christ was divine and was to be worshiped. He calls him "Lord" in the same way he calls God "Lord." But Paul never completely equates Jesus with "God."[8] In fact, there are places where Paul implies that Jesus is inferior to God in ways that many in the church would later consider heretical. In 1 Corinthians 11:2–16, Paul is trying to persuade women to veil their heads when praying or prophesying. In order to explain why women should be veiled but not men, Paul constructs a hierarchy: Christ is the head of man; man is the head of woman; and God is the head of Christ (11:3). Just as Paul needs a hierarchical relationship between man and woman for his argument to work, and just as he obviously accepts a hierarchical relationship between Christ and man, so he must be assuming one also between God and Christ. God is superior to Christ.

Later in 1 Corinthians, in his explanation and defense of the resurrection of the body, Paul also makes statements that imply a "subordinationist" Christology. Paul says that when Jesus returns in glory, he will first defeat all evil, "every ruler and authority" (1 Cor 15:24). He will subdue all his enemies "under his feet" (15:25). But then, "When all things are subjected to him, then the Son himself will also be subjected to the one who put all things in subjection under him, so that God may be all in all" (15:28). Paul's Christology is not as "high" as that of the author of Colossians, for whom Christ is "the fullness of God" himself.

I am not saying this makes Paul a "heretic." He was writing long before the orthodox developments of later Christianity. He is just innocent of any doctrine of the Trinity or the fully developed Christology of such creeds as those of Nicea and Chalcedon. In fact, those creeds owe much more to other texts, including the Gospel of John and Colossians, than to Paul himself. But the difference is one more piece of evidence that Paul did not write Colossians.

The Letter to the Ephesians as Treatise

The author of Ephesians uses Colossians as one of his sources and builds on it even further in the same direction. Colossians had implied that the Colossian Christians already resided with Christ in heaven, but Ephesians says so explicitly. First, the author describes the resurrection of Christ and his enthronement "in the heavenly places, far above all rule and authority and power and dominion, and above every name that is named, not only in this age but also in the age to come" (Eph 1:20–21).

But he also says that Christians are seated there too, even now: "But God, who is rich in mercy, out of the great love with which he loved us even when we were dead through our trespasses, made us alive together with Christ—by grace you have been saved—and raised us up with him and seated us with him in the heavenly places in Christ Jesus" (Eph 2:4–6). Note that this author, like that of Colossians, insists that Christians have also "been saved"; but even more than that, they have ascended already into heaven, in some sense, "in Christ Jesus," and that is where they are "sitting." Ephesians, therefore, takes many cues from Colossians and in many cases strengthens them or takes them further.

There are many other theological differences between Ephesians and Paul. There are also minor differences between Ephesians and Colossians, but these differences are such that the two documents must not have been written by the same person. One small but significant indication is how the two authors have different views of "shameful speech," that is, what kind of language Christians should avoid. In a recent book, Jeremy Hultin explores what counted as "shameful speech" or dirty language in the ancient world.

Both authors advise Christians to avoid shameful speech, but what counts as prohibited speech is different for each of them. Hultin notes that the prohibitions on speech in Ephesians, in comparison with those in Colossians, are more extreme. Not only is obscene speech prohibited in Ephesians, but "wittiness" is as well (Eph 5:4). The author of Ephesians uses the Greek word *eutrapelia* to refer to the kind of talk Christians must avoid. Although the word is translated in the NRSV as "silly talk," it was much more often used by Greek writers, including philosophers, to mean "witty talk," which they praised. The author of Colossians looks much more like the philosophers when he encourages "witty talk," although he uses the expression "seasoned with salt" to indicate it (Col 4:6). As Hultin argues, the writer of Ephesians is copying moral teachings from Colossians but changing the advice about speech because he considers "witty talk" bad, although the author of Colossians thought that it was fine.[9] We are dealing with two different authors, even though the writer of Ephesians used Colossians as a model and source.

Another important difference between Colossians and Ephesians is that Colossians is polemic addressed to particular beliefs and practices the author opposes. The letter criticizes other Christians and attempts to persuade the Colossians to change their behavior. We need not assume that the letter was actually sent to Colossae. In order for it to function as a forged letter from Paul, probably written after his death, the author would have done better to pretend to have "found" the letter and then produced it for some other social situation with which he was concerned. But the letter is intended as "Pauline" polemic against other Christians.

Ephesians reads more like a theological treatise. In fact, it looks like one with two complementary parts. The first three chapters elaborate doctrinal teachings about God, Christ, Jews, gentiles, the law, works, and salvation by grace through faith. One of its main concerns is the abolition of the law in the death of Christ and the bringing together of Jews and gentiles into one unity in the church, the body whose head is Christ. So the first half of the letter deals mainly with theological and doctrinal teaching.

The last three chapters, however, turn to ethics, morality, or how to live out the Christian life. It even has a section on "household management," what scholars call a "household code." The author instructs male heads of households, wives, children, and slaves in how they should behave. All the others must submit to the men who head the households (Eph 5:22–6:9). This was also something addressed by Colossians, but it is, as usual, much lengthened and elaborated by the author of Ephesians. The second part of the letter, therefore, looks like a section on ethics. Scholars call this sort of thing by the Greek term *paraenesis*, which means something like moral instruction about everyday life. Ephesians, that is, looks less like a letter to a particular church and more like a general treatise on Pauline Christianity, including doctrine and moral instruction.

In fact, we can't be certain that the original writer addressed the letter to the Ephesian church in particular. There are Greek manuscripts that don't have the letter addressed "to the Ephesians," but have instead some kind of general address to "saints who are faithful." Some early Christians don't seem to know that the letter was addressed to Ephesus.[10] Some scholars, in fact, have suggested that Ephesians was actually written as a general or circular letter. Some even suggest that it may have been composed with the intention that it would function as something like a "general treatise" of Paul's gospel and ethics, placed first as a general introduction to a collection of Paul's letters. That view is highly speculative, but it does make well the point that Ephesians reads more like a general treatise than a letter to a particular location or addressing a particular problem.

In Colossians and Ephesians, we have glimpses of what "Paulinism," or at least one form of Paulinism, looked like after Paul. Paul is now a revered figure of the past, someone in whose name people compose forged letters in order to gain a more receptive hearing for their own theological views, which have evolved to be now a bit different from those of Paul. The "reserved eschatology" Paul himself advocated—insisting that Christians had to await their future salvation and the full blessings it would bestow—has become a "realized eschatology," teaching that Christians already possess those blessings; at least in some sense, they are already sitting "in heavenly places."

We have also seen here two fascinating attempts at what will become a very common practice among early Christians: pseudepigraphy in the name of past "greats" of the Jesus movement. What makes this example especially interesting is that one author has forged a letter in Paul's name by using as a model another letter he no doubt believed Paul actually wrote, but which was forged as well. Paul has receded into the past, and later admirers of his are writing letters in his name promoting their own brands of Christianity that have similarities to Paul's but are also different in significant ways. This will become the way Christianity develops, from its "primitive" phase of the first generation of believers to its more mature phases in the second, third, and fourth centuries, when the great ecumenical councils attempt to establish "orthodoxy."

CHAPTER 18

Differing Christians: Christology, Faith, and Works

Overview: Early Christianity presents us with a wide diversity in attitudes about Christology (the nature of Christ) and the relationship of faith to works. The book of James presents one perspective. It is written in the tradition of Jewish wisdom literature in its presentation of sayings. James also presents a view of works and faith that seems to oppose Pauline teaching. The terms "faith" and "works," however, have different meanings for the two different authors.

Christologies in Early Christianity

We have already encountered different forms of early Christian views of Jesus. Who was he? If he was divine, to what extent? If he was human, how so? Was he equal or subordinate to God the Father? It is important for a history of early Christianity—as distinct from, say, a theological account of Christian doctrine—to recognize how Christians disagreed on central aspects of faith and doctrine. To get from the "Jesus movement" during the life of Jesus of Nazareth to what much later became orthodox Christianity required many debates and choices. Why did what later became the orthodox church make the decisions it did at each stage?

We have already seen the high Christologies of Colossians and Ephesians. The Christology of John may be higher still, since in that work Jesus is explicitly made "equal with the Father" and bears the name "I am." Paul seems to have a somewhat "lower" Christology, since he has no hesitance in portraying Jesus as subordinate to God, as we saw in the last chapter. We have also seen that the author of the letters of John knew of Christians who accepted that Christ was divine but seem to have doubted that he was fully "human." They seem to have questioned whether Jesus' body was a flesh-and-blood body or only "seemed" to be so. In the second century, such Christians would be labeled "Docetists" by their opponents. A Docetic Christology was one that admitted the divinity of Jesus but denied that he was completely human in a physical sense.

Another form of early Christianity that was later declared heretical is what we call "adoptionist." Some early followers of Jesus believed that Jesus was divine but had not always been divine. They taught that Jesus was a very good man, but merely a man. Because of his exceptional righteousness, God "chose" Jesus at some point to be his son. God therefore "adopted" Jesus as his divine son. Such Christians variously placed that adoption at Jesus' birth, or perhaps at his baptism, or perhaps at his resurrection.

We have hints within the New Testament itself of these ideas. For instance, according to the Gospel of Luke, after Jesus' baptism, he was praying. Suddenly the heavens opened, the Holy Spirit in the form of a dove descended on him, and a voice from heaven said, "You are my Son, the Beloved; with you I am well pleased" (Luke 3:22). That happens to be a loose quotation from Jewish scripture (see Ps 2:7 and Isa 42:1). Most English translations have a footnote here, though, pointing out that some ancient manuscripts had the quotation as "You are my Son; today I have begotten you," which is actually closer to Psalm 2:7 as it appears in our Bibles. What that footnote is telling the reader is that the editors of the Greek text on which this English translation is based decided to print what they did, and not to print what does occur in some other Greek manuscripts, "today I have begotten you." Why? The editors believe that what they chose to print was most likely what the original author wrote, and that some later scribe changed the text to what is now just in the footnote.

But their decision may be mistaken. Other modern scholars make a good case that the original text did say, "Today I have begotten you," and that other scribes later changed it, probably in the second century, because they knew that those words could support the idea that Jesus had not been born the son of God, but was only "adopted" as God's son at his baptism.

Luke's original text, with the quotation of "today" in it, was perhaps used to promote an adoptionist Christology, which the later scribes believed was heretical. So they changed Luke's "today I have begotten you" to "with you I am well pleased." The latter carries no hint of adoptionism.[1]

We see a similar discrepancy in the different Greek texts of Luke 9:35, and probably for a similar reason. This is in the story of the transfiguration of Jesus on the mountain. Here again, a voice comes from above, this time from a cloud, and says, "This is my Son, my Chosen; listen to him!" The term "chosen" could be taken to mean that Jesus was not the "begotten" son of God, but was "chosen" by God at some point during his lifetime. Sure enough, as a footnote will say in many English versions, some ancient Greek manuscripts here do not have "my chosen," but "my beloved" instead. That may be a case in which our version has the original text, but later, more "orthodox" scribes changed "chosen" to "beloved" to make sure that people would not use this text to promote an adoptionist Christology.[2]

In Acts 2:36, in the first sermon preached in Acts, Peter, at the climax of his sermon, says, "Therefore let the entire house of Israel know with certainty that God has made him both Lord and Messiah, this Jesus whom you crucified." The words "made him" could imply that Jesus was not "eternally" Lord and Messiah, but was merely "made" those things at some point by God. In a sermon Paul later preaches in Acts, he says, "And we bring you the good news that what God promised to our ancestors he has fulfilled for us, their children, by raising Jesus; as also it is written in the second psalm, 'You are my Son; today I have begotten you'" (Acts 13:32–33). Here Paul quotes Psalm 2:7, including the "today" phrase. This constitutes another hint at early Christian adoptionism, this time at the resurrection of Jesus.

Finally, let's look at a quotation of Paul. We know that Paul himself does not seem to be an adoptionist. He certainly believed that Jesus was divine in preexistence, as Philippians 2:5–11 shows: Jesus was "in the form of God" and decided himself to give up higher status and voluntarily take on human form. Yet elsewhere, Paul lets slip a statement that could easily have made him seem to hold an adoptionist Christology. In Romans 1:4, Paul says that Jesus, here in the NRSV translation, "was declared to be Son of God with power according to the spirit of holiness by resurrection from the dead." I believe the translation "declared" here is misleading. The Greek word should be translated by something like "designated." The Greek makes it sound as if Paul is saying that God "designated" or "appointed" Jesus to be his son at his resurrection. Now, since I said that Paul is not himself an adoptionist, we may suppose that it is overinterpreting to take the Greek to imply an adoptionist assumption. Or we may imagine that Paul is here quoting something he has picked up from somewhere else. At any rate, the text does provide, I argue, one more piece of evidence for the presence, in earliest Christianity, of adoptionist Christology: the belief that Jesus was not always divine but became divine at some point in history.

With all these different Christologies in mind (see Fig. 10), let us imagine the choices early Christians had to make about what to believe and teach about Jesus and his nature. We may helpfully think of these as forks in a theological road. Let's start with the belief by Jesus' followers that he was a prophet, and perhaps even that he was a "king," a Jewish messiah. To call Jesus the Messiah or, in the Greek translation, Christ was in no way to make any kind of statement about whether he was a mere human or divine in some way. The "anointed ones" of Jewish scripture and tradition, even if they were called "sons of God," were generally not thought to be divine. Contrary to modern assumptions, Jesus was not divine because he was "the Christ" (except later in Christian theological thinking). Jewish messiahs were generally assumed to be human beings.

After his death, though, his followers had to decide whether Jesus was merely a man, or whether he was divine in some way. The decision made at this fork in the road by those who became "orthodox" was that he was in some way divine. But once that decision was made, Christians debated about when Jesus was divine. Some insisted that he became divine at some point (adoptionism). If they believed that, they then had to decide whether he became divine at his birth, at his baptism, or at his resurrection. That choice was deemed heretical by other Christians, who made the choice to believe that Jesus always was divine. But even then, Christians debated about the nature of his divinity and what that had to say about

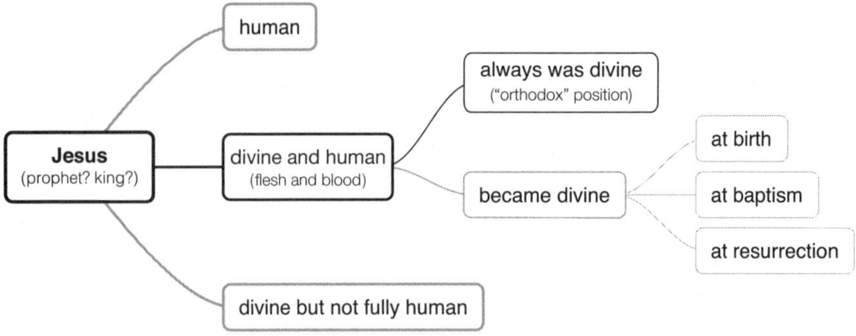

Fig. 10 Development of Ancient Christologies

whether he was human. The "heretical" choice here was that chosen by the Docetists: Jesus was divine, but he was not fully human; he only seemed to be flesh and blood. The "orthodox" choice at this fork in the road was to insist that Jesus was both God and man. Christ is fully divine and fully human.

This is, of course, a schematized and shorthand depiction of what was really a very long and messy historical process, but it shows us something of a picture of several different decisions that the early church had to make about the nature of Jesus, a branching tree of Christological options. It is important to see that at each fork, only one of the choices led to "orthodoxy" in Christianity. What later developed as orthodox Christology required the "correct" decision at each of several different forks in the theological road. If you made one bad choice, you would end up in one or another of several Christian heresies.

Christians, of course, may just chalk all this up to the providence of God. God, leading the church through the Holy Spirit, providentially caused it to make the right choice at each point, so that the orthodox Christologies of Nicea and Chalcedon eventually won out. Historians, however, can offer no such narrative. As historians, we must point out the many different directions Christianity could have taken in history. Christianity ended up the way it did because of social and cultural forces, political struggle, and the single-minded elimination of many different options for one "right" answer. The diversity of early Christologies is a fact of history. We can only marvel that one won out over all the others, and we must do our best to explain the process using only historical factors, such as social forces and politics.

James as Jewish Wisdom Literature

The varieties of early Christianity may be illustrated for other theological issues. Thus far I have concentrated in this chapter on Christology. But we may also consider soteriology, which refers to theology of salvation: how is it that people are saved? We have spent much energy already considering how Paul answers that question: people are justified by grace through faith apart from works of the law, and they will be saved by Jesus on the basis of that faith at his appearing in the future. We get a different answer with James.

James is an example of what scholars call "wisdom literature," a genre found in the Hebrew Bible in addition to books of history, poetry, law, and prophecy. This term refers to those writings that look like "advice" literature; that is, they comment on life and how to live it. (In fact, what scholars call "wisdom literature" is included in the wider part of the Hebrew Bible designated by Jews as "writings," in Hebrew, Ketuvim, which also, though, includes the Psalms, the Song of Songs, Ezra-Nehemiah, and other books.) This kind of literature reads less like narrative and more like straightforward instruction.

Proverbs begins:

> For learning about wisdom and instruction, for understanding words of insight, for gaining instruction in wise dealing, righteousness, justice and equity; to teach shrewdness to the simple, knowledge and prudence to the young—let the wise also hear and gain in learning, and the discerning acquire skill, to understand a proverb and a figure, the words of the wise and their riddles. The fear of the Lord is the beginning of knowledge; fools despise wisdom and instruction. (Pro 1:2–7)

The kinds of advice found in wisdom literature vary from how to find a good wife to how to run a household, warnings about loose women, or even how to eat properly. This literature reads as general life-instruction manuals—though written in poetic form—for young, upper-class men.

Sometimes one finds simply gnomic-like sayings or aphorisms, such as this one from Job that emphasizes natural human mortality: "A mortal, born of woman, few of days and full of trouble, comes up like a flower and withers, flees like a shadow and does not last" (Job 14:1). A lot of wisdom literature, as a matter of fact, is about the difficulty of life and how to survive it.

Much of this literature, of course, praises wisdom, even hypostatizing Wisdom (Sophia in the Greek) as a divine consort of God, as in this passage from the Wisdom of Solomon, a book found in the Christian Apocrypha but not in the Hebrew Bible:

> The beginning of wisdom is the most sincere desire for instruction,
> and concern for instruction is love of her,
> and love of her is the keeping of her laws,
> and giving heed to her laws is assurance of immortality,
> and immortality brings one near to God;
> so desire for wisdom leads to a kingdom. (Wis Sol 6:17–20)

Although much of this kind of literature sounds as if it was written by upper-class men for other upper-class men, some of it does advocate justice and assistance for the poor. The author of the book of Sirach emphasizes such concerns:[3] "Do not cheat the poor of their living, and do not keep needy eyes waiting" (Sir 4:1). "Give a hearing to the poor, and return their greeting politely" (4:8). We will see these concerns heavily stressed also in James.

As one might expect in advice literature intended for the training of young men, perhaps even for service in the "court" of a ruler, there is much emphasis on proper speech and the dangers of speech itself. Sirach advises, "Pleasant speech multiplies friends, and a gracious tongue multiplies courtesies" (Sir 6:5). But speech can harm as well: "For a bad name incurs shame and reproach; so it is with the double-tongued sinner" (6:1).

If we are familiar with this kind of literature, we can recognize it in James as well. James has this to say about speech, comparing the tongue to a rudder and people to ships. "Though they are so large that it takes strong winds to drive them, yet they are guided by a very small rudder wherever the will of the pilot directs. So also the tongue is a small member, yet it boasts of great exploits" (James 3:4–5). The author is aware of the burden and dangers of being a teacher: "Not many of you should become teachers, my brothers, for you know that we who teach will be judged with greater strictness. For all of us make many mistakes" (3:1–2). James, therefore, is a representative, in many ways, of typical Jewish wisdom literature. This book is certainly a Christian one, although it mentions Christ only twice (1:1, 2:1). With only a few such references removed, it could be read as a rather typical example of Jewish wisdom and instruction literature.

Faith and Works in James in Comparison with Paul

The one aspect of James that best demonstrates its setting in early Christianity, however, is its furious attack on what certainly appears to be some kind of Paulinism. The author opposes any doctrine of justification by faith apart from works. We remember what Paul had to say about this topic, and how he explicitly referred to Abraham as his prime example of justification by faith apart from works of the law: "What then are we to say was gained by Abraham, our ancestor according to the flesh? For if Abraham was justified by works, he has something to boast about, but not before God. For what does the scripture say? 'Abraham believed God, and it was reckoned to him as righteousness'" (Rom 4:1–3). Paul quotes Genesis 15:6 as proof that justification is by faith, not by works. "Now to one who works, wages are not reckoned as a gift but as something due. But to one who without works trusts him who justifies the ungodly, such faith is reckoned as righteousness" (Rom 4:4–5).

Paul had already made the same point even more strongly, as we have seen, in Galatians, even quoting the same passage: "Just as Abraham 'believed God, and it was reckoned to him as righteousness,' so, you see, those who believe are the descendants of Abraham," including gentiles (Gal 3:6–7). Paul teaches that Abraham was circumcised after being justified by his faith, which proves for Paul that it was precisely the faith, and not the work of circumcision, that justified him.

James completely disagrees. As he says, "Be doers of the word, and not merely hearers who deceive themselves" (James 1:22). James puts his points using the very same words Paul had, but insisting that works must be present also for salvation.

> What good is it, my brothers and sisters, if you say you have faith but do not have works? Can faith save you? If a brother or sister is naked and lacks daily food, and one of you says to them, "Go in peace; keep warm and eat your fill," and yet you do not supply their bodily needs, what is the good of that? So faith by itself, if it has no works, is dead. (James 2:14–17)

What is even more striking is that the author of James also appeals to Abraham as proof of his position:

> Was not our ancestor Abraham justified by works when he offered his son Isaac on the altar? You see that faith was active along with his works, and faith was brought to completion by the works. Thus the scripture was fulfilled that says, "Abraham believed God, and it was reckoned to him as righteousness," and he was called the friend of God. You see that a person is justified by works and not by faith alone. . . . For just as the body without the spirit is dead, so faith without works is dead. (James 2:21–24, 2:26)

James quotes precisely the same scripture from Genesis Paul had used, but to make the opposite point: Abraham was not justified by faith alone, but by works and faith.

Many scholars point out that the author of James is fighting something he may think is the theology of Paul, but that what he is against is not anything Paul actually taught. This is clear when we realize what James means by "faith" and "works" and how both are different from what Paul meant by the same terms.

About "faith," James says, "You believe that God is one; you do well. Even the demons believe—and shudder" (James 2:19). Paul would never have said that demons have the kind of "faith" he believes is sufficient for justification. "Faith" for Paul is not mere acceptance of a proposition about "fact." Rather, it is the total trust in God of Christian life. It is a throwing oneself completely onto and into Christ, making oneself dependent on the love and grace of God through Christ. It is a relationship and a way of life, not mere acquiescence to some "fact" or proposition. That is obvious in all that Paul says about "faith" in his letters, but particularly in Galatians and Romans. In fact, much of Romans, especially chapter 6, was written to demonstrate that if someone had "real" faith in Christ, one simply would not live in sin. That is not what James means by "faith." He means simply a belief in monotheism, an admission that God exists. And if that is all one means by "faith," then of course it is not "saving" faith, even in Paul's mind.

Likewise with "works." When Paul speaks of the "works" that cannot justify someone, he is referring to works of the Torah, the law of Moses (almost always, if not always, although that is somewhat debated by scholars). Paul does not mean by "works" just any act of kindness or mercy in his discussions of "faith" and "works." He might indeed believe that even those kinds of "good deeds" cannot in themselves justify or save someone. But in Galatians and Romans, when he is addressing the issue, he is thinking predominantly, if not completely, of circumcision and other requirements of the law of Moses.

James, on the other hand, never refers explicitly to the law of Moses itself. He never mentions circumcision, or keeping the Sabbath, or keeping kosher, the three main parts of "the law" for which Jews were best known in the ancient world. James instead speaks of the "law of liberty" (James 1:25, 2:12), which seems mainly just to refer to "morality" and general ethics, along with, of course, belief in God. The "work" of Abraham that James cites as justifying him was his willingness to sacrifice Isaac, not his circumcision (2:21). And when James speaks of his hearers' "works," he means simply their "good life" (3:13).

So also, when he castigates people for "transgressing the law," he is referring not to circumcision or dietary restrictions (although we can't exclude the possibility that he may have included those also), but "murder" (2:11) or "speaking evil" of another person (4:11). Most especially, he is concerned about the treatment of the poor and justice. The author in one place makes this summation of his view: "Religion that is pure and undefiled before God, the Father, is this: to care for orphans and widows in their distress, and to keep oneself unstained by the world" (James 1:27). This reveals no concern about the law of Moses at all. It is simply a concern for common morality and ethics, common among ancient Jews, even apart from any special interest in the Torah.

So the author of James may indeed think he is countering some form of Paulinism. In fact, since he uses the same words to refer to the issue as does Paul ("faith" and "works"), and since he quotes the same passage from Genesis 15:6 to back up his argument, it may well be that he has seen Galatians or Romans and wishes to use the same scripture in an attempt to "correct" Paul's views or a later "Paulinism" such as that of Colossians or Ephesians. After all, in Ephesians, "works" has come to be represented by "good deeds" in general (see Eph 2:9–10), and "trespasses" and sins are not specifically sins against the law of Moses, but any sinful deed committed even by gentiles in their former life (Eph 2:1–9). In fact, one may easily imagine that the letter of James was written to attack the kind of Paulinism of Ephesians, which explicitly teaches, "By grace you have been saved through faith, and this is not your own doing; it is the gift of God—not the result of works" (Eph 2:8–9; see also 2:5). Since James bases his argument also on Genesis 15:6, I think it likely that he had Paul and his arguments in Galatians and Romans in mind, but he is more accurately attacking a kind of Paulinism we find in Ephesians rather than Paul's position itself.

The Social Situation of James

I have sometimes used the phrase "the author of James," although I have also used the simple name "James" as a convenient designation for the author. I do not believe, however, that any actual "James" wrote the letter, as I mentioned in the last chapter. By claiming to be "James," the author is portraying himself as James, the brother of Jesus and the early leader of the church in Jerusalem. Since James had a reputation for piety and keeping the law, and since people were clearly traveling around claiming to be his representatives and urging gentiles to keep the law, this author is casting himself in a tradition of Jewish piety. We have already seen in Paul's letter to the Galatians that "James" was associated with opponents of Paul (Gal 2:12). This author, therefore, writes in the name of James to provide cover for what he intends to be a "correction" of writings of Paul.

But the historical James was almost certainly not the author. The historical James, brother of Jesus, was no more literate than Jesus may have been. If he could read at all, it might have been Hebrew or Aramaic, but almost certainly not Greek. Even if he could understand or read a bit of Greek, writing it would have required much more schooling and skill than he would have been able to acquire. And even if he could write a little Greek, he certainly would not have been able to attain the level of style evinced by this letter. The facts that this author shows no concern at all for the law of Moses, but advocates merely a certain form of morality, and that the style of the letter shows high education mean that James, the probably illiterate peasant or craftsman from Nazareth, could not have written it.

But we can say something about the social situation of the author, and that helps explain his need to emphasize that "works" must be added to "faith." He assumes that the churches to which he writes contain mostly poor people, some even destitute and desperate, but also a very few richer people. He writes to admonish the poor not to kowtow to the rich, and the rich not to mistreat the poor.

> My brothers and sisters, do you with your acts of favoritism really believe in our glorious Lord Jesus Christ? For if a person with gold rings and in fine clothes comes into your assembly, and if a poor person in dirty clothes also comes in, and if you take notice of the one wearing the fine clothes and say, "Have a seat here, please," while to the one who is poor you say, "Stand there," or, "Sit at my feet," have you not made distinctions among yourselves, and become judges with evil thoughts? Listen, my beloved brothers and sisters. Has not God chosen the poor in the world to be rich in faith and to be heirs of the kingdom that he has promised to those who love him? But you have dishonored the poor. Is it not the rich who oppress you? Is it not they who drag you into court? Is it not they who blaspheme the excellent name that was invoked over you? (James 2:1–7)

From this quotation, we might get the impression that the author is simply urging mutual respect of the rich and the poor, something like a respectful egalitarianism.

But he actually seems to believe that the "rich" are evil merely by the fact that they are rich. There are no "good" rich people in this letter. He seems to believe, in fact, that the wealthy are automatically corrupted by their wealth. This comes across when he gets even more heated later in the letter, in a passage that reads like a sermon of condemnation:

> Come now, you rich people, weep and wail for the miseries that are coming on you. Your riches have rotted, and your clothes are moth-eaten. Your gold and silver have rusted, and their rust will be evidence against you, and it will eat your flesh like fire. You have laid up treasure for the last days. Listen! The wages of the laborers who mowed your fields, which you kept back by fraud, cry out, and the cries of the harvesters have reached the ears of the Lord of Hosts. You have lived on the earth in luxury and in pleasure; you have fattened your hearts in a day of slaughter. You have condemned and murdered the righteous one, who does not resist you. (James 5:1–6)

This is more than just an appeal for the rich to treat their workers better. It is a screed against the rich entirely, apparently assuming that the only reason they are rich is that they oppressed the poor.

The author of James is a highly educated Jew, deeply familiar with the long tradition of Jewish wisdom literature. He uses that genre to write a letter of encouragement to churches that are composed mostly of poor, working people. When he says that "works" must supplement "faith," he means, at least to a great extent, basic justice—proper treatment of one's fellow human beings, especially proper treatment of the poor by their employers, the rich. The rich cannot get themselves off at the day of judgment by pious claims that they have "faith." His message is much like the popular left-wing bumper sticker that says, "If you want peace, work for justice." It is unfair to complain about conflict and do nothing to alleviate the social injustices that lie at the root of those conflicts. The author seems not particularly worried about circumcision, or the Sabbath, or kosher dietary laws. He is concerned about proper treatment of fellow human beings. And he is most exercised about the injustices the rich inflict on the poor.

If things are viewed from his perspective rather than the traditional "Pauline" or Protestant one, it is almost as if James didn't have the luxury of teaching salvation by faith alone. It is as if the author looked at some Christian texts that taught salvation by faith alone, apart from works, and said, "Well, that's nice and convenient for those people who don't want to work for justice." Perhaps he intended to oppose Paul's own writings. Perhaps what he was attacking was some modified form of Paulinism like that found in Ephesians, or even some form about which we now know nothing. But he clearly sends the message that if people want salvation and peace, they must also work for justice, and that means to a great extent the alleviation of the suffering of the poor. Even if he is not writing directly against Paul, he is opposing some kind of early Christianity, which demonstrates again the movement's remarkable diversity in its beginnings.

Women and Household

CHAPTER 19
The Pro-household Paul: The Pastoral Epistles

Overview: In the undisputed Pauline letters, marriage is seen as a way to extirpate sexual desire. Paul did not view marriage as a "good" for purposes of procreation, and he preferred that all Christians remain celibate, like him. The Pastoral Epistles, written to give instructions about church organization and management, present quite different attitudes. In the Pastoral Epistles, the church becomes a household, a specifically patriarchal structure in which men hold offices and women are not to have authority over them—this in contrast to the church as *ekklēsia*, a "town assembly," as it was in Paul's own letters. In contrast to Paul's letters, the Pastoral Epistles present a pro-family, antiascetic message.

Marriage, Family, Sex, and Women in Paul's Letters

As mentioned in a previous chapter, the Pastoral Epistles are called "pastoral" because they present Paul as instructing two of his followers, Timothy and Titus, on how to "pastor" a church, and on how to appoint other men to be pastors of churches. Very few scholars consider these letters to have been written by Paul. Many studies have shown that the vocabulary of the letters is very different from that of Paul's undisputed letters. The theology is different, and as this chapter will show, Paul's approach to marriage, sex, the household, and women is very different from that promoted here. Most scholars feel certain that the Pastoral Epistles were not written by Paul. They base their opinion on writing style, theology, and the more developed state of the church exemplified there, compared with the state of the church (and its structures of authority) exemplified in Paul's letters. Most scholars believe that these letters were written in the first half of the second century. We may imagine a date around 125, although that is merely a speculative number. The writing, in any case, must be from a time at which the "offices" of the church—"overseer" or bishop; presbyter ("elder") or priest; deacon—were much more firmly established than they could have been anytime during or immediately after the life of Paul.

These letters demonstrate why I needed to spend so much effort earlier in this book describing the traditional Roman household. The Pastoral Epistles attempt to reshape the church from reflecting the social reality of the ekklēsia, the "town assembly" of a Greek democratic *polis*, to that of the Roman household, with its *paterfamilias* at the top, its hierarchy, and the subordinated roles for women, children, and slaves. Not only does the author of these forged letters of Paul advocate the values of the hierarchical Roman household, but he also attempts to turn the church into a household, in fact, as he says in 1 Timothy 3:15, "the household of God." In doing so, he must depart from Paul's own ideas about women's place in the church and home, sex, and family.

Paul and the Household

To observe the sharp contrasts between Paul and the author of the Pastoral Epistles, we need to review Paul's own writings in some depth. In 1 Corinthians, Paul addresses the issue of sex and marriage. "Now concerning the matters about which you wrote: 'It is well for a man not to touch a woman.' But because of cases of sexual immorality, each man should have his own wife and each woman her own husband. The husband should give to his wife her conjugal rights, and likewise the wife to her husband" (1 Cor 7:1–3). The statement "It is well for a man not to touch a woman" seems to be a slogan used by at least some Corinthians, perhaps advocating an early form of Christian asceticism. Paul quotes it, probably, from a letter they had written to him, and he does not completely disagree with it. As the rest of the chapter demonstrates, Paul himself believes that avoiding sexual intercourse entirely is the preferred option, but he also does not believe that all Christians are up to the task. So he gives advice that attempts a balance of asceticism with some leniency toward those who are "weak" in the matter.

The point I here emphasize is how Paul balances his advice to the woman with that to the man. There is a reciprocity between male and female members in marriage that is striking, given the gender hierarchy assumed in the ancient world among Greeks, Romans, Jews, and early Christians for the most part. Paul, rather surprisingly, continues: "For the wife does not have authority over her own body, but the husband does; likewise the husband does not have authority over his own body, but the wife does" (1 Cor 7:4). The Greek terms here translated "wife" and "husband" can also mean simply "woman" and "man." The Greek language does not have special terms in the New Testament for "wife" or "husband" other than the general terms "woman" and "man." Here, it is certain what Paul means, but in other contexts his meaning is debatable. At any rate, it is remarkable that Paul does not simply put the wife under the control of her husband, as most people would assume, but gives her equal rights over the body of her husband, at least when it comes to sexual intercourse.

Then Paul gets to the issue of sex:

> Do not deprive one another except perhaps by agreement for a set time, to devote yourselves to prayer, and then come together again, so that Satan may not tempt you because of your lack of self-control. This I say by way of concession, not of command. I wish that all were as I myself am. But each has a particular gift from God, one having one kind and another a different kind. (1 Cor 7:5–7)

Paul himself was, as far as we know (and I think it certain), unmarried, at least at the time of his ministry as an apostle, and he would prefer that all Christians be. But he does not want people to be consumed by erotic desire, so he insists that married people continue to have sexual relations if they are unable to control their desire and quench it. He does not "command" people to have sex; he only "concedes" it. His preference would be celibacy for all who can endure it without experiencing desire.

We later get a hint of the reasons for Paul's wariness about sex and desire when he addresses those Corinthians who are single at the time. "To the unmarried and the widows I say that it is well for them to remain unmarried as I am. But if they are not practicing self-control, they should marry. For it is better to marry than to burn" (7:8–9). I have changed the last sentence from the NRSV ("it is better to marry than to be aflame with passion") to a more literal translation of the Greek. But what does Paul mean by "burn"? Some interpreters have suggested that he means "burning in hell"; that is, if single Christians are not able to avoid sex and have sex outside marriage, they will be destroyed in the burning of hell. I have argued elsewhere that it is much more likely that Paul means by "burning" the experience of sexual desire itself.[1]

In ancient Greek and Roman cultures, sexual desire was portrayed as a disease, a physical burning. Greek and Roman doctors prescribed all kinds of remedies to relieve people of the burning disease of erotic desire. They advocated sexual intercourse on a limited basis (they also tended to believe that the less sex people had, the healthier they would be), but they also recommended certain "cooling" diets or drugs to counteract the heat of desire. For many people in ancient Mediterranean cultures, desire was unhealthy, and sex was dangerous. Paul seems to share these common cultural presuppositions, and thus he is most concerned about the burning of erotic desire.

Paul's solution is that people should avoid sexual intercourse completely if they are able to quench their desire. But if they cannot, and they do experience erotic desire, they should get married and have sex. Interestingly, Paul does not recommend that they have sex in order to "control" their desire or as the proper expression of erotic desire. He says that they should have sex if they must so that they will not experience desire at all, the "burning" of erotic passion. Contrary to the way this passage is almost always read by modern Christians, Paul does not say that they should have sex so they may burn only a little; he is not recommending a little "simmering." He poses a radical "either-or": have sex if you must so that you will not experience erotic desire at all.

It sounds completely counterintuitive to us moderns that Paul could recommend sex within marriage as a way to preclude the feelings of erotic desire, but that is just what he is doing, as any literal interpretation of his words shows. And although the notion is completely strange—perhaps even inscrutable—to us, it was thought to be an available option by others in the ancient world. The Stoics were well known as philosophers who also believed that the true wise man could extinguish desire and passion entirely. They considered it very rare, but it was a goal of theirs. They even believed that married men could experience sexual intercourse with their wives without experiencing the passion of erotic desire—sex without sexual desire. Paul, therefore, was not the only person in the ancient world who believed that one could have sexual relations without desire.

But this means that Paul's beliefs about marriage and sex are very different from those of almost all modern people, especially Christians. First, Paul prefers that all Christians remain single and never marry. Second, Paul believes that the main problem is not the sex act itself, but the erotic desire that compels it. Third, Paul recommends marriage and sex within marriage not as the "good expression" of sexual desire, but as the tool with which Christians can preclude desire entirely. And fourth, the purpose of sexual intercourse in marriage for Paul is simply to keep from experiencing desire, and procreation has nothing to do with it. It is significant that Paul shows no concern at all for childbirth. It is quite likely that he did not because he believed that the end of this world was coming very soon, and there was no need to bring new people into this world to replace those who were passing away. As remarkable as it may seem from the perspective of modern Christians, Paul cared nothing about procreation in marriage, he advocated celibacy if possible, and he allowed sex within marriage only for the purpose of precluding sexual desire.

That this was Paul's considered opinion and not just an aberration of 1 Corinthians 7 is demonstrated also by 1 Thessalonians 4:5, as we have seen already. There, Paul addresses the men of the church in Thessalonica and concedes that they should have sex, only with their own wives, but not "in the experience of desire as indeed the gentiles do, those who do not know God" (my translation, more literal than most English versions). In that context, it is notable that Paul addressed only the men of the church. Here in 1 Corinthians, Paul addresses both the men and the women of the church, the married and the unmarried, widows and virgins. In all cases, Paul's preferred recommendation is that people not be married. If they are not able to avoid experiencing sexual desire, however, he allows them to marry, but he insists that they have sex only within the confines of marriage, and that they do so not as the "proper expression" of desire, nor for the purpose of procreation, but in order to preclude desire entirely.

I noted that in 1 Corinthians 7 Paul addresses both the women and the men in an equal fashion. And by the time of the writing of 1 Corinthians—whatever we make of the gender issues raised by 1 Thessalonians—Paul has come to include women in his churches, even in leadership positions. He mentions Prisca as a coworker along with her husband Aquila (1 Cor 16:19); they both are mentioned as the hosts of a house church in Ephesus. In

Romans 16, he mentions several women. Phoebe seems to be a deacon in the church at Cenchreae (Rom 16:1). In this context, Paul even puts Prisca's name before that of her husband, which may indicate that she enjoyed higher status than he (16:3).[2] Paul offers greetings to a "Mary" whom he commends for her work in the Roman church (16:6).

All in all, Paul mentions ten women in Romans 16, implying that they are leaders of churches or at least respected coworkers. Of two people, Andronicus and Junia, Paul says that they were followers of Christ before he was, and that they were in prison at some time with him, and he even calls them "apostles" (16:7). For much of history, the woman's name was translated as a man's name, "Junias," simply because scholars could not imagine that Paul would call a woman an apostle. But recent research has shown that "Junias" was very rare as a man's name, while "Junia" for a woman was common. Scholars nowadays admit that it was mere prejudice that kept the name from being translated as that of a woman. Paul, we now admit, recognized a woman as "among the apostles."[3]

Scholars have taken these references to women in Paul's letters as indicating that women enjoyed complete equality with men in Paul's churches. People commonly cite Galatians 3:28 to support the idea: "There is no longer Jew or Greek, there is no longer slave or free, there is no longer male and female; for all of you are one in Christ Jesus." But to make Paul a modern feminist or gender egalitarian goes too far. I have already noted that Paul believes that women are subordinate to men in God's plan. That hierarchy is presupposed when Paul says that the man is the "head" of woman, just as Christ is the "head" of man, and God is the "head" of Christ (1 Cor 11:3). Paul's argument that women must be veiled when they prophesy, but men must not, makes no sense if we do not also acknowledge his assumption of a gender hierarchy.

I have argued elsewhere that Galatians 3:28 probably refers to a baptismal slogan that held up a postresurrection, androgynous body as that created "in Christ." It was common in early Christianity to believe that the tragic division of humanity into male and female would be healed in the end-time by God turning all saved human bodies into androgynous bodies, as they were before some "fall" in ancient history. But the male aspects of that androgynous body would still be superior to the female aspects, if it retained the "female" at all. One way of thinking of it was that the masculine "presence" would simply swallow up the feminine "absence" within the body. Galatians 3:28 does not teach the maintenance of a two-gender humanity, now in equality. Rather, it teaches the swallowing up of two-gender humanity into an androgynous unity. It teaches unity of a one-gender body, not separate but equal genders.[4]

We need not consider Paul to make male and female completely equal in order to appreciate that he allowed women central roles, even leadership roles, in his churches. He recognized women as the hosts of house churches, as deacons (whatever that may have meant in his day, which is not at all clear), and as apostles, and he respected them as prophets, although he did insist that they veil themselves while praying or prophesying in church.

We might have a contradiction of all this if 1 Corinthians 14:34–35 actually was part of the original letter written by Paul. There, the writer says, "Women should be silent in the churches. For they are not permitted to speak, but should be subordinate, as the law also says. If there is anything they desire to know, let them ask their husbands at home. For it is shameful for a woman to speak in church." Many scholars, however, believe that these sentences were not written by Paul. They were later inserted into the letter by a scribe (maybe influenced by non-Pauline forgeries) who believed that Paul would not have allowed women to speak or hold authority in his churches. There are good reasons for this hypothesis. First, the vocabulary sounds less like the authentic Paul than it does like that of the Pastoral Epistles. Second, the sentences interrupt the flow of the prose before and after them. Third, the passage seems flatly to contradict what Paul said just a few chapters earlier, when he did allow women to pray and prophesy. The best argument, though, that it is an "interpolation" by a later scribe is that these two verses do not appear at this point in all ancient Greek manuscripts or other witnesses to the text (such as versions in other languages or quotations in church fathers). Some manuscripts place verses 34–35 after verse 40.

The fact that we do not have any manuscripts that leave out the verses altogether could be an argument in favor of their inclusion. It has been argued that since all our surviving Greek manuscripts include the verses, though in different locations, surely they were part of the original letter. But it is hard to explain why the verses occur in two different places in different manuscripts unless we assume that scribes found the verses written not in the text before them, but in the margins of a manuscript. And it is not hard to imagine why someone would have put them there. A scribe who could not imagine Paul actually permitting women to be preachers and prophets in church, a scribe perhaps even influenced by other forms of "Paulinism" such as that of the Pastoral Epistles, could have written them in the margin of a manuscript he was reading. Later scribes came along, saw the marginal gloss, and inserted it into the manuscript they were copying from the older manuscript before them. But different scribes placed the verses in different places in their copies, thus preserving verses 34–35 as part of 1 Corinthians 14, but in two different locations. This would explain how something that seems to contradict Paul's statements and practices elsewhere made it into 1 Corinthians.

At any rate, all this is to make the point that Paul recognized women as coworkers, as leaders in his churches, and as preachers and prophets. Although Paul still retained some notion about "female" being subordinate in some way to "male," women enjoyed remarkably free roles in his churches. Paul also gave wives the same kind of "ownership" over the bodies of their husbands as he gave husbands over the bodies of their wives. Paul's instructions on marriage were reciprocal, and women in his churches were important. As we will see, however, in this chapter and the next, later churches that took very different positions toward women, marriage, and sex nonetheless claimed to be the proper heirs of Paul.

The Pro-family and Antiascetic Stance in the Pastoral Epistles

I believe that all three of the Pastoral Epistles were written by the same person. They share a vocabulary and a writing style that are very different from Paul's but consistent in all three letters. The author writes in Paul's name to argue against a form of early Christianity he opposes. "I urge you, as I did when I was on my way to Macedonia, to remain in Ephesus so that you may instruct certain people not to teach any different doctrine, and not to occupy themselves with myths and endless genealogies that promote speculations rather than the divine training that is known by faith" (1 Tim 1:3–4; see also 4:7). We do not know many of the specifics of these "myths and genealogies." It has been speculated that they may be Gnostic, but there is no sufficient evidence to be certain on that score.

The author says that these teachers teach "the law" (1 Tim 1:6–7), and in Titus he mentions "those of the circumcision" (1:10) and "Jewish myths" and "commandments" (1:14). Apparently at least some of the people our author has in mind are Jews. We should not assume that the same opposition group is the reference of all the condemnations from all three letters. The condemnations of 1 Timothy and Titus sound remarkably alike, so perhaps those two letters were written to oppose the same brand of Christianity. But 2 Timothy evokes a different context (fictional, of course). It seems intended to sound like Paul's "last will and testament" while he is in prison awaiting his death. But it also mentions people who are claiming, heretically from our author's perspective, "that the resurrection has already taken place" (2 Tim 2:18).

Of more interest here, however, are the author's indications that he is opposing a kind of Christianity that teaches asceticism:

> Now the Spirit expressly says that in later times some will renounce the faith by paying attention to deceitful spirits and teachings of demons, through the hypocrisy of liars whose consciences are seared with a hot iron. They forbid marriage and demand abstinence from foods, which God created to be received with thanksgiving by those who believe and know the truth. For everything created by God is good, and nothing is to be rejected, provided it is received with thanksgiving; for it is sanctified by God's word and by prayer. (1 Tim 4:1–4)

Against the kind of early Christian asceticism that attempted strict controls over sex and eating, this author advocates eating and marriage. He explicitly later tells Timothy, "No longer drink only water, but take a little wine for the sake of your stomach and your frequent ailments" (1 Tim 5:23). The author opposes the kind of Christianity—and we know it existed—that forbade wine and certain kinds of foods, and he promotes marriage and the traditional household.

The Church as Household

In his attempt to defend marriage, the household, and traditional morality, the author ends up modeling the church on the household. Every person in the church is given a role in the household: "Do not speak harshly to an older man, but speak to him as to a father; to younger men as brothers, to older women as mothers, to younger women as sisters—with absolute purity" (1 Tim 5:1–2). Titus is given similar instructions and is told how to teach the church members their proper roles. Older women, for instance, are supposed to teach the younger women "to love their husbands, to love their children, to be self-controlled, chaste, good managers of the household, kind, being submissive to their husbands" (Titus 2:4–5).

Men have their own particular roles: "I desire, then, that in every place the men should pray, lifting up holy hands without anger or argument" (1 Tim 2:8). Women have very different roles, including a role in the church that matches their submission in the home:

> The women should dress themselves modestly and decently in suitable clothing, not with their hair braided, or with gold, pearls, or expensive clothes, but with good works, as is proper for women who profess reverence for God. Let a woman learn in silence with full submission. I permit no woman to teach or to have authority over a man; she is to keep silent. For Adam was formed first, then Eve; and Adam was not deceived, but the woman was deceived and became a transgressor. Yet she will be saved through childbearing, provided they continue in faith and love and holiness, with modesty. (1 Tim 2:9–15)

It is not clear how "childbearing" functions in this passage. Is the author saying that women can "earn" their salvation by bearing children? That is, they can redeem themselves from the curse brought on by Eve if they give birth? Or is he saying that they may be saved from the dangers of childbirth as long as they live in submission and modesty? Either interpretation could be supported by the Greek. We may even imagine that the text supports both readings at the same time. In any case, the author certainly wants the women of his churches to be childbearers and homemakers. That is their role in their own homes as well as in the church, the "household of God."

The Offices of the Church

The way the author instructs Timothy and Titus on how to appoint leaders of the churches also draws on the traditional household. One of the leadership positions is that of the "bishop" or "overseer." The Greek word may be translated either way. The Greek word *episkopos* could be used for any "overseer" or manager. We get the English word "bishop" from it, as can be seen simply by comparing the pronunciation of the two words. It need not here refer to what a bishop is and does in the Roman Catholic, Eastern Orthodox, or Episcopal churches (or others that have them, including Lutheran, Methodist, and other denominations). In those churches, bishops usually preside over not one church but many different parishes or churches in a broader area. The Pastoral Epistles seem to envision a "bishop" or a group of them over one church, even one house church, or the different house churches in one city. The author also gives their qualifications:

> Now a bishop must be above reproach, married only once, temperate, sensible, respectable, hospitable, an apt teacher, not a

> drunkard, not violent but gentle, not quarrelsome, and not a lover of money. He must manage his own household well, keeping his children submissive and respectful in every way—for if someone does not know how to manage his own household, how can he take care of God's church? (1 Tim 3:2–5)

The author adds that a bishop must not be a recent convert, and he must have a good reputation in the wider community of the city.

This is all very traditional morality of Greek and Roman culture, with its emphasis on the traditional, patriarchal household. It is telling, given the fact that the later church came to require that bishops were not to be married, that this author insists that leaders of his churches must be family men. The bishop occupies the role in the church that the paterfamilias does in a conservative Roman family. And all the traits here mentioned could have been read out of almost any middle-of-the-road philosophical treatise on morality and household management. The social model is all completely conservative and traditional.

The author next gives instructions for "deacons," a word that may also be translated simply as "servant," but which here obviously refers to an office of the church. They also must be heads of households, married only once, and with obedient and submissive children (1 Tim 3:12). There is some confusion about the "women" mentioned in this context (3:11). Does this verse mean that women were appointed as female deacons? Or are these simply the wives of the male deacons? It is not clear from the Greek or the context. There were female deacons in Paul's churches, as we have seen, so perhaps this is still an office in the present author's churches.

There may have been another office for male leaders in these churches. In 1 Timothy 4:14, the author mentions a "council of elders" that commissioned Timothy through the "laying on of hands." Later, the author says that elders who "rule well," and especially those who preach and teach, should be supported financially (1 Tim 5:17–18). The Greek word for "elder" is *presbyteros*, which normally just refers to an old man, but from which we get the word "presbyterian." Presbyterian churches are led by a group of persons, usually elected by the congregation. They take their name from this role in ancient Christianity. It is likely that the English word "priest" derives from the ancient "presbyter" also. Since it appears in Titus that presbyteros may just be another title for the "overseer" (the episkopos), or that the two roles overlapped (see Titus 1:5–9), it is not certain that it is here a separate, third office for men in the churches represented by the Pastoral Epistles.

In all these cases, the male leaders of churches are expected to be married heads of households. In the beginning of Christianity, there was no expectation of a celibate priesthood. There are examples of unmarried Christian leaders, as we have seen to be the case with Paul himself, but that seems to have been the exception, not the norm. For the author of the Pastoral Epistles, that fact is used in his attempt to shape the church, the ekklēsia, to be a "household" instead.

There were also roles and offices for at least some women in these churches. We have already seen that there may have been female deacons. But in 1 Timothy we see a new office that will later become highly important in the Christianity of late antiquity: the widow. The author gives elaborate instructions on how to deal with both older and younger widows in the church:

> Honor widows who are really widows. If a widow has children or grandchildren, they should first learn their religious duty to their own family and make some repayment to their parents; for this is pleasing in God's sight. The real widow, left alone, has set her hope on God and continues in supplications and prayers night and day; but the widow who lives for pleasure is dead even while she lives. Give these commands as well, so that they may be above reproach. And whoever does not provide for relatives, and especially for family members, has denied the faith and is worse than an unbeliever. (1 Tim 5:3–8)

The author, though, goes on to speak of "registering" widows. There is some kind of official list of "real widows." They must be sixty years old or older, must have been married only once, and must show several other traits, as is the case with the bishops and deacons.

Several times we have seen the author of the Pastoral Epistles recommend people who have been married only once. He is enthusiastic about people in the church being married, but he prefers that they be married only once. So as was the case for the men, women who become "official" widows must have been married, but only once.

It is clear why the author would want some kind of official church role for widows. If they really were without other family members, especially children or grandchildren, they would likely have had no resources at all for living. The church, therefore, would become their "family." In later Christianity, in the church of late antiquity, the role of "widow" did become an official one. They were registered, recognized, and financially supported by the churches. Rich widows, who of course did not need financial support, became important patrons of the church and sometimes used their wealth to establish monasteries and especially convents for women.

Our author, however, is careful to exclude younger widows from the registry of widows. He does not trust them. He believes that their sexual desires will lead them astray, and if they are given financial support, they will just become gossips and busybodies. So even though he especially values those who are married only once, he instructs the church to make sure younger widows marry again, bear children, and become good, female managers of a household (1 Tim 5:11–15). All other women, as he concludes this section, must be supported by their own families and households (5:16).

The author of the Pastoral Epistles is not inventing all these different roles for leaders of his churches. It is clear from his language that he is not establishing the offices of bishop or deacon, although he may be doing so for widows. He is relying on the existence of those offices and is strengthening them in order to use the organization of the church to oppose other forms of Christianity, along with their doctrines he rejects, including asceticism. He stresses the offices of bishop or overseer and deacon, and also presbyter (if that is indeed a separate office and not just another word for the overseers), so that he can solidify his vision of what the church should be and teach.

But he is doing something with his rhetoric that is quite unlike much Christianity before him: he is taking what was an ekklēsia model for the church and turning it into an organization modeled on the traditional Roman household. The churches of Paul took inspiration for their organization and self-identity from at least three kinds of organizations of the ancient Mediterranean.[5] They were perhaps modeled in part on the Jewish synagogue—although it is interesting that they did not call themselves "synagogues." Early Christian house churches also resembled ancient Greek "voluntary associations," such as clubs.[6] Like those voluntary associations, the Christian churches met regularly, had some kind of religious cultic activities, and ate and drank together. The third ancient social model used by early Christians, however, was the town assembly as a political unit in the Greek city.

It is likely that Christians used the term *ekklēsia* for themselves partly because they found that word in the Greek translation of Jewish scripture. But the connotations of the Greek use of the term as "town assembly" could not be avoided. Even though they met in houses, Paul's churches were not so much modeled on the traditional family or household as on other, more political, models.

The author of the Pastoral Epistles does his best to change all that. He tries to turn his "town assemblies" into traditional, patriarchal households. Every member has a familial role to play, as paterfamilias, mother, brother, sister, child, or slave. Those women who have no households of their own must be forced into some other household, either by remarriage for younger women or by enrollment in the office of "widow" in the household of God. Everyone is forced in one way or another into the household, which is hierarchically arranged, ruled by men, and served by women, who keep house and bear children. This is not the same house church Paul knew. This is the hierarchically enforced, patriarchal, traditional household of conservative Greco-Roman ideology.

Household Codes

We have already seen moves in this direction in Colossians and Ephesians. They departed from Paul in several ways theologically, as I pointed out in Chapter 17. Paul tended not to emphasize gender hierarchy in his churches; he assumed some gender hierarchy, as I have shown, but he had little interest in belaboring it. Paul had little to say that would enforce the traditional family or roles within it—although admittedly there are some remarks, such as that on the veiling of women. Colossians, however, introduces traditional Greco-Roman "household codes" in its instructions. These were common in popular philosophical morality: instructions that told heads of households how to order and manage the different people in their houses. Thus Colossians instructs wives to be subject to their husbands, and husbands to love and take care of their wives. Children are to obey their parents, and fathers are not to provoke their children. Slaves are to obey their masters, and masters must not mistreat their slaves (Col 3:18–4:1).

That rather bare version of a household code is much expanded by Ephesians (5:22–6:9). The author of Ephesians takes over the instructions of Colossians that wives, children, and slaves must submit to the male master, but strengthens it by comparing the relationship of husband and wife to that of Christ and the church. It also elaborates the instructions to slaves, likening their submission to their masters as service to Christ and telling them that they must be not only obedient slaves but also enthusiastic ones. The point of view is clearly that of the paterfamilias. Only brief instructions are given to the male heads of household, perhaps because the author assumes that they know already how to behave.

We do not have one special section for the "household code" in the Pastoral Epistles. Rather, it is as if each of the letters has become a household code itself. Both 1 Timothy and Titus are full of admonitions about the familial role expected of every Christian: old men, young men, old women, young women, husbands, wives, and even widows are brought back into the household in one way or another. Slaves get less attention, but they are noticed, nonetheless (1 Tim 6:1–2; Titus 2:9–10). Although 2 Timothy reads less like a household code and more like a last testament of Paul, it still maintains the tone by making Paul sound like the dying father addressing his son, Timothy (2 Tim 1:2, 2:1, 2:22, 3:14–15). It is as if the author of the Pastoral Epistles did not need a special section for his household code because each letter is one in itself.

The advocacy of marriage and sexual relations for procreation within marriage marks this brand of Christianity as a departure from Pauline Christianity—and probably from the ministry of Jesus himself, who seems to have been famous for calling disciples away from their families.[7] Turning the church, the ekklēsia, into a household, an *oikos*, is something Paul did not do. This change was made by some of his "followers" many years after his death, first to some extent in Colossians and Ephesians and then with a vengeance in the Pastoral Epistles.

Although this is what most modern Christians expect the church to be—the promoter and defender of marriage and family—it is actually a form of Christianity that contradicts the teachings of Jesus and Paul. In fact, it is a version of Christianity that later lost out as the more ascetic versions of Christianity came to predominate until the Renaissance and the Reformation. As we will see in the next chapter, other authors used the name and fame of Paul to critique the traditional household and to advocate instead an antifamily, antisex form of ascetic Christianity. They were fighting against people like the author of the Pastoral Epistles.

CHAPTER 20

The Anti-household Paul: The *Acts of Paul and Thecla*

Overview: The *Acts of Paul and Thecla* has a narrative quite similar to those in ancient Greco-Roman novels: Thecla becomes enamored of Paul, and they share a number of adventures. The *Acts*, however, redirects eroticism toward a belief in a gospel of purity and asceticism. It presents an ascetic, antimarriage, antifamily message that would break the cycle of sex, birth, death, and decay that was so obvious in the ancient world. Given that Thecla emerges from the story as the true hero (and not Paul), could it be possible that the story is a feminist one?

The *Acts of Paul and Thecla* in Literary Context

Religious studies as a discipline focuses on the beliefs, literature, and practices of different religions from a secular point of view. Religious studies grew out of the theological study of, mainly, Christianity and Judaism in the twentieth century. But whereas previous generations, even until the 1960s, had generally studied religious traditions from a confessional point of view—people even in universities studying what were their own religious beliefs and traditions—religious studies departments intentionally set themselves up to study those materials in a comparative and secular manner, not presupposing faith and not concerning themselves with the "truth" of religious claims. This means that students who take courses in departments of religious studies in modern American universities are often trained to come to different religions, even their own, as something new, foreign, or even strange. Religious studies courses often attempt to teach students how to look at something they may initially see as irrational, false, or even making no sense, and to continue to study that phenomenon—a text, a ritual, an institution—until they see how it can in fact make sense, at least to adherents of those religions. This is one of the by-products, and one of the significant values, of the approach to religion usually practiced in the discipline of religious studies: we learn to see as rational something that we initially may see as irrational or strange.

For the topic of early Christian literature and history, this becomes easier when we get outside the Bible and analyze documents we may never have heard of and that represent a kind of Christianity with which we are not familiar. We have already done this with the *Gospel of Thomas*, and we saw that, compared with the canonical Gospels, it does seem odd, both in form and in what it teaches. Much other literature survives from earliest Christianity about which most modern Christians know nothing. We have many such documents—gospels, acts of different apostles, apocalypses, letters, and more—from the first few centuries of Christianity. They are all works of fiction, although they often claim not to be. They usually pose as actual historical accounts or actual "gospels" written by "real" apostles. Most are pseudonymous, but even those that are anonymous provide us with almost no "historical facts" about "what really happened." They are pious legends. They are often fascinating stories nonetheless.

Sometimes scholars use the label "New Testament Apocrypha" for this literature simply as a catchall frame. That term, though, is rather misleading. For one thing, "apocrypha" means "things hidden," and much of this literature has never been really hidden (although some has been, only to be discovered later, such as the Nag Hammadi codices or the *Gospel of Judas*). For another, the term "New Testament Apocrypha" gives the impression that this is the Christian parallel to the Apocrypha published in Roman Catholic, Eastern Orthodox, and Anglican Bibles, as well as study Bibles that include the Apocrypha between the Old and New Testaments (see the explanation in Chapter 2 of this book). That Apocrypha is a collection of Greek translations of Jewish texts that have been passed down as a collection for centuries. What people call the "New Testament Apocrypha" has not experienced that history. The term just refers to all kinds of early Christian writings that did not fall under the categories of official church documents, patristic literature (the church fathers), or the canonical New Testament. Thus people should be aware that when they encounter the term "New Testament Apocrypha," it does not refer to a recognized body of literature in the sense of the Apocrypha in Catholic and Anglican Bibles.[1]

The *Acts of Paul and Thecla* looks odd to modern audiences partly just because it fashions itself narratively along the lines, as I will explain later, of the ancient Greek romance novel, a genre not generally familiar to modern audiences. But another reason the document may even be off-putting to modern audiences is its message: it is radically ascetic, claiming that the only true form of Christianity teaches the complete avoidance of sex, even in marriage, and rejects the family and the traditional household. This is a version of Paulinism that is "anti-household."

The radical asceticism of some early Christianity initially strikes many of my students as almost incomprehensible. For most Americans (this is less true, I believe, for Christians in Europe or many other cultures), the two things that Christianity stands for more than anything else are the family and patriotism. Christians often will fail to bat an eye if they encounter other people who don't really believe in the Trinity, or Christians who don't know what they believe about the Eucharist, or the precise doctrine of the divinity and humanity of Christ, or the nature of the Holy Spirit. What would have been considered in centuries past the most central beliefs and doctrines of Christianity are hardly important to many American Christians. But they will usually be absolutely shocked if they meet another Christian who believes that Christianity teaches against the modern idea of the family, or teaches that nationalism or patriotism is a sin. Indeed, as I have argued elsewhere, patriotism and the family are the only two things most American Christians regard as indispensable to Christian values.[2] I have claimed that the family and the nation are the two most central gods of American Christian idolatry. So it comes as a surprise to my students when they encounter the kind of Christianity represented in the *Acts of Paul and Thecla* precisely because it teaches that the gospel demands the rejection of the traditional family and of the nation.

The *Acts of Paul and Thecla* makes its points, as I mentioned, by imitating the ancient Greek romance novel.[3] Typically, these novels are set in the Hellenistic period (that is, from the time of Alexander the Great to the rise of Rome as the main imperial power in the Mediterranean), although they were written later than that, from the first century through late antiquity. The stories are often set in Greek cities in the eastern part of the Mediterranean. Most of the time, the main characters are from the upper class. The novels usually star a young man and woman who fall in love. Sometimes they even are able to be married for a time before they are tragically separated, but most often they are separated before they can get married or consummate their love.

I have already described this kind of literature in Chapter 1. To recapitulate briefly, these stories are driven by the attempts of a separated, star-crossed young couple to find each other again. The story is also driven by the beauty of the man and the woman and the erotic pull they have on other characters in the story. People regularly think, for instance, that they are in the presence of a goddess when they first see the woman. Both men and women try to seduce the gorgeous young man. But usually the woman and sometimes, but less usually, the man are able to maintain their sexual purity, keeping themselves for the other in case they are reunited. The focus of the stories is always on sexual desire, the unspeakable beauty of both lovers, and their attempt to find each other and finally unite, make love, set up a household, and live happily ever after. The novels are full of the erotic—especially the erotic of the eye, the visual allure of beauty. The *Acts of Paul and Thecla* steps into this kind of erotic literary world with its radically ascetic message.

The Gospel of Asceticism in the *Acts of Paul and Thecla*

The story opens with Paul, fleeing persecution in Antioch, arriving in the city of Iconium. While Paul is preaching in a church meeting in the house of his host, he is overheard by Thecla, who is sitting nearby at a window. She is enraptured by Paul's teaching, the content of which is that the gospel calls people to virginity for those not yet married, and to abstinence from sex for those who are. The problem is that Thecla is an upper-class woman engaged to be married to one of the most important men in town.

When Thecla shows her unwillingness to go through with the marriage, her fiancé has Paul arrested as the instigator of the trouble. He eventually also hauls Thecla before the governor, who has Paul beaten and expelled from the city and orders Thecla to be burned at the urging even of her mother. Thecla is miraculously saved by God, who sends rain and hail to put out the fire. This is only one of the many miraculous escapes Thecla will make in the story. Thecla then leaves Iconium and seeks out Paul.

To make a long story short, the narrative continues with Thecla allowed to follow Paul for a while, but then comes another scene in which she rejects the love of a rich and powerful man in Antioch. She endures another trial and punishment in which she must be saved this time from being eaten by beasts. After more miraculous escapes, Thecla basically turns herself into an apostle, and a rather male-looking one at that. She had already baptized herself, and now she dresses like a man (she had earlier told Paul that she was going to cut her hair off, another reference to her masculinization; §25). She gathers a band of celibate young men and virgins around her and again finds Paul. Thecla announces that she is going to preach the gospel herself, a plan Paul blesses. The story concludes with Thecla going off as a missionary preaching an ascetic gospel.

Those are the bare bones of the story. But it becomes much more interesting in an analysis of its rhetoric, and especially of the way it uses eroticism to teach the avoidance of sex. One tool the author uses repeatedly is the beauty of Thecla, and although she ends up "male," she starts off in the story as very feminine indeed. From the beginning, her status as a virgin girl is emphasized (§§7, 9). When Thecla goes to visit Paul in prison (during the night, which is probably another hint of eroticism), she bribes the gatekeeper by giving him her bracelets and the jailor by giving him her silver mirror (§18). Jewelry is a sign of femininity in ancient culture, and mirrors are especially so. Funeral monuments of young women, for instance, often feature a carved mirror as part of the decoration. Thecla's girlish, even clinging, dependence on Paul also emphasizes her femininity.

The author goes even further, however, and repeatedly eroticizes Thecla as an object of the gaze of onlookers—and the reader. In one scene, after being condemned to be burned, Thecla is brought naked to the site of execution (§22). All the people look on in admiration and sadness. Even the governor, who had just condemned her to death, "wept and admired the power that was in her." It is difficult not to read "the power" also as a veiled reference to her naked but beautiful body, exposed for all to see. When Thecla is later condemned to be killed by the beasts, we are again reminded of her beauty. A rich woman weeps that "such beauty was to be thrown to the wild beasts" (§29). When Thecla later actually has to face the beasts, the reader's gaze is again focused on her body: the author points out that she was stripped again (§33). After being miraculously saved from the beasts, she sees a pool nearby, filled with man-eating seals (yes, that's right). She takes this as an opportunity to baptize herself, intending to throw herself in. This time the governor weeps "because the seals were to devour such beauty" (§34). We should remember that Christians at this time were likely baptized naked. So as we read, we are to imagine a beautiful young virgin, standing, fighting, and making speeches stark naked before all the people of the city. This is no accidental occurrence of eroticism. It is orchestrated by the author to heighten the eroticism of the story and to pull the narrative and the readers along.

The last point I will make about the story's eroticism is the way Thecla is portrayed as yearning after Paul. Also here, there are unmistakable signals of desire. In many Greek romance novels, the two lovers first taste their desire for one another at a chance sighting, perhaps at a parade, or by simply overhearing the other speak with friends. A similar scene introduces Thecla, who falls in love with Paul just by hearing his voice through a window. When she visits him in prison, she kisses his bonds (§18). She regularly gazes longingly at him (§§20–21). Thecla is said to "long for Paul" (§40) and to search for him like a lamb (§21); she is "chained to him by affection" (§19). Her fiancé complains that Thecla "loves" Paul rather than himself (§13).

With all this emphasis on erotic desire and physical beauty, and with the "gaze" of the story so intensely trained on this young virgin, we are likely to be surprised when we realize that it is all put to the service of a gospel that forbids sexual activity entirely. Paul, sounding like the Jesus of Matthew and Luke, offers his own "beatitudes":

> Blessed are the pure in heart, for they shall see God; blessed are those who have kept the flesh chaste, for they shall become a temple of God; blessed are the continent, for God shall speak with them; blessed are those who have kept aloof from this world, for they shall be pleasing to God; blessed are those who have wives as not having them, for they shall experience God; blessed are those who have fear of God, for they shall become angels of God. (§5)

When the author uses the words "chaste" and "continent," he means rejecting all sexual contact whatsoever. When he invokes the Pauline phrase about having wives "as not having them" (see 1 Cor 7:29), he means avoiding sexual contact even in marriage. The gospel Paul preaches in this document is the radical rejection of all sexual contact, even in marriage. It reflects what became the acknowledged "orthodoxy" of the Catholic Church until the Renaissance and Reformation: a hierarchy of virtue and reward exists on earth and in heaven, with those who have never experienced sexual activity (virgins, both men and women) held in highest honor.[4]

But the *Acts of Paul and Thecla* goes even further. It insists that the avoidance of sexual activity is the only way to preserve the purity of one's baptism and be assured of future resurrection. In another of his "beatitudes," Paul says, "Blessed are those who have kept the baptism" (§6), by which is meant that they have avoided sex after their baptism. Paul at one point even refuses to baptize Thecla, explaining that she is so beautiful that she may not be able to avoid sexual encounter in the future, so she should put off her baptism (§25). This reflects a common belief among Christians in late antiquity that baptism worked to forgive sins one had already committed, but any serious sin committed after baptism might not be forgiven.[5] Christian emperors, therefore, often put off baptism until their deathbeds, since they knew that they might have to commit actions, such as killing or sexual intercourse, as part of their office. The *Acts of Paul and Thecla* reflects this assumption in its insistence that only the "chaste" life will "keep baptism" (see §§6, 9, 31).

The *Acts* also reflects the ancient view, held by both Jews and Christians at different times and places, that angels are sexless, androgynous beings, and that the resurrected bodies of Christians will be sexless or androgynous just like those of the angels. This is doubtless the meaning of Jesus' saying in Mark 12:25 (and parallels in Matt 22:30; Luke 20:35). It is probably the scenario assumed by Paul in Galatians 3:28 when he says that "in Christ" there is no "male and female."[6] So Paul in the *Acts of Paul and Thecla* says that those who avoid sex "become a temple of God," and that God "shall speak with them" (§5).

The *Acts of Paul and Thecla* not only presents its radical message on the lips of Paul and Thecla; it also furnishes "bad guys" who represent the opposing position, the nonascetic position. Thecla's mother provides one such portrait. She, like many mothers of the ancient world, as in the world today, is eager for Thecla to enter into a profitable marriage. She is desperate when Thecla refuses a rich and powerful citizen, and at first she even urges the burning of her daughter (§20). Paul's falsely flattering companions Demas and Hermogenes provide another foil. In contrast to the dietary asceticism of Paul—who alternates between fasting completely and contenting himself with plain bread, vegetables, and water (§§5, 23, 25)—Paul's two "false" disciples accept an invitation from Thecla's rejected fiancé to feast and drink in his home: "a sumptuous supper and much wine and great wealth and a splendid table" (§13). It is from them, in their condemnations of Paul, that we get the clearest summary of Paul's message: "He deprives the husbands of wives and maidens of husbands, saying, 'There is for you no resurrection unless you remain chaste and do not pollute the flesh'" (§12). Demas and Hermogenes, in fact, are given a position not unlike that of the author of the Pastoral Epistles, who recommends drinking wine, condemns dietary restrictions and food laws, recommends marriage and childbearing, and condemns those who forbid marriage. The *Acts of Paul and Thecla* is written precisely to attack the kind of Christianity represented in the Pastoral Epistles.

The Cultural Context of Ancient Sexuality

When I am teaching the *Acts of Paul and Thecla* and other radically ascetic literature from ancient Christianity, I often have to explain why this kind of Christianity was so popular among early Christians. And it was popular. The ascetic movements of ancient Christianity drew many people, especially women, and perhaps young people as well. What made this kind of radical asceticism so attractive to ancient persons?

Many people do not realize how the meaning of sex has changed over the past few decades. One could argue, in fact, that sex just doesn't mean the same thing for people now, especially young people, as it did before the 1970s. At least two things began changing modern society around the 1970s that altered the meaning of sex, probably forever: the feminist movement and the pill. Young students do not realize how inextricably linked heterosexual intercourse was to gender hierarchy and pregnancy. Every time a man and woman had sex, they faced the possibility that the woman might become pregnant. And before the rise, or we should say the resurgence, of the women's movement in the 1960s and 1970s, every sex act tended to be scripted to reflect the gender hierarchy of male on top and female on bottom. Modern feminism has forced even those who ridicule it and would not consider themselves feminists at all to think about gender relations—and therefore sex—in more egalitarian ways than were possible in the ancient world. And reliable contraception has decoupled the sex act from conception, certainly in many cases and therefore in the minds of people. There have been other cultural and social factors that have caused a recent reconceptualization of sexuality, but at least those two, both of which became culturally significant around the 1970s, have been central: feminism and reliable contraception.

The linkage of sex to gender hierarchy and procreation was even more pronounced in the ancient world. All ancient societies were built on assumptions of a rigid gender hierarchy. Opposition to sex acts considered not "normal" was almost without exception based on the assumption that it was "male" to penetrate and "female" to be penetrated. Therefore, it was considered abnormal for a man to be penetrated in any way, orally or anally, by another person, whether male or female. It was considered "monstrous" for a woman to penetrate another woman or a man. Homosexual acts were not considered "abnormal" because of any idea that sexual desire for members of one's own sex was wrong or unthinkable. In fact, people most often assumed that women were sexually voracious and that most men were naturally attracted to beautiful young men as well as women. What made homosexual practices "unnatural"—wrong or even disgusting—was the idea that one of the men would have to be penetrated (they imagined) or one of the women would have to penetrate. Ancient people were unable to conceptualize any sex act without imagining it reenacting—or disrupting—the natural hierarchy of male over female.

Likewise, for ancient persons, even more than for modern persons before the 1970s, heterosexual intercourse was always linked to the possibility of pregnancy. Ancient women experienced many more pregnancies than modern women. Even demographics show this. For the population of the Roman Empire to remain the same—not for it to increase, but only to remain stable—the average number of childbirths per woman had to be around six or seven.[7] Given the dangers of childbirth, infant mortality rates, and range of life spans, many more births were necessary then than now just to maintain population levels. This fact means that ancient people almost always had to think about pregnancy when they were having heterosexual sex.

All this also led ancient people to connect sex to death in ways scarcely imaginable to moderns. We tend to think of life when a child is born. Ancient people did also, of course, but they could scarcely avoid thinking of death. Why have births at all? Because all of us know how ubiquitous death is. We regularly see in ancient culture the assumption of a cycle. Birth is followed by life. But living bodies necessarily age, or become ill, or are damaged, and death is the result. Death is followed by corruption. And that is followed by other births in order for the human race to survive. This cycle—sex, birth, death, decay, followed by more sex, birth, death, decay, and on and on—occupied a central place in ancient notions of life. Philosophers and poets bemoaned it as the Sisyphean predicament of all human existence: sex, birth, death, decay.

The Early Christian Answer to the Cycle of Birth and Death

Many early Christians believed that they had found an answer to the hopeless cycle of birth, death, and decay. They believed they could break the cycle at the very beginning: don't have sex. This does not seem at all intuitive to us moderns, precisely because we do not share the feeling of being entrapped in the cycle that begins with sex and ends with death and decay. But we see this as one apparent motive for early Christian asceticism: the desire to gain release from the natural trap that began with sex and ended with decay and corruption. Do you want to break out of the cycle of death and despair? Nip it in the bud: at sex. Don't have sex, and you break the cycle. Don't have sex, don't have childbirth, don't have death.

Of course, these Christians already believed that there was a solution to the ultimate state of death: resurrection. But Christian ascetics seemed to go further and assume that one could break out of death's cycle even more by living a life of celibacy and chastity. This comes out in their texts. In the *Acts of Paul and Thecla*, Paul says, for instance, that his goal is to "rescue" people "from corruption and uncleanness and from all pleasure, and from death" (§17). Paul promises rescue from death for those who first refuse sex. Paul's gospel explicitly links abstinence with resurrection (§5). He teaches that those who die will be resurrected if they keep their baptism "pure" by avoiding sex. But ascetics already partially partake in that resurrected state by nature of their angelic purity. As counterintuitive as it may seem to us moderns, many ancient people were drawn to the asceticism of some forms of Christianity because they saw it as the first blow in breaking the ineluctable cycle of sex, birth, death, and decay.

It is also clear that women saw asceticism as a means of escaping from their inferior status as female. When Thecla asks Paul to baptize her and allow her to join his ministry, she tells him that she intends to cut her hair (§25). At the end of the story, before she launches her own independent mission, she begins dressing like a man (§40). As an ascetic, by rejecting sex, Thecla escapes from the typical role of woman as baby factory and takes on the higher and more powerful role of the free and independent man. But she has to reject sex and its consequence, childbirth, in order to escape the role of a woman. This proved attractive to a substantial minority of ancient Christian women. For them, because sex was imprisoning, asceticism was liberating.

Naturally, that meant that asceticism was threatening for at least one dominant social segment: male heads of households. We should note how the two sides of the conflict in the *Acts of Paul and Thecla* line up. On one side is Thecla, attempting to escape her normal fate in the household, along with other women, including young women as well as many young men. Paul first comes to Thecla's attention when she sees "many women and virgins going in to Paul" (§7). Thecla's mother, complaining about the fact, says that "all the women and the young men" are following Paul (§9). She later complains that women in particular have been badly influenced by him (§20). When Thecla is later condemned to be killed by the beasts, we are told that it was the women who objected the loudest (§§27, 32, 38), or elsewhere, "the women and children" (§28). Even the lioness meant to kill Thecla in the arena sides with her instead. First, the lioness just licks her feet, to the amazement of the crowd (§28). But later, when a bear and a lion are also set on Thecla, the lioness comes to her aid, first killing the bear and then turning on her own kind and fighting the lion until both of them lie dead (§33). Even the female of the lion species sides with Thecla.

So on one side are the majority of the women in the story, along with many "young men" and children. On the other are the male heads of households and their compatriots who fear the destruction of the traditional family. Thecla's fiancé correctly sees what is at stake: if Paul is successful, he says, he will be deprived of his marriage (§13). The men of the city shout against Paul, saying, "He has misled all our wives!" (§15). The rich and powerful man Alexander, after he is publicly rebuffed by Thecla, plots to have her killed precisely because he knows that he, as an upper-class man, has been shamefully humiliated—and by a woman (§§26–27). Even the members of Thecla's own household, her mother and her own slaves, regret Thecla's choices more, it seems, out of their own self-concerns for the household. In this text, the freed-up, masculinized, ascetic woman is the most powerful threat imaginable by the men who quite correctly see its potential to destroy their households. Without women willing to have sex, there will be no babies, and without children, there will be no future for the household. Asceticism was perceived by many men in antiquity as a clear threat to their own position as *paterfamilias*, and to the very existence of their families and households.

Indeed, they recognize that if the household is threatened, so is the entire society. In ancient social reality, as well as ideology, the foundational institution of society was the household—not the nuclear family, note, but the broader household as an economic unit. Thus the governors and other rulers who condemn Thecla and Paul correctly recognize the social threat embodied in ascetic female bodies. The men perceive Paul's teaching as threatening not just their households, but the entire city (§15), a point made also by Thecla's mother (§9). By teaching women and young people to keep themselves from sexual relations, the ancient ascetic missionary threatened the very foundation of the ancient city and society: the patriarchal household.

Thecla, the Heroine (Hero?)

Paul is rendered in the *Acts of Paul and Thecla* in a rather ambiguous light. He is certainly, at least on the surface, the great apostle. He is, of course, praised and pictured as the man of God. But he also says and does a few things that do not pose him in an entirely positive light. In a subculture that honored martyrdom, for instance, which characterizes much of ancient Christianity, it seems interesting that Paul suffers much less in the story than does Thecla. Thecla here is the great "confessor," a term that referred to someone who had been condemned to death but was later delivered in some way (for more on this role, see Chapter 25 in this book). She faces torture and death not just once, but twice. Paul, in contrast, is merely beaten, released, and expelled from the city (§21). Paul refuses to baptize Thecla, apparently afraid that she is not strong enough to resist temptation and may not remain a virgin after all (§25). This means that Thecla has to turn "apostle" and baptize herself, which she does in the vat of killer seals (§34). After they arrive together in Antioch, and the rich man Alexander asks Paul about Thecla, Paul denies that he even knows her: "I know not the woman of whom you speak, nor is she mine" (§26). It is hard to resist the idea that this is a deliberate echo of Peter's denial of Jesus. Just after this, Thecla is arrested, but Paul vanishes from the scene entirely. He certainly doesn't hang around to try to rescue or defend Thecla. Through much of the story, while Thecla is enduring trial after trial and crisis after crisis, Paul is hiding in an unoccupied tomb in the country (§§23–25). I doubt that the author was intentionally trying to cast Paul in a negative light, but Paul's actions and words here are sometimes at least ambiguous.

The true hero is Thecla. She endures awful trials with bravery. She begs for death if that will save her from losing her virginity (§27). She baptizes herself. After enduring all her trials and emerging victorious with her virginity intact, she turns herself male, gathers a band of ascetic women and young men around her, and goes off to preach as an apostle of erotic asceticism. The gospel commands asceticism, but it uses a highly eroticized story to do so. She spreads the message of this ascetic, antifamily, antihousehold gospel she had received from the apostle Paul himself.

This is a form of Christianity, indeed a form of Paulinism, that has nothing of the modern idolatry of the family and patriotism. This is not pro-family, and it is certainly no form of nationalism—unless it is the nationalism of the kingdom of God. Indeed, in this kind of Christianity, people have put all their eggs (literally, we may think, if we are thinking ovaries) in one basket: the kingdom of God.

The message is cast in erotic form. The *Acts of Paul and Thecla* does not really throw eroticism or sexual desire out the window. It rather uses them, along with Thecla's physical beauty, and capitalizes on that currency. The author is trying to persuade people, perhaps especially young people most susceptible to the appeal of the erotic and beautiful, to meet their fear of death by striking a blow right at the beginning of the cycle of death: at sex. If you choose the household, you necessarily will be caught in the cycle of sex, birth, death, and decay. But if you accept the life of erotic asceticism, you escape corruption and decay and free yourself for life and resurrection.

Is this a feminist document? Perhaps in the context of ancient patriarchal culture we could imagine it functioning for the liberation of at least some women. But from our situation informed by modern feminism, we can see that it offers no critique of the basic hierarchy of male over female. It promotes, like many ancient Christian documents, the liberation of individual women from the trap of the male-dominated household, but only by having them shed their "feminine" traits and take on those recognized as "masculine." None of our surviving ancient Christian documents teach the true equality of male and female. If they offer any kind of social improvement for women, it is in the form of masculinization even in an androgynous body. Angels in that world, for instance, could be male or androgynous. I have never, though, encountered a female angel in ancient Christian texts. And the androgynous body assumed by Paul and other ancient Christian authors is still an overwhelmingly "male" body. The *Acts of Paul and Thecla* may have worked to disrupt the ancient male-dominated household and city, but it is not feminist by modern standards.

It may well, though, have been written as a direct attack on the Pastoral Epistles, or at least the kind of Paulinism represented in them.[8] These texts—1 and 2 Timothy and Titus on one side, the *Acts of Paul and Thecla* on the other—represent two diametrically opposed visions of Paul and Christianity. They both claim Paul as their authority. They both claim to embody Paul's true teachings. But one of them is staunchly pro-household, marriage, sex, and childbirth, and the other is opposed to all of them.

In fact, neither of them got Paul just right. Paul was an ascetic in his own sense—much more ascetic than is admitted by any modern church—but he allowed marriage and sex within marriage for those Christians too weak for asceticism. Paul was not, however, as pro-household as the Pastoral Epistles. Paul was not concerned to keep women down, nor to keep them bearing children. Paul's churches were not modeled on the patriarchal household in the way the author of the Pastoral Epistles wants. So we have here three different visions of what Christianity teaches about sex, marriage, and family—the diversity of early Christianity.

Biblical Interpretation

CHAPTER 21
Hebrews and Biblical Interpretation

Overview: There are many ways of interpreting a text, and ancient methods of interpretation may seem bizarre to our modern sensibilities. The New Testament offers us many examples of how early Christians interpreted Jewish scripture, which was the Greek translation of the Hebrew Bible, also Christian scripture. The Letter to the Hebrews, which is more like a speech of encouragement than a real letter, structures its argument around the thesis that Jesus' liturgy and priesthood are superior to those represented in Jewish scripture. The author of Hebrews attempts to prove this through several interesting interpretations of passages.

Ancient Christian Interpretation of Scripture

The method of interpretation I have been using throughout this book has been modern historical criticism, in which we imagine an ancient author and ancient readers and attempt to figure out how they would have read these texts. We do not read them like poetry, or allegorically. We imagine them in their original contexts and then guess what they would have meant in those contexts. In the next chapter, I explain in more detail the different assumptions of historical criticism as a method and examine a bit how it developed in the modern world.

It is already clear, though, that this was not the way ancient Christians read texts they took to be scripture. We have seen how Paul interprets the text of Genesis and its stories about Sarah and Hagar. He reads these as allegories in which Sarah stands for those who believe in Christ, and Hagar stands for those Jews who do not believe in Christ. That is an interpretation—even a method of interpretation—that few modern people would invent today. If Paul were to offer to us that kind of reading of Genesis, we might well object that he was just "reading into" the text what he wanted to find there, and that the original author—whomever we imagine that to be—certainly didn't mean that.

Jesus takes just as much liberty (from our modern point of view) in his interpretations of texts as portrayed in the Gospels. When some Pharisees ask Jesus whether it is lawful for a man to divorce his wife, Jesus first asks them (according to Mark's version) what Moses had commanded, meaning that he first looks to scripture for the answer (Mark 10:2–9). The Pharisees quite rightly point out that the law of Moses did indeed allow it as long as the man gave her a certificate of divorce (presumably so she would be able to marry another man, if necessary). This is the most obvious reading of Deuteronomy 24:1–4, which addresses the issue of divorce and remarriage explicitly.

Jesus, though, is unhappy with their answer, so he quotes back to them Genesis 1:27 ("male and female he created them") and Genesis 2:24 ("Therefore a man leaves his father and his mother and clings to his wife, and they become one flesh"). Then Jesus adds his interpretation of those statements: "Therefore what God has joined together, let no one separate" (Mark 10:9). It is not often noted that the texts Jesus quotes actually say nothing at all about divorce. They certainly do not in any literal way forbid divorce. Jesus rejects a passage of scripture that permits divorce explicitly and instead chooses to interpret a different passage that says nothing about divorce to forbid it.

Jesus is here breaking a fundamental rule of textual interpretation that was as common in the ancient world as it is in ours: interpret the obscure by reference to the clear, not the clear by reference to the obscure.[1] When the meaning of one passage is puzzling, try to find a passage on the same topic whose meaning is more obvious, and use the latter passage to shed light on the former. Jesus does the opposite. He rejects a plain text and offers an interpretation of another that seems not to be on the topic at all.

From a modern point of view (and even from an ancient one, since they knew that "rule" also), the Pharisees' interpretation was better, and

Jesus' was far fetched. But Jesus was not a historical critic. Ancient readers just did not feel constrained by the rules of interpretation that constrain us. But one thing the examples prove is that texts cannot interpret themselves. They cannot speak to Jesus and say, "Wait, that's not what Genesis 1 and 2 mean!" Texts cannot control their own interpretation. In fact, since texts have no meaning until they are interpreted by some human being, they have no meaning in themselves apart from human interpretation.[2]

Another example that brings out the difference between modern historical interpretations and ancient ones is a reading offered by ancient Christians of the "dove" that descends on Jesus at his baptism. I have explained what "adoptionist" Christologies were in previous chapters. Some Christians who believed that Jesus was "adopted" by God at his baptism used the dove as proof. As is commonly known, ancient Greek (and Hebrew) letters all had numerical values: alpha was one, beta was two, and so on. Some of these Christians apparently pointed out that the numeral values of the letters in the Greek word for "dove," *peristera*, added up to 801.[3] That number also happens to be the sum of alpha (1) and omega (800). As we know from Revelation, God (and Christ, in his divinity) is "the Alpha and Omega" (Rev 21:6, 22:13). This is scriptural proof that "divinity" came on Jesus at his baptism: 801.

This is a form of textual interpretation we moderns are not likely to find convincing. But how would we convince these Christians that their interpretation was incorrect? We could argue that Luke must not have had any such intention, since he gives us no clues in the text that we are supposed to interpret the dove "numerically." But they could say that the dove, accompanied by the voice from heaven, was all the clue they needed (see Luke 3:22). We could point out that Luke likely did not know Revelation at all, since he wrote around 70, and Revelation wasn't written until much later in the first century. But they could say that didn't matter; Luke certainly knew as well as the author of Revelation that God and Christ were the Alpha and Omega. We may imagine that we could, by many different examples, arguments, and other texts, persuade them to leave their "meaning" of the text and accept ours. But we would have to do so precisely by rhetoric and persuasion, and we would have to begin with common presuppositions about right and wrong methods of interpretation. Just pointing to the text and expecting it to "speak" won't do anything to resolve the issue. Texts don't "say" anything. In fact, texts don't "mean"; people "mean" with texts.

Thus we should be clear that the interpretations of the New Testament and other texts I have been offering in this book are based on the method of modern historical interpretation. Hebrews, though, provides us with an excellent example of ancient interpretive methods. So one of the reasons for reading it—besides what it can tell us about early Christian theology—is to see ancient interpreters at work. Hebrews is a sermon that constructs most of its arguments by interpreting Jewish scripture.

The Letter to the Hebrews: A Speech of Encouragement

As I said in Chapter 1, in spite of being titled "Epistle to the Hebrews," Hebrews is not really a letter. In fact, in Hebrews 13:22 it tells us what it is: a "word of exhortation" or, differently translated, a "speech of encouragement" (the same term is used in Acts 13:15 for a speech by Paul in a synagogue). The author has tacked on a very brief conclusion that sounds a bit like a Pauline letter, but there is no greeting at the beginning, no address, none of the typical elements of the beginning of a letter. The author just dives into his topic: "Long ago God spoke to our ancestors in many and various ways by the prophets, but in these last days he has spoken to us by a Son, whom he appointed heir of all things, through whom he also created the worlds" (Heb 1:1–2).

Although the author begins with a reference to "our ancestors," I also don't believe it is necessary to imagine that Hebrews was addressed to a Jewish audience. At least, I find no firm evidence in the letter that it was intended for Jews, and certainly none that it was intended exclusively for them. So for different reasons, the document seems to me mistitled: it is not a letter, and it probably is not just to Jews.

We also don't know who wrote it. The letter was accepted as part of the canon, no doubt, because people thought it was by Paul. In some ancient collections, it is placed among Paul's letters, after Romans and before 1 Corinthians. Perhaps its placement in our canon—just after Paul's last letter in the canon, Philemon—indicates something of a compromise: people connected the letter to Paul, and Paul's authority gave Hebrews more respectability, but people knew that its authenticity was in doubt. In fact, ancient Christian scholars, notably Origen, but others as well, recognized that the style differed from Paul's. They guessed that it might have been written by Luke, or Apollos, or someone else of Paul's followers. Since we know of no book of the Bible written by a woman, some people have enjoyed imagining that Hebrews was written by Prisca, intentionally anonymous precisely because she was a woman. But in the end, we have no idea who the author was.[4] We also have no idea when it was published; guesses range from 60 to 100.

The author, though, was clearly well educated. In fact, the Greek of Hebrews may well be the best Greek of the New Testament. The sermon uses Hellenistic Jewish speech styles, rhetoric, and exegetical techniques. It may even be thought of as exhibiting a certain kind of Jewish Platonism, or "popular" Platonism, in that it contrasts "the real" and "the apparent," the eternal and the temporal. The spiritual is superior to the physical, as light is superior to shadow. The rhetoric plays on all sorts of dualisms, as much popular philosophy would have. I wouldn't say that the author is deeply immersed in any one philosophical "school." It is more likely that he has been exposed, probably more through rhetorical than philosophical training per se, to popular tropes of general philosophy. This also need not mean that the author was Jewish. He could have been a gentile. But if so, he had long been well acquainted with Jewish scripture and "symbolic" or even allegorical interpretation of it.

Greeks and Romans also used this kind of "spiritual" exegesis. Greek philosophers, for instance, had long interpreted Homer's *Iliad* or *Odyssey* as allegories for physical science, ethics, or other philosophical ideas. Philosophers and grammarians had long taken different gods of popular piety to represent different elements of nature, such as air or fire. By the first century, when Hebrews was composed, typological or allegorical interpretation of authoritative texts was common among Greeks, as well as Jews. The most famous Jewish representative in the early first century was Philo of Alexandria. We must imagine that the author of Hebrews was well educated and a skillful writer and rhetorician, though not nearly at the level—whether of wealth, education, or philosophical sophistication—of Philo. But this author was sophisticated.

The Outline of Hebrews

One way to see the sophistication of the author is to note the intricacies of the composition of Hebrews (see Fig. 11). A look even at its organization, in outline, brings this out. Instead of a letter salutation, the document begins with a statement of the thesis of the entire sermon: "Long ago God spoke to our ancestors in many and various ways by the prophets" (Heb 1:1). So we know already that this will be a message about the "old." We may also gather that it will provide interpretation of Jewish scriptures. "But in these last

I. Introduction and Thesis: the old and new (1:1–2)
II. Introduction to the superiority of Jesus (1:3–5:10)
  A. Superior to angels (1:3–2:18)
  B. Superior to Moses (and Joshua) (3:1–4:13)
  C. Superior to the old high priesthood (4:15–5:10)

  [Mention of Melchizedek here foreshadows section V below]

III. Digression: Invitation to a Higher Doctrine (5:11–6:12)

  [Mention of examples of faith here (6:12) foreshadows section VII.C below]

IV. Introduction to Second Half of Sermon: our assurances (6:13–20)
V. Jesus compared to Melchizedek (7:1–28)
  A. Melchizedek as superior to Abraham and Levitical priesthood (7:1–14)
  B. Jesus as new Melchizedek (7:15–28)
VI. "Reality" compared to "Shadow" (8:1–10:18)
  A comparison of the earthly to the heavenly "liturgy"
VII. Parenesis ("Therefore . . .") 10:19–13:21
  A. Introduction 10:19–25 (since all these things are true, let us "hold fast" to the new covenant) . . .
  B. In spite of sufferings (10:26–39)
  C. Examples of faith (11:1–40)
  D. Encouragement (12:1–29)
  E. Practical, detailed parenesis (13:1–7)
  F. Call to "leave the camp" (13:8–16)
VIII. Closing admonitions and benediction (13:17–25)

Fig. 11 Outline of Hebrews (A Sermon of Synkrisis: Comparison)

days he has spoken to us by a Son" (1:2). So we know that the author is going to contrast that "old" with what is "new" in Jesus Christ. The thesis of the whole work is a comparison and contrast of old and new, and the superiority of the new over the old.

The first major section argues for the superiority of Jesus, first in comparison with the angels (1:3–2:18), then to Moses and Joshua (3:1–4:13), and finally when compared with the old high priesthood (4:15–5:10). At the end of this section, we have the first mention of Melchizedek, which functions as foreshadowing for a major discussion of him that will come up in chapter 7. Then we have a digression in which the author invites his readers to move from "basic teaching about Christ" and onward "toward perfection" in higher knowledge of the gospel (5:11–6:12). The last line, with its emphasis on "those who through faith and patience inherit the promises" (6:12), functions as another piece of foreshadowing, this time looking forward to the "examples of faith" that will come in chapter 11.

The second half of the sermon begins with its own introduction (6:13–20), followed by a lengthy "exegesis" of the Genesis story of Melchizedek, hinted at in 5:6 and 10. The author explains how the text of scripture, if it is read correctly (that is, as he interprets it), teaches that Melchizedek was superior to Abraham, the father of all the Jews (7:1–14). This is followed by a section proving that Jesus is the new Melchizedek (7:15–28).

The next major section is a long one in which "reality" is compared with "shadow," and in which the "earthly liturgy," or service to God described in Exodus and Leviticus, is shown to be inferior now to the "heavenly liturgy" inaugurated by Christ, its high priest (8:1–10:18). This is the most "Platonic"-sounding part of the sermon, with elaborate comparisons of the inferior "shadow" with the superior "reality."

The sermon concludes with a long section of what biblical scholars call "paraenesis." This technical word, from the Greek, refers to "moral exhortation," the kind of ethical advice that commonly repeats well-known moralisms, as we saw in James. It "reminds" the audience of ethical commonplaces they already know. The section begins, as is often the case, with a "therefore." It is as if the author is saying, "Since everything I have said so far is true, here is how we ought to live." As shown in the outline, this section may be divided further into parts on different topics or examples, but it all hangs together in the manner of a paraenetic exhortation at the end of a speech. The very last part of the text comprises closing admonitions and a benediction (13:17–25).

Hebrews as *Synkrisis*: A Comparison of the Superior and the Inferior

We have, then, a well-structured and organized sermon. The author has hinted at times about what will come later, and he has drawn his audience along by citing examples with which they are familiar, even though he is probably offering innovative interpretations of those texts and persons. The basic point, however, is the superiority of Jesus' *leitourgia* over that of Moses. We get our English word "liturgy" from this term, and it can mean in Greek also what liturgy or ritual means in English. In Greek, though, it also carried broader and more varied meanings. When a town, for instance, wanted a celebration for a festival, with a parade, a sacrifice, and the distribution of food to the people, it would often depend on rich citizens to supply the funding. All such activities were considered something done in service to the gods and were leitourgiai. Moreover, although a leitourgia was a service to the god, it was also to the entire town. In fact, the benefactor could be called the *leitourgos*, as could others who worked in the sacrifice and festivities in service to the god. That term, in fact, is the one the author uses when he refers to the angels in Hebrews 1:7 and 14. They are the servants, the "liturgists," of God.

The sermon therefore compares two leitourgiai, two liturgies, two ways of serving and worshiping God: that of Moses and the tabernacle as commanded in Exodus and Leviticus, and that initiated by Jesus. Here, I must introduce another Greek word. Speeches of comparison were common in ancient Greek rhetoric. Boys would be taught to compose, memorize, and deliver for the rest of the class a speech comparing, say, the bravery of Alexander with that of Julius Caesar, or the poetry of Homer with that of Hesiod, or any other paired subjects. The term for a speech of comparison was *synkrisis*, which means "judging" two or more things "together with" one another. It means comparison and contrast. Hebrews is a sermon of synkrisis.

The different arguments our author marshals to prove the superiority of the liturgy of Jesus over that of Moses are fascinating. We have to keep in mind that he is preaching to the choir, no doubt. The people who would be hearing this or reading it would almost certainly already all be Christians. So even where his argument might strike us as weak, we probably should imagine that it was well received. And even where his rhetorical moves or logical arguments seem strained to us, as I think they must to modern people, they are actually good examples of ancient rhetoric.

For example, in Hebrews 8:6–7, he says, "But Jesus has now obtained a more excellent ministry [*leitourgia*], and to that degree he is the mediator of a better covenant, which has been enacted through better promises. For if that first covenant had been faultless, there would have been no need to look for a second one." His argument is that the very existence now of the Christian service to God proves that the Mosaic covenant and service were not fully adequate. Christianity wouldn't exist if the Mosaic covenant were sufficient. So the existence of Christianity proves its superiority to Judaism (to put it in modern terms, which he doesn't actually use). As I admitted, this is an argument not likely to convince any who aren't already believers.

One of the most common means of proving his point, however, is less through such (dubious?) logic and more often through citation and interpretation of scripture. The author is not using the Hebrew Bible, though. We must remember that he no doubt was dependent on Greek translations of the Hebrew Bible. And when he talks about the sacrificial cult laid out in Exodus and Leviticus, he is not talking about the Jerusalem temple. If he is writing after 70 C.E., as I think is probable, that temple and its sacrificial practices no longer exist anyway. But that is not important for his argument, because he is comparing Christian "sacrifice," "priesthood," and worship with descriptions of the tabernacle, the "tent" of God used by the Israelites as they sojourned in the desert and in Israel before the building of the Temple of Solomon. He reads descriptions of the tabernacle given in Exodus and Leviticus, but he reads them all through the lens now of Christ. Christ provides the interpretive key for everything in Jewish scripture.

Notice also that although the author almost certainly believed that Moses wrote scripture, and that David wrote the Psalms, he takes the "real" author to be God. Our author is unconcerned with what meaning Moses or David or anyone else would have assigned to his words; the ultimate author of scripture is God, so when we read it, we hear God speaking, not just Moses or David or an individual prophet. The author also sometimes imagines the speaker of scripture to be the Holy Spirit (see Heb 3:7, 10:15) or even Jesus (Heb 2:11–12, 10:5). God, the Holy Spirit, and Christ may all be considered authors of scripture, even though they speak "through David" or some other human author (see Heb 4:7). The author of Hebrews quotes Jewish scripture extensively to prove the superiority of Jesus' ministry and service—that is, what we, though not he, would call Christianity—over Judaism.[5]

Some of the most fascinating exegesis occurs in chapter 7, in the author's interpretation of the meaning of Melchizedek from Genesis 14:17–24 and a brief mention of him in Psalms 110:4 (cited at Heb 5:6, 5:10, and 6:20). According to the story in Genesis, Abraham was returning from a battle in which he and some of his allies had defeated several other "kings" who had themselves previously defeated the city of Sodom, among several others. Abraham's nephew and all his household and goods had been hauled away after the fall of Sodom, where they had lived. Abraham and his forces had rescued the people and were returning home with Lot and his household and the spoils of war. On their way home, they were met by a man identified as Melchizedek, the king of Salem, who offered bread and wine and blessed Abraham. Abraham gave Melchizedek a tenth of everything he had captured. That is just about all we know of Melchizedek from Genesis.

The author of Hebrews, though, gets a lot more than that out of the text. First, he interprets Melchizedek's name and title. Although I think it doubtful that our author actually knew Hebrew, he did know the meaning of some words, which one could glean from different kinds of "study aids" available to Greek-speaking Jews. So he explains that the name itself means "king" (*melech*) of "righteousness" (*zedek*). He also notes that his city Salem is from the Hebrew word *shalom*, "peace" (7:2). So this is already building up Melchizedek as a "type" for Christ, who will come later.

He next states that Melchizedek had no father or mother and no genealogy at all. He adds that Melchizedek had "neither beginning of days nor end of life," so he was eternally existing. Now, there is nothing in the Bible that says that about Melchizedek. The author is noticing that Melchizedek seemed to come into the narrative in Genesis out of nowhere. He is obviously a hugely important figure, as is shown by the fact that the great Abraham tithed to him and received his blessing. Why do we know nothing more about this shadowy but significant person? The author of Hebrews takes this to mean that Melchizedek really didn't have a genealogy to tell. He always existed, he never died, and therefore "he remains a priest forever." Who else has eternally existed and will eternally exist? Jesus, of course. Thus Melchizedek "resembles the Son of God" (7:3). He is a "type" of the Christ to come.

One of the reasons the author does this is that he intends to make Jesus the great high priest of the new covenant, but he knows that Jesus was not of the tribe and lineage of Aaron and Levi, from whom all Jewish priests were supposed to descend. How can Jesus be a high priest if he is not from the tribe of priests? Because he is a priest not "after the order" of Levi, but "after the order" of Melchizedek (7:15–17).

But another benefit the author gets from this interpretation is that it is one more demonstration that Jesus is superior to Abraham:

> See how great he is! Even Abraham the patriarch gave him a tenth of the spoils. And those descendants of Levi who receive the priestly office have a commandment in the law to collect tithes from the people, that is, from their kindred, though these also are descended from Abraham. But this man, who does not belong to their ancestry, collected tithes from Abraham and blessed him who had received the promises. It is beyond dispute that the inferior is blessed by the superior. In the one case, tithes are received by those who are mortal; in the other, by one of

> whom it is testified that he lives. One might even say that Levi himself, who receives tithes, paid tithes through Abraham, for he was still in the loins of his ancestor when Melchizedek met him. (Heb 7:4–10)

In order to understand this argument, it is helpful to know a bit about ancient genetic theories. Many ancient cultures believed that very, very tiny versions of human beings existed physically in the bodies of their ancestors (or at least the male ancestors). They did not believe that just sperm were swimming around in Abraham's body, therefore, but tiny, invisible, but real and physical homunculi. Inside Abraham's loins, therefore, were all the Jews who ever existed, including those who existed at the time of the Exodus, the time of the establishing of the law of Moses and the Levitical priesthood. They all were present in Abraham's body, therefore, when he was in the act of tithing to Melchizedek.

Therefore, even Levi and all his descendants, as well as Aaron and his—that is, every man who ever after served as a Jewish priest—had also tithed to Melchizedek. Add that to the "indisputable" fact that the one who gives the tithe is inferior to the one who receives the tithe, and to the fact that Jesus is Melchizedek and a high priest in his order of priesthood, and we have the proof that Jesus and his priesthood and covenant are all superior to the current priesthood and covenant of the Jews. The Jewish priesthood itself recognizes (even if its members don't realize it themselves) the superiority of the Christian covenant and liturgy in their tithing to Melchizedek. The covenant with Abraham recognizes the superiority of the covenant of Christ in receiving Melchizedek's blessing. "It is beyond dispute that the inferior is blessed by the superior" (7:7).

This is all surprising enough: the methods of reading texts; the kinds of arguments considered convincing; the kinds of "facts" that are "indisputable." But they make perfect sense given the goals of the writer. And the argument all comes to an even more striking climax at the end of the sermon. There is no direct evidence that the author is writing to people who are actively "judaizing," that is, gentile Christians who are taking up Jewish dietary restrictions, observing Sabbaths, or seeking to be circumcised. But the author warns against any such temptations, portraying these acts as "returning" to a covenant that has been superseded by the superior covenant of Christ. He warns them against "regulations about food, which have not benefited those who observe them" (13:9).

The author then contrasts the sacrificial cult of the Jews with that of Christians: "We have an altar from which those who officiate in the tent have no right to eat" (13:10). He then explains how the sacrifices worked at the tabernacle. He notes that the actual killing of the sacrificial victims and the disposal of the materials were done not in the tent or temple themselves but "outside the camp": "For the bodies of those animals whose blood is brought into the sanctuary by the high priest as a sacrifice for sin are burned outside the camp. Therefore Jesus also suffered outside the city gate [of Jerusalem] in order to sanctify the people by his own blood" (13:11–12). But not willing to leave the comparison there, he continues to urge Christians to leave "the city" entirely. "Let us then go to him outside the camp and bear the abuse he endured" (13:13). This is not just an appeal to his hearers to leave the actual city of Jerusalem; it is an appeal to leave behind Judaism itself, with all its trappings. Christianity is portrayed as a new covenant between God and his people that has superseded the covenant of Moses as superior to it.

Many Christians are naively "supersessionists" in how they think about Christianity in relation to Judaism. They have a view of history in which God had an "old testament" or "covenant" with the Jews. But with the coming of Christ, Christians have a "new testament" or "covenant" with God that is not only different from the "old" but has taken its place. The "old covenant" of "works" and "judgment" has been replaced, superseded, by the "new covenant" of grace and love. This is a starkly anti-Jewish, perhaps even anti-Semitic, view, but it is common nonetheless.

Contrary to the way many people have read him over the centuries, I would argue that Paul was not supersessionist in his views of the covenant God made with Abraham. Although he fought hard to keep his gentile converts from submitting to the law of Moses, he claimed that he himself was perfectly willing to be "under the law" when it was the proper thing to do; that is, I assume he meant when he was among Jews (1 Cor 9:20). Paul was against gentiles keeping the law of Moses, but he thought the law was still an important player in the history of salvation of all human beings. His letter to the Romans is a complicated attempt to explain his very confusing ideas of the relation of the law of Moses to the new covenant in Christ. But Paul never acts as if the law of Moses and Judaism is something now superseded by Christianity and therefore purely a thing of the past.

The writer of Hebrews, however, advocates about as supersessionist a view as one can find in the New Testament. His language about "inferior" and "superior," about "shadow" and "reality," and about "leaving the camp" and "the city," which clearly refer to the Judaism of his day, are all striking in their advocacy of the supersession of Judaism accomplished, he believes, in the covenant of Christ. As we have seen, in order to use the very scriptures of the Jews to make a case that Judaism was obsolete, he had to engage in some pretty fancy exegetical footwork. It is all a great example of premodern biblical interpretation, as we will explore further in the next chapter.

CHAPTER 22

Premodern Biblical Interpretation

Overview: The principles of interpreting the New Testament in this book assume a historical-critical perspective. The historical-critical method of interpreting a text privileges the intended meaning of the ancient author, the interpretation of a text's original audience, the original language the text was written in, and the avoidance of anachronism. For most of the last two thousand years, however, this has not been the method used to interpret the Bible. Premodern interpreters, such as Origen, Augustine, and Bernard of Clairvaux, felt free to allegorize and interpret the text with theological rather than historical questions foremost. It was only through the Reformation and other events in modern history that the historical-critical method became the predominant method of interpretation for Western societies.

Principles of the Historical-Critical Method

The method of textual interpretation I have been using throughout this book has been some form of modern historical criticism. Most of this chapter will be devoted to showing that there have existed—and do exist—other ways of reading texts, and so other ways of reading the Bible, all of which I believe may be completely appropriate. In fact, I have elsewhere argued that the historical-critical method is inadequate for a Christian theological appropriation of the Bible. I have said that schools educating future ministers should spend much more time and effort teaching their students how to "think theologically" and how to move from historical readings of biblical texts to appropriate theological and ethical readings.[1] It is important for modern people, whether they are religious or not, to be able to recognize the different ways different people may interpret the Bible. Thus, although I teach biblical studies mostly from the point of view of modern historical criticism when I am teaching in a secular university setting, I want to insist that this method provides only one among several valuable ways of reading this text.

Many people will find it "natural" to assume the point of view of modern historical criticism, by which I mean that they will almost automatically think that "the meaning" of the text must be what the original, historical, human author "intended" to say. When they are puzzled over, say, what the text means by "principalities and powers" in Paul's letters, they will naturally ask, "What could Paul have meant by this?" That is a historical-critical question. Although I have been using this method throughout this book, I think it important to explain how the historical-critical method works and to make explicit some of its often-unspoken assumptions. Many textbooks on biblical interpretation don't lay out the unwritten "rules" of modern interpretation, as I do here. But these are the assumptions usually present in modern academic teaching of biblical interpretation, whether in secular or theological contexts. These are the "rules" of modern historical interpretation of the Bible.

1. The meaning of a text according to historical criticism is what the ancient human author intended it to mean. Jeremiah 3:6 says, "The Lord said to me in the days of King Josiah." If I wanted to be creative in my interpretation, I might say that the "me" here must refer to "me": Dale B. Martin. That might be a "fictive" or "poetic" way to appropriate the text, but it would not be legitimate within historical criticism, which would normally take the "me" to refer to the prophet Jeremiah himself, unless there was some other indication that the author was referring to someone else in his own time. And we would take the "King Josiah" to refer to the king of Judah at the time we have historically decided was when the prophet Jeremiah likely wrote. We would assume that that is what the historical author meant.

2. Scholars have increasingly recognized how difficult it is to discern the intentions of an author, especially an author who lived thousands of years ago and about whom we know very little. We know much more about

ancient language and customs. So the goal of interpretation for many scholars has expanded beyond the single author's intention to the range of ways competent speakers of the ancient language around the time of the writing of the document would understand the text. How would a person—or different people—living in Corinth likely understand Paul's text if they heard it read aloud in their church? This means that the "meaning" of Paul's text may not be one thing, but a range of probable meanings, arrived at by historical study in order to decide how people living in Paul's society would understand him. This "imagination," for it is still a practice of our modern imagination informed by historical research, is an expansion of the rule about "the author's intention" as constituting the goal of interpretation. It is still a historical endeavor, not one of completely free creative imagination, as would be expected in a fantasy novel about Paul.

3. Part of "being modern" is the assumption that people who lived in historical periods much removed from our own lived therefore in a "world" that was to a great extent different from our own. The "ancient world" was not like "our world." Ancient inhabitants of the Mediterranean cultures, for instance, tended to assume that the cosmos was a layered universe of hierarchical stories, like a building. We tend to think of the universe as many different spheres in something like infinite space.[2] The ancients tended to assume that the earth was a flat level, under which was water, and over which was a firm ceiling (the "firmament" of Genesis). Above that was more water or other levels of the world.

Students trained in the historical-critical method of biblical interpretation, therefore, are often taught something about the Greek, Roman, and Jewish "worlds." They may be taught something about the ancient Near East so that when they read about Baal and other gods in the Hebrew Bible, they have some idea of how ancient people conceived of those beings. A corollary of these assumptions is that people should, if they can, read the Hebrew Bible in Hebrew and the New Testament in Greek. It used to be the case that students training to be ministers were taught Greek and Hebrew in theological education, along with the Latin they had learned from childhood. Nowadays, most denominations have given up requirements that all their ministers be trained in Greek and Hebrew, but almost all theological schools nonetheless teach both subjects. This reflects the modern assumption that the world that created these texts was significantly different from ours, and our leaders who teach about these texts should be educated in the languages and cultures of those ancient worlds.

Part of the "historical consciousness" of the modern world—the realization that we live in a "different world" from that of our predecessors—is the assumption of a "gap" between their world and ours also in customs and values. Even conservative interpreters, for instance, will often insist that women in their churches need not wear veils in church, in spite of Paul's instructions to women in 1 Corinthians 11, because our culture is different from his. Paul and his hearers, they might say, assumed that an unveiled woman was thereby "shamed" and could be seen as a "loose woman" or "available" if she were seen in public without a veil. Since such assumptions and values are not present in our society, they argue, women in their churches need not veil themselves. The difference in cultures warrants a difference in values and customs. The awareness that there is a "gap" between their world and ours, even in the case of worldview and values, is part of modern historical consciousness.

4. Historical criticism teaches that we should not interpret the Bible primarily through the meaning these texts have within the canon as a whole. Students are regularly told not to interpret Paul by appeal to doctrines or themes found in John, or vice versa. They are taught that Matthew may have his own particular understanding of the law of Moses, so they should not import into their interpretation of Matthew something they have read in Mark about the law. Historical criticism—in contrast to the entire history of biblical interpretation in the church—takes the canon apart and insists that each individual document must be studied in its own right and for its own content. Even when we are studying Romans, as I demonstrated in a previous chapter, we may consult other letters of Paul, such as Galatians, for comparative purposes, but we should not assume that Paul's statements about the law in Romans must mean the same thing as what he says about it in Galatians. Historical criticism teaches students to avoid harmonizing the different documents in the Bible so that they all speak with the same voice. It insists that the Christian canon not influence the historical interpretation of the texts.

5. In spite of the fact that we do not study the Bible canonically in historical criticism, we do compare the different documents within the Bible and their authors. In fact, we use "source analysis" to suggest what kinds of sources the authors used and how they used them. I have said, for instance, that Matthew and Luke both used Mark as one of their sources, and analyzing how they did so—how they "edited" Mark to fit their own purposes—gives us ideas of what their own goals were, and what they wanted to "do"

with their own Gospels that may have been different from what Mark was "doing" with his. I will demonstrate in Chapter 24 that the author of 2 Peter used Jude as his source. The author of 2 Thessalonians used 1 Thessalonians as his source.

Students are regularly taught that the first five books of the Bible—Genesis, Exodus, Leviticus, Numbers, and Deuteronomy—were not written by Moses, as tradition teaches. They were written by several different authors or even groups of authors. The first five books, known as the Torah by Jews and sometimes called the Pentateuch (from the Greek for "five"), have been broken down into four different "sources," J, E, P, and D. Some parts of Genesis, for example, use the name "Yahweh" for God, which is spelled in German with an initial J. Since it was mainly German scholars who invented this theory, we still use J to mean this source. Other parts of those same books use the name "Elohim" for God, so scholars hypothesize that there was another source, which they call E. The P stands for "priestly," since scholars suggested that priests came up with one edition of these documents. Finally, an author designated as D put the five books in order, the same author (or authors) mainly responsible for the book of Deuteronomy. Almost every student taking a modern course in the Hebrew Bible or the Old Testament will be taught some version of this theory, even if they are then told that it is wrong. This is modern "source criticism," and some form of it is practiced in all modern historical criticism.

6. I have spoken about the different authors of these biblical documents, and one of the common practices of modern criticism—obviously setting it apart from most premodern interpretation—is to question the authenticity of authorship. As I have noted, the four canonical Gospels were not actually written by Matthew, Mark, Luke, and John, but were published anonymously. In other cases, I have said that documents were published pseudonymously. They claim to have been written by, say, Paul, but we do not believe that they actually were. Even in conservative seminaries, where professors teach that 1 and 2 Timothy and Titus were actually written by Paul, they will often defend the texts' authenticity precisely because they are working in a modern situation. In a premodern situation, the authenticity of biblical documents was assumed and needed no defense. The questioning of the authorship of biblical documents comes with modern criticism.

7. In historical criticism, as in the practice of modern historiography more broadly, a great sin is the commission of "anachronism": one must not retroject an idea or practice into the ancient text or its context that didn't

exist at the time. For example, most historical critics would agree that although New Testament authors do speak of the Father, Jesus as the Son, and a Holy Spirit (although it is seldom clear precisely what they mean by the last term, whether it was a "thing" or a "person"), it would be anachronistic to read the New Testament as teaching the full doctrine of the Trinity as it became developed later, especially in the fourth-century church councils. It would be even more objectionable to read Genesis as referring to the Trinity. A premodern interpreter may be perfectly happy to say that the "spirit" (or "wind" in more recent translations) that "hovers over the space of the deep" in Genesis 1:2 is the Holy Spirit. But a modern critic would object that such a reading is anachronistic, retrojecting a later Christian doctrine into a text whose author could not possibly have known it.

8. That last point leads to a word that represents the big bogeyman of historical criticism: "eisegesis." Almost every student trained in a seminary or divinity school in the twentieth century was taught that he or she should practice "exegesis," not "eisegesis." As the Greek implies, students will be told, "exegesis" is reading the meaning that is "really in the text" "out of" (*ek*) the text. Eisegesis is "reading into" (*eis*) the text a meaning not "really there in the text." This idea that one kind of interpretation is simply the objective practice of "listening" to the text, whereas another is the inappropriate, biased "reading into" the text of foreign meanings, is a simplistic and mostly mistaken representation of what actually happens when human beings interpret texts. But such theoretical sophistication is often absent in modern biblical education. The difference between "exegesis" and "eisegesis" is a staple of modern theological education and another factor that characterizes modern historical criticism as a method.

Very rarely will students be taught these rules of modern criticism so explicitly, but they are indeed some of the central assumptions of historical criticism as developed and practiced in the modern world, as even my own comments throughout this book illustrate. It is important to realize that this is one way of interpreting the Bible, and not necessarily the only way or even the best way for all purposes. The development of historical criticism also has its own history.

The History of Historical Criticism

For much of Christian history, laypeople for the most part depended on the clergy for what knowledge they had about the Bible. Premodern Christian scholars realized that people could read just about any "meaning" they liked from scripture, so bishops and priests regularly insisted that interpretations of scripture must be led by and agree with those of the church hierarchy. The ultimate arbiter of doctrine and scriptural meaning was the Vatican, through the office of the *magisterium* and ultimately, eventually, the pope himself. Since indeterminacy of meaning in multiple interpretations was believed to be a threat to orthodoxy, the institution of the church itself was put forward as a control on interpretation. The meaning of the text was what the church, in the persons of its hierarchy of leaders, said it was.

Even before the Reformation, there was a movement away from that kind of top-down control. The humanist movement of the Renaissance began advocating new interpretive practices, with a "return to the fount" of the origins of Christianity. Scholars began learning Greek and Hebrew and departed from sole reliance on the Latin Vulgate for studying scripture. The Reformation accelerated this movement, but there were Roman Catholic scholars who never became Protestants who also advocated newer, more modern practices of biblical interpretation, Erasmus being perhaps the most famous.

In the Reformation, however, the move away from depending on the institution of the church for the meaning of the text and toward individual interpretation took hold. The Reformers Martin Luther, John Calvin, and Philipp Melanchthon were all biblical scholars well trained in the ancient languages. They led the way toward free interpretation and away from the constraints of tradition and the church. The Reformation advocated the rejection of the authority of the pope or bishops and appealed to scripture alone, *sola scriptura*, for authority in matters of doctrine and morality.[3]

Of course, this inevitably led to the realization that scripture itself could not actually control its own interpretation. There were different methods known for scriptural interpretation. Medieval exegetes had been taught that there was the "literal" meaning, but also a "spiritual" meaning. Other divisions of methods were also taught, such as the allegorical and the analogical. The Reformers attempted to bring a bit of security and order to varieties of interpretations by insisting that the predominant, though not necessarily the only, meaning of the text should be its "literal sense," the *sensus literalis.*

Admittedly, it is not always clear what these authors meant by the "literal sense." They seem to have believed that even the literal sense could contain a "prophetic" sense. So when a psalm says, "The Lord says to my Lord, 'Sit at my right hand'" (Ps 110:1), it certainly refers to the Davidic king of Israel. But it is also legitimate to take it as a prophecy about Christ, and so the writer of Hebrews is nonetheless still promoting the "literal" meaning of the text (see Heb 1:13). This is perhaps not what many modern scholars would consider the "literal" meaning of Psalm 110:1, but it seems to have fit within that category for the Reformers and their like. The "literal sense" of the Reformers was not exactly what we would accept as the meaning arrived at by modern historical criticism.

As Protestantism split into many different churches, with different doctrines and practices all needing to be supported by the "literal" reading of the same texts, Christian scholars increasingly came to insist that the science of historiography, as it was developing mainly in German academic circles in the nineteenth century, be used as the guide for interpretation. After all, scholars had long practiced the new and developing disciplines of history and philology to reconstruct "what really happened" behind the accounts of Greek and Latin classics. The various myths of Near Eastern cultures were being analyzed through increasingly critical modern historical methods. It eventually seemed natural, though not without controversy, that the critical gaze of modern historiography be turned on the Bible also.

This development took a while to be imported from Germany to theological schools in the United States, but by the middle of the twentieth century, just about all theological schools in the United States were teaching some form of modern historical criticism as the dominant way to study the Bible.[4] Movements springing originally from Protestantism led to what became "modern" ways to teach biblical studies.

We should note that this is not "the natural" way to read the Bible. It is not the only way. It is not even the best way if one wants to use the Bible as Christian scripture. That would require "theological" interpretation. In order to illustrate how premodern Christian interpreters did it differently, the rest of this chapter looks at three examples, ones provided by Origen, Augustine, and Bernard of Clairvaux.

Origen

Origen was one of the greatest scholars of ancient Christianity, although his reputation later suffered because he was considered not quite "orthodox" enough in many Christian circles. He is also famous as a great allegorizer in biblical interpretation. That is, he usually taught that texts of the Bible have more than one meaning: a "literal" meaning (often the Greek word here is *historia*, but it doesn't mean "historical" in our sense), and a "spiritual" meaning, which could be called a "higher" meaning or allegory. In fact,

Origen taught that sometimes God or the Holy Spirit had planted obvious "errors" in the Bible, such as historical mistakes or simply things that couldn't be true because they contradicted nature or logic, and that God did so in order to lead the reader to a "higher," more "Christian" meaning of the text. Origen knew his history—insofar as a scholar of his time and place could know "history"—but he looked for other meanings in biblical texts without denying their literal meaning.

One fascinating example of Origen's exegesis, however, shows that what he regarded as the literal meaning of the text is not really what a modern scholar would regard as a literal meaning of the text read through the method of historical criticism. Origen offers an interpretation of the passage from 1 Samuel 28 (called "1 Kingdoms" in the Greek Bible) that tells how King Saul, just before an important battle, consults a medium in order to question the dead prophet Samuel about what will happen at the battle. The story is traditionally known as "Saul and the Witch of Endor." The term "witch," however, might be better interpreted by the very literal translation of the Greek term for the woman, the "belly-myther."[5] The Greek indicates that these figures were mediums who made people believe that voices arising from deep within their bellies could tell "fabulous stories" (the meaning of "myth" here). They may have been something like ventriloquists who could make it seem as if ghostly or miraculous voices were speaking from their bellies, conveying hidden or spiritual messages through them from another world. At least, that seems to be the best understanding of the Greek version of this story originally from the Hebrew Bible.

King Saul has to go to the woman in disguise precisely because he has outlawed any such kind of magic or witchcraft in his kingdom. Anxious on the eve of battle, however, he searches out just such a woman and asks her to call up Samuel from hell, the realm of the dead. Ancient people often assumed that the dead could predict the future because they lived in a realm not constrained by the same limits we experience. As the story goes, the woman does call up Samuel, who appears and rebukes Saul for calling him up. Samuel then says that God has turned his back on Saul and chosen David to be king in his place, and that Saul and his sons will be killed in battle with the Philistines.

This story seems to have caused problems for pious Christian interpreters. They assumed, in the first place, that if the woman had any power of divination at all, it must have been because either she herself was a demon, or she made use of a demon, and they asked why a petty demon would have such power over a great prophet like Samuel. Other interpreters said that the woman didn't really see Samuel, but was merely lying. Others objected that a great prophet of God wouldn't be in hell in the first place. These other interpreters said that the entire story was just the fabrication of a demon-possessed, lying woman. The story, that is, didn't "mean" what it appeared to "say" at first blush.

Origen, in spite of his great reputation as an allegorist, insists that the story must be read literally. The text does not say that the woman "thought" that she saw Samuel, or that she "pretended" to see Samuel. It says that she saw Samuel. To the objection that it was not Samuel she saw but a demon pretending to be Samuel, Origen points out that the text does not say that either. It says that she saw Samuel. Next, Origen points out that the prophecy Samuel gives in the text—that Saul and his sons would be killed by the Philistines and the kingdom would pass to David—actually came true. Demons may fake prophecies, Origen notes, but they are powerless to provide true, dependable prophecies. No, this was Samuel, risen from hell, prophesying about Saul's demise.

To the objection that a holy man such as Samuel would not be in hell, Origen notes that even Christ descended into hell to preach to the righteous people who died before the coming of Christ (see 1 Pet 3:19). Origen says that other prophets had gone to hell to preach God's message there, and that they had even been accompanied by angels. According to Origen, who is here just reflecting some common Christian ideas of the time, before the coming of Christ, "paradise" was closed to all human beings, dead or alive. So even the righteous dead had to reside in hell, awaiting the coming of Christ. But with the "harrowing of hell," the entry of Christ into hell, the power of hell has been broken, and the righteous have been freed.

Origen here outliteralizes his opponents. He insists that the text must mean precisely what it says: a medium called Samuel up from hell, and Samuel arose and delivered the message of doom to Saul. But the literal meaning of the text is not just that it narrates a real, historical account of something that actually happened. Origen also says that another literal meaning of the text is that it teaches that "every place has need of Jesus Christ" (*Homily on 1 Kingdoms 28* 7.4). Origen takes a Christian theological teaching about Jesus to be also part of the literal meaning of the text.

Origen ends his sermon by exploring still another meaning of the text, which is now apparently the "elevated sense" of the passage, that is, a meaning "further" than the literal sense (see *Homily* 2.1–2). He says that the text gives Christians "even more." The text also teaches Christians that with the "harrowing of hell" completed by Christ, virtuous Christians will be allowed to pass "through the flaming sword" unharmed and proceed straight to paradise. Christians will receive a blessing that even the great prophets and patriarchs of old could not: entrance directly into paradise without a sojourn in any other "place of the dead."

Note that Origen claims to have arrived at a "narratival" or "literal" meaning of the text. In fact, from our perspective, he has more than one. The first is simply the "historical" account: a woman called Samuel up from hell at the request of Saul, and Samuel prophesied Saul's destruction. But another literal meaning for Origen is the text's teaching that "every place is in need of Jesus Christ." There is no part of the universe closed off from the salvation Christ offers. And then the "elevated" meaning identified by Origen is that Christians may proceed straight to paradise without spending time in hell, unlike even the righteous prophets of old. This "elevated" meaning is one no modern historical critic would take to be the meaning of the text. It doesn't even look like what we expect from an allegorical interpretation. Origen's exegesis is a great illustration of how premodern interpreters could see several different meanings in a text, even on the literal level, in a way not allowed by historical criticism.

Augustine

Augustine, even in his *Confessions*, which is not overtly a sermon or a book of biblical interpretation, provides wonderful examples of premodern exegesis. I use that work here to illustrate only two interpretive practices used by Augustine that differentiate his methods from modern ones.

First, Augustine's *Confessions* provides great examples of the practice of "praying through scripture." Augustine takes the Psalms, for instance, to speak with many different voices. Sometimes they are the words of God addressed to David or another ancient character. Sometimes, though, they are the words God directs straight to Augustine personally. Sometimes they are Augustine's words to God. In one example, Augustine takes a quotation as the Spirit speaking about God and Jesus to Augustine and his friends on retreat: "How long will you be heavy-hearted, human creatures? Why love emptiness and chase falsehood? Be sure of this: the Lord has glorified his Holy One" (*Conf.* 9.4.9, quoting Ps 4:2–3).[6] The scriptures speak with many voices, and the Christian reader must be open to communication coming from many directions and meaning many different things.

"Praying through scripture" is possible because of the ability of scripture to have many voices. The practice was common throughout premodern Christianity and has been revived by many churches, schools, and individual Christians in the past few decades. It is called *lectio divina*, "divine reading," and it takes the words of scripture as furnishing a dialogue between God and oneself. Augustine, for example, takes Psalm 4:4 to be God's address to him personally. "Then I read, 'Let your anger deter you from sin,' and how these words moved me, my God! I had already learned to feel for my past sins an anger with myself that would hold me back from sinning again" (*Conf.* 9.4.10). In this method of reading, Christians quote a scriptural text as their own voice to God and then read other texts as God's response to them.

The other way of reading I wish to highlight from Augustine's *Confessions* is his insistence that scripture has many different meanings simultaneously, and he takes the "six days of creation" from Genesis to teach this principle. When God gives the command to "increase and multiply" (Gen 1:22, 1:28), this means that it is God's will that we "multiply" the various "meanings" we get from scripture (*Conf.* 13.24.36). The "fecundity" of sea creatures and human beings instructs us to respect the fecundity of meaning in scripture.

Augustine illustrates this fecundity with his own various interpretations. For example, Augustine interprets the "firmament" of Genesis, what we would call the "sky," as meaningful even for our understanding of the nature of scripture and its interpretation. In ancient thought, as we have already seen from other passages in the New Testament, what we take to be the sky was considered a dome of matter, like a canvas stretched high above us and anchored to the earth at its edges. That is why older translations called it the "firmament": it was something "firm." The sky is blue, it was believed, because water is behind the firmament, held back by it. Augustine compares the firmament, moreover, to the leather, or vellum, of a scroll. It is stretched over us. The making of the firmament in heaven describes, Augustine believes, the actual creation of the sky in the beginning. But it also teaches us about God's creation of scripture as a gift to human beings.

Augustine points out that the writing of that vellum occurs only on one side, the side facing us human beings below. That is because the angels, who live above the firmament, above the vellum, need no scripture to inform them what to believe and how to live. They live with God himself (*Conf.* 13.15.18). But we human beings need to be able to read the writing of scripture. We need scripture for proper knowledge of God. The creation of the "firmament" teaches also a message about our dependence on scripture.

When Genesis describes the separation of dry land from the waters of the sea, that also refers to the actual creation (Gen 1:9–10). But Augustine interprets it further to represent the division between the two different parts of humanity. The sea represents the "bitter" part of humanity, even for us individuals, the "unruly urges of our souls," whereas the dry land represents "souls athirst" for God. The good works of human beings are represented by the fruitfulness of the earth (*Conf.* 13.17.20–21). Many other examples could be given, for Augustine goes page by page interpreting each detail of the six days of creation as representing "higher truths" about God, the universe, and ourselves. Augustine is urging his readers to imitate his creativity, his "fecundity" in practicing biblical interpretation. The meanings of scripture cannot be constrained.

Bernard of Clairvaux

The last example of a premodern interpreter I provide in this chapter is Bernard of Clairvaux, who lived and taught much later, from 1090 to 1153. By this time, the most popular book of the Bible for commentators was the Song of Songs, also the most erotic book of the Bible. Whereas we moderns usually read the book now as a straightforward poem of love and desire between a woman and a man, the book had mostly been read from the beginning of Christianity through the medieval period as an allegory. Jews read it as an allegory of the love between Israel and God. Patristic commentators, such as Origen, read it as an allegory of the love between the church and Christ. In both cases, the man was taken to be God or Christ. And usually in both cases, the stark eroticism and sexuality of the poem were downplayed or "interpreted away" allegorically.

In the Middle Ages, this tendency was reversed as many commentators used the erotic aspects of the poem, including its emphasis on beauty, to reclaim something of a Platonic message that beauty creates desire, which leads to higher "goods," especially the love of God. Bernard represents this tradition, but he manipulates the eroticism of the poem in ways that are surprising to most modern Christians. Bernard, if anything, exaggerates the emphasis in the poem on physical beauty, physical feelings, and the tug of erotic desire.

We must remember that these interpretations of the Song of Songs come from homilies Bernard delivered to fellow monks in a monastery, an all-male environment. When we keep that social setting in mind—all male and in the closeness of a medieval monastery—Bernard's use of the Song of Songs becomes remarkable.

Let's note one long quotation. Bernard has already spent several sermons without getting much beyond the first sentence of the Song: "Let him kiss me with the kiss of his mouth." Here, he speaks in the voice of the young girl, who is speaking about her bridegroom (*Sermons* 9.2.2):

> I cannot rest until he kisses me with the kiss of his mouth. I thank him for the kiss of the feet, I thank him too for the kiss of the hand; but if he has genuine regard for me, let him kiss me with the kiss of his mouth. There is no question of ingratitude on my part, it's simply that I am in love. . . . It is desire that drives me on, not reason. Please do not accuse me of presumption if I yield to this impulse of love. My shame indeed rebukes me, but love is stronger than all. . . . I ask, I crave, I implore; let him kiss me with the kiss of his mouth.[7]

Up to this point, we naturally envision the young girl as the speaker. But gradually the speaker seems to change. Bernard continues:

> Don't you see? That by his grace I have been for many years now careful to lead a chaste and sober life, I concentrate on spiritual studies, resist vices, and pray often; I am watchful against temptations, I recount all my years in the bitterness of my soul. As far as I can judge I have lived among the brethren without quarrel. I have been submissive to authority, responding to the beck and call of my superior.

Suddenly, we realize that we are no longer listening to the girl, but to a monk. The monk complains that even though he willingly follows the harsh discipline of the monastery, he has not experienced the full blessing of the direct presence of Christ. "I obey the commandments to the best of my ability, I hope, but in doing so 'my soul thirsts like a parched land' [quoting Ps 19:4]. If therefore he is to find my holocaust acceptable, let him kiss me, I entreat, with the kiss of his mouth." This is a male monk, speaking in the voice of a desirous young girl, about his yearning for his male lover, Christ.

Bernard does not get rid of the eroticism of the Song. He capitalizes on it. He is attempting to encourage young monks who may be weary of the daily office, of the dreary tasks of monastic life, who have attempted to feel the presence of Christ in their prayers and meditations, but who despair that they have no such feelings. Bernard has the young girl morph into a young monk and then instills in the monk the erotic desire for Christ in order to encourage endurance and strength. Bernard uses the eroticism of the Song to enliven the daily office of the monks in their monastery.[8]

Later, Bernard goes even further in his titillating interpretations. He has his monks imagine their girlish feelings when the Bridegroom actually arrives and kisses them. Like a girl's, their breasts, he says, swell, "rounded with the fruitfulness of conception, bearing witness, as it were, with this milky abundance" (9.5.7). And again, at this height of erotic tension, Bernard turns the girl into the monk.

> Men with an urge to frequent prayer will have experience of what I say. Often enough when we approach the altar to pray our hearts are dry and lukewarm. But if we persevere, there comes an unexpected infusion of grace, our breast expands as it were, and our interior is filled with an overflowing of love; and if somebody should press upon it then, this milk of sweet fecundity would gush forth in streaming richness. (9.5.7)

Bernard is talking about orgasm, and orgasm experienced the way Bernard, at least, seems to imagine a woman would. But he is speaking in an all-male environment to young monks, arousing in them not only erotic desire, but even homoerotic desire, although I rather doubt that Bernard would have put it that way. Bernard feels free to interpret the Song of Songs in a way that plays with the imagination of the monks, who are led to identify with the beauty and desire of a young girl for her beautiful male lover. This is all for the purpose, of course, of encouraging the monks to continue faithfully in their monastic duties with a bit more zeal.

Opening the Imagination

Many other such examples from many other premodern interpreters can easily be found.[9] I believe we should pay more attention to premodern biblical interpretations than has been typically the case in modern education and churches. They show us how recent and limited are the methods of modern historical criticism. They may spark our imaginations about different ways people could interpret the Bible—and other texts, for that matter.

Without dismissing historical criticism, we must keep in mind that other perfectly good ways of interpreting the Bible do exist. I have been illustrating here mostly theological interpretations, that is, interpretations that have Christian theology as the goal and use Christian theological criteria for how to distinguish a "good" interpretation from a "bad" one. But we may also imagine other methods, such as literary criticism. Literary critics and even biblical scholars have for years been offering more literary-critical approaches, especially to certain biblical books. The Gospel of Mark, for instance, has been interpreted with a view not to its theological meanings or its historical value, but to issues such as rhetoric, character, plot, and the effects it may have on even a nonreligious reader.[10]

In this book, I have concentrated on readings of early Christian literature, especially the New Testament, via the method of historical criticism. I think that is appropriate, for one thing, simply because that happens to be the dominant way the discipline is still conducted and taught in North American (and European, for that matter) academic contexts, both secular and theological. But the previous chapter and this one are intended to signal that there are other fruitful and interesting ways of reading these texts. We need not limit ourselves to one method or one "meaning."

Apocalypticism and Politics

CHAPTER 23
Apocalypticism as Resistance

Overview: The Apocalypse, or the Revelation of John, exhibits many of the traits found in apocalyptic literature. It operates in dualisms—earthly events contrasted with heavenly ones, present time with the imminent future. Apocalyptic literature sometimes calls for cultural and political resistance. The structure of Revelation is like a spiral, presenting cycle after cycle of building tension and reprieve, so that the reader who hears the text also experiences crisis and then catharsis. Politically, Revelation equates Rome with Babylon and the Roman Empire with the domain of Satan.

The Revelation of John and the Genre of Apocalyptic Literature

The word "apocalypse" is derived from the Greek *apokalypsis*, usually translated as "revelation." The word means any sort of uncovering or unveiling. The Revelation of John is therefore sometimes called the Apocalypse of John. Although people often refer to it as the book of "Revelations," the proper title is in the singular: it records one great revelation, not several of them. Revelation is not the earliest example of the genre. In fact, the book of Daniel in the Old Testament is one of the earliest examples of the genre and doubtless influenced the author of Revelation. But the entire genre takes its name from the Apocalypse of John.

"Apocalyptic" is used, for one thing, as the label for what modern scholars have delineated as an ancient genre of Jewish and Christian writings. Although ancient readers would certainly have recognized that different documents looked like one another in their apocalyptic styles or tendencies, they did not have a term for the genre as we do, except for calling the documents "prophecies." Modern scholars distinguish between a broader genre of prophetic writings (including most of the prophets of the Old Testament) and that narrower group of prophetic writings we call "apocalypses."

"Apocalyptic," however, may also be used to describe various characteristics of both style and content we find in different kinds of writing, even writings that are not "apocalypses." For instance, everyone agrees that Paul's letters are heavily influenced by apocalyptic themes: the wrath of God coming in judgment, the imminent "coming" (*parousia*) of the Messiah, and the setting up of the kingdom of God, to name only a few of the many we will discuss in this chapter. The adjective "apocalyptic," therefore, refers to all these elements that derive from ancient apocalypses even when they are found in sources that are not apocalypses. Finally, scholars sometimes use the term "apocalypticism" to refer not to the texts themselves but to a certain worldview, a way of seeing the universe and time that we associate with ancient apocalypses and those persons and writings under their influence.

There are several features we identify as typical of apocalypses. They are almost always pseudonymous, are set deep in the past, and are said to have been authored by a famous holy person. Daniel claims to have been written by a wise man, Daniel, who lived in Babylon in the sixth century B.C.E. As we have already seen, it was actually composed sometime between 168 and 164 B.C.E. We also have apocalyptic literature claiming to have been authored by Enoch, Ezra, Abraham, and even Adam.[1] Importantly, we have no reason to believe that the author who wrote Revelation was anyone other than an actual man named John, although this is not the same person as the apostle John. Therefore, the book that gave apocalyptic literature its name may be the only one not written under a pseudonym.

These books usually narrate a chronological span of time. They have all kinds of images, angels, demons, and sometimes beasts, which may be quite monstrous, as we see in Revelation. They are often written as narratives. Sometimes they narrate a journey taken by the author. He claims that he was in a certain place or state of mind, perhaps praying, and that an angel or some other sort of "heavenly guide" took him up and led him around the cosmos or up to the heavens. These books therefore express themselves through ancient cosmologies: their universe may have four corners, different layers of "skies," a storied universe with layers below the earth, and different "hells." The books, that is, pass along "special" information both about things that will happen in the future and the geography and state of the universe.

Apocalypticism as a worldview has recurring characteristics. It often has three kinds of dualism: ethical, spatial, and chronological. The ethical dualism is seen in the fact that every character in the world is either good or bad, even terribly evil. The world contains both good angels and bad angels, good men and bad men, with almost no one in between. The cosmos is constructed along the lines of a spatial dualism in that what goes on here on earth is only a shadow and the result of what goes on up above, in the heavens. Each nation has its own guardian (or rather, oppressing) angel. When nations here on earth battle one another, that is merely an earthly version of a spiritual battle going on between the angels or other superhuman beings battling in the skies. Everything that happens in our earthly world is simply a mirror of the "truer" events taking place above us.

Then there is the extremely important chronological dualism. We human beings are living in the "now" time, the time before the great event that will usher in the future "reign of God." As we have seen in Daniel, the prophet describes history. Of course, he pretends that he is predicting the future, but he is actually narrating political events and wars that he knows have already occurred. In the future, he says, some great event will split time in two, and a heavenly son of man will intervene, along with angels and human actors. God, through his agents such as the Messiah, a "son of man," or angels, will destroy evil, judge the world, and set up a moral and blessed society ruled by God, again usually through chosen agents. We have seen this dualism of time many places already in the New Testament; one of the central aspects of an apocalyptic worldview divides all time into the "before" and the "after."

As we have seen, Jesus himself was an apocalyptic Jewish prophet. He almost certainly expected the apocalyptic intervention of God, perhaps a "son of man" not himself, or perhaps he saw himself playing that eschatological role. He taught about the characteristics of the kingdom of God and how it would be different from the current world and society. After his death, his followers were doubtless shocked. If they thought he was the Messiah, they would have been expecting him to triumph over the powers of evil, including the Romans. No one had previously thought of a "dead Messiah." Followers of Jesus, therefore, altered their apocalyptic expectations. Now they decided that the coming of Jesus as the man they had known must be only the forewarning, the foretaste, of his future coming, when he would come in power rather than as a poor peasant. As they came to believe that Jesus had been resurrected and had appeared after his death, they interpreted his resurrection, as we have seen in Paul, as merely the "first fruits" of the future, eschatological resurrection. There were many more adjustments early Christians were forced to make in order to retain their belief that Jesus was the Messiah. They had to adjust their apocalyptic expectations in order to retain some kind of dualism of the "now" time, before the glorious victory of the kingdom of God, and the "time to come," when Jesus would finally be truly triumphant. They made adjustments from traditional Jewish apocalyptic dualism to a new version that took into account the resurrection of Jesus and the expectation that he would still "return" in glory in the future.

As is already apparent, apocalypses could serve as a form of cultural and political resistance. The author of Daniel was obviously chafing at the rule of Antiochus IV Epiphanes. He published his book to warn Jews of what was to come, but also to encourage them and urge them not to give in to those who wanted to push a "hellenizing" program onto the Jews. Apocalypticism, therefore, often makes special sense to those who consider themselves oppressed by a more powerful cultural force. The weakened nation of Israel couldn't always see itself as able to throw off the yoke of the Greeks or, later, the Romans. The Christian minority could never have overthrown the idolatrous Romans in order to establish what they would have seen as a more just world. The apocalyptic idea was that the oppressed would endure for a while, remaining faithful to their God and their own view of the world, and that soon God would intervene in history with angelic armies. Those armies would fight the oppressor, defeat the overlords, and establish a world of justice, mercy, and peace.

It is certainly not true that people who adhere to apocalyptic beliefs are always truly the "oppressed." There are many Americans who are very well-off and enjoy the benefits of all the injustices of capitalism but who still believe that God will intervene soon, overthrow current governments, and establish their own vision of the world. President Ronald Reagan, even while he was the most powerful man on earth, accepted what he was told were biblical prophecies that before the coming of Jesus, which he believed was imminent, there would be a major apocalyptic war in which evil nations would attack and try to destroy Israel. Why do some people who actually are rich and powerful nonetheless hold apocalyptic views of the world? I expect that it is often just because they believe that these views are "biblical" and something they are expected to believe as good Jews or Christians. In other cases, it seems clear that they perceive themselves as an "oppressed" minority, even if the only "oppressors" they can point to are "eastern elites," or "the media," or "liberals" who wreak havoc on "traditional values." As we will see, not all early Christian apocalyptic literature functions as "resistance literature" for a people suffering real oppression, but it often does so. It is a means of dealing with a sense—or reality—of powerlessness in the face of more powerful but putatively unjust opponents. This is precisely the function of Revelation.

As I said, it is remarkable that Revelation is not pseudepigraphic. If the author claimed to be the apostle John, brother of James and son of Zebedee, scholars would have cause to doubt this. It is also clear that this author is not the person who wrote the Fourth Gospel or the letters of John in our New Testament (whatever his name; remember, originally that Gospel was anonymous and was given the name of John only later). The styles of the Gospel of John and Revelation could hardly be more different. Whereas the Greek of the Gospel is perfectly fine Greek (if rather simplistic and odd in itself), the Greek of Revelation is atrocious, seeming almost illiterate at times. The theologies of the Gospel and the letters of John, on the one hand, and Revelation, on the other, are also quite different, although the Gospel and the letters do show strong influences from apocalypticism. But the author of Revelation does not claim to be any well-known "John," and since that was a common name for Jews at the time, scholars simply accept it as the name of our author, often distinguishing this "John" from others by calling him "John the Seer."

John also sees no need to claim that he exists somewhere deep in the past or that he hid his apocalypse so that it could be discovered later, closer to the time of the end of the world. He places his work in his own time. He does not believe that there will be much of a future before the intervention of God. He believes that he is a prophet just as important as Daniel or any other, but he is prophesying about things that will happen any day now. He feels no need to cast himself in the past or to project his book far into the future.

The Structure of Revelation

Compared with many other ancient apocalypses, Revelation has a rather peculiar structure. For one thing, the content of the vision itself is preceded by seven letters addressed to seven churches in Asia Minor. I return later to a closer examination of these letters, but their very presence at the beginning of the book is notable. I will argue, though, that the structure of the rest of the book—something like its "outline"—is also significant for its meaning and function. In the chapter on Hebrews, I argued that the document was an elaborately structured sermon. Hebrews is written in fine Greek, some of the best Greek of the New Testament. But even beyond its Greek style, its outline is impressive. In spite of the fact that the Greek of Revelation is terrible, I will argue that its structure or outline is elaborate and important for how it accomplishes its purposes.

Revelation is structured in a series of cycles. In fact, I imagine it as a spiral: circles that come around and around again, but nonetheless progress higher and higher to a climax and then an anticlimactic ending. I have noted that many apocalypses provide narratives, and some of those narratives are fairly straightforward: first this happened, then this; next this will happen, then this, and the end will look like this. In fact, many Christians through the centuries have attempted to read Revelation as a prophecy of events that will follow a linear time line. A book that was the best-selling book in the 1970s was Hal Lindsey's *The Late, Great Planet Earth*, which attempted to read Daniel and Revelation to predict future wars between the United States and the Soviet Union, wars between the ten countries of a United Europe and Israel, and many more such fantastic notions. Of course, because things didn't happen the way Lindsey promised they would—the Soviet Union dissolved, the European Union ended up being much larger than he had predicted, and geopolitical "things on the ground" just changed all over the place—later editions of the book had to be updated (that is, changed) repeatedly. Lindsey's was just one of the many failed attempts to read Revelation as predicting one linear time line of future events.

I argue instead that the narrative of Revelation circles around on itself several times (see Fig. 12). It does tell of expected events that will happen on earth and in heaven, but it does so in cycles. After we get past the letters to the seven churches and the introduction to the vision, including John's vision of the throne room of God, we encounter a cycle of seven seals, which will be the first of at least three large cycles of things or events. Following an introduction to the entire issue of the scroll and the seven seals, includ-

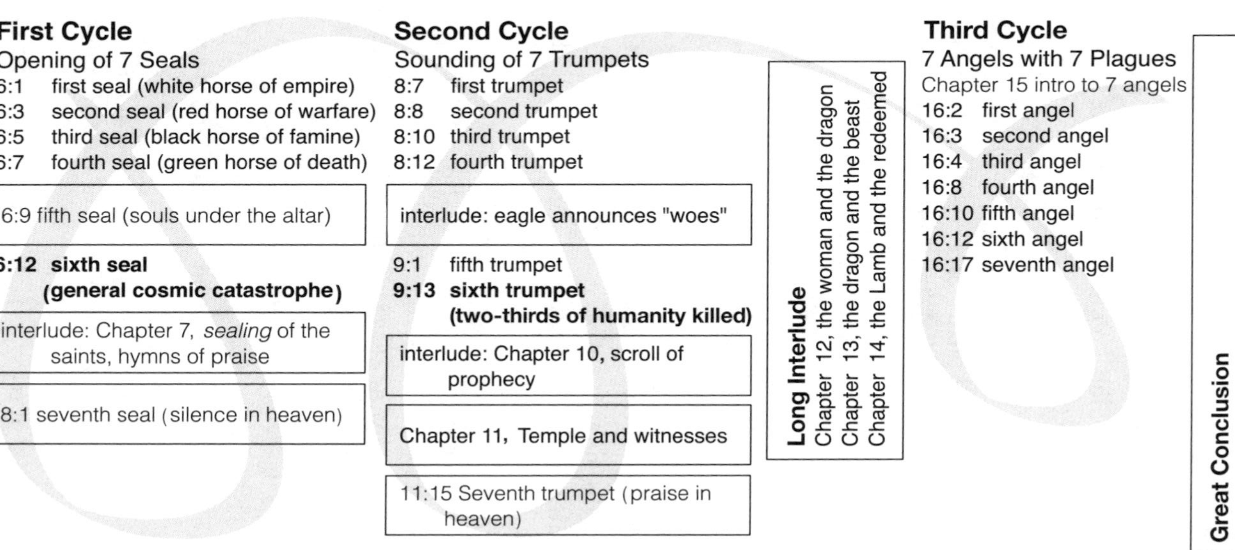

Fig. 12 Spiral Outline of Revelation

ing praise for God and the Lamb, who is capable and worthy of opening the seals, John begins the first cycle: "Then I saw the Lamb open one of the seven seals, and I heard one of the four living creatures call out, as with a voice of thunder, 'Come!' I looked, and there was a white horse! Its rider had a bow; a crown was given to him, and he came out conquering and to conquer" (6:1–2).

We modern people may have some difficulty picturing how this book and its seals work. First, we must remember that we are supposed to imagine a huge scroll, which is how almost all books of this time were made, not a book with cut-up pages sewn together. Books, letters, and other documents were often sealed shut with wax; the book would be rolled up, and a sealed lump of wax would keep the last flap closed. It seems that this special scroll with seven seals has its different seals lined up along the edge of the scroll, so that as each seal is broken, a bit of the "page" can be opened. But I imagine the scroll as having seven seals on and within the rolled-up scroll. The Lamb breaks the first seal, and the scroll is able to be unrolled just a bit, with a white horse and rider jumping out and riding off. To open the scroll further, however, the Lamb must break another seal that has kept the scroll from being completely unrolled, and so on through the seven seals. The process of going through the seals and knowing that others will be following is what sustains the expectations of the readers and hearers. The device of movement through a scroll with several seals adds suspense to the text.

The first four seals release four horses and riders, each symbolizing some kind of warfare or disaster (6:1–8): conquering or perhaps "empire" (white), the slaughter of warfare (red), famine (black), and death and Hades (pale green). But suddenly with the fifth seal, the expected pattern is disrupted. The fifth seal has nothing to do with horses, riders, or even disasters: "When he opened the fifth seal, I saw under the altar the souls of those who had been slaughtered for the word of God and for the testimony they had given" (6:9). The breaking of the fifth seal reveals the souls of Christian martyrs, who cry to the Lord asking for relief and vengeance. And they do find some relief, though not the final relief. They are given white robes and told to rest "a little longer" until the fullness of time and events bring about their release. Notice how the sequence of disasters, the first four seals, is followed not by another disaster but by a reassurance, a slight relief from the parade of disasters. This "interlude" type of interruption will recur in different ways throughout Revelation.

After the interlude of reassurance represented by the fifth seal, the breaking of the sixth seal releases the greatest concatenation of disasters of all: the earth quakes, the sun blackens, the moon turns to blood, the stars fall to earth, and the sky itself vanishes "like a scroll rolling itself up" (6:14). Again, we moderns have to think ourselves back into an ancient cosmology. As I have explained in previous chapters, in ancient notions the sky was actually something firm, like a leather scroll that stretched high above us. We are supposed to look up and imagine the actual physical scroll of the sky rolling itself up, and thus the entire cosmos being ripped apart and falling in on itself. This is the great day of "wrath" (6:17) that is so terrifying that even the most powerful men on earth run and hide, begging that the rocks and mountains fall on them and crush them just so they will not have to endure the worse fate of God's anger (6:15–16).

At this point, we must be thinking that if the sixth seal was such a disaster, the seventh must be even worse. Yet just when we are expecting it, just after the devastation of the sixth seal, we don't encounter the seventh seal after all. Our expectations (our dread?) are disrupted by another interruption, another interlude. At 7:1 in our Bibles, right where we expect to meet the seventh seal, we find something else entirely.[2] The destruction is in fact halted, with four angels assigned to the four corners of the earth (another aspect of ancient cosmology ancient people took to be perfectly physical) to make sure that things are, at least for the moment, peaceful and protected.

Chapter 7 is occupied first with "sealing" the 144,000 faithful people, that is, 12,000 from each of the twelve tribes of Israel, the faithful remnant who are sealed to protect them from all disasters. Then an even greater number of faithful arrive, "a great multitude that no one could count, from every nation, from all tribes and peoples and languages" (7:9). These people are all wearing white robes and carrying palm branches of peace in their hands. In other words, first the faithful remnant of those from the Jews are sealed for protection, and then they are joined by the faithful gentiles from all over the world. They provide the first song of praise (7:10), which is followed by a second song of praise sung by the angels, the elders, and the four living creatures standing around God's throne (7:11) and finally by a third song of praise that closes the chapter with the assurance that "God will wipe away every tear from their eyes" (7:17).

We must note the elaborate structure and plays on words. The use of "seal" first for the four disasters and then the great disaster of the sixth seal is followed by the use of "sealing" for the activity of protecting the faithful—the faithful Jews and gentiles. The thing that frightened the reader at first provides in the interlude after the terrible sixth seal protection and promise and peace: a sealing of protection for the faithful in place of the sealing of disaster for the rest of the world.

But we have not forgotten that there are seven seals, and we have not yet seen the seventh. In fact, the author has been stringing us along, moving us from disaster to reassurance, back to disaster and again to reassurance, all through the "seals" and the songs. But finally, he turns our attention again to the seventh seal: "When the Lamb opened the seventh seal" (8:1). Surely at this point his hearers are holding their breath. The narrative has built up tension, and we await the seventh seal with a mixture of dread and hope. What will happen when the seventh seal is opened? "When the Lamb opened the seventh seal . . . there was silence in heaven for about half an hour." If we pause right at the ellipsis (which I added) and then just matter-of-factly say the rest, the last phrase sounds like a great letdown in the tension. Even the words "about half an hour" in English sound abruptly informal and anticlimactic. But no explanation is given for this strange ending to a progression of tension. For immediately after that strange statement—"there was silence in heaven for about half an hour"—the author has us off on more "sevens," this time seven angels and seven trumpets. The whole vision takes off into another cycle.

The second cycle, this time of seven trumpets, begins at 8:2 and continues until 11:19. Although many other things will happen, they are fitted into the cycle of seven. Again, we have the juxtaposition of disaster and reassurance, of condemnation and praise. We have the first four trumpets announcing four different cosmic disasters (8:1–12). We have then the first interruption in this cycle, with an eagle flying through the scene announcing woes on the "inhabitants of the earth" and the coming of the last three trumpets (8:13). The fifth trumpet brings "the first woe." Again, the narrator ratchets up the tension and suffering: the trumpet calls forth inhuman and seemingly invincible beasts that torture people (9:1–11). The sixth trumpet releases four angels who proceed to slaughter a third of humankind. An army of two hundred million troops, bestial riders on fire-breathing horses with lions' heads and stings in their tails, kills another third of humanity (9:13–19).

But again, we are made to wait for the seventh angel and the seventh trumpet. Instead, another angel comes down from heaven with a scroll of prophecy, which John is told to eat, and he is informed that he must prophesy (10:1–11). This interruption is followed by a second one in which John is instructed to measure the temple. The activities of two mysterious prophets are described, including their martyrdom and resurrection after "three and a half days" (11:1–13). Only after these interludes do we finally get to the seventh trumpet. Like the seventh seal earlier, it does not usher in a disaster, but rather relief and praise: another song is sung, and God's temple in heaven is opened, accompanied by celestial fireworks (11:15–19). So ends the second cycle of seven.

Another cycle of seven, this time seven angels with seven plagues, is announced at 15:1. But in the intervening chapters we encounter other episodes that function as interludes or interruptions, as had other episodes within the previous cycles of seven. In other words, the book of Revelation exhibits internal structures of cycles of disasters interrupted by interludes that introduce different images and information, and the entire book is structured as sections of disaster interrupted by larger interludes. Thus the end of the second cycle of seven, at the end of chapter 11, is followed by chapter 12, which narrates the tale of the woman and her male child who are attacked by a great red dragon, which is fought by the angel Michael and his army of angels. That episode ends with the rescue of the woman. The woman may represent the church or Israel (or may have many different meanings); it seems that her child certainly represents the Messiah (12:5). The main "meaning" of the entire episode, in any case, is to depict danger and disaster followed by rescue and salvation. That scene is followed by a vivid portrayal of the dragon and a beast that serves it, with all their destruction, certainly representing Rome and Nero (chapter 13). Chapter 14 is about the horned Lamb that is wounded, that is, Jesus. And then, with 15:1, we have the introduction of the last cycle of seven: angels, plagues, bowls (chapters 15 and 16).

It is not accidental that we have found three cycles of seven. Both numbers were important symbols in antiquity and could evoke many different meanings. The conclusion, in any case, of the third cycle of sevens brings us to the climax of the entire book: the destruction of Rome (chapters 17–19); the final battle between evil and good (19:11–21); the imprisonment and eventual destruction of enemies of God (chapter 20); and the establishment of peace and the new Jerusalem (chapters 21 and 22).

What I have given here is, of course, a brief, foreshortened outline and sketch of the book, but its purpose is to demonstrate that Revelation, in spite of appearing initially confused and confusing, actually exhibits an intricate elaboration of a repetitive structure: series of repeated disasters are interspersed with events and images intended to offer salvation and encouragement; repetitions are ratcheted up to reach climaxes of destruction and woe, which are inevitably followed by assurances of salvation and peace; anticlimaxes follow climaxes.

Crisis, Catharsis, and Politics in Revelation

What does this structure—or these Chinese boxes of repetitions of an inlaid structure—tell us about the meaning and purpose of Revelation? In *Crisis and Catharsis: The Power of the Apocalypse*, Adela Yarbro Collins argues that the purpose of Revelation was to build a sense of crisis among early followers of Jesus. A famous slogan about great preaching says that a good sermon should "comfort the afflicted and afflict the comfortable." According to Yarbro Collins, that is precisely the goal of the author of Revelation. If his readers are feeling oppressed by the Romans, if they have experienced persecution from the Romans or just from their neighbors in Asia Minor, or if they have suffered because of their faith, they should experience, through following the narrative flow of the text, a move from suffering to relief, from pain to peace, from crisis to catharsis.

But as we will see in an analysis of the seven letters at the beginning of the book, the author also wants to address those he feels are too comfortable in a Roman-dominated Asia Minor. If they are wealthy and prospering from the so-called Roman Peace, they should recognize the foundation of murder and injustice on which that "peace" is built. If they get along just fine with their idolatrous neighbors, they should instead come to see them as servants of a bloodthirsty dragon or the lovers of a blood-dripping whore. His goal is not just to give suffering Christians hope, but also to alter the vision of those Christians who are ignoring the injustices of Rome. Crisis is created by the book's narrative in order to allow the reader to experience a catharsis of salvation. The looping structure of the book is designed to work psychologically on its hearers.

My use of "hearers" in that last sentence is deliberate. As we have seen in other situations addressed by this book, the fact that ancient documents were almost always read aloud, even when the reader was alone, should influence the way we imagine them being "read" or, for most people, "heard." Furthermore, when a document was read in a group, the "group dynamic" of public reading would have altered the experience of the text. All these dynamics would have been heightened by a document as "visual," dramatic, and psychological as Revelation. The way ancient Christians experienced the message of Revelation would have been affected as much by the way they encountered it—together with other Christians, read out loud, and probably in a darkened room lit by a few lamps and candles in the evening—as by the "content" of the text itself.

Revelation, that is, would have been "performed" rather than merely "read," and the structures and elements of the text would have enhanced the performance. Revelation alternates, for example, narrative about visions or events with "songs." Between the sixth and the seventh seal occur three episodes of chanting or singing (7:10, 7:12, 7:15–17). After the seventh trumpet occur one chant (11:15) and one longer song (11:16–18). In this case, it helps us moderns imagine the ancient effect if, when we hear them read, we recall their setting in famous modern music, such as the "Hallelujah Chorus" of Handel's *Messiah*: "The kingdom of this world has become the kingdom of our Lord and of his Christ!" This alternation of narrative with chanting and music occurs throughout the book. It is almost like a Broadway musical: action and dialogue take place, and then the chorus runs on the stage for a musical number, which is then followed by another scene of acting and dialogue.

We must use our imaginations to get an inkling of what an ancient Christian would have experienced in hearing the text read aloud in a group. We envision a group of Christians in Asia Minor gathered, as they usually do, in someone's dining room, after dark, with someone having presented a new document from a prophet. We hear of visions, beasts, creatures, angels, people singing, angels singing, elders chanting. The spookiness begins with the beginning of the narration of how John first entered God's throne room:

> After this I looked, and there in heaven a door stood open! And the first voice, which I had heard speaking to me like a trumpet, said, "Come up here, and I will show you what must take place after this." At once I was in the spirit, and there in heaven stood a throne, with one seated on the throne! And the one seated there looks like jasper and carnelian, and around the throne is a rainbow that looks like an emerald. Around the throne are twenty-four thrones, and seated on the thrones are twenty-four elders, dressed in white robes, with golden crowns on their heads. Coming from the throne are flashes of lightening, and rumblings and peals of thunder, and in front of the throne burn seven flaming torches, which are the seven spirits of God. (Rev 4:1–6a)

We sit in the dark, seeing in our mind's eye four living creatures with monstrous combinations of body parts, chanting over and over, night and day,

Holy, holy, holy,
The Lord God Almighty
Who was, and who is, and who is to come.

The twenty-four elders compete with them, shouting, "Worthy is the Lamb that was slain!" Then all this chanting and noise are joined by the voices of "every creature in heaven and on earth and under the earth, and in the sea" (5:13), singing,

Glory, honor, power
To thee our God most high.

In all the noise, we see the beasts flapping their wings, smoke and lightening surrounding the throne, and fear and praise and awe mingled as we have never felt them before.

Contrary to the way Revelation has often been read throughout the centuries, its purpose is not simply to pass along information, but to create a state of emotion and psychology. It is attempting to comfort those who are suffering under Roman rule—and there were many who were—but also to instill in all its hearers a fear and loathing for Rome. And it does so through dramatic narration, imagery, music, and chants. Its depiction of Rome is intended to provoke both fear and disgust:

> After this I saw another angel coming down from heaven, having great authority; and the earth was made bright with his splendor.
> He called out with a mighty voice,
> "Fallen, fallen is Babylon the great!
> It has become a dwelling place of demons,
> a haunt of every foul spirit,
> a haunt of every foul bird,
> a haunt of every foul and hateful beast.
> For all the nations have drunk of the wine of the wrath of her fornication,
> and the kings of the earth have committed fornication with her,
> and the merchants of the earth have grown rich from the power of her luxury." (18:1–3)

That "Babylon" is code for Rome is clear; in 17:9 and 18, the author had already described it as a city on seven hills, referring to the famous seven hills of Rome.

Rome is also identified by the mysterious symbol of the "mark of the beast": 666 (13:18). Many interpreters have tried to identify this number with the name of every imaginable "beast," from the pope in the minds of some Protestants to the six, six, six letters in the name Ronald Wilson Reagan for leftists with a sense of humor in the 1980s. Modern scholars, though, think the most compelling theory identifies the number with Nero. In many ancient languages, as we have already seen in Chapter 21, the letters of the alphabet functioned also as numerals. If one adds up the letters of the name Neron Caesar (spelled in Hebrew, which used the "n" for the ending of the name), the sum is 666. This also makes sense of a textual variant here found in certain ancient manuscripts. Some scribes, thinking of the name as it would appear in Greek rather than Hebrew (and thus without that one "n"), changed the number to 616, which would be the correct addition of the letters of the name spelled in Greek. Thus we know that at least those ancient scribes also took the number to be a reference to Nero.

Most scholars, though, believe that Revelation was not written in the 60s, when Nero was emperor, but late in the first century, perhaps closer to 100 C.E. Nero had committed suicide in 68 C.E., but he was so feared by some portions of the population, especially by Christians, apparently, that a legend developed that either he was not dead and was just in hiding somewhere in the East, or he had died but would rise from the dead, gather a new army, and wage war again to regain the throne. Thus the reference that the beast had suffered a "mortal wound" but had been healed (13:3; one does not "heal" from a truly "mortal" wound) and another account of the beast ascending "from the bottomless pit" intent on destruction (17:8). This would have been especially terrifying for Christians, who remembered Nero as the first Roman emperor to target Christians for persecution, torture, and death.[3]

The Social Context of Revelation

Having imagined the psychological effect of hearing Revelation read aloud, we must also imagine what kind of social context is reflected in the document. For this, we concentrate on the letters at the beginning of the document. First, we note where these seven churches are located: Ephesus, Smyrna, Pergamum, Thyatira, Sardis, Philadelphia, and Laodicea. It may be no accident that some of these churches are important for the ministry of Paul, who would have been long dead by the writing of Revelation (on my assumption of a later dating around 100 rather than an earlier dating in the 60s). Paul's churches, however, would still have been there. We know, for instance, that Paul spent much time with the church in Ephesus; although he did not found the church in Colossae, he was enough connected to it that a forged letter to Colossae supposed to be by him survives. Laodicea, a town near Colossae, is implied as being in a "Pauline circle" in Colossians 2:1 and 4:13–16, and a forged letter to Laodicea also survives. According to Acts, one of Paul's first converts was a female dealer in purple cloth from Thyatira (Acts 16:14–15). John, therefore, is addressing his document, by including these "literary" letters within it, to a circle of churches concentrated in a region of Asia Minor long associated with Paul's ministry.

Next, we may find some clues in seeing what sorts of actions John praises in the churches. He singles out those who have been or are experiencing suffering or persecution (2:3). He praises poverty (2:9), and we know from the rest of Revelation that he condemns the rich. He praises those who have separated themselves from and reject "those who say that they are Jews and are not, but are a synagogue of Satan" (2:9; see also 3:9). And we can list those things John is against. He strongly condemns any church that he perceives as less than perfectly enthusiastic about its faith, calling it "lukewarm" (2:4, 3:15–16), and he urges churches to regain their previous fervor (3:2–3).

John becomes the most riled, though, when he is addressing those people who are less strict than he believes they must be in their resistance to idolatry and fornication. He praises some of the Christians in Pergamum, but he condemns them for tolerating in their midst others "who would eat food sacrificed to idols and practice fornication" (2:14). This seems especially galling to him because they are living in a city "where Satan's throne is" (2:13). Pergamum was (and for scholars still is) famous for a huge altar to Zeus built on the mountain that served as the city's acropolis. The altar, with its fantastic depictions of the gods and their battles, was built in the Hellenistic period and was still well known in the Roman period. Its reconstruction now resides in the Pergamonmuseum in Berlin. There were also major temples and altars dedicated to the imperial cult in Pergamum. John, therefore, may have particularly idolatry, and even the cult of the emperor and Roma especially, in mind when he is addressing the church in Pergamum.

John takes the church in Thyatira to task for tolerating in its midst a woman teacher he calls "Jezebel," whom he accuses also of leading other Christians to "practice fornication and to eat food sacrificed to idols" (2:20). This may refer to an actual woman in the church, although of course her real name would not have been Jezebel, which John chooses for its connotations of both female sexuality and idolatry associated with the Phoenician queen of King Ahab (see 1 Kings 16, 19).

What do we make of these clues? First, I think it important to point out that John's references to "fornication" may not mean that these churches were actually practicing or promoting real "fornication" among its members, that is, promiscuous sexual relations outside the bonds of marriage. It is sometimes not adequately noted that all John's references to faithful followers of Christ in Revelation, whom he calls "slaves" although they are not literally slaves, are male, as are God, Christ, and apparently all the angels. They are also described as entirely celibate, a kingdom of male slave priests and prophets who have "not been defiled by women" (14:4). John's ideal church, therefore, would probably have been a completely male community (or one in which women were invisible) of sexual ascetics.[4] Since the Greek word translated here as "fornication" is *porneia*, which for Greek-speaking Jews of the time could refer to any and all sexual activity (masturbation, oral sex, or whatever) they considered immoral, and not just what we mean by the English "fornication," we probably would be closer to the mark to translate it as something like "sexual impropriety" or "sexual immorality" in Revelation.

With that in mind, we can draw a fuller picture of the kind of early Christianity here condemned by John, and it could have been nothing more than the slightly more "lenient" or "accommodating" Christianity we find in many of Paul's churches. After all, Paul's churches sometimes had female leaders and teachers. Paul had taught that Christians should not be condemned for eating meat that had been sacrificed to idols. And contrary to many early Christians, who advocated complete sexual renunciation even for those in marriages, Paul allowed members of his churches to continue having sexual relations with their spouses, even if that spouse was not a Christian.[5] Moreover, many people in Paul's churches, especially in 1 Corinthians, seem to have been relatively comfortable in their social and cultural surroundings, and even with Roman rule, as we will see in the next chapter. It is entirely possible, as surprising as it may be for modern Christians, that Revelation was written, at least in part, to condemn a form of Pauline Christianity existing in western Asia Minor at the end of the first century. Those are the kinds of comfortable Christians John wants to afflict.

Who Was This John?

Modern scholars are convinced that the John who wrote Revelation was not the apostle John or the anonymous author who wrote the Gospel of

John or any of the three letters. We know little else about him with certainty or detail, but I would like to suggest that we again use our imagination to construct a profile of him. First, note his virulent anti-Roman attitude. It seeps through the pages like venom. He views Rome as not only depraved and unjust but thoroughly blood soaked. He condemns wealthy people and praises the poor. He praises those who have suffered for the faith, some even to martyrdom. He is radically opposed to idolatry, especially the imperial cult, and he opposes idolatry even to the extent of taking a very hard line on Christians, like some in Paul's churches, who believe that eating food previously offered to an idol is permissible as long as one does not participate in the cult itself. John also can be placed in the kind of Christianity that advocated not merely sexual propriety within marriage, but radical sexual asceticism. True "slaves of Christ," priests, and prophets must not be "tainted by women" at all.

John also seems to be jealous of the name "Jew." He believes that those Jews who attend synagogues but do not recognize Jesus as the Messiah are Jews in name only. But he himself seems separated from the Jewish synagogue and believes that all followers of Jesus should be. Last but not least, his Greek is not very good. He writes in Greek, but probably not as a native speaker or one highly educated.

Although it is pure speculation, I think it is intriguing to imagine that John is a Jewish follower of Jesus who has been in situations where he has experienced the worst of Roman rule. We may imagine him as a Jew from Palestine who perhaps lived through the Jewish War, the destruction of much of Palestine, the destruction of the temple, the enslavement of thousands of Jews, and the transfer of many of them to slavery in Rome. He has seen the sporadic mistreatment of Christians, perhaps in Judea and even in Rome. While he is traveling around the Mediterranean, prophesying to the churches in different areas, his anti-Romanism gets him in trouble, and he is imprisoned on the island of Patmos, off the coast of Asia Minor and not far from Ephesus, a major port city in the area.

In his travels, he has come across Christian churches that are unlike those from which he came, perhaps in Palestine and elsewhere. They are rather healthy and growing. They seem comfortable with Roman rule and Greek culture. They live in comfortable Greek and urbane cities. They are sometimes, unlike him, fairly well educated. They may have their own businesses—that is, they may themselves be merchants profiting from the "peace" engineered by Roman violence. They have their own slaves. There are women leaders in their churches. Some of them even eat meat sold in the marketplace that has probably been sacrificed to idols. And they enjoy fairly normal sexual relations with their spouses, or maybe even with their slaves.[6]

Precisely because he is so horrified both by Rome and by those "followers" of Jesus who have accommodated to Roman rule, John writes his magnum opus of terrifying visions, but one with a happy ending for those who share his brand of the faith. For those slaves of Christ who suffer in poverty and patience, stoutly resisting Rome and their wealthy, idolatrous neighbors, the bloody, horned Lamb will finally bring salvation, happiness, and peace, a city better than Rome, a new Jerusalem.

CHAPTER 24

Apocalypticism as Accommodation

Overview: The Apocalypse of John showed an anti-Roman, politically revolutionary perspective. This is in contrast with Paul's writing in Romans 13, which calls for submission to governmental authorities—although passages in 1 Corinthians may be said to contradict this. Second Thessalonians, a pseudonymous letter, also preaches a politically conservative and accommodating message, as does 1 Peter. Interestingly, these letters do not discard or ignore apocalypticism but use it quite differently from the author of Revelation to further their message of political conservatism. Second Peter seems to be a letter dating from the second century, from the postapostolic age. In 2 Peter, the apocalypse is no longer imminent and is not used to further any admonition. Instead, it has become simply a part of Christian doctrine.

The Politics of Early Christianities

In the last chapter, we encountered a kind of Christian apocalypticism that bitterly opposed Roman rule and power. Although almost all earliest Christianity was apocalyptic in some sense—that is, expecting that the "end" would come soon and that Jesus would return from the heavens as a victorious conqueror to establish the kingdom of God—not all early Christians used that apocalypticism to oppose Rome, or at least not openly and vigorously. Some early Christians tolerated Roman rule, and some early Christian sources teach what later became the more typical stance of most churches: to submit to rulers and governmental authorities. Although it was not the position of all early followers of Jesus—Jesus had been executed, remember, by the Romans as an insurrectionist and pretender to the throne of Judea, and some early Christians seem to have remembered that—the more "accommodationist" attitude to Roman authority and human rulers also found a place among early Christian groups.

In Romans 13, Paul wrote what became his famous (or perhaps infamous) sentences on submission to ruling authorities: "Let every person be subject to the governing authorities; for there is no authority except from God, and those authorities that exist have been instituted by God. Therefore whoever resists authority resists what God has appointed." According to Paul here, God himself had appointed the Roman governors. "Those who resist will incur judgment, for rulers are not a terror to good conduct, but to bad" (Rom 13:1–3a). Only those who are bad need fear the Romans? Jesus might have been surprised to hear that. Certainly the author of Revelation would have completely disagreed. Paul continues, "Do you wish to have no fear of the authority? Then do what is good and you will receive its approval; for it is God's servant for your good. But if you do what is wrong you should be afraid, for the authority does not bear the sword in vain. It is the servant of God to execute wrath on the wrongdoer" (13:3b–4). The Roman governor, from Paul's perspective—judging at least from this passage—is actually God's servant to punish wrongdoing.

Paul does sound a bit different in some other letters of his, for example, in 1 Corinthians 2:6–8: "Yet among the mature we do speak wisdom, though it is not a wisdom of this age or of the rulers of this age, who are doomed to perish. But we speak God's wisdom, secret and hidden, which God decreed before the ages for our glory. None of the rulers of this age understood this; for if they had, they would not have crucified the Lord of glory." Paul, of course, knows that the Romans crucified Jesus. In spite of the history of Christian anti-Semitism, which blamed the Jews, and often only the Jews, for killing Christ, everyone in the ancient world knew that crucifixion was a method of execution much favored by the Romans.[1] It was not a Jewish punishment. Stoning was the usual means of execution by Jewish authorities or mobs, while crucifixion was the usual Roman method for those not lucky enough to be Roman citizens or elites from other ethnic groups in Roman territories. Paul knows this.

So when Paul talks about the "rulers of this age" who unknowingly crucified "the Lord of glory," is he thinking of the Romans? Pilate was the ruler of Judea at the time of Jesus' death, but he was simply the representative of the Senate and the emperor. Is Paul therefore blaming the Senate and Emperor Tiberius for the crucifixion of Jesus? In spite of what he says in Romans 13, Paul may very well have had little fondness for the Roman overlords. And in this passage, if they are whom he means by "the rulers of this age," he is predicting their eventual destruction. He is saying that the Roman rulers are even now in the process of perishing, and they will be completely destroyed by God when Jesus comes back on the clouds with his holy army of angels. This would not be very different from the prophecies of John in Revelation.

But the Greek word here translated as "ruler" (*archōn*) could also refer to superhuman, angelic powers. Paul does believe that evil angels exist who will be judged in the Last Judgment. In fact, he believes that Christians will be the ones who judge evil angels (if that is the meaning of Paul's "we" in 1 Cor 6:3, as I think must be the case).[2] Is Paul, therefore, talking here about some kind of satanic angelic powers that ruled the cosmos? One of the aspects of an apocalyptic worldview, as we have seen, is that different nations have angelic forces as their rulers. In Daniel, they are called the "princes" of the nations; the "prince of Persia" is an angel who rules Persia (Dan 10:13; see also Deut 32:8; Sir 17:17). According to this mythology, every nation has an assigned angelic or satanic power (they are usually understood as satanic angels, that is, "angels of Satan" or angels who do satanic-like work). Satan, in this view, is just one, perhaps the highest and chief, of many kinds of powers, rulers of "this cosmos." If that is what Paul is talking about here, he is blaming the crucifixion of Jesus on evil angelic powers.

Scholars have tended to line up behind one or the other of these proposals: with terms such as "principalities and powers" Paul is referring either to human ruling authorities or to "superhuman," angelic-demonic powers. I tend to believe that Paul is talking about both. We have seen that the apocalyptic prophet of Daniel believed that Persia and other countries had human kings and governors, but those human rulers were under the control of evil powers that ruled them. In some forms of apocalypticism, the evil, oppressive human rulers are just puppets in the hands of superhuman, spiritual evil powers, and the wars and fighting that take place here on earth are merely the shadow of the greater wars and fighting going on in the heavens between the powers of good and those of evil. I think it highly likely, therefore, that when Paul condemns those "rulers," "principalities," and "powers" of evil, he means both the human and the superhuman species. But if that is so, Paul's less negative comments about human rulers in Romans 13 must be seen in a somewhat different light. He is writing there to Christians in Rome, after all; he knows that Rome will suffer destruction as an evil overlord, but until that final destruction by the hand of Jesus, Christians are in the meantime to submit and not rebel.

It is not easy, therefore, to answer the question, was early Christianity politically revolutionary and anti-Rome, or was it politically accommodating? Some scholars may answer that in spite of a few revolutionary documents or statements, early Christianity was basically quietistic and accommodating to the ruling political powers. Others will say that in spite of a few texts such as Romans 13 and others I will analyze in this chapter, early Christianity was a movement of resistance to oppressive rulers, although it did not usually express that resistance openly or by means of actual rebellion. The reason scholars can line up on both sides of the issue is that both sides have some ammunition in the New Testament to support their positions.

Even in Luke-Acts itself, taking it as two volumes of one work, we find some strange ambiguities in its attitude toward the Romans. On the one hand, the author goes out of his way to depict Roman governor after Roman governor declaring that Jesus or Paul or the Christian "way" is politically innocuous.[3] Paul is eventually taken to Rome as a prisoner, but by that time in the narrative we have already seen a governor declaring that he could have released Paul as completely innocent, but Paul has appealed to the emperor, and so he must go to the emperor (Acts 26:32). Any conflict between Paul or other Christians and Jews is declared to be merely a dispute about religious beliefs or some kind of internal family spat. Everyone in authority in Acts is there to demonstrate that Christianity is not politically insurrectionist.

It would appear that the author of Luke and Acts is writing a defense, an apology, about the Romans, except that all these Roman rulers come across as rather incompetent and feckless. They can just barely control the mobs that attack Christians. They can't seem to act decisively against Jewish leaders who want to kill Paul. Rome and its leaders at various levels come across in Luke and Acts ambiguously: they are neither evil oppressors of Christians nor noble rulers of the earth who protect Christians from their enemies.

Second Thessalonians, the Lawless One, and Politics

Second Thessalonians is one of those letters whose authorship is disputed. Many scholars believe that Paul did write it. I join many others in believing that it is a forgery in Paul's name. Unlike Colossians and Ephesians, however, this is not demonstrable on the basis of the style of writing. Other disputed Pauline letters, Colossians and Ephesians, as well as the Pastoral Epistles, survive in styles that are so unlike the style of Paul's seven undisputed letters that the style alone argues for pseudonymity. The Greek of 2 Thessalonians looks much like Paul's Greek. In fact, I believe the writer of 2 Thessalonians had access to a copy of 1 Thessalonians and used it as a model for his forgery. If one lines up the first parts of the two letters next to each other (see Fig. 13), one sees not only similarities, but almost exact matches in the wording of the opening (1 Thess 1:1–2; 2 Thess 1:2–3) and in other sections (compare 1 Thess 3:11–13 with 2 Thess 2:16–17, to name only one such case; there are more).

On the other hand, the two letters are very different on a central issue: the timing of the coming of Jesus. Paul writes in 1 Thessalonians as if he expects the coming of Jesus very soon indeed; he seems to expect that perhaps he, but certainly some of those now living, will be living also at the *parousia* (the appearance or coming) of Jesus from the heavens (1 Thess 4:15–18). He urges the Thessalonians to watch and stay awake because it could happen any day now (5:1–6).

1 Thess 1:1	Paul, Silvanus, and Timothy, To the church of the Thessalonians in God the Father and the Lord Jesus Christ: Grace to you and peace.	2 Thess 1:1–2a
1 Thess 1:2	We always give thanks to God for you	2 Thess 1:3
1 Thess 1:4	brothers and sisters beloved by God/the Lord	2 Thess 2:13
1 Thess 2:9	labor and toil. . . we worked night and day, so that we might not burden any of you.	2 Thess 3:8
1 Thess 3:11–13	Now may our God and Father himself and our Lord Jesus . . . strengthen your hearts	2 Thess 2:16–17

Fig. 13 Comparison of First and Second Thessalonians

The author of 2 Thessalonians, on the other hand, seems to write his letter precisely to cool down expectations of an imminent parousia. He not only says that the day is not yet "here," but he also gives a fairly elaborate time line of events that must take place before Jesus returns, as I will explain later. He tells them that they should not quit their jobs, and that those who are unwilling to continue working for their living should not be supported by others: "Anyone unwilling to work should not eat" (2 Thess 3:10). He writes with the express purpose of insisting that the coming of Jesus will be further in the future than they are expecting. They should not look for it any day now.

So any theory about the authorship of 2 Thessalonians has to make sense of both these facts: the style and even the wording of 2 Thessalonians look very much like those of 1 Thessalonians, almost as if the writer of the second letter had a copy of the first in front of him as he wrote, but the main point of 2 Thessalonians—that the coming of Jesus is not going to be really soon, and people should not expect it to happen any day now—seems directly to contradict Paul's teaching about the coming of Jesus in 1 Thessalonians. Scholars who argue for the authenticity of 2 Thessalonians say that Paul must have written it so soon after sending 1 Thessalonians that he just happened to use the same wording in places, either out of habit or precisely because he had written it so recently. They also argue that he wrote 2 Thessalonians precisely because he had heard that some people in Thessalonica had taken his previous letter too much to heart and were expecting Jesus so soon that they had quit working. He needed the second letter to say: Jesus is coming soon, but not that soon.

I believe those are weak arguments. When I sit down to write a letter to someone, I do not usually copy parts out of a previous letter I sent that person for inclusion in the second. I think it much more likely that the author of 2 Thessalonians used 1 Thessalonians as a model to make sure he was imitating Paul's style correctly. Ancient forgers knew that they needed to do their best to imitate the writing style of the person in whose name they were writing. Having Paul's own letter to the Thessalonians beside him would have made that easier. There are also signs in 2 Thessalonians that the author went out of his way to provide his forged letter with the kind of marks of verisimilitude popular among ancient forgers. He alludes to the dangers of paying attention to letters that might be circulating in Paul's name but that have been forged (2 Thess 2:2). He insists that the signature at the close of the letter is by himself, Paul: "I, Paul, write this greeting with my own hand. This is the mark in every letter of mine; it is the way I write" (2 Thess 3:17). Whereas some scholars have thought that these personal references make it more likely that the letter really is by Paul, other scholars think the author was doing what we know forgers did: adding urgent protestations of the authenticity of their letters and warning about forgeries in their name.[4] Those who doubt the authenticity of 2 Thessalonians think the author simply protests too much and thereby shows his hand—a hand that is not Paul's.

The one place where 2 Thessalonians looks very different from 1 Thessalonians is precisely where its author is attempting to "correct" 1 Thessalonians: in the time line that delays the parousia of Jesus (2:1–12). That section begins: "As to the coming of our Lord Jesus Christ, and our being gathered together to him, we beg you brothers not to be quickly shaken in mind or alarmed, either by spirit or by word or by letter, as though from us, to the effect that the day of the Lord is already here" (2:1–2).[5] Notice that if this letter is pseudonymous, as I claim, we have here a reference to a pseudonymous letter in a pseudonymous letter. As I have argued, although that may seem strange to us, it was not at all uncommon in ancient forgeries.

He continues, "Let no one deceive you in any way; for that day will not come unless the rebellion comes first and the lawless one is revealed, the one destined for destruction. He opposes and exalts himself above every so-called god or object of worship, so that he takes his seat in the temple of God, declaring himself to be God" (2:3–4). As we have seen in Daniel and the synoptic Gospels, references to men who set themselves up as false messiahs or even as a god occur in early Christian texts and the Jewish texts they used as models. The false god or "object of worship" is called the "abomination of desolation" (or "the abomination that makes desolate") elsewhere (Mark 13:14, translated as "desolating sacrilege" in the NRSV; see Dan 9:27, 11:31, 12:11). The author here also prophesies about a false Christ, the same kind of figure elsewhere called an "Antichrist" (1 John 2:18).

The author then claims that Paul himself was supposed to have warned them about these events: "Do you not remember that I told you these things when I was still with you? And you know what is now restraining [the lawless one] so that he may be revealed when his time comes" (2 Thess 2:5–6). The word for "restraining" comes from the Greek word *katechō* and means something "holding back" something else. At this point, we cannot tell whether the author is referring to a thing, a power or institution, or a person, although the participle used here is neuter, so it seems to be referring to "the restraining thing." "For the mystery of lawlessness is already at work, but only until the one who now restrains is removed" (2:7). Here the participle is masculine. That may mean that we should be thinking of a person who is functioning as the current restraint on this "lawless one." But this is not necessarily the case, since a masculine word could be referring to something that occurs as a masculine noun in Greek, such as an institution or other force.

At any rate, whatever is now working to restrain the lawless one will be removed at some time in the future, allowing him to do his evil, self-promoting work.

> And then the lawless one will be revealed, whom the Lord Jesus will destroy with the breath of his mouth, annihilating him by the manifestation of his coming. The coming of the lawless one is apparent in the working of Satan, who uses all power, signs, lying wonders, and every kind of wicked deception for those who are perishing, because they refused to love the truth and so be saved. For this reason God sends them a powerful delusion, leading them to believe what is false, so that all who have not believed the truth but took pleasure in unrighteousness will be condemned. (2:8–12)

There is no agreement among scholars about what this "restraining one" is or how it or he is working to restrain the lawless one. I believe that although this author doesn't use the word, by "the lawless one" he means some Antichrist figure who will occupy the Jerusalem temple and set himself up as divine. I believe, that is, that this is a reference to a false messiah who must appear before the final coming of Jesus in glory. The author is imagining a Jewish false messiah now hidden but already in existence, perhaps in Palestine, awaiting his moment to proclaim himself.

But what is the "restraining" force? It could be God. It could be some other superhuman force, such as a very powerful angel. But I think the author could be thinking of Rome and the emperor. That could also explain his use of both a neuter and a masculine term to refer to it and him. The emperor, who is now "holding back" the rise of any potential Jewish competitor, is going to be removed by some other power, by God or at least according to God's will. With the removal of Roman power and its armies, a false Jewish messiah will be able to arise and take over Jerusalem and the temple. After all, the one thing in the ancient Mediterranean that kept other men from proclaiming themselves kings was the power of Rome. Jesus had been executed on the charge of illegally posing as a king (no one could be a king except by appointment of the Senate). But the Romans had executed other pretenders to various thrones as well. The one visible power that was keeping any legitimate or illegitimate kings from arising was that of Rome. The Roman emperor and power will someday be removed. The lawless one will use that opportunity to claim the messianic title and power for himself in Jerusalem. And that will be the signal for Jesus to lead his own army, destroy the lawless one, and set up the true kingdom of God.

This is all my speculation, of course. We don't have enough evidence to solve the puzzle. But I believe it is a good hypothesis. If it is true, this author doesn't see Rome as a completely negative power in the world. Rome actually has a purpose in God's plan. Of course, once that purpose is completed, and God is ready for the end-time events to begin, Rome and the emperor will be destroyed, so Rome doesn't get off either.

We have here, therefore, a case in which someone writes a letter in Paul's name precisely to counter the idea that Jesus is coming back really soon. The coming is still fairly soon in the future. The author seems clearly not to be thinking of a thousand years or so. But he puts forward a series of geopolitical events that will precede the coming of Jesus and that must be endured by Paul's churches before they can rejoice in the reign of God at the end.

First Peter and Politics

The First Letter of Peter is another example of a pseudepigraphic letter in the New Testament. There are several reasons for believing it is a forgery and not actually by the apostle Peter. The most glaring is that all our evidence indicates that Peter was an illiterate peasant fisherman from Galilee. He is called "uneducated and ordinary" in Acts 4:13. As I have argued concerning other early figures whose names are attached to letters, such as James and Jude, if Peter could read or write at all, it is all but certain that he would not have been able to write the quality of Greek represented in 1 Peter. Moreover, to historians, who sketch out the development of Christianity over many years, the letter seems to represent a kind of Christianity that developed only later in the first century, not likely in the first three decades of the movement, when Peter was active. Arguments and evidence for the pseudonymity of 1 Peter, however, are easily found elsewhere, so I do not dwell on the topic further here.

The letter begins: "Peter an apostle of Jesus Christ to the exiles of the Dispersion in Pontus, Galatia, Cappadocia, Asia, and Bithynia" (1:1). At first glance, it would seem that he is writing a general letter, a circulating letter, to dispersed Jews who now live not in Palestine but in major geographic regions of what is now central and western Turkey. But he is clearly addressing gentiles who used to be sinful idolaters (1:14, 1:18, 4:3). Only recently, he believes, have they become members of the people of God (2:9–10). The author does use the term "gentile" to refer only to "outsiders," not to the people he is addressing (2:12, 4:3), but Paul does that also, usually reserving the word "gentile" only for people who are not Jews but also not members of the church.

The author calls them exiles, but it is almost certain that he is using the term metaphorically and "spiritually," implying that followers of Jesus must conduct themselves as aliens in a strange land because their "true home" is with God (1:17, 2:11). He is attempting to get them to see themselves as "illegal aliens" or, if legal, as people who don't really belong in a strange and hostile country, the world itself.

What are his politics? "For the Lord's sake accept the authority of every human institution" (2:13). This is clearly a reference to human authorities, not angelic powers. "Whether of the emperor as supreme, or of governors, as sent by him to punish those who do wrong and to praise those who do right" (2:13–14). The governors of the different parts of the Roman Empire were appointed either by the Senate or by the emperor himself. Our author seems to believe that all Roman governors are appointed directly by the emperor, which was in fact not the case. But I doubt that he cares about the niceties of Roman governmental appointments.

The main reason he urges his audience to submit to the authorities and cause no trouble has to do with perceptions of the churches and Christians by their non-Christian neighbors: "For it is God's will that by doing right you should silence the ignorance of the foolish. As servants of God, live as free people, yet do not use your freedom as a pretext for evil. Honor everyone. Love the family of believers. Fear God. Honor the emperor" (2:15–17). To see properly how different this sentiment is from those of other Christians of the time, we must try to imagine the author of Revelation saying such a thing. It would have been impossible for him to have urged people to "honor the emperor." The author of Revelation does have concern and loyalty for other Christians, but apparently none at all for outsiders. Compared with Revelation, therefore, the Christianity of 1 Peter is remarkably conservative in its politics.

That politics plays itself out also in some other social issues. Just after urging honor for the emperor and governors, he also insists that slaves completely accept their slavery and defer to their owners: "Slaves, accept the authority of your masters with all deference, not only those who are kind and gentle but also those who are harsh. For it is a credit to you if, being aware of God, you endure pain while suffering unjustly. If you endure when you are beaten for doing wrong, what credit is that? But if you endure when you do right and suffer for it, you have God's approval" (2:18–20). This is precisely the kind of religion ("the opiate of the masses") condemned by Marx and Lenin: a religion that exists to keep the slave a slave, to keep the poor poor, and to keep the downtrodden down.

So it is not surprising to see the author's instructions to women: "Wives, in the same way, accept the authority of your husbands, so that, even if some of them do not obey the word, they may be won over without a word by their wives' conduct" (3:1). Some of the women in these churches are followers of Jesus, but their husbands are not. They should still obey them. The author doesn't allow women to use their Christian allegiance and the lordship of Christ to get out from under the lordship of their husbands. "Do not adorn yourselves outwardly by braiding your hair, and by wearing gold ornaments or fine clothing; rather, let your adornment be the inner self with the lasting beauty of a gentle and quiet spirit, which is very precious in God's sight. It was in this way long ago that the holy women who hoped in God used to adorn themselves by accepting the authority of their husbands" (3:3–5).

The author's assumption of the hierarchies of society in the household of the church extends to the need for young people to submit to the old, or at least older men: "In the same way, you who are younger must accept the authority of the elders" (5:5). As came to be true for much of Christianity through the ages, this author, writing in the name of Peter, commands people to stay in their places. There is to be no revolution, no insurrection, no bucking of traditional social hierarchy. This is clearly political quietism, accommodation, accepted and nurtured so that Christians will cause no offense to their neighbors and thereby provoke condemnation of Christians as troublemakers. "Conduct yourselves honorably among the gentiles, so that, though they malign you as evildoers, they may see your honorable deeds and glorify God when he comes to judge" (2:12).

Note that the author has not left apocalypticism behind. He admits, "The end of all things is near" (4:7). He invokes typical images of apocalyptic fire: "Beloved, do not be surprised at the fiery ordeal that is taking place among you to test you, as though something strange were happening to you" (4:12). He warns of coming judgment: "For the time has come for judgment to begin with the household of God; if it begins with us, what will be the end for those who do not obey the gospel of God?" (4:17). But the apocalyptic material functions quite differently here than it did in Revelation. The apocalypticism is not here to provide an answer for suffering (as in "We suffer now because the world is momentarily under the grip of evil, but only for a short time more"), or to rectify a sense of injustice by promising vengeance ("Yes, the Romans are evil rulers, but they will get theirs in the end"). The apocalypticism of 1 Peter does little, if any, work to help anyone in a fight against injustice. Rather, it seems to be present in 1 Peter simply as part of the furniture of early Christianity. It is the apocalypticism of accommodation.

Second Peter: A Letter from the Postapostolic Age

The Second Letter of Peter is also pseudonymous and was not written by the same person who wrote 1 Peter. Moreover, it was probably written decades after the letters of Paul, perhaps as late as the first half of the second century. Second Peter, in fact, shows us a form of Christianity much more developed than that of the first century. Notice the way chapter 3 begins: "This is now, beloved, the second letter I am writing to you; in them I am trying to arouse your sincere intention by reminding you that you should remember the words spoken in the past by the holy prophets, and the commandment of the Lord and Savior spoken through your apostles" (2 Pet 3:1–2). It is as if he is speaking of himself in the third person, since of course Peter was one of those "apostles." He sounds as if he is hearkening back to a now-distant "apostolic age." They are to "remember" a time of the living voices of prophets and apostles. He also knows of another letter in Peter's name, and this may very well be our document 1 Peter. He knows that he is writing in a tradition that goes back many years.

The writer also knows at least some of the Gospels: "For we did not follow cleverly devised myths when we made known to you the power and coming of our Lord Jesus Christ, but we had been eyewitnesses of his majesty. For he received honor and glory from God the Father when that voice was conveyed to him by the Majestic Glory, saying, 'This is my Son, my Beloved, with whom I am well pleased.' We ourselves heard this voice come from heaven, when we were with him on the holy mountain" (1:16–18). This, of course, is a reference to the story of the transfiguration of Jesus on the mountain while he was with Moses and Elijah, which was witnessed by

Peter, James, and John (see Mark 9:2–8 and parallels). The author knows the story and that Peter was one of three disciples to see the transfiguration.

In one of the most interesting passages, he refers to the letters of Paul, as I mentioned already in Chapter 2:

> Therefore, beloved, while you are waiting for these things, strive to be found by him at peace, without spot or blemish; and regard the patience of our Lord as salvation. So also our beloved brother Paul wrote to you according to the wisdom given him, speaking of this as he does in all his letters. There are some things in them hard to understand, which the ignorant and unstable twist to their own destruction, as they do the other scriptures. (3:14–16)

What makes this quotation significant—and important for demonstrating the relatively late date of its composition—is that the author knows that collections of Paul's letters have been circulating for a long time and that some Christians have used them to advance doctrines this author considers not adequately orthodox. Most important, however, he ranks the letters of Paul on the level of "scripture."

Paul had no idea when he wrote his letters that he was writing "scripture." For Paul, and for all other New Testament writers except this one, "scripture" referred to Jewish scripture, usually read in Greek translation. Paul probably did consider his letters authoritative, but they had authority only for his own churches. It must have taken many decades after the death of Paul for churches to begin considering his letters scripture, and even, by the tone of these sentences, on a par with the older scriptures, those that now make up the Old Testament. This author is living in a time when the Gospels and collections of Paul's letters are circulating among networks of churches and are revered as "scripture."

Another indication that the author of 2 Peter is writing in a later time comes from the way he uses the Letter of Jude. He uses Jude, though without naming it, as a source for his own writing. Second Peter 2:1–22 reproduces much of the material found in Jude 4–18, though abbreviated and rearranged. Among the huge amount of Jewish writings from the Second Temple period, we have several different documents published in the name of Enoch. According to Genesis 5:21–24, Enoch was a seventh-generation descendant of Adam; he "walked with God" and was "taken" by God. This passage was interpreted in ancient Judaism and Christianity to signify that Enoch had been so righteous that he did not die but was raised still alive to heaven by God. That made Enoch, who was therefore still living, a useful source for pseudepigraphic prophecies; he has been living all this time with God, so he must know what he is talking about. Jude alludes in different places to Enochic material and in one place quotes it explicitly.

To back up his warning about the Lord coming with his angelic army to bring judgment and punishment, Jude quotes a passage from *1 Enoch* 9: "Enoch, in the seventh generation from Adam, prophesied, saying, 'See, the Lord is coming with ten thousands of his holy ones, to execute judgment on all, and to convict everyone of the deeds of ungodliness that they have committed in such an ungodly way, and of all the harsh things that ungodly sinners have spoken against him'" (Jude 14–15). The author of Jude therefore takes Enochic materials to be true prophecy on the same level as other biblical prophecy.

What is interesting is that the author of 2 Peter leaves out this quotation when he takes material from Jude. That may indicate that he does not consider *Enoch* to be scripture on a par with biblical prophecy. If that is so, it may indicate that he is writing at a time, later in the development of Christianity, when the Old Testament canon was becoming a bit more settled, and the Enochic materials were being sidelined.

Jude alludes to other noncanonical Jewish writings that 2 Peter omits. Jude mentions a story that the angel Michael, after the death of Moses, argued with the devil over the body of Moses (Jude 9). This is a story that is also not in our Bible but is found in other Second Temple Jewish documents.[6] It may not be an accident that the author of 2 Peter leaves out these details also. He may be providing evidence of a somewhat more conservative canon of adopted Jewish scripture than that assumed by Jude. All these differences between the letters of Paul and the Letter of Jude, on the one hand, and 2 Peter, on the other, suggest that we are dealing here with forgery in the name of Peter from much later in the postapostolic period, perhaps from the second century.

In spite of writing many decades after the earliest period of Christian apocalypticism, the author of 2 Peter nonetheless retains apocalyptic elements. He refers to the future coming of Jesus and rejects those who mock such expectations: "First of all you must understand this, that in the last days scoffers will come, scoffing and indulging their own lusts and saying, 'Where is the promise of his coming? For ever since our ancestors died, all things continue as they were from the beginning of creation!'" (3:3–4). "Our ancestors?" Even though he is writing in Peter's name, the author writes as if those in the first generation or so after the death of Jesus are "our ancestors."

And he has to answer doubters who point to the long time since the first "coming" of Jesus to cast doubt on a second coming. To answer such doubts, he rehearses his own apocalyptic scenario:

> They deliberately ignore this fact, that by the word of God heavens existed long ago and an earth was formed out of water and by means of water, through which the world of that time was deluged with water and perished. But by the same word the present heavens and earth have been reserved for fire, being kept until the day of judgment and destruction of the godless. But do not ignore this one fact, beloved, that with the Lord one day is like a thousand years, and a thousand years are like one day. The Lord is not slow about his promises, as some think of slowness, but is patient with you, not wanting any to perish, but all to come to repentance. But the day of the Lord will come like a thief, and then the heavens will pass away with a loud noise, the elements will be dissolved with fire, and the earth and everything that is done on it will be disclosed. (3:5–10)

But we must ask, even if he does have an apocalyptic scenario, what "work" does it do for him? There is no sense of imminence. It may happen thousands of years from now. There is no heightened sense of injustice and crisis. The apocalypticism does not do anything like what it does for John in Revelation, or for Paul in his letters.

With 2 Peter, we are no longer in a kind of Christianity caught in eschatological fervor. We are in a Christianity that has its own scripture, that looks back to the apostolic age deep in the past, and that is politically rather conservative—there are no curses against Rome, nor even hints that it is an "evil power." The apocalyptic elements of 2 Peter seem to function as nothing more than doctrines one is supposed to accept, elements of "correct belief" that separate the "right" Christians from the "wrong" Christians. In other words, even though we are still not at a time when "orthodoxy" has been clearly defined, apocalyptic elements are called forth as doctrines that separate the "orthodox" from the "heterodox." Otherwise, the apocalypticism itself has lost fire and steam.

Apocalypticism is a political ideology, but the kinds of politics it advocates and supports may vary substantially. Indeed, the apocalypticism of different branches of early Christianity promoted different political ends. Apocalypticism could provide hope in desperate situations. It could label the Roman rulers as evil and Rome as a great whore or monster. It could encourage resistance and even open rebellion, as it certainly did among Jews in the first century, though apparently not among Christians. But we also find in early Christianity certain expressions of apocalypticism that taught quietism and urged Christians simply to go about their own business and wait. The varieties of early Christianities are expressed in the various ways apocalypticism served as an ideological and political force.

Development

CHAPTER 25

The Development of Ecclesiastical Institutions: Ignatius and the *Didache*

Overview: The letters of Ignatius of Antioch contain evidence of a move toward the institutionalization of early Christianity. Ignatius mentions, for example, three different church offices: bishops, presbyters, and deacons. He also emphasizes the authority held by those with these titles. The *Didache* contains liturgical and ritual instructions for rites such as baptism, the Lord's Prayer, and the Eucharist. All these documents show the change in early Christianity toward greater church structure and institutionalization.

From "Charismatic" to "Official" Institutions

When Paul was attempting to influence or control the house churches he had founded, he could draw on no official church structures or leaders to reinforce his rhetoric. All he had were his power of persuasion and his personal authority. Even his claim to be an apostle was not an appeal to an "office." He had never been appointed an apostle by any human institution. He claimed to be one on the basis of a revelation of Jesus that came to him alone. And there were no bishops, or priests, or even deacons in his churches in any official sense. When Paul uses those terms ("overseer," "elder," or "servant," to use their less official-sounding translations), he is referring to roles people play in his churches, not to institutionally established "offices."

To use a word made famous by the early sociologist of religion Max Weber, these leaders were "charismatic" leaders in a social group based on "charismatic" organization. The use of that word in this context means that any leaders who have influence must exercise it by their power of persuasion and personality. They are not "official" leaders occupying set institutional "offices." They lead by the power of personality and unofficial authority. Christianity did eventually establish regular offices for leaders, and this chapter shows that happening in its very early stages and by way of only two examples: the letters of Ignatius and the *Didache*, or, in its longer and translated title, *The Teaching of the Twelve Apostles.*

Ignatius and the Cult of the Martyr

Very early in Christianity, suffering was taken to confer respect and even honor. The example of the suffering of Jesus, of course, stood at the center of any Christian valuation of suffering. We have seen how Paul often appeals to his imprisonments, his beatings, and several other ways he has suffered for the gospel as a badge of his apostleship. Suffering for the cause, therefore, was part of Christianity from the beginning. It led to an entire theology surrounding martyrdom. In fact, we can also call it an "ideology" because it was the use of language in struggles for power and authority.

Martyrs enjoyed some immediate benefits. Whereas the belief developed in early Christianity that ordinary Christians could enter some state of blessedness at death, they had to wait until the end of time and the resurrection actually to enter heaven.[1] But martyrs, as a reward for their supreme sacrifice, earned with their deaths immediate entry into heaven. Martyrs were already, therefore, in the presence of God and Christ.[2] This again gave them a place of honor and authority.

A martyr, of course, could be honored—and could even "rule from heaven" by appearances in dreams or visions or via prophecies—but could no longer take part in the day-to-day life of a church. A martyr could receive prayers and even "votives" (gifts and offerings left at a grave or shrine), but couldn't "use" her or his martyrdom actually to wield authority in a church in precisely the way a living person could. Early Christians, however, also held high regard for "confessors." Confessors were persons who had been arrested and perhaps condemned to martyrdom, but who for some reason had not yet been killed or who had been released. Confessors were martyrs in all but the actual death. Many Christians took confessors to be especially close to God and Christ, to "have the ear" of the Lord more than other Christians, perhaps even more than bishops and priests, the "official" leaders of the churches. Because they had been so close to death and therefore heaven, confessors were sought out for advice, miracles, or intercession. Indeed, at some times and in some places, bishops had to counter the power of confessors, and this led to something like a rivalry for authority and ecclesiastical status between the official leaders, bishops, and the unofficial ones, martyrs and confessors.[3]

In the letters of Ignatius, we see a fascinating attempt to combine both these forms of authority and power: that of the bishop and that of the martyr. Ignatius was bishop of Antioch in Syria in the early second century. Sometime probably around the year 110, he was arrested and condemned in Antioch, but was sent under guard to Rome to be executed. During his extended journey, he was allowed to stop and spend time with churches on the way. He seems to have stayed in, at least, Smyrna and Troas in Asia Minor, and in Philippi in Macedonia. He also, though, got to know leaders from other churches in those areas, who came from their own towns and cities to visit him during those stays. He wrote letters to the churches in Ephesus, Magnesia on the Maeander, Tralles, Philadelphia, and Smyrna. He also wrote ahead to the Christians in Rome. And he wrote back to the bishop of Smyrna, Polycarp, after having left that city. We have, therefore, seven letters he wrote during the trip.

There are references to his upcoming martyrdom in all the letters. In the letter to the Ephesians, for instance, Ignatius refers to his chains as his "spiritual pearls" (*Eph* 11). This emphasis comes out most emphatically in his letter to the Romans because one of his main purposes for sending it was to instruct them that he was intent on dying and that they should make no attempt to save him:

> I am writing all the churches and giving instruction to all, that I am willingly dying for God, unless you hinder me. I urge you, do not become an untimely kindness to me. Allow me to be bread for the wild beasts; through them I am able to attain to God. I am the wheat of God and am ground by the teeth of the wild beasts, that I may be found to be the pure bread of Christ. Rather, coax the wild beasts, that they may become a tomb for me and leave no part of my body behind, that I may burden no

> one once I have died. Then I will truly be a disciple of Jesus Christ, when the world does not see even my body.[4] (*Rom* 4.1–2)

We see the beginnings of what can only appear to modern sensibilities a gory and grotesque celebration of death, torture, and suffering. But this has had a long and broad history in Christianity, as well as in other religions.

Just after that passage, Ignatius prays that the beasts will be eager to tear him apart. If they are not, he says, he will grab them and force them to eat him. "Fire and cross and packs of wild beasts, cuttings and being torn apart, the scattering of bones, the mangling of limbs, the grinding of the whole body, the evil torments of the devil—let them come upon me, only that I may attain to Jesus Christ" (*Rom* 5.3).

Although Ignatius emphasizes the "gain" he gets by his self-sacrifice, he is also clearly manipulating the currency of martyrdom valued in the early church. He has already insisted on his authority as bishop of Antioch. That authority, of course, would not have extended outside Antioch's own region. Ignatius was not the bishop of any other area. But his condition as a condemned and soon-to-be-martyred man gives him a universally recognized status among all the churches. The tone of his letters clearly shows his recognition of that status and his intention to use it.

Ignatius and Church Office

Besides commenting on his expected martyrdom, Ignatius addresses a few issues of doctrine and controversy. Rather than detailing the specifics of those disputes, however, I will focus instead on Ignatius's appeal to now-established church offices as a means of enforcing his version of orthodoxy and unity. Ignatius repeatedly mentions three distinct offices he expects to exist throughout Christianity: bishop, presbyter (priest), and deacon. Indeed, this is the earliest Christian writing that so explicitly cites these roles and gives them such an elevated status.

Even more surprising, however, is the way Ignatius describes—or, no doubt more accurately put, prescribes—the role of the bishop. As we have seen in the Pastoral Epistles, "overseers" (*episkopoi*) seem to have been appointed or elected in different churches, and there may have been several for the church in each town or city. In Ignatius's letters, we see for the first time at least an attempt to establish the "monarchical bishop"—that is, the practice of having one bishop over each city and its surrounding area who "ruled" as the sole, highest authority for that area. I say "attempt" because we don't know how successful Ignatius initially was. Almost certainly at this time (around 110 C.E.), different churches in different regions still had different practices. I believe it almost impossible that the way Ignatius portrays these offices, along with the unquestioned authority of a single bishop per city, characterized all of Christianity at this early date. In fact, I read Ignatius's letters as one powerful rhetorical intervention attempting to move the church in that direction.

Ignatius gives the bishop a very elevated status indeed. He compares the authority of the bishop to that of Jesus Christ, as he writes to the Trallians: "For when you are subject to the bishop as to Jesus Christ, you appear to me to live not in a human way but according to Jesus Christ, who died for us that you may escape dying by believing in his death. And so—as is already the case—you must not engage in any activity apart from the bishop" (*Trall* 2.1–2). The church is to be completely ruled by the bishop, and any activity not approved by him is forbidden. Elsewhere, Ignatius compares the bishop's authority to God's (*Magn* 6). The bishop is to be regarded as "the Lord himself," and just as the Lord Jesus "did nothing" apart from the Father, so the church should "do nothing" apart from the bishop and the presbyters (*Magn* 7).

Ignatius also insists on the authority and centrality of the other two offices, presbyter and deacon. At one place in his letter to the Magnesians, he places the bishop in the place occupied by God, the presbyters as "the apostolic council," and the deacons with the "service" of Jesus Christ (*Magn* 6; the Greek *diakonia* means "service"). Later in the same letter, though, he makes an even more explicit comparison of the three offices of the church to the three persons of the Trinity. "Father, Son, and Spirit" seem mirrored by bishop, presbyters, and deacons (*Magn* 13).

This hierarchical, three-tiered authority structure is meant by Ignatius to make sure that churches are united within themselves and with other churches not only in doctrine, but also in liturgy and biblical interpretation. He tells them to assemble "frequently" to take the Eucharist (*Eph* 13). Those meetings also must be under the supervision of the bishop and presbyters: "Obey the bishop and the presbytery . . . breaking one bread, which is a medicine that brings immortality, an antidote that allows us not to die but to live at all times in Jesus Christ" (*Eph* 20). This emphasis on the Eucharist, the insistence that the bishop and priests preside, and the naming of the elements of the Eucharist as "the medicine of immortality" all show a more developed stage in Christianity. The Lord's Supper is no longer a free-for-all potluck or even an "agape feast," but a carefully controlled enforcement of church unity under proper offices of authority.

Ignatius also attempts to bring the vagaries of scriptural interpretation under control. He mentions people in the church ("judaizers"; see *Phila* 6) who appeal directly to scripture as their authority: "If I do not find it in the ancient records, I do not believe in the gospel." When Ignatius attempts to interpret the texts for them, saying, "It is written," they object with, "That is just the question" (*Phila* 8). Ignatius therefore depends on the basic message of Jesus Christ, his death and resurrection and "the faith that comes through him," rather than simply an appeal to the scriptures (by which here he probably is thinking of the Old Testament). Even in this context, Ignatius appeals to his authority as bishop to trump private interpretation of scripture. He really means it when he says, "Do nothing apart from the bishop," not even interpreting the scriptures.

With the letters of Ignatius, we see remarkable developments in early Christianity. There are attempts at solidifying church offices, liturgy, doctrine, and practice. The institutional hierarchy over all the churches in a locality is wielded as a tool to bring unity and uniformity, as much as possible, to the church universal.[5]

The *Didache* and the Development of Liturgy

In 1873, a scholar discovered an ancient Christian document in a larger manuscript in the library of the Holy Sepulchre in Constantinople (now Istanbul). Scholars tend to refer to this document by the first word of the Greek title, the *Didache* ("teaching"). Scholars had known about this document from citations in ancient church fathers and a few fragments, but the discovery of the full text (or at least most of it, since the ending may be lacking) gave us one of the best glimpses into ancient church practices, and especially liturgy, from a very early period of Christian history.[6]

Scholars tend to believe that the document was a composite of probably previous sources, edited and published around 100 C.E., give or take around ten years. That means that the *Didache* predates some of the books of the New Testament and comes perhaps only a few years after, or even around the same time as, the Gospel of John or other New Testament books. It is therefore one of our earliest noncanonical Christian documents, and it is remarkable because it gives us information we never had before on how some churches were practicing baptism and the Eucharist. It also gives us some idea of leadership roles, both itinerant and settled, in churches before the system of bishops, presbyters, and deacons was widespread.

The book, indeed, looks like it represents a form of Christianity even more "primitive" than that portrayed in the letters of Ignatius, although it may have been written only a few years earlier. This again shows that we cannot take the letters of Ignatius—or any other Christian writing from this early period—as representing "Christianity." The movement was simply too diverse to be represented by any one document, or even by any small list of documents. The *Didache* certainly looks as "orthodox" as the letters of Ignatius (using that term, as I have explained, anachronistically for this early period), but its form of church organization is not nearly as settled as we might suppose on the basis of Ignatius's letters. That is, incidentally, another piece of evidence that Ignatius was not simply "representing" reality but attempting to create it.

The *Didache* is not pseudonymous because it makes no claim actually to have been written by the twelve apostles. It just claims to reproduce their teaching. The *Didache* seems to be heavily dependent on ethical themes derived from Judaism. It is also obviously influenced by the Gospel of Matthew. It begins with six chapters of ethical teaching, organized in the form of "two ways": the "way of life" and the "way of death." This was a common topos in Judaism of the time. Parallels can be found in other Christian documents, as well as in the *Manual of Discipline* (or *Community Rule*) from the Dead Sea Scrolls. These chapters offer, therefore, a fairly typical "paraenesis," or ethical admonition, regularly encountered in Judaism and early Christianity.

It is with the next major section of the document that we get the more interesting material on Christian liturgy. The author says that people should be baptized in the name of the Father, the Son, and the Holy Spirit (see Matt 28:19), and in running water (the Greek is "living water," so there may be some kind of double meaning, but that was the common way of designating "running water"). If that is not possible, baptism in still water in a pool is acceptable. It should be cold water if possible, but warmer water will do in a pinch. And if no pool is available, one may pour water over the head three times. The writer instructs that both the one baptizing and the one baptized should fast beforehand, joined by others if possible. But at any rate, the one being baptized must fast for one or two days first (*Didache* 7).

The next paragraph gives instructions about fasting and prayer. Readers are told not to fast on Mondays and Thursdays, because that is when "the hypocrites" fast. I think that the author must be thinking of Jews who do not believe in Christ. He tells his Christian readers to fast instead on Wednesdays and Fridays. He then says that they should pray the Lord's Prayer three times per day. It is interesting that the form of the Lord's Prayer he recites is much closer to the form recited in most Christian churches today than to either the form found in Matthew or that of Luke (*Didache* 8; compare Matt 6:9–13; Luke 11:2–4): it has a doxology at the end. This is because the common modern church version came from older Bibles, such as the King James Version, that had longer versions of the prayer later emended by scholars using better and more ancient Greek manuscripts for more modern versions of the Bible. But the longer version in the *Didache* must have been used by at least some churches around the end of the first century. In fact, the longer version in the *Didache* may have influenced Christian scribes to alter the shorter version originally found in Matthew.

Next, the author addresses issues surrounding the Eucharist. A couple of things from this section are of interest. First, he says that the cup of wine, with an accompanying prayer that he prescribes, is to be taken first, followed by the bread. This order is the reverse of what we find in Matthew, Mark, and Paul.[7] (Luke has first a cup, then the bread, and then another cup "after supper"; Luke 22:14–20.) He also says that only baptized people should be allowed to take the Eucharist. This will become common practice in later Christianity, but this is the first time we see it laid out explicitly as a rule. Incidentally, the next section prefaces its recommended prayers by saying, "And when you have had enough to eat" (*Didache* 10; the Greek more literally is "After you are full").[8] This indicates that the Eucharist at this time and place must have also included a full meal, or at least that enough bread and wine were offered that one could get "full."

After prescribing a long posteucharistic prayer, the author addresses the issue of itinerant teachers. He uses the word "apostle" for at least some of these traveling figures; recall that the word just means "someone sent out." The term has obviously not come to designate for all Christian groups (unlike its use in Acts) only the founding "apostles" of the Jesus movement and Paul; it still can be used more broadly. He also speaks of "prophets." It is unclear whether "apostle" and "prophet" designate two separate roles or are used interchangeably for itinerant prophets and teachers in general.

He says that itinerant teachers generally should be welcomed as long as they teach proper doctrines, but they should stay only one day, or at most two (*Didache* 11). If they stay three days, they are false prophets. When they leave, they may take some bread with them, but if any prophet asks for money, he is a false prophet. Apparently, prophets could order meals for the poor, but if they do, he says, they must not eat any of it themselves (11:9). He also speaks of prophets speaking "in the Spirit," and that they shouldn't be contradicted when they are doing so. This may refer to some kind of ecstatic prophetic activity, similar to the "speaking in tongues" Paul discusses (1 Cor 12–14). But even if a prophet is "speaking in the Spirit," he should be ignored if he asks for money for himself (*Didache* 11:12).

As we have seen elsewhere, ordinary Christians also used churches to provide temporary lodging when they were traveling (*Didache* 12),[9] and the author gives instructions about them also. They should be welcomed as long as they are "simply passing through," but only for two or three days. If they want to stay longer, they should settle down and practice a trade or find some other way to work and make a living. He seems very concerned about freeloaders, even calling them "Christmongers" (12:5: *Christemporoi*).

He leaves open the possibility that prophets and teachers may decide to settle down with them also. He calls these people "your high priests" and says that if they are true prophets and teachers, which their behavior is expected to demonstrate, they deserve support from the church: wine, grain, meat, oil, and even money and clothing if possible. If a church has no such local prophet to support, it should give the same amount to the poor (13).

After prescribing appropriate actions for "the Lord's day"—reconciling with one another and gathering to eat the Eucharist, which he calls their "sacrifice"—he turns his attention to the topic of bishops and deacons (14–15). It is interesting that he differentiates these roles from those of teacher and prophet. It also appears that we have here a plurality of bishops in each location. They are to be elected by the people (not appointed by higher authority). We should note that the "offices" in the *Didache* don't match those of Ignatius. There is no mention of presbyters, for instance. We probably do not have here the monarchical bishop. So the firm three-tiered system of clergy is not yet in place everywhere.

The *Didache* concludes with warnings about "end-time" events, the resurrection of the dead, and the coming of the Lord "on the clouds of the sky" (16). The document ends so abruptly that most scholars assume that the conclusion is lost.

"Christianity" Evolving

Even though we still have a great deal of diversity in the movement that will later become "Christianity," we can see here, at the end of the first century and the beginning of the second, a development toward later forms. But we have moved a long way from the tiny band of followers of the Jewish apocalyptic prophet Jesus of Nazareth. We have also moved significantly from the more informal, "charismatic" house churches planted by the apostle Paul. In the future, Christians will fight many battles among themselves about what is "true" doctrine and what is "false," what are the right liturgical practices and what are wrong, and even what are the right way and time to celebrate Easter. The churches around the Mediterranean will eventually develop the ecclesiastical structures of late antiquity: full church institutions, creeds, social networks, monasticism, and the canon, to name only a few. In the letters of Ignatius and the *Didache*, however, we see early steps toward those later institutions of Christianity.

Epilogue: Christianity after the New Testament Period

Overview: In this book, I have focused attention on the earliest period of Christian history, from Jesus to the house churches of Paul, the writing of the earliest Gospels, and the developments of the Christian movement during the late first century and early second century. The major theme has been the diversities of early Christian groups. What eventually became "orthodox" Christianity as represented in the creeds, councils, and established doctrines of most Christian denominations took centuries to develop; it did not spring simply from the teachings of Jesus or any later disciple of Jesus.

Diversities in Early Christianity

I have highlighted how different followers of Jesus developed, after his death, different notions of "who he was." Some doubtless saw him simply as a great prophet of Israel, preaching an apocalyptic message about an imminent "kingdom of God." Some believed that he was divine in some way, perhaps as an eminently righteous man who was elevated to some kind of semidivine status by God. Others came to believe that he was so divine that the "real" Christ, perhaps as differentiated from the "man" Jesus, was a pure spirit and not "flesh and blood." Still others came to believe that he was a fully divine being, though nonetheless subordinate to the highest God. And some came to believe that he was equal in divine status to God the Father. Jesus himself was also the "I am" who appeared to Moses in the burning bush. The Christologies developed in the first hundred years of Christianity were all over the map.

In the same way, our earliest Christian texts show remarkable diversity in how they viewed the Jewish law, the law of Moses. Matthew seems to have expected that all followers of Jesus, whether Jew or gentile, would keep the law and submit to its regulations with even greater care and piety than those of the Pharisees. Paul, at the other extreme, taught that although Jews could continue with their observations of the law of Moses, if gentiles even attempted to observe the law, they would by that action "cut themselves off from Christ"; they would "fall from grace." Law observance was not even an option for gentiles, in Paul's mind. Luke, we might imagine, occupied a middle position. He took the law of Moses to be simply the ethnic law of the Jews, just as Greeks, Romans, Egyptians, and other peoples had their own ethnic customs, traditions, and laws. Luke likely had none of the grand theological problems with the law entertained by Paul, but he likewise did not expect gentile converts to observe it, as did Matthew. The author of Hebrews saw the law as a code that one could "read" in order to discern previously hidden truths about the now-revealed "liturgy" of Christ. It was a clue, but not a problem, as long as Christians made no attempt actually to live by it.

We have seen that early Christians took diametrically opposed positions on the role of women in their churches and the place of the traditional patriarchal household. Jesus himself allowed women to be among his closest followers. He seems to have had no concern to support the traditional household or family, but instead called his disciples away from their households to be members of a new, eschatological, itinerant community awaiting the kingdom of God. Paul likewise allowed women dominant roles in his churches, although he was not truly a modern "egalitarian" in regard to gender. And Paul had no particular desire to reinforce the traditional household. For Paul, marriage existed only to quench sexual desire. The *Acts of Paul and Thecla* is only one document from a later generation of Paulinism that carried the anti-household brand of Christianity even further. The Pastoral Epistles did the opposite: they turned the church into a household, with women in silent, subordinate, childbearing roles in the church, just as they had been in the patriarchal household.

Indeed, once we compare the varieties of ancient Christianity represented in our sources, we notice a pattern: whenever a writer wishes to support the traditional family structures, he subordinates women; whenever he wishes to give women a greater and higher role in society or the church, he attacks the household. The two go together precisely in that way in earliest Christianity. It is only much later that a kind of asceticism is placed simply in parallel structure with the traditional patriarchal household. Later, one may be a monk or nun, or one may exist in a "normal" household, but asceticism is not allowed to challenge the traditional patriarchy of the household. In the earliest days of Christianity, it was different: asceticism seems regularly to have gone hand in hand with more powerful roles for women, and the subordination of women went hand in hand with promoting the traditional family.

Finally, the end-times. Most of early Christianity held eschatological views to some extent. Those documents that lean toward views later attributed to the Gnostics, such as the *Gospel of Thomas*, may have radically deemphasized earlier Christian apocalyptic expectations, but even there the traces of eschatology survive. The historical Jesus was himself, I have argued, an apocalyptic Jewish prophet, which is to say that he was expecting God and his angels to break into current world events, overthrow oppressors of the Jews, and establish the reign of God on earth. Jesus may have entertained the idea that he himself was to be the Messiah used by God for these deeds. Or perhaps he merely saw himself as a prophet and precursor for the Messiah, as John the Baptist may have seen himself. At any rate, Jesus was executed by the Romans on the charge of pretension to the throne of Judea, which indicates that either he himself or other people were claiming that he was a messiah. That, I and many scholars believe, is the only way to make sense of how and by whom he was killed.

Paul also assumed Jewish apocalyptic notions, although in his brand things had to be changed a bit to allow for the "fact" that the Messiah had already come, though in a "humble" form. Paul and other followers of Jesus had to alter older Jewish apocalypticism because they believed that the end-times were already in the making through the resurrection of Jesus, the "first" of the future resurrections of the righteous at the very end. Other early Christian documents likewise nurtured strongly apocalyptic views and expectations, such as the three synoptic Gospels (though more strongly in Mark than in Luke) and especially Revelation. Apocalyptic expectations declined later in different strands of Christianity, with even the deutero-Pauline letters (Colossians and Ephesians) muting apocalyptic expectations. Eschatological ideas have never died out among all Christians—predictions of the "end" and the "rapture" regularly return in our own societies—but for most of Christianity, apocalypticism has acted as a framework for theology rather than the prime driving force of it.

And in the ancient world, though not in the modern, Jewish apocalyptic beliefs almost always went hand in hand with opposition to the current ruling powers. The Jewish apocalypticism of Daniel opposed the hegemony of Hellenistic rulers. That of early Christianity usually was accompanied by suspicion of and hostility toward the Romans and their local "retainers" among the upper class of the provinces. Even Paul, who never openly urges opposition to the Roman overlords, is probably signaling hostility to them in his references to the "principalities and powers" that rule the cosmos and unknowingly killed "the Lord of glory" (1 Cor 2:8). That opposition becomes overt in documents such as the Revelation of John. The diversity of Christianity includes a variety of reliance on an apocalyptic worldview, along with a diversity of political orientation, from the radical revolutionary rhetoric of Revelation to the quietistic conservatism of "honoring the Emperor" of other documents (see 1 Pet 2:13–17).

These are only the topics I have emphasized by the structure of this book. I could point to other issues in which we see difference and diversity in the first hundred years of the Christian movement. Of course, Christianity has always exhibited and still exhibits many more differences among its different branches than is often noticed in popular ideas, which tend to emphasize rigid "orthodoxies" and conformity. But especially in its first few centuries, Christians experienced many differences among themselves, and many were more radical than those we experience today. It is important for people to realize that Christianity did not spring from the ground or fall from heaven in one shape or form. Its development was long, and the struggle at times for one doctrine or another was fierce. It was history happening.

After the New Testament

In some ways, the more important story for how Christianity came to be what it later was is the story of what happened after the New Testament, in the several centuries following the first.[1] In the second century, we have the beginnings of truly upper-class, educated people entering the ranks of the churches. Along the way, some of them make the first moves toward turning the religious movement of Christianity into a "philosophy." In the second and third centuries, we see the remarkable growth of Christian asceticism, both in numbers of adherents and in power of influence over the entire church. Monasticism, for both women and men, becomes one of the most powerful and notable social forces of late antiquity.[2]

As we have already seen to some extent in the letters of Ignatius and in the *Didache*, the different local, regional churches eventually developed institutional structures, formed mainly along the lines of known Roman governmental institutions, leading to monarchical bishops and a clergy comprising priests and deacons. Only much later, of course, was the bishop of Rome able to establish himself as the "first among equals" of the more powerful bishops, just as Augustus had earlier established himself as the first among equals in the Roman Senate. Indeed, it was well into the Middle Ages before the pope would be able to exert imperial status for himself and the Vatican, and "papal infallibility" wasn't declared dogma until the nineteenth century. But the beginnings of this centralization and institutionalization can be seen already in the late antiquity of the second through sixth centuries.

Perhaps the most important event in the historical establishment of Christianity and its eventual "triumph" over the ancient Roman world was the victory and conversion of Constantine. Because Constantine was such a powerful and long-lived emperor, and also because his dynasty after him mostly followed his lead in sponsoring the Christian church, Christianity was able, during the eventful fourth century, to become, eventually, the religion not only of a strong minority and the imperial household but also of the entire empire. It took many years for "paganism" to shrink to the extent that it was a negligible factor in society generally.[3] And of course, it hardly ever truly died out, because traces of the worship of "the gods" survived even in popular forms of Christianity. But the patronage of the church by Constantine and his descendants was the turning point toward the "triumph of Christianity" over its ancient rivals. What began as a ragtag bunch of poor, illiterate, Jewish peasants from Galilee eventually became the official religion of the Roman Empire. One could make good arguments that that story, the post–New Testament story, is the story of greater historical import than the first one hundred years represented by the documents studied in this book.

Christianity as "World Religion"

My students are often surprised when they realize just how unimportant Jesus of Nazareth was during his life, and just how insignificant the movement begun in his name was for a couple of centuries afterward. They think, like most people, that Jesus must have been a very important person, and that his followers must have taken the world by storm after his death. Once they hear the story of how diverse the early Jesus movement was, how weak it was for so long, and how it took centuries for its adherents to become even a powerful minority in the ancient Mediterranean, they ask, "So how did this tiny group of illiterate peasant followers of an apocalyptic Jewish prophet become a world religion? How, why, and when did that happen?"

To some extent, these are trick questions. One could say that Christianity did not become a "world religion" until the late nineteenth or early twentieth century because the category of "world religion" wasn't invented until then.[4] Scholars in religious studies for the past few decades have increasingly come to realize that even the category of "religion" in the way modern people use it did not exist in the ancient world. We generally mean by "religion" a system of beliefs (doctrines), practices (ritual), and ethics (morality) that conceives of supernatural beings (God, gods, angels, or others) in certain ways and structures human beings' relationship with those beings. We consider "religion" a general, even universal category that subsumes different "religions" within the larger, universal category of "religion." Critical theorists and historians of religious studies have pointed out that this entire way of thinking of "religion" is a modern invention, beginning mainly from the period of Europe's world explorations and modern colonialism.[5]

The category of "world religions" is even more recent, having been invented by different scholars in the late nineteenth and early twentieth centuries. What seems obvious—that Christianity is one great world religion among other world religions—is actually a fairly recent idea, given the grand sweep of all the history of Christianity. So in some sense, one could say that Christianity became a world religion only when that category became thinkable, in the late nineteenth and twentieth centuries.

But let's leave that more theoretical and critical discussion aside and ask the more specific question, when did all the major regions of the globe host some form of the Christian church? Unfortunately, that is also a very difficult question, in part because of our lack of historical information from many regions and periods, but also because of how we gauge the importance of the presence of a few "Christians" in otherwise "non-Christian" areas.[6]

In the beginning, of course, Christianity was limited to the Mediterranean basin. A bit of it certainly spread farther north in Europe during the first several centuries, but it was not until the Middle Ages that one would be able to think of all of Europe as "Christianized." A bit of Christianity certainly spread eastward, even reaching India, where some form of Christianity has existed since ancient times, albeit represented by only a small minority of the population. The ancient Near East (including Syria, Persia, Mesopotamia, and the lands that would later be "Arab") experienced vibrant Christianization in early years, but with the huge success of Islam, many of those regions could scarcely be called "Christian" today. Egypt was in the ancient world one of the most heavily "Christianized" areas very early on. But again, in the centuries after the arrival of Islam in Egypt, and especially today, one certainly wouldn't call Egypt a "Christian nation." And the same would have to be said of China and the Far East; there may well have been minorities of certain kinds of Christians there for centuries, but that is not particularly important from a sociological or political point of view.

For most of history of the past two thousand years, what was meant by "Christendom" was Europe. With the spread of European hegemony to the New World, the Western Hemisphere also became predominantly "Christian," too often by either the forced conversion or manufactured extinction of the native population. But the concentrated effort to spread Christianity "throughout the world"—that is, including Africa and all of Asia—took place mainly in the nineteenth century. So again, one could say that Christianity became a world religion—that is, not just the religion of Europe and those areas under the control of Europe—finally in the nineteenth century.

All of this is to say that the question, "When did Christianity finally become a world religion?" is much more complicated and debatable than many people realize. An answer depends on how one defines the terms, on what counts as Christianity, and whether we are also considering how significant Christianity is for a geographic region or a given society. It also depends on what someone means by "world religion." As I have indicated, one could easily defend the thesis, although it would surely be debatable, that it was only in the nineteenth century that Christianity became not just a European but a world religion. And much of that development would have to be chalked up to modern technology, communications, travel, and, not least, ideology.

One of the points of this book, in any case, is to say that a book on the New Testament and earliest Christianity can't answer the question. I don't believe that any historian can point to any kernel within or aspect of ancient Christianity that "caused" it to grow historically the way it did. There is no "universalism" inherent in the Christian story of Jesus or in early Christian teachings that caused Christianity to become, eventually, universally influential. It is part of the messiness of history, not some quality inherent either in Jesus or in the early Christian movement. In other words, from the point of view of the historian, there was nothing inevitable about the later growth of Christianity. Christians may indeed believe that the seed planted on Golgotha came to fruition in the "universal body of Christ" that is the church, and they may believe that it happened by divine providence and the agency of the Holy Spirit. But that is a matter of Christian faith that historians, if they are decent historians, will attempt neither to prove nor to disprove.

Of course, I believe that the beginning of Christianity warrants study and is fascinating on its own merits, regardless of the later history of Christianity. Entering into the sometimes-bizarre world of Jesus and his earliest followers is fun. Attempting to eavesdrop on the churches of Paul or the followers of Thecla provides a fascinating pastime. It also helps us broaden our own worlds of experience. We travel through time and space in our imaginations to wonder at the diversity of human belief and experience—even within Christianity. That is not only fun. It is also good.

Notes

CHAPTER 1
Introduction

1. Pius IX, *Ineffabilis deus* (1854).
2. See Marx, "Critique of the Gotha Program," 531.
3. In John 21:18–19, Jesus prophesies about Peter's death: he will "stretch out his hands," be bound at the waist, and be taken where he does not wish to go. That is not much to go on. If it is a reference to crucifixion, it is an obscure one.
4. See Martin, "When Did Angels Become Demons?"
5. Matthew (19:3–9) takes the story from Mark and modifies it somewhat. For analysis and an argument that the historical Jesus most likely forbade divorce entirely, see Martin, *Sex and the Single Savior*, 125–147.
6. For an argument that the New Testament's "theological" meaning is in some cases more important than its "historical" meaning, see Martin, *Pedagogy of the Bible.*
7. See, for example, Plato, *Phaedo* 80b.
8. For a collection and translation of Greek novels, see Reardon, *Collected Ancient Greek Novels.*
9. Pliny, *Epistles* 10.96. See also Minucius Felix, *Octavius* 8.
10. For remarks about the Christian god having no name, see *Martyrs of Lyon* 52, found in Eusebius, *Ecclesiastical History* 5.1.52.
11. For example, see *Martyrdom of Polycarp* 3; Athenagoras, *Embassy for the Christians* 3.
12. Minucius Felix, *Octavius* 9.
13. See Pliny, *Epistles* 10.96; 1 Cor 10:28.
14. *Apostolic Tradition* 21. The date and authorship of this work, traditionally attributed to the early third-century Roman bishop Hippolytus, are debated. It does, however, seem to preserve some material from as early as the second century. On its historical background, see Bradshaw, Johnson, and Phillips, *Apostolic Tradition.*
15. Minucius Felix, *Octavius* 9; Athenagoras, *Embassy for the Christians* 3, 31.

CHAPTER 2
The Development of the Canon

1. On the circulation of Paul's letters, and of early Christian literature in general, see Gamble, *Books and Readers in the Early Church*, 88–143.
2. Papyrus 46 (early third century) and the uncorrected versions of the Codex Sinaiticus and the Codex Vaticanus lack the phrase "To those in Ephesus" (Eph 1:1). Tertullian, *Against Marcion* 5.11, notes that the letter to the Ephesians

is known by "heretics" as the letter to the Laodiceans. For an introduction to the study of manuscripts, see Metzger and Ehrman, *The Text of the New Testament.*

3. "But I say to you, Love your enemies and pray for those who persecute you."
4. "Remain in the same house, eating and drinking whatever they provide, for the laborer deserves to be paid. Do not move about from house to house."
5. 1 Corinthians 9:15–18: "But I have made no use of any of these rights, nor am I writing this so that they may be applied in my case. Indeed, I would rather die than that—no one will deprive me of my ground for boasting! If I proclaim the gospel, this gives me no ground for boasting, for an obligation is laid on me, and woe to me if I do not proclaim the gospel! For if I do this of my own will, I have a reward; but if not of my own will, I am entrusted with a commission. What then is my reward? Just this: that in my proclamation I may make the gospel free of charge, so as not to make full use of my rights in the gospel."
6. The most famous account is in Plato's *Phaedrus,* and its most famous modern commentary is contained in Derrida, *Dissemination.*
7. This fragment of Papias's writings is preserved by Eusebius, *Ecclesiastical History* 3.39.3–4. For the Greek text and this English translation, see Ehrman, *Apostolic Fathers,* 2:99.
8. Justin Martyr, *First Apology* 67.
9. See Ehrman and Pleša, *The Apocryphal Gospels.*
10. The standard study of Marcion, on which virtually all later studies depend, is Harnack, *Marcion: Das Evangelium vom fremden Gott.* For a partial English translation that omits the appendixes of the original German, see Harnack, *Marcion: The Gospel of the Alien God.* Foster, "Marcion," presents a concise and recent overview of Marcion.
11. Tertullian, *Against Marcion* 1.18, 3.6, 5.1; *Prescription against Heretics* 30 (spurious); Rhodo, preserved in Eusebius, *Ecclesiastical History* 5.13.3. For the donation, see Tertullian, *Against Marcion* 4.4; *Prescription against Heretics* 30 (spurious).
12. See reactions and descriptions in Irenaeus, *Against Heresies* 3.3.4; Tertullian, *Against Marcion* 4.4; Epiphanius, *Panarion* I.42.2.1–42.2.8; Justin Martyr, *First Apology* 58.
13. Justin Martyr, *First Apology* 26; Tertullian, *Against Marcion* 1.19; Irenaeus, *Against Heresies* 1.27.2, 3.12.12.
14. Irenaeus, *Against Heresies* 1.27.2; Epiphanius, *Panarion* I.42.9.1.
15. Tertullian, *Against Marcion* 1.19–21.
16. See Foster's chart of these letters according to Tertullian (*Against Marcion* 5) and Epiphanius (*Panarion* I.42.9.3–42.9.4, I.42.11.9) in his "Marcion," 274. The letters are Galatians, 1 and 2 Corinthians, Romans, 1 and 2 Thessalonians, Laodiceans/Ephesians (Epiphanius considers these to be two distinct letters), Colossians, Philippians, and Philemon.
17. See Chapter 14 in this book.
18. Tertullian, *Against Marcion* 4.3–5; Irenaeus, *Against Heresies* 3.2.2; Epiphanius, *Panarion* I.42.11.3–42.11.12.
19. Against this view, see Barton, "Marcion Revisited," 341–354.
20. Tertullian, *Against Marcion* 4.4.
21. See Ehrman, *New Testament,* 6–7.

22. The classic case was made by Harnack, *Marcion*; followed by Campenhausen, *Formation of the Christian Bible.*
23. See, for example, the essays collected in McDonald and Sanders, *Canon Debate*, and other works there cited.
24. See Petersen, *Tatian's Diatessaron*. For an English translation, see Hogg, "Diatessaron of Tatian."
25. Preserved in Eusebius, *Ecclesiastical History* 3.39.15.
26. Tertullian, *Against Marcion* 4.5. Origen is also of this opinion in his *First Book on Matthew's Gospel* (preserved in Eusebius, *Ecclesiastical History* 6.25.4–6).
27. Papias, fragments (preserved in Eusebius, *Ecclesiastical History* 3.39.16); Origen, *First Book on Matthew's Gospel* (preserved in Eusebius, *Ecclesiastical History* 6.25.4).
28. One of the most obvious examples is Matthew's repeated use of the Greek word *hypocritēs*, "hypocrite" (for example, Matt 15:7, 23:13, 23:23, 23:25, 23:27, 23:29), which was a classical (one might even say technical) term for an actor. His quotation of Isa 7:14 as a prophecy of a "virgin" birth presupposes that he was dependent on a Greek translation of the Hebrew Bible, since the Hebrew word that occurs in the original meant simply a "young woman," as modern English translations demonstrate. There are many other pieces of such evidence.
29. See Metzger, *Canon of the New Testament*, 191–201; Hahneman, "Muratorian Fragment," 405–415. Metzger argued for a late second-century date. See also E. Ferguson, "Canon Muratori." For a fourth-century date, see Sundberg, "Canon Muratori"; Hahneman, *Muratorian Fragment.*
30. Ehrman, *Apostolic Fathers*; Holmes, *Apostolic Fathers.*
31. *Festal Letter* 39; translated in Schaff and Wace, *Nicene and Post-Nicene Fathers*, 4:552.
32. Metzger, *Canon of the New Testament*; Gamble, *Books and Readers in the Early Church*; McDonald and Sanders, *Canon Debate.*
33. Kraft, "Codex and Canon Consciousness." Metzger also seems to find this a plausible explanation; see his *Canon of the New Testament*, 108–109.
34. Scholars arguing against the idea include Roberts and Skeat, *Birth of the Codex*, 45–61; Gamble, *Books and Readers in the Early Church.*
35. See Metzger, *Canon of the New Testament*, 109.
36. Metzger, *Canon of the New Testament*, 311. It was discovered in 1886 by Theodor Mommsen, a German classicist, and thus is sometimes referred to as the Canon of Mommsen.
37. Brakke, "Scriptural Practices in Early Christianity."
38. A comparative chart showing the canon lists of different churches may be found in *New Oxford Annotated Bible*, 2187.
39. See Francis, "'Blessed is the One Who Reads Aloud.'"
40. For a list of the books considered canonical by the Roman Catholic Church, see "Session 4" of the Council of Trent in Tanner, *Decrees of the Ecumenical Councils*, 2:663. "Masoretic" refers to the official version of the Hebrew Bible for Judaism.
41. Lightstone, "Rabbis' Bible"; J. Sanders, "Canonical Process."
42. Episcopalians, that is, the Anglican communion in the United States, and other churches associated with the Church of England tend to accept the Apocrypha also, though in something of a "secondary" status to the other books of the Old

Testament. On the status of the apocryphal books in Anglicanism, see "An Outline of the Faith, Commonly Called the Catechism" and Article VI of the "Articles of Religion" in the *Book of Common Prayer*, 853 and 868–869, respectively.

43. See Dungan, *Constantine's Bible.*
44. Such is the conclusion of E. Ferguson in his "Factors Leading to the Selection and Closure of the New Testament Canon."
45. See Metzger, *Canon of the New Testament*, 254–257.
46. These are taken from Metzger, *Canon of the New Testament*, 251–254.
47. For a concise introduction to the diversity present within early Christianity, see King, "Which Early Christianity?"

CHAPTER 3
The Greco-Roman World

1. For a study of the problems of using the term "religion" for ancient institutions, practices, and beliefs, see Nongbri, "Paul without Religion"; Nongbri, *Before Religion.*
2. On the Hellenistic age, see Green, *Alexander to Actium*; Koester, *Introduction to the New Testament.*
3. On Alexander's life and conquests, see Green, *Alexander to Actium*; Bosworth, *Conquest and Empire*; Bosworth, "Alexander III," 57–59; Ehrman, *New Testament*, 31.
4. Wycherley, *How the Greeks Built Cities.* On the general features and structure of the Hellenistic city, see 41–96, "Society and Economics," in Koester, *Introduction to the New Testament*, 1:41–96; Meeks, *First Urban Christians.*
5. Clarke, *Higher Education in the Ancient World.*
6. S. Miller, *Ancient Greek Athletics*; Newby, *Athletics in the Ancient World*; on Sparta, see Kennell, *Gymnasium of Virtue.*
7. For one description of the advent of democracy in Athens and its impact on other aspects of ancient culture, see Martin, *Inventing Superstition*, 229–237.
8. McDonald and Walton, *Cambridge Companion to Greek and Roman Theatre.*
9. See the sources on athletics cited in note 6.
10. Yegül, *Baths and Bathing in Classical Antiquity*; Yegül, *Bathing in the Roman World.*
11. On Greek religion in general, see Ehrman, *New Testament*, 34–48; Buxton, *Oxford Readings in Greek Religion*; Zaidman and Schmitt Pantel, *Religion in the Ancient Greek City*; Koester, *Introduction to the New Testament*, vol. 1, 137–196; Garland, *Religion and the Greeks*; Klauck, *Religious Context of Early Christianity.*
12. On the rhetoric of universalism in the ancient world, see Schott, *Christianity, Empire, and the Making of Religion in Late Antiquity.*
13. Price, *Rituals and Power*; Koester, *Introduction to the New Testament*, vol. 1, 34–39 and 347–356.
14. Bosworth, *Conquest and Empire.*
15. Schwartz, *Imperialism and Jewish Society.*
16. Saller, *Personal Patronage.* See also MacMullen, *Corruption and the Decline of Rome*, chap. 2.
17. See especially Meeks, *Origins of Christian Morality*, chap. 3; and Meeks, *First Urban Christians*, chap. 3.

18. Martin, "Construction of the Ancient Family," 40–46.
19. For a short survey of women in antiquity, see G. Clark, *Women in the Ancient World*; see also Just, *Women in Athenian Law and Life*; Gardner, *Women in Roman Law and Society.*
20. See Martin, *Slavery as Salvation*, 1–49.
21. For a basic introduction to Roman law, see Johnston, *Roman Law in Context.*
22. On Julius Caesar, see Gelzer, *Caesar*; Wistrand, *Caesar and Contemporary Society.*
23. On Octavius, see Green, *Alexander to Actium.*
24. Velleius Paterculus, *Res gestae* 2.89. For an English translation, see Shipley, *Velleius Paterculus: Res Gestae.*
25. Velleius Paterculus, *Res gestae* 4.34.
26. Wells, *Roman Empire*; Garnsey and Saller, *Early Principate.*
27. Finley, *Ancient Economy*; Jones, "Taxation in Antiquity."
28. Casson, *Travel in the Ancient World.*
29. Plutarch, *Life of Pompey.*
30. Ehrman, *New Testament*, 455–459.
31. Rabello, "Legal Condition of the Jews in the Roman Empire"; Schäfer, *History of the Jews in the Greco-Roman World.*
32. See Beard, North, and Price, *Religions of Rome*, vol. 1, chap. 5; Rüpke, *Religion of the Romans.*

CHAPTER 4
Ancient Judaism

1. For an overview of the historical background of the books of the Hebrew Bible, see Collins, *Introduction to the Hebrew Bible.*
2. On Alexander and hellenization, see Green, *Alexander to Actium.*
3. For a time line of the Seleucid and Ptolemaic rulers, see Koester, *Introduction to the New Testament*, 1:24 and 28; E. Ferguson, *Backgrounds of Early Christianity*, 16–17.
4. 2 Macc 4:9.
5. See 2 Macc 4:24 and 4:32: "But [Menelaus], when presented to the king, extolled him with an air of authority, and secured the high priesthood for himself, outbidding Jason by three hundred talents of silver. . . . But Menelaus, thinking he had obtained a suitable opportunity, stole some of the gold vessels of the temple and gave them to Andronicus; other vessels, as it happened, he had sold to Tyre and the neighboring cities." See also Mørkholm, "Antiochus IV," 281–282.
6. On the effects of hellenization on Judaism in particular, see Cohen, *From the Maccabees to the Mishnah*, 26–37. See also Koester, *Introduction to the New Testament*, 1:197–271.
7. 2 Macc 4:8–10 describes the incident: "[Jason promised] the king at an interview three hundred sixty talents of silver, and from another source of revenue eighty talents. In addition to this he promised to pay one hundred fifty more if permission were given to establish by his authority a gymnasium and a body of youth [*ephēbeion*] for it, and to enroll the people of Jerusalem as citizens of Antioch. When the king assented and Jason came to office, he at once shifted his compatriots over to the Greek way of life." See also Mørkholm, "Antiochus IV."
8. See Gruen, "Hellenism and Persecution"; and Mørkholm, "Antiochus IV," 286.

9. 2 Macc 6:1–2: "Not long after this, the king sent an Athenian senator to compel the Jews to forsake the laws of their ancestors and no longer to live by the laws of God; also to pollute the temple in Jerusalem and to call it the temple of Olympian Zeus."
10. Consider, for instance, the remark at 1 Macc 1:11: "In those days certain renegades came out from Israel and misled many, saying, 'Let us go and make a covenant with the Gentiles around us, for since we separated from them many disasters have come upon us.'"
11. On the Qumran community and the Dead Sea Scrolls, see VanderKam, *Dead Sea Scrolls Today*; Lim and Collins, *Oxford Handbook of the Dead Sea Scrolls*.
12. See 1 Macc 2:42 and 2 Macc 14:6–13.
13. Goldstein, "Hasmonean Revolt and the Hasmonean Dynasty." Judas's battles are described in 2 Macc 5:27 and 8:1–15:39.
14. On the Hasmonean dynasty, see Goldstein, "Hasmonean Revolt and the Hasmonean Dynasty."
15. For a fuller treatment of the genre and this aspect of it, see Chapter 23 in this book.
16. For an introduction to apocalyptic literature, see Collins, *Apocalyptic Imagination*.
17. On the history of Roman Palestine, see Gabba, "Social, Economic, and Political History of Palestine," 96–160; Koester, *Introduction to the New Testament*, 1:371–391.
18. See, for example, Josephus, *Antiquities* 20.169–170.
19. On messianic expectations, see Yarbro Collins and Collins, *King and Messiah as Son of God*; Ehrman, *New Testament*, 63–64, 90.
20. On the Jewish War, see Goodman, *Ruling Class of Judaea*; Gabba, "Social, Economic, and Political History of Palestine," 156–167.
21. On the aftermath of the destruction and the rise of rabbinic Judaism, see Cohen, *From the Maccabees to the Mishnah*; Schwartz, *Imperialism and Jewish Society*; Boyarin, "Tale of Two Synods."

CHAPTER 5
The New Testament as a Historical Source

1. The Greek for the amount of time Paul stayed in Damascus ("some time") is an indistinct expression meaning something like "after some days" or "several days."
2. I think that this must be the meaning of the verse. Many Greek editions and English translations say that they "returned to Jerusalem." Some Greek manuscripts do have some form of "from Jerusalem," although they use different Greek words for "from." It may be that the author actually wrote "to," and that later scribes, seeing that it hardly makes sense in the context (which is depicting Barnabas and Paul returning from Jerusalem to Antioch), changed it to some form of "from." In any case, I think that "to" must be either a slip of the pen by the original author or a textual variant supplied by a later scribe. The context seems to demand that the narrator intends to describe their return from Jerusalem to Antioch.
3. On the difference between historical-critical and theological approaches to the Bible, see Martin, *Pedagogy of the Bible*, especially the first chapter, "The Bible in Theological Education."

CHAPTER 6
The Gospel of Mark

1. Kähler, *So-Called Historical Jesus.*
2. See Wrede, *Messianic Secret.*
3. For other "misunderstanding" passages and Jesus' rebukes, see Mark 4:41, 7:18.
4. On the suffering servant, see Isa 50:4–9, 52:13–53:12. On the messianic passages, see, for example, Isa 9:2–7, 11:1–5; Mic 5:2–4; Jer 23:5–6; Ezek 34:23–24; Ps 89, 110, 132.
5. The hypothesis was famously proposed in the middle of the twentieth century by Marxsen, *Mark the Evangelist.*

CHAPTER 7
The Gospel of Matthew

1. The earliest citation with this suggestion I know of is Bacon, "'Five Books' of Matthew against the Jews"; see also Bacon, *Studies in Matthew*; Kingsbury, *Matthew.*
2. See also Matt 23:2–3, where Jesus admits that the scribes and Pharisees "sit on Moses' seat." He tells the people to do what they say, just not the hypocrisy they practice.
3. John was not arrested by Herod the Great, of course, who died in 4 B.C.E., but his son Herod Antipas, who had been given the rule of Galilee and Perea by the Romans.
4. The original German, "Die Sturmstillung im Matthäusevangelium," was published in an English translation in Bornkamm, "Stilling of the Storm in Matthew."
5. See Matt 6:30, 8:26, 14:31, 16:8, 17:20.

CHAPTER 8
The *Gospel of Thomas*

1. For a full introduction, as well as translations of many of these documents, see Layton, *Gnostic Scriptures.*
2. For an English translation of the *Infancy Gospel*, see Elliott, *Apocryphal New Testament*; or Erhman and Pleša, *Apocryphal Gospels*, which also provides the text in the original Greek.
3. An excellent study of the ancient "Gnostics" that addresses the question whether such a group can be said to have existed is Brakke, *Gnostics.* Brakke argues against some scholars, insisting that it is perfectly permissible to use the term "Gnostics" for adherents to a certain kind of Christianity in late antiquity. Unlike myself, Brakke demurs at using the term "Gnosticism." In my view, it is no more objectionable than speaking of ancient "Neoplatonism." I give a fuller exposition of my position on "Gnostics" and "Gnosticism" later in this chapter.
4. I use the translation from Layton, *Gnostic Scriptures.* The numbers refer to the logion (or saying) numbers there. Other reference numbers may also be found. In Layton, a bold number in the *Gospel of Thomas* refers to the page number of the original Coptic manuscript, and smaller numbers in the margins refer to the line

number on that page. Thus the first line of the prologue is also numbered 32.10 (page 32, line 10, of the Coptic manuscript). I cite simply the saying (logion) number as provided in Layton.

5. For a couple of references to the use of the word "rest" or "repose" in what sounds like a special, Gnostic sense, see Brakke, *Gnostics*, 56.
6. The words in brackets were supplied by the editor (Layton); they seem to have dropped out, probably by mistake, from the Coptic manuscript.
7. See, for example, Williams, *Rethinking "Gnosticism"*; King, *What Is Gnosticism?*
8. For one discussion of both theories about it and horror of it, see Martin, "Contradictions of Masculinity."
9. This summary of the "Gnostic myth" can be found more fully in Layton, *Gnostic Scriptures*, 12–17.
10. For this designation and a discussion, see Layton, *Gnostic Scriptures*, 267–275.
11. This translation is from Duling and Perrin, *New Testament*, 73. For the full text of the *Excerpta ex Theodoto*, see Casey, *Excerpta ex Theodoto*.
12. A translation of this text can be found in Layton, *Gnostic Scriptures*. See also the recent annotated translation by Attridge, *Acts of Thomas*.
13. See, for example, Matt 21:33–43; Mark 12:1–12; Luke 20:9–19.
14. Layton, *Gnostic Scriptures*, xxxii: "Words in parentheses have been added by the modern translator, as an interpretive supplement implied by the text but not literally present within it. They may be retained whenever the translation is being quoted."

CHAPTER 9
The Gospel of Luke and the Acts of the Apostles, Part 1

1. Parts of Acts may be open to debate since the author does include sections of Paul's travel narratives given in the first person, using "we" at times (16:10–17, 20:5–15, 21:1–18, 27:1–28:16). But the portrait of Paul provided by Acts is so at odds with Paul's letters that most critical scholars believe that the "we" passages are from a source used by the author or are simply attempts at verisimilitude. There is no mention of Paul's letters, and the author of Acts doesn't consider Paul an "apostle" (apostles have to have been disciples of Jesus during Jesus' lifetime; see Acts 1:22). It is hard to imagine a close companion of Paul going against Paul on that score (compare Gal 1). As shown in Chapter 5 in this book, Acts' account of Paul's comings and goings doesn't match Paul's own account. The author of Acts, therefore, was not likely an eyewitness either to Jesus' ministry or to Paul's.
2. There must be some question about the man's actual status vis-à-vis Judaism. According to Deut 23:1, no man whose testicles had been crushed or whose penis had been cut off could be admitted into "the assembly." That was taken to prohibit eunuchs from converting to Judaism officially. But the Ethiopian eunuch could have been born Jewish and enslaved in Ethiopia, or he could have been a "follower" of Judaism without officially converting as a proselyte. In any case, since what could count as being a "eunuch" varied in the ancient world, we simply can't know what the author considered the status of this "eunuch" to be with regard to the law of Moses. We must also remember that we are here speaking about a character in a narrative, not necessarily a historical person about whom we may conduct

independent research. On eunuchs in early Christianity, see Kuefler, *Manly Eunuchs*; Brower, "Ambivalent Bodies."

3. I interpret 9:32–43 also as something of a transition or preparation for the section that follows. In those verses, coming after the section on the conversion of Paul, Peter is portrayed as advancing his ministry outside Jerusalem but still among Jews, in Lydda and then Joppa. This region, along the coast of Palestine, would have had many gentile inhabitants, perhaps even a majority. But Peter's ministry at this time is still limited to Jews living there. That section ends with Peter residing with a Jew in Joppa, which is where he will be when he is called to deliver the first sermon (according to the author of Acts, at any rate) to a gentile audience (9:43).
4. Among these are Papyrus 74 (seventh century) and the Codex Alexandrinus (fifth century). The difference is slight: *hellēnistas* for "hellenists"; *hellēnas* for "Greeks."

CHAPTER 10
The Gospel of Luke and the Acts of the Apostles, Part 2

1. See Josephus, *Jewish War* 6.5.3, §§300–309.
2. See 2 Sam 7:5; 1 Chron 17:4; 1 Kings 8:27.
3. See Gal 3:19; Martyn, *Galatians*, 356–357; Callan, "Pauline Midrash."
4. Heb 2:2; *Jubilees* 1:27–2:1; Josephus, *Antiquities* 15.5.3, §136.
5. There are several good editions. For one that includes only the synoptic Gospels in the New Revised Standard Version translation, see Throckmorton, *Gospel Parallels*. Another edition includes also the Gospel of John and is available in an English (Revised Standard Version) translation, a bilingual English-Greek edition, and a Greek-only edition: Aland, *Synopsis of the Four Gospels*.

CHAPTER 11
The Gospel of John

1. For an overview of some of the major debates in the study of the Gospel of John, see Sloyan, *What Are They Saying about John?*
2. A classic study of John's narrative is Culpepper, *Anatomy of the Fourth Gospel*.
3. For an overview of some of the themes that make John distinct, see Smith, *Theology of John*. See also Kysar, *John the Maverick Gospel*.
4. The classic work on the Johannine community is R. Brown, *Community of the Beloved Disciple*.

CHAPTER 12
The Letters of John and the Spread of Christianity

1. On the doctrine established at the first four "ecumenical councils"—Nicea, Constantinople, Ephesus, and Chalcedon—see Young, *From Nicaea to Chalcedon*; Hanson, *Search for the Christian Doctrine of God*.
2. I cite the Creed here as found in the 1979 *Book of Common Prayer*, Rite I of the Holy Eucharist.

3. The Chalcedonian Creed affirms that Jesus possesses two "natures," human and divine, in one "substantial" (hypostatic) union.
4. The NRSV, in an attempt at gender inclusivity, probably mostly for liturgical purposes, includes "and sister," but that is not in the Greek. Since my concern here is not liturgical but historical, I retain the gender exclusivity of the original texts. To put "and sister(s)" in all places renders the ancient church and the text more "egalitarian" than they actually were, and it is important from a historical point of view to have the texts reflect the patriarchal reality of the society and the church.
5. On the *Gospel of Peter*, see Elliott, *Apocryphal New Testament*, 150–158.

CHAPTER 13
The Historical Jesus

1. Some recommended books on the subject are Ehrman, *Jesus*; and Allison, *Historical Christ*.
2. We may imagine that the light from past historical events is still traveling in some way through space. When Albert Einstein was still a child, he wondered what it would be like to ride a beam of light. If we could travel faster than the speed of light, couldn't we theoretically outrun the light from past events on earth and see what "really happened"? This is something like knowing that when we see the light of a distant star, we are actually seeing not the star as it is "right now," but as it appeared many years ago. We are seeing not the "present" star, but its "history." But thought experiments such as these cannot render the past of our own world present for us in any way. Einstein convinced most scientists that nothing can travel faster than the speed of light. The past, therefore, in any way that matters for us, no longer exists. Therefore, we can have no access to it. (For the Einstein story, see Isaacson, *Einstein*, 3.)
3. See Martin, *Pedagogy of the Bible*, 40–42; and Martin, *Sex and the Single Savior*, 1–16. See also E. Clark, *History, Theory, Text*.
4. For a fuller discussion, see Meeks, *Christ Is the Question*.
5. The source of the story, first published in 1800, is Weems's *Life of Washington*.
6. See Dahl, "Crucified Messiah"; Ehrman, *Jesus*, 217–218.
7. For a fuller discussion of marriage, divorce, and asceticism in ancient Judaism, see Martin, *Sex and the Single Savior*, 91–102 and 125–147.
8. The suggestion that some author invented the event in order to "fulfill scripture" is totally unpersuasive. Only Luke makes that case, and the scripture he cites says nothing about swords or violence at all. It just says, "He was counted among the lawless" (Isa 53:12). Luke comes up with the scripture in order to excuse the fact that Jesus' disciples were armed.
9. See Allison, *Constructing Jesus*, 31–164.
10. This is much the way the point is laid out by E. Sanders, *Jesus and Judaism*, 326–327.
11. For an overview of some of the major constructions of the historical Jesus, see Powell, *Jesus as a Figure in History*.
12. See Funk, Hoover, and the Jesus Seminar, *Five Gospels*. For an accessible overview of the debate over whether Jesus should be called an apocalyptic prophet, see R. Miller, *Apocalyptic Jesus*.

13. For a few examples, see Ehrman, *Jesus*; Allison, *Jesus of Nazareth*; Allison, *Constructing Jesus*, 31–164; E. Sanders, *Jesus and Judaism*; and references there cited.
14. E. Sanders, *Jesus and Judaism*, 69.
15. See, for example, Matt 24:27–44.
16. See, for instance, Matt 24:27–44, 26:64; Mark 2:10, 8:38, 14:21, 14:41; Luke 6:5, 9:58, 12:10, 17:22.

CHAPTER 14
Paul as Missionary

1. Meeks and Fitzgerald, *Writings of St. Paul*, 689–694. Cf. Homer, *Odyssey* 4.456–458.
2. See the new study by Eastman, *Paul the Martyr.*
3. On the persistence of this view in modern Pauline scholarship, see Stendahl, "Apostle Paul and the Introspective Conscience of the West."
4. Meeks and Fitzgerald, *Writings of St. Paul*, 413; emphasis in the original.
5. Meeks and Fitzgerald, *Writings of St. Paul*, 417.
6. Meeks and Fitzgerald, *Writings of St. Paul*, 419.
7. When I say "critical scholars" in this book, I mean those scholars who feel no compulsion to accept Pauline authorship as a matter of faith or doctrine about the historical reliability of the Bible. Many scholars believe that the Bible cannot contain significant errors—or, for some people, any errors—even about "history" or "science." They are inclined, therefore, to maintain that all or most of the letters that claim to be by Paul in the New Testament were actually written by him. My term "critical scholars" refers to scholars who work without those theological or methodological inclinations.
8. The language spoken commonly would have been Aramaic by our modern standards. But the biblical writers make no distinction between what we would consider classical Hebrew and the Aramaic spoken popularly in the first century.
9. This is mentioned more than once in Acts; see 21:39, 22:25–29, 23:27.
10. The NRSV adds "and sisters" for gender inclusivity. As usual, I alter the translation slightly to correctly reflect the Greek. As will become clear later, I think the masculine gender of the language is, in this case, historically significant.
11. For a study of reading in the ancient Roman world, see Johnson, *Readers and Reading Culture.*
12. See Martin, *Slavery as Salvation*. The main place Paul speaks of his self-lowering in these ways is 1 Corinthians 9, where he explains why he has not accepted financial support from the Corinthians. Note that Paul speaks of his self-support as something he has had to "endure" (9:12); he compares it with enslavement (9:19, 9:27) and becoming one of "the weak" (9:22) and portrays it as "punishing" (9:27).
13. See Hock, *Social Context of Paul's Ministry.*
14. For a full defense of this rather counterintuitive interpretation of Paul's ethics, see Martin, *Sex and the Single Savior*, 65–76.
15. Fatum, "Brotherhood in Christ."
16. Incidentally, the English term "the rapture," found in some kinds of millenarian Christianity, comes from the Latin equivalent of the Greek word that is here

translated "caught up," quite literally "snatched up." It refers to the sweeping up of living Christians expected at the coming of Jesus.

CHAPTER 15
Paul as Pastor

1. On the mechanics of letter writing and sending in antiquity, see Richards, *Paul and First-Century Letter Writing*; Epp, "New Testament Papyrus Manuscripts."
2. I have argued and documented all the main points of this section on 1 Corinthians much more fully in Martin, *Corinthian Body.*
3. Besides Martin, *Corinthian Body*, see also Engberg-Pedersen, *Cosmology and Self in the Apostle Paul.*
4. See Meeks, *First Urban Christians*; Theissen, *Social Setting*; Martin, *Slavery as Salvation.*
5. Martin, *Slavery as Salvation*; Martin, *Corinthian Body.*
6. On this, see Martin, *Inventing Superstition.*
7. For analysis of this strategy of Paul's and my argument that the other issues in 1 Corinthians may also be seen as reflecting status conflicts, see Martin, *Corinthian Body.*
8. I first noted this fact in my Yale dissertation of 1988, later published as Martin, *Slavery as Salvation* (for this characterization of the letter, see 143–145); the definitive case for the thesis is now Mitchell, *Paul and the Rhetoric of Reconciliation.*

CHAPTER 16
Paul as Jewish Theologian

1. Such references occur several times in Genesis. See Gen 12:7, 15:5, 17:8, 22:17.
2. I have translated a Greek word as "slipped in" rather than simply "came in," as in the NRSV, because I think there is a connotation of sneakiness in the word here. After all, it is the same word Paul used in Galatians 2:4 when he was describing some "false brothers" who "slipped into" the Jerusalem meeting, implying that their presence was not truly legitimate. I believe the NRSV translation ("with the result that the trespass multiplied") also misleads in that the Greek words do not imply merely that a "result" just "happened"; rather, the most likely meaning of Paul's Greek is that the "slipping in" of the law had as its very purpose to increase trespasses.
3. The dating of both letters is uncertain, of course, but it seems that Paul must have founded the churches in Galatia before his arrival in Greece. Even if we don't trust Acts for much historical knowledge about Paul's travels, it seems that he must have moved gradually in his missions from east to west, arriving in Galatia well before Macedonia and Greece. And since, as we saw in the previous chapter, there must have been some time between the founding of the Corinthian church, the growth of that church into what I have called "adolescence," and the passing of at least two letters between the Corinthians and Paul, I take it that the letter to the Galatians

was written before the Corinthian correspondence. In fact, since Paul does not mention the collection at all in Galatians, some have suggested that it was written before the "Jerusalem council" that reached an agreement about that collection. I find that argument unconvincing, however, since it would be unreasonable to expect Paul to interrupt his angry diatribe that is the letter to the Galatians with an appeal for a contribution from them to his collection. Paul was a better rhetorician than that.

4. It has been proposed that Romans 16 was not part of the original letter Paul sent to Rome, but was another letter, or a fragment of another letter, added to the end of Romans later. For an overview of the issue, see Myers, "Romans." I have never been convinced by those arguments and so take Romans 16 to be part of the original letter.
5. Notice that Paul says nothing here about any participation of the Galatians in the collection. Is this an indication, after all, that he has broken with the churches there? Could it be that his letter to Galatia was not a success, and therefore the Galatians are not participating in the collection, as we thought they were when we read 1 Cor 16:1?

CHAPTER 17
Colossians and Ephesians

1. Quoted in Eusebius, *Ecclesiastical History* 1.13.10; translated in Williamson, *Eusebius.*
2. See Augustine, *Against Faustus* 28.4, in Schaff, *Nicene and Post-Nicene Fathers*, vol. 4.
3. The best scholarship in English on ancient pseudonymity, especially Christian, is now Ehrman, *Forgery and Counter-forgery.*
4. See Rothschild, *Hebrews as Pseudepigraphon.*
5. For the best and most detailed account of the debate, with lists of numbers of words, etc., see Ehrman, *Forgery and Counter-forgery.*
6. I say "according to one count" because there are some textual variants, that is, some disagreements among different ancient Greek manuscripts about the inclusion of a few words.
7. A possible exception is when he says that through the "stumbling" of the Jews, "salvation has come to the Gentiles" (Rom 11:11). In Rom 8:24, Paul does use a past tense that "we have been saved," but in that context he is still thinking of it as something we experience now only "in hope."
8. Scholars regularly read back later Christological orthodoxy into the earliest period of the movement in ways that are hard to defend historically. For one such example, see Hurtado, *Lord Jesus Christ.* I agree more with the critical review of that book by Fredriksen in *Journal of Early Christian Studies.*
9. See the summary of the argument made more fully elsewhere in the book: Hultin, *Ethics of Obscene Speech*, xix–xx.
10. On the variants and Basil of Caesarea's and Origen's ignorance of the designation "to the Ephesians," see Metzger, *Textual Commentary*, 532.

CHAPTER 18
Differing Christians

1. For a full defense of this position, and of the other examples here discussed, see Ehrman, *Orthodox Corruption of Scripture*.
2. A scribe might be encouraged to make the change also because the parallel passages in Matt 17:5 and Mark 9:7 have "beloved."
3. Sirach is also not in the Hebrew Bible, but is in the Christian Apocrypha. The book is sometimes known by the Hebrew version of the author's name, Ben Sira, or by the title it bears in the Latin Vulgate, Ecclesiasticus (not to be confused with the biblical book Ecclesiastes).

CHAPTER 19
The Pro-household Paul

1. See Martin, *Corinthian Body*, 198–228; Martin, *Sex and the Single Savior*, 65–76.
2. It seems that in funerary inscriptions of the time, a woman's name often preceded her husband's if she was of higher social status than he. She might be a free woman, while he was a slave or freedman. See Flory, "Where Women Precede Men"; Martin, *Slavery As Salvation*, 182n2; and Martin, "Slave Families and Slaves in Families," 221–222.
3. See Epp, *Junia*. We have to remember also that for Paul, the term "apostle" was broader than "the twelve" disciples of Jesus mentioned in the Gospels, Acts, and 1 Cor 15:5. For Paul, the term apparently referred to people especially chosen by God to preach the gospel, a larger contingent than "the twelve."
4. For much more elaborate demonstrations of these arguments, see Martin, *Corinthian Body*, 229–233; and Martin, *Sex and the Single Savior*, 77–90.
5. See Meeks, *First Urban Christians*, 74–84.
6. On voluntary associations, see Gillihan, *Civic Ideology*.
7. On this, see Martin, *Sex and the Single Savior*, 103–124.

CHAPTER 20
The Anti-household Paul

1. A good recent collection and translation of much of this literature is Elliott, *Apocryphal New Testament*. I cite this translation of the *Acts of Paul and Thecla* by paragraph numbers rather than page numbers so any edition may be consulted.
2. See Martin, *Sex and the Single Savior*, 103–124.
3. For an introduction to these texts, along with translations of the few that survive whole and fragments of others, see Reardon, *Collected Ancient Greek Novels*.
4. See Martin, *Sex and the Single Savior*, 114–118.
5. On the early Christian controversy over whether postbaptismal sin could be forgiven, see Le Saint, *Tertullian*; and comments in E. Ferguson, *Baptism in the Early Church*.
6. Martin, *Sex and the Single Savior*, 82–87.

7. See Scheidel, "Demography," esp. 41; see also Frier, "Roman Life Expectancy." As ranges of numbers and differences among studies show, these are only rough estimates.
8. On this argument for the *Acts of Paul and Thecla*, see MacDonald, *Legend and the Apostle*.

CHAPTER 21
Hebrews and Biblical Interpretation

1. See Augustine, *De doctrina christiana* 3.83 (26.37); D. Ferguson, *Biblical Hermeneutics*, 161.
2. I provide much more explanation and defense of these points in Martin, *Sex and the Single Savior*, 1–35; and Martin, *Pedagogy of the Bible*, 29–45.
3. This interpretation is related by a church father who rejects it: Irenaeus, *Against Heresies* 1.14.6; see also 1.15.1, 1.26.1.
4. Rothschild, *Hebrews as Pseudepigraphon*, makes a fervent case that the author of Hebrews intended his readers to take the letter as by Paul. In other words, this is an anonymous but still pseudepigraphic letter.
5. It may well be that the author doesn't know the term "Christianity" yet. It may not have been "invented" when he wrote. But in any case, he doesn't use it.

CHAPTER 22
Premodern Biblical Interpretation

1. See Martin, *Pedogogy of the Bible*. The materials of this chapter are taken mostly from that book, especially from chapters 1 and 3.
2. Even if we know that physicists and cosmologists now tell us that the universe is finite after all, it is really difficult for most people to comprehend a finite universe in which there is nothing on the "other side."
3. For an overview of the study of the Bible during the Reformation and the Enlightenment, see Sheehan, *Enlightenment Bible*.
4. The most thorough history of this importation of German influences into American theological education is E. Clark, *Founding the Fathers*. As Clark's title indicates, the book is mainly about changes in patristic scholarship and teaching, but the book also demonstrates how biblical studies were likewise changed in the same period.
5. See Greer and Mitchell, *"Belly-Myther."* The book includes the text and an analysis of Origen's *Homily on 1 Kingdoms 28*. The Greek text and translation may be found in Greer and Mitchell, along with an introduction and notes.
6. I quote the translation of Maria Boulding in Augustine, *Confessions*. Different ways of referring to the text by number exist in different books. I provide book number, chapter number, and then paragraph number, following Boulding's translation.
7. I use the translation by Kilian Walsh in Bernard of Clairvaux, *On the Song of Songs*.
8. For more discussion of the erotic in interpretation of the Song of Songs, see Moore, *God's Beauty Parlor*, 21–89.

9. I provide analyses of two more—the Venerable Bede and Thomas Aquinas—in Martin, *Pedagogy of the Bible*, in chapter 3, from which these were taken.
10. One of the most famous interpretations of this kind is *The Genesis of Secrecy*, by literary critic Frank Kermode.

CHAPTER 23
Apocalypticism as Resistance

1. See Charlesworth, *Old Testament Pseudepigrapha*, vol. 1.
2. All chapter and verse numbers were added to Bibles centuries later. The ancient reader would have had a text that was not divided with these numbers, but was simply for the most part continuous. The chapter numbers for the New Testament were probably added in late antiquity, although those numbers would not necessarily match ours. Verse numbers matching ours did not occur in Bibles until the sixteenth century. See Specht, "Chapter and Verse Divisions."
3. See Tacitus, *Annals* 15.44; see also Suetonius, *Nero* 16.2.
4. For fuller discussion, see Martin, *Sex and the Single Savior*, 109–111.
5. Again, for more discussion and demonstration, see Martin, *Sex and the Single Savior*, 111–118.
6. For the possibility that slaves in Christian households may have been sexual partners with their owners or other members of the household, see Glancy, *Slavery in Early Christianity*.

CHAPTER 24
Apocalypticism as Accommodation

1. A classic study is Hengel, *Crucifixion in the Ancient World*.
2. 1 Cor 6:3: "Do you not know that we are to judge angels—to say nothing of ordinary matters?"
3. See, for example, Acts 18:12–17, 19:35–41, 23:26–30, 25:18–20, 25:24–27, 26:31–32.
4. For examples of all these aspects of ancient pseudepigraphy, see Ehrman, *Forgery*.
5. As I often do in this book, I have omitted the words "and sisters" added by modern editors to the NRSV.
6. On the possible sources for this story, see Bauckham, *Jude, 2 Peter*, 65–76.

CHAPTER 25
The Development of Ecclesiastical Institutions

1. See the discussion of this issue in the biblical interpretation of Origen in Chapter 22.
2. See, for example, John's vision of martyrs under the altar in heaven (Rev 6:9).
3. See the conflict in Cyprian's church in third-century North Africa discussed in Burns, *Cyprian the Bishop*.
4. I use the Greek text and English translation in Ehrman, *Apostolic Fathers*.
5. See further Schoedel, *Ignatius of Antioch*.
6. See further Niederwimmer, *Didache*.

7. Matthew 26:26–29; Mark 14:22–25; 1 Cor 11:23–26.
8. As with Ignatius, for the *Didache* I am using the Greek and English provided in Ehrman, *Apostolic Fathers.*
9. See, for instance, Philem 22, where Paul asks Philemon to prepare a guest room for him.

Epilogue

1. For studies of the development of Christianity in late antiquity, see White, *From Jesus to Christianity*; MacMullen, *Second Church*. For a thorough topical overview, with extensive bibliography, see Harvey and Hunter, *Oxford Handbook of Early Christian Studies.* See also the primary texts collected in Ehrman, *After the New Testament*; and in Ehrman and Jacobs, *Christianity in Late Antiquity.* For an older, but still-classic, study, see Chadwick, *Early Church.*
2. A classic study of the development of asceticism in late antiquity is P. Brown, *Body and Society.* See also Harmless, *Desert Christians.*
3. For a new account of the "pagans" of late antiquity, see Cameron, *Last Pagans of Rome.*
4. The best study of this history is now Masuzawa, *Invention of World Religions.*
5. See Nongbri, "Paul without Religion"; and Nongbri, *Before Religion.*
6. A very old, but in many ways unsurpassed, region-by-region chronicle of the spread of Christianity is Harnack, *Expansion of Christianity.*

Bibliography

Aland, Kurt. *Synopsis of the Four Gospels*. New York: American Bible Society, 1985.

Allison, Dale C. *Constructing Jesus: Memory, Imagination, and History*. Grand Rapids, MI: Baker Academic, 2010.

Allison, Dale C. *The Historical Christ and the Theological Jesus*. Grand Rapids, MI: Eerdmans, 2009.

Allison, Dale C. *Jesus of Nazareth: Millenarian Prophet*. Philadelphia: Fortress Press, 1998.

Attridge, Harold W. *Acts of Thomas*. Salem, OR: Polebridge, 2010.

Augustine, *The Confessions*. Trans. Maria Boulding. Vintage Spiritual Classics. New York: Vintage, 1998.

Bacon, B. W. "The 'Five Books' of Matthew against the Jews." *Expositor* 15 (1918): 56–66.

Bacon, B. W. *Studies in Matthew*. London: Constable, 1930.

Barton, John. "Marcion Revisited." In *The Canon Debate*, ed. Lee Martin McDonald and James A. Sanders, 341–354. Peabody, MA: Hendrickson, 2002.

Bauckham, Richard. *Jude, 2 Peter*. Word Biblical Commentary. Waco, TX: Word Publishing, 1983.

Beard, Mary, John North, and Simon Price. *Religions of Rome*. Vol. 1, *A History*. Cambridge: Cambridge University Press, 1998.

Bernard of Clairvaux. *On the Song of Songs: Sermones super Cantica Canticorum*. 4 vols. Trans. Kilian Walsh. Introduction by Corneille Halfants. Spencer, MA: Cistercian, 1971–1980.

Bornkamm, Günther. "The Stilling of the Storm in Matthew." In G. Bornkamm, G. Barth, and H. J. Held, *Tradition and Interpretation in Matthew*, 52–57. Trans. Percy Scott. Philadelphia: Westminster Press, 1963.

Bosworth, A. B. "Alexander III." In *The Oxford Classical Dictionary*, 3rd ed., ed. Simon Hornblower and Anthony Spawforth, 57–59. New York: Oxford University Press, 2003.

Bosworth, A. B. *Conquest and Empire: The Reign of Alexander the Great*. New York: Cambridge University Press, 1993.

Boyarin, Daniel. "A Tale of Two Synods: Nicaea, Yavneh, and Rabbinic Ecclesiology." *Exemplaria* 12 (2002): 21–62.

Bradshaw, Paul, Maxwell E. Johnson, and Edward L. Phillips. *The Apostolic Tradition: A Commentary*. Hermeneia. Minneapolis: Fortress Press, 2002.

Brakke, David. *The Gnostics: Myth, Ritual, and Diversity in Early Christianity*. Cambridge, MA: Harvard University Press, 2010.

Brakke, David. "Scriptural Practices in Early Christianity: Towards a New History of the New Testament Canon." In *Invention, Rewriting, Usurpation: Discursive Fights over Religious Traditions in Antiquity*, ed. David Brakke, Anders-Christian Jacobsen, and Jörg Ulrich. Early Christianity in the Context of Antiquity 11. Frankfurt: Peter Lang, 2011.

Brower, Gary. "Ambivalent Bodies: Making Christian Eunuchs." Ph.D. diss., Duke University, 1996.

Brown, Peter. *The Body and Society: Men, Women, and Sexual Renunciation in Early Christianity.* New York: Columbia University Press, 1988.

Brown, Raymond. *The Community of the Beloved Disciple.* New York: Paulist Press, 1979.

Burns, J. Patout. *Cyprian the Bishop.* New York: Routledge, 2002.

Buxton, R. G. A., ed. *Oxford Readings in Greek Religion.* Oxford: Oxford University Press, 2000.

Callan, T. "Pauline Midrash: The Exegetical Background of Gal. 3:19b." *Journal of Biblical Literature* 99 (1980): 549–567.

Cameron, Alan. *The Last Pagans of Rome.* New York: Oxford University Press, 2011.

Campenhausen, Hans von. *The Formation of the Christian Bible.* Philadelphia: Fortress Press, 1972.

Casey, Robert Pierce, ed. and trans. *The Excerpta ex Theodoto of Clement of Alexandria.* London: Christophers, 1934.

Casson, Lionel. *Travel in the Ancient World.* Baltimore: Johns Hopkins University Press, 1994.

Chadwick, Henry. *The Early Church.* London: Hodder and Stoughton, 1968.

Charlesworth, James H., ed. *Old Testament Pseudepigrapha.* 2 vols. New York: Doubleday, 1983.

Clark, Elizabeth A. *Founding the Fathers: Early Church History and Protestant Professors in Nineteenth-Century America.* Philadelphia: University of Pennsylvania Press, 2011.

Clark, Elizabeth A. *History, Theory, Text: Historians and the Linguistic Turn.* Cambridge, MA: Harvard University Press, 2004.

Clark, Gillian. *Women in the Ancient World.* New York: Oxford University Press, 1989.

Clarke, M. L. *Higher Education in the Ancient World.* London: Routledge, 1971.

Cohen, Shaye D. *From the Maccabees to the Mishnah.* 2nd ed. Louisville, KY: Westminster John Knox Press, 2006.

Collins, John J. *The Apocalyptic Imagination: An Introduction to Jewish Apocalyptic Literature.* Rev. ed. Grand Rapids, MI: Eerdmans, 1998.

Collins, John J. *Introduction to the Hebrew Bible.* Minneapolis: Fortress Press, 2004.

Culpepper, Alan. *The Anatomy of the Fourth Gospel: A Study in Literary Design.* Philadelphia: Fortress Press, 1983.

Dahl, Nils A. "The Crucified Messiah." In Dahl, *The Crucified Messiah and Other Essays,* 10–36. Minneapolis: Augsburg, 1974.

Derrida, Jacques. *Dissemination.* Trans. with introduction and additional notes by Barbara Johnson. Chicago: University of Chicago Press, 1981.

Duling, Dennis C., and Norman Perrin. *The New Testament: Proclamation and Parenesis, Myth and History.* 3rd ed. Fort Worth, TX: Harcourt Brace, 1994.

Dungan, David L. *Constantine's Bible: Politics and the Making of the New Testament.* Minneapolis: Fortress Press, 2007.

Eastman, David L. *Paul the Martyr: The Cult of the Apostle in the Latin West.* Atlanta, GA: Society of Biblical Literature, 2011.

Ehrman, Bart D. *After the New Testament: A Reader in Early Christianity.* New York: Oxford University Press, 2004.

Ehrman, Bart D., ed. and trans. *The Apostolic Fathers.* 2 vols. Loeb Classical Library. Cambridge, MA: Harvard University Press, 2003.

Ehrman, Bart D. *Forgery and Counter-forgery in Early Christian Polemics*. Oxford: Oxford University Press, 2012.

Ehrman, Bart D. *Jesus: Apocalyptic Prophet of the New Millennium*. New York: Oxford University Press, 1999.

Ehrman, Bart D. *The New Testament: A Historical Introduction to the Early Christian Writings*. 5th ed. New York: Oxford University Press, 2012.

Ehrman, Bart D. *The Orthodox Corruption of Scripture: The Effect of Early Christological Controversies on the Text of the New Testament*. New York: Oxford University Press, 1993.

Ehrman, Bart D., and Andrew S. Jacobs. *Christianity in Late Antiquity, 300–450 C.E.: A Reader*. New York: Oxford University Press, 2004.

Ehrman, Bart D., and Zlatko Pleše. *The Apocryphal Gospels*. New York: Oxford University Press, 2011.

Elliott, J. K. *The Apocryphal New Testament: A Collection of Apocryphal Christian Literature in an English Translation*. Oxford: Clarendon Press, 2nd ed. 2005.

Engberg-Pedersen, Troels. *Cosmology and Self in the Apostle Paul: The Material Spirit*. New York: Oxford University Press, 2010.

Epp, Eldon J. *Junia: The First Woman Apostle*. Minneapolis: Fortress Press, 2005.

Epp, Eldon J. "New Testament Papyrus Manuscripts and Letter Carrying in Greco-Roman Times." In *The Future of Early Christianity: Essays in Honor of Helmut Koester*, ed. Birger A. Pearson, 35–56. Minneapolis: Fortress Press, 1991.

Fatum, Lone. "Brotherhood in Christ: A Gender Hermeneutical Reading of 1 Thessalonians." In *Constructing Early Christian Families: Family as Social Reality and Metaphor*, ed. Halvor Moxnes, 183–197. London: Routledge, 1997.

Ferguson, Duncan S. *Biblical Hermeneutics: An Introduction*. Atlanta: John Knox Press, 1986.

Ferguson, Everett. *Backgrounds of Early Christianity*. 2nd ed. Grand Rapids, MI: Eerdmans, 1993.

Ferguson, Everett. *Baptism in the Early Church: History, Theology, and Liturgy in the First Five Centuries*. Grand Rapids, MI: Eerdmans, 2009.

Ferguson, Everett. "Canon Muratori: Date and Provenance." *Studia Patristica* 18 (1982): 677–683.

Ferguson, Everett. "Factors Leading to the Selection and Closure of the New Testament Canon." In *The Canon Debate*, ed. Lee Martin McDonald and James A. Sanders, 295–320. Peabody, MA: Hendrickson, 2002.

Finley, Moses I. *The Ancient Economy*. Updated ed. Berkeley: University of California Press, 1999.

Flory, Marlene Boudreau. "Where Women Precede Men: Factors Influencing the Order of Names in Roman Epitaphs." *Classical Journal* 79 (1983): 216–224.

Foster, Paul. "Marcion: His Life, Works, Beliefs, and Impact." *Expository Times* 121, no. 6 (2010): 269–280.

Francis, Matthew W. G. "'Blessed is the One Who Reads Aloud . . .': The Book of Revelation in Orthodox Lectionary Traditions." In *Exegesis and Hermeneutics in the Churches of the East: Select Papers from the SBL Meeting in San Diego, 2007*, ed. Vahan S. Hovhanessian, 67–78. New York: Peter Lang, 2009.

Fredriksen, Paula. Review of *Lord Jesus Christ*, by Larry W. Hurtado. *Journal of Early Christian Studies* 12 (2004): 537–541.

Frier, Bruce. "Roman Life Expectancy." *Harvard Studies in Classical Philology* 86 (1982): 213–251.

Funk, Robert W., Roy W. Hoover, and the Jesus Seminar. *The Five Gospels: The Search for the Authentic Words of Jesus; New Translation and Commentary.* New York: Macmillan, 1993.

Gabba, Emilio. "The Social, Economic, and Political History of Palestine: 63 BCE–CE 70." In *The Cambridge History of Judaism*, vol. 3, *The Early Roman Period*, ed. William Horbury, W. D. Davies, and John Sturdy, 94–167. New York: Cambridge University Press, 2008.

Gamble, Harry Y. *Books and Readers in the Early Church: A History of Early Christian Texts.* New Haven, CT: Yale University Press, 1995.

Gardner, Jane F. *Women in Roman Law and Society.* Bloomington: Indiana University Press, 1991.

Garland, Robert. *Religion and the Greeks.* London: Bristol Classical Press, 2000.

Garnsey, Peter, and Richard Saller. *The Early Principate: Augustus to Trajan.* New Surveys in the Classics 15. Oxford: Clarendon Press, 1982.

Gelzer, Matthias. *Caesar: Politician and Statesman.* Trans. Peter Needham. Cambridge, MA: Harvard University Press, 1968.

Gillihan, Yonder. *Civic Ideology, Organization, and Law in the Rule Scrolls: A Comparative Study of the Covenanters' Sect and Contemporary Voluntary Associations in Political Context.* Leiden: Brill, 2011.

Glancy, Jennifer. *Slavery in Early Christianity.* New York: Oxford University Press, 2002.

Goldstein, Jonathan A. "The Hasmonean Revolt and the Hasmonean Dynasty." In *The Cambridge History of Judaism*, vol. 2, *Hellenistic Age*, ed. W. D. Davies and Louis Finkelstein, 292–351. New York: Cambridge University Press, 2008.

Goodman, Martin. *The Ruling Class of Judaea: The Origins of the Jewish Revolt against Rome, A.D. 66–70.* New York: Cambridge University Press, 1993.

Green, Peter. *Alexander to Actium: The Historical Evolution of the Hellenistic Age.* Berkeley: University of California Press, 1990.

Greer, Rowan A., and Margaret M. Mitchell. *The "Belly-Myther" of Endor: Interpretations of 1 Kingdoms 28 in the Early Church.* Atlanta, GA: Society of Biblical Literature, 2007.

Gruen, Erich S. "Hellenism and Persecution." In *Hellenistic History and Culture*, ed. Peter Green, 238–264. Berkeley: University of California Press, 1993.

Hahneman, Geoffrey Mark. *The Muratorian Fragment and the Development of the Canon.* Oxford: Clarendon Press, 1992.

Hahneman, Geoffrey Mark. "The Muratorian Fragment and the Origins of the New Testament Canon." In *The Canon Debate*, ed. Lee Martin McDonald and James A. Sanders, 405–415. Peabody, MA: Hendrickson, 2002.

Hanson, R. P. C. *The Search for the Christian Doctrine of God: The Arian Controversy, 318–381.* Edinburgh: T&T Clark, 1988.

Harmless, William. *Desert Christians: An Introduction to the Literature of Early Christian Monasticism.* New York: Oxford University Press, 2004.

Harnack, Adolf von. *The Expansion of Christianity in the First Three Centuries.* Vol. 2. Trans. and ed. James Moffatt. Repr. Eugene, OR: Wipf and Stock Publishers, 1996.

Harnack, Adolf von. *Marcion: Das Evangelium vom fremden Gott; Eine Monographie zur Geschichte der Grundlegung der katholischen Kirche.* Berlin: Akademie-Verlag, 1960.

Harnack, Adolf von. *Marcion: The Gospel of the Alien God*. Trans. John E. Steely and Lyle D. Bierma. Durham, NC: Labyrinth Press, 1990.

Harvey, Susan Ashbrook, and David G. Hunter, eds. *The Oxford Handbook of Early Christian Studies*. New York: Oxford University Press, 2008.

Hengel, Martin. *Crucifixion in the Ancient World and the Folly of the Message of the Cross*. Philadelphia: Fortress Press, 1997.

Hock, Ronald F. *The Social Context of Paul's Ministry: Tentmaking and Apostleship*. Philadelphia: Fortress Press, 1980.

Hogg, H. W., trans. "The Diatessaron of Tatian." In *Ante-Nicene Fathers*, ed. Allan Menzies, 9.33–129. Peabody, MA: Hendrickson, 1995.

Holmes, Michael W. *The Apostolic Fathers: Greek Texts and English Translations*. 3rd ed. Grand Rapids, MI: Baker Academic, 2007.

Hultin, Jeremy F. *The Ethics of Obscene Speech in Early Christianity and Its Environment*. Supplements to Novum Testamentum, vol. 128. Boston: Brill, 2008.

Hurtado, Larry W. *Lord Jesus Christ: Devotion to Jesus in Earliest Christianity*. Grand Rapids, MI: Eerdmans, 2003.

Isaacson, Walter. *Einstein: His Life and Universe*. New York: Simon & Schuster, 2007.

Johnson, William A. *Readers and Reading Culture in the High Roman Empire: A Study of Elite Communities*. New York: Oxford University Press, 2010.

Johnston, David. *Roman Law in Context*. Key Themes in Ancient History. New York: Cambridge University Press, 1999.

Jones, A. H. M. "Taxation in Antiquity." In *The Roman Economy: Studies in Ancient Economic and Administrative History*, ed. P. A. Brunt, 151–185. Oxford: Blackwell, 1974.

Just, Roger. *Women in Athenian Law and Life*. New York: Routledge, 1989.

Kähler, Martin. *The So-Called Historical Jesus and the Historic Biblical Christ*. Trans. C. Braaten. Philadelphia: Fortress Press, 1964.

Kennell, Nigel M. *The Gymnasium of Virtue: Education and Culture in Ancient Sparta*. Chapel Hill: University of North Carolina Press, 1995.

Kermode, Frank. *The Genesis of Secrecy: On the Interpretation of Narrative*. Cambridge, MA: Harvard University Press, 1979.

King, Karen L. *What Is Gnosticism?* Cambridge, MA: Harvard University Press, 2005.

King, Karen L. "Which Early Christianity?" In *The Oxford Handbook of Early Christian Studies*, ed. Susan Ashbrook Harvey and David G. Hunter, 66–84. New York: Oxford University Press, 2008.

Kingsbury, Jack Dean. *Matthew: Structure, Christology, Kingdom*. Philadelphia: Fortress Press, 1991.

Klauck, Hans-Josef. *The Religious Context of Early Christianity: A Guide to Graeco-Roman Religions*. Minneapolis: Fortress Press, 2003.

Koester, Helmut. *Introduction to the New Testament*. Vol. 1, *History, Culture, and Religion of the Hellenistic Age*. 2nd ed. New York: Walter de Gruyter, 1995.

Kraft, Robert A. "The Codex and Canon Consciousness." In *The Canon Debate*, ed. Lee Martin McDonald and James A. Sanders, 229–233. Peabody, MA: Hendrickson, 2002.

Kuefler, Mathew. *Manly Eunuchs: Masculinity, Gender Ambiguity, and Christian Ideology in Late Antiquity*. Chicago: University of Chicago Press, 2001.

Kysar, Robert. *John the Maverick Gospel*. Atlanta, GA: John Knox Press, 1976.

Layton, Bentley. *The Gnostic Scriptures: A New Translation with Annotations and Introductions*. Anchor Bible Reference Library. New Haven, CT: Yale University Press, 1995.

Le Saint, William P. *Tertullian: Treatises on Penance*. Ancient Christian Writers. Westminster, MD: Paulist Press, 1959.

Lightstone, Jack N. "The Rabbis' Bible: The Canon of the Hebrew Bible and the Early Rabbinic Guild." In *The Canon Debate*, ed. Lee Martin McDonald and James A. Sanders, 163–184. Peabody, MA: Hendrickson, 2002.

Lim, Timothy H., and John J. Collins. *The Oxford Handbook of the Dead Sea Scrolls*. New York: Oxford University Press, 2010.

MacDonald, Dennis R. *The Legend and the Apostle: The Battle for Paul in Story and Canon*. Philadelphia: Westminster Press, 1983.

MacMullen, Ramsay. *Corruption and the Decline of Rome*. New Haven, CT: Yale University Press, 1988.

MacMullen, Ramsay. *The Second Church: Popular Christianity, A.D. 200–400*. Atlanta, GA: Society of Biblical Literature, 2009.

Martin, Dale B. "The Construction of the Ancient Family: Methodological Considerations." *Journal of Roman Studies* 86 (1996): 40–46.

Martin, Dale B. "Contradictions of Masculinity: Ascetic Inseminators and Menstruating Men in Greco-Roman Culture." In *Generation and Degeneration: Tropes of Reproduction in Literature and History from Antiquity through Early Modern Europe*, ed. Valeria Finucci and Kevin Brownlee, 81–108. Durham, NC: Duke University Press, 2001.

Martin, Dale B. *The Corinthian Body*. New Haven, CT: Yale University Press, 1995.

Martin, Dale B. *Inventing Superstition: From the Hippocratics to the Christians*. Cambridge, MA: Harvard University Press, 2004.

Martin, Dale B. *Pedagogy of the Bible: Analysis and Proposal*. Louisville, KY: Westminster John Knox Press, 2008.

Martin, Dale B. *Sex and the Single Savior: Gender and Sexuality in Biblical Interpretation*. Louisville, KY: Westminster John Knox Press, 2006.

Martin, Dale B. "Slave Families and Slaves in Families." In *Early Christian Families in Context*, ed. David L. Balch and Carolyn Osiek, 207–230. Grand Rapids, MI: Eerdmans, 2003.

Martin, Dale B. *Slavery as Salvation: The Metaphor of Slavery in Pauline Christianity*. New Haven, CT: Yale University Press, 1990.

Martin, Dale B. "When Did Angels Become Demons?" *Journal of Biblical Literature* 129 (2010): 657–677.

Martyn, J. Louis. *Galatians*. The Anchor Bible. New York: Doubleday, 1997.

Marx, Karl. "Critique of the Gotha Program." In *The Marx-Engels Reader*, ed. Robert C. Tucker, 525–541. New York: W. W. Norton, 1978.

Marxsen, Willi. *Mark the Evangelist: Studies on the Redaction History of the Gospel*, trans. James Boyce et al. Nashville, TN: Abingdon Press, 1969.

Masuzawa, Tomoko. *The Invention of World Religions; or, How European Universalism Was Preserved in the Language of Pluralism*. Chicago: University of Chicago Press, 2005.

McDonald, Lee Martin, and James A. Sanders, eds. *The Canon Debate*. Peabody, MA: Hendrickson, 2002.

McDonald, Marianne, and J. Michael Walton. *The Cambridge Companion to Greek and Roman Theatre*. New York: Cambridge University Press, 2011.

Meeks, Wayne A. *Christ Is the Question*. Louisville, KY: Westminster John Knox Press, 2006.

Meeks, Wayne A. *The First Urban Christians: The Social World of the Apostle Paul*. 2nd ed. New Haven, CT: Yale University Press, 2003.

Meeks, Wayne A. *The Origins of Christian Morality: The First Two Centuries*. New Haven, CT: Yale University Press, 1993.

Meeks, Wayne A., and John T. Fitzgerald, eds. *The Writings of St. Paul*. 2nd ed. New York: W. W. Norton, 2007.

Metzger, Bruce M. *The Canon of the New Testament: Its Origin, Development, and Significance*. Oxford: Clarendon Press, 1987.

Metzger, Bruce M. *A Textual Commentary on the Greek New Testament*. 2nd ed. Stuttgart: Deutsche Bibelgesellschaft, 1994.

Metzger, Bruce M., and Bart D. Ehrman. *The Text of the New Testament: Its Transmission, Corruption, and Restoration*. 4th ed. New York: Oxford University Press, 2005.

Miller, Robert J., ed. *The Apocalyptic Jesus: A Debate*. Santa Rosa, CA: Polebridge Press, 2001.

Miller, Stephen G. *Ancient Greek Athletics*. New Haven, CT: Yale University Press, 2006.

Mitchell, Margaret M. *Paul and the Rhetoric of Reconciliation: An Exegetical Investigation of the Language and Composition of 1 Corinthians*. Tübingen: Mohr Siebeck, 1991.

Moore, Stephen D. *God's Beauty Parlor and Other Queer Spaces in and around the Bible*. Stanford, CA: Stanford University Press, 2002.

Mørkholm, Otto. "Antiochus IV." In *The Cambridge History of Judaism*, vol. 2, *Hellenistic Age*, ed. W. D. Davies and Louis Finkelstein, 278–291. New York: Cambridge University Press, 2008.

Murray, Oswyn, and Simon Price, eds. *The Greek City from Homer to Alexander*. Oxford: Clarendon Press, 1990.

Myers, Charles D. "Romans." In *The Anchor Bible Dictionary*, ed. David Noel Freedman. New York: Doubleday, 1992.

Newby, Zahra. *Athletics in the Ancient World*. London: Bristol Classical Press, 2006.

The New Oxford Annotated Bible: New Revised Edition with the Apocrypha. 3rd ed. Oxford: Oxford University Press, 2001.

Niederwimmer, Kurt. *The Didache: A Commentary*. Hermeneia. Philadelphia: Fortress Press, 1998.

Nongbri, Brent. *Before Religion: A History of a Modern Concept*. New Haven, CT: Yale University Press, 2012.

Nongbri, Brent. "Paul without Religion: The Creation of a Category and the Search for an Apostle beyond the New Perspective." Ph.D. diss., Yale University, 2008.

Petersen, William L. *Tatian's Diatessaron: Its Creation, Dissemination, Significance, and History in Scholarship*. Supplements to Vigiliae Christianae, vol. 25. Leiden: Brill, 1997.

Pius IX. *Ineffabilis deus*. 1854. www.vatican.va.

Powell, Mark Alan. *Jesus as a Figure in History: How Modern Historians View the Man from Galilee*. Louisville, KY: Westminster John Knox Press, 1998.

Price, Simon R. *Rituals and Power: The Roman Imperial Cult in Asia Minor*. New York: Cambridge University Press, 1984.

Rabello, A. M. "The Legal Condition of the Jews in the Roman Empire." In *Aufstieg und Niedergang der Römischen Welt II*. 13, 662–762. New York: Walter de Gruyter, 1980.

Reardon, B. P., ed. *Collected Ancient Greek Novels*. Berkeley: University of California Press, 2008.

Richards, Randolph E. *Paul and First-Century Letter Writing: Secretaries, Composition, and Collection*. Downers Grove, IL: InterVarsity, 2004.

Roberts, Colin H., and T. C. Skeat. *The Birth of the Codex*. New York: Oxford University Press, 1983.

Rothschild, Clare K. *Hebrews as Pseudepigraphon: The History and Significance of the Pauline Attribution of Hebrews*. Tübingen: Mohr Siebeck, 2009.

Rüpke, Jörg. *Religion of the Romans*. Malden, MA: Polity, 2007.

Saller, R. P. *Personal Patronage under the Early Empire*. New York: Cambridge University Press, 1982.

Sanders, E. P. *Jesus and Judaism*. Philadelphia: Fortress Press, 1985.

Sanders, James A. "The Canonical Process." In *The Cambridge History of Judaism*, vol. 4, *The Late Roman-Rabbinic Period*, ed. Steven T. Katz, 230–243. Cambridge: Cambridge University Press, 2008.

Schäfer, Peter. *The History of the Jews in the Greco-Roman World: The Jews of Palestine from Alexander the Great to the Arab Conquest*. New York: Routledge, 2003.

Schaff, Philip, and Henry Wace, eds. *Nicene and Post-Nicene Fathers*. Second Series. Vol. 4. Peabody, MA: Hendrickson, 1994.

Scheidel, Walter. "Demography." In *The Cambridge Economic History of the Greco-Roman World*, ed. W. Scheidel, I. Morris, and R. Saller, 38–86. Cambridge: Cambridge University Press, 2007.

Schoedel, William. *Ignatius of Antioch: A Commentary*. Hermeneia. Philadelphia: Fortress Press, 1998.

Schott, Jeremy M. *Christianity, Empire, and the Making of Religion in Late Antiquity*. Philadelphia: University of Pennsylvania Press, 2008.

Schwartz, Seth. *Imperialism and Jewish Society: 200 BCE to 640 CE*. Princeton, NJ: Princeton University Press, 2004.

Sheehan, Jonathan. *The Enlightenment Bible: Translation, Scholarship, Culture*. Princeton, NJ: Princeton University Press, 2005.

Shipley, Frederick W., trans. *Velleius Paterculus: Res Gestae Divi Augusti*. Loeb Classical Library. Cambridge, MA: Harvard University Press, 1961.

Sloyan, Garard S. *What Are They Saying about John?* New York: Paulist Press, 1991.

Smith, D. Moody. *The Theology of John*. Cambridge: Cambridge University Press, 1994.

Specht, Walter. "Chapter and Verse Divisions." In *The Oxford Companion to the Bible*, ed. Bruce M. Metzger and Michael D. Coogan, 105–107. New York: Oxford University Press, 1993.

Stendahl, Krister. "The Apostle Paul and the Introspective Conscience of the West." *Harvard Theological Review* 56 (1963): 199–215.

Sundberg, A. C., Jr. "Canon Muratori: A Fourth-Century List." *Harvard Theological Review* 66 (1973): 1–41.

Tanner, Norman P., ed. *Decrees of the Ecumenical Councils*. Vol. 2. Washington, DC: Georgetown University Press, 1990.

Theissen, Gerd. *The Social Setting of Pauline Christianity: Essays on Corinth*. Philadelphia: Fortress Press, 1982.

Throckmorton, Burton H. *Gospel Parallels: A Comparison of the Synoptic Gospels*. 5th ed. Nashville, TN: Thomas Nelson, 1992.

VanderKam, James C. *The Dead Sea Scrolls Today*. 2nd ed. Grand Rapids, MI: Eerdmans, 2010.

Weems, Mason Locke. *The Life of Washington*. Ed. Marcus Cunliffe. Cambridge, MA: Belknap Press of Harvard University Press, 1962.

Wells, Colin. *The Roman Empire*. 2nd ed. Cambridge, MA: Harvard University Press, 1995.

White, L. Michael. *From Jesus to Christianity: How Four Generations of Visionaries and Storytellers Created the New Testament and Christian Faith*. San Francisco: HarperSanFrancisco, 2004.

Williams, Michael L. *Rethinking "Gnosticism": An Argument for Dismantling a Dubious Category*. Princeton, NJ: Princeton University Press, 1999.

Williamson, G. A., trans. *Eusebius: The History of the Church from Christ to Constantine*. Rev. and ed. Andrew Louth. New York: Penguin, 1989.

Wistrand, Erik. *Caesar and Contemporary Society*. Göteborg: Kungl. Vetenskaps- och Vitterhets-Samhället, 1978.

Wrede, William. *The Messianic Secret*. Trans. J. C. G. Greig. Cambridge: James Clarke, 1971.

Wycherley, R. E. *How the Greeks Built Cities*. 2nd ed. New York: W. W. Norton, 1976.

Yarbro Collins, Adela. *Crisis and Catharsis: The Power of the Apocalypse*. Philadelphia: Westminster John Knox Press, 1984.

Yarbro Collins, Adela, and John J. Collins. *King and Messiah as Son of God: Divine, Human, and Angelic Messianic Figures in Biblical and Related Literature*. Grand Rapids, MI: Eerdmans, 2008.

Yegül, Fikret K. *Bathing in the Roman World*. New York: Cambridge University Press, 2010.

Yegül, Fikret K. *Baths and Bathing in Classical Antiquity*. Cambridge, MA: MIT Press, 1992.

Young, Frances M. *From Nicaea to Chalcedon: A Guide to the Literature and Its Background*. Philadelphia: Fortress Press, 1983.

Zaidman, Louise Bruit, and Pauline Schmitt Pantel. *Religion in the Ancient Greek City*. Trans. Paul Cartledge. New York: Cambridge University Press, 1992.

Subject and Author Index

Index of Scripture Citations